Praise for *Music Marketing for the D...*

"Bobby Borg leads the charge of today's modern rockpreneurs. He has lived and breathed the business from multiple perspectives. There is no more credible source for marketing your music than Bobby!"   —BLASKO, Ozzy Osbourne/Mercenary Management, Inc.

"The music industry today is a wild wilderness of ideas and directions. Bobby's book helps you find your footing and make your way through an ever-changing and beautiful landscape."

—JOHN PANTLE, talent agent at Agency for the Performing Arts (APA)

"Bobby has been on both sides of the desk so he knows the real-life ins and outs from each perspective. His matter-of-fact approach is refreshing in that he is providing actual strategies based on practical day-to-day information that can help form the basis of successful creative careers. Required reading in my view."   —NEIL GILLIS, president, Round Hill Music

"As a veteran of both the creative and business sides of the industry, Bobby has the background necessary to assist artists in becoming successful. The book explains the changes in the business in a way that is easily understood and offers advice on how musicians can capture a share of the DIY marketplace."

—STEVE WINOGRADSKY, attorney and author of *Music Publishing: The Complete Guide*

"Bobby Borg makes music marketing easy to understand *and* execute for people who don't know where to start or how to do it, and fear that marketing is beyond their reach. Buy this book!"

—MICHAEL LASKOW, founder, TAXI Independent A&R

"Bobby Borg's book is the arrow that every musician needs in their quiver. His experience as a professional musician and his study of the industry gives him a complete understanding of all sides of the music business and marketing. While it's difficult to get a break in this business, Bobby's book almost guarantees that you'll make your own."

—JONAH DAVID, drummer for Matisyahu and the Live Debate

Music Marketing
for the DIY Musician

music **PRO**
guides

Music Marketing for the DIY Musician

Creating and Executing a Plan of
Attack on a Low Budget

Bobby Borg

Hal Leonard Books
An Imprint of Hal Leonard Corporation

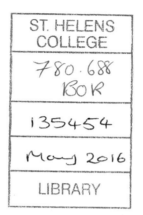
Published in 2014 by Hal Leonard Books
An Imprint of Hal Leonard Corporation
7777 West Bluemound Road
Milwaukee, WI 53213

Trade Book Division Editorial Offices
33 Plymouth St., Montclair, NJ 07042

Permissions to reproduce images in this book are noted in the Acknowledgments section on pages xxi–xxii.

Printed in the United States of America

Book design by Kristina Rolander

Library of Congress Cataloging-in-Publication Data

Borg, Bobby.
 Music marketing for the DIY musician : creating and executing a plan of attack on a low budget / Bobby Borg.
-- 1st paperback edition.
     pages cm
 Includes index.
 ISBN 978-1-4803-6952-8
 1. Music trade--Vocational guidance. 2. Musicians. I. Title.
 ML3790.B679 2014
 780.68'8--dc23
                    2014020267

www.halleonardbooks.com

Contents

9. DEVELOP A BRAND STRATEGY FOR YOUR PRODUCTS/SERVICES: Achieving the Desired Image for Your Tours, Records, Merch, and More   87

21. CONTINUE TO LEARN ABOUT MARKETING:
Strengthening Your Marketing Muscles with 20 Exercises

Preface

So, why should you spend your time and money reading this book? More and more artists are taking advantage of new technologies to independently build awareness, make sales, and leverage favorable industry deals. But in this expanding competitive marketplace overflowing largely with hopeful artists and fly-by-night services, serious do-it-yourself musicians need "structured" advice more than ever from an artist who's lived through the business and succeeded.

Written for musicians by a veteran musician, *Music Marketing for the DIY Musician* is a strategic, step-by-step guide to producing a fully customized, low-budget plan of attack for marketing one's music. Presented in a conversational tone, it reveals the *complete marketing process* using the same fundamental concepts used by top innovative companies, while always encouraging musicians to find their creative niche and uphold their artistic vision. *It's the perfect blend of left-brain and right-brain marketing.*

Rest assured, ladies and gentlemen, that this book is not about using "hope" as a strategy, or just trendy tools and services that can help you "do things" right. It's about taking more control of your own destiny and *doing the right things* by professionally planning, strategizing, and executing a fully integrated, customized Marketing Plan of Attack™. It will help you save time and money, rise above all of the clutter, and eventually attract the attention of top industry pros. Ultimately, this book is about making quality *music that matters, and music that's heard!*

What inspired me to write this book? As a musician, consultant, and educator, my mission has always been simple: *to help music professionals turn their art into a more successful business.* But over the years I've identified an important void in the marketplace: nothing has been written for musicians by a musician with extensive professional experience that includes fundamental marketing concepts used by the most successful companies and contains easy-to-follow templates to help DIY artists budget their precious time and money. At a time when new technologies enable talented artists to act as their own independent record labels, there is clearly a need for a practical, DIY, step-by-step guide that presents tried-and-tested marketing advice in a modern way. *Music Marketing for the DIY Musician* is the culmination of 25 years in the trenches as a professional musician and entrepreneur, and over a decade in academic and practical research that has involved thousands of independent artists and marketing experts from around the world.

How is this book different? And why is it relevant to you? While there are other resources available, this book is unique and has several competitive advantages, including:

- It is written specifically for DIY musicians by a musician with DIY, indie, and major-label success, making it a more credible, focused, practical, and relatable resource for artists.
- It covers the complete marketing process—from *vision* through *execution*—with handy templates and samples in each chapter to help artists create fully customized marketing plans one step at a time.
- It provides an integrated mix of online and offline strategies extending far beyond just the traditional "four P's" of marketing and the latest Internet and social media promotion tips.
- It introduces sophisticated business and research tools (SWOT, SMART, AIDA, and PFB charts) not found in most music marketing books, enabling artists to choose more confidently *and even scientifically* the right strategies for their own career paths.
- It includes both real-world anecdotes and short tips in text boxes and afterthoughts to break up the text, and exclusive interviews with noted professionals to provide broad perspectives. *Interviews include Jeff Hinkle, Business Manager at GSO Business Management; Nance Rosen, Business Consultant at Sandler Training; and Ira Kalb, President of Kalb & Associates.*

- It contains a detailed glossary of key marketing terms, a resource guide of over 300 DIY and low-budget services, a complete sample Marketing Plan of Attack™, and 20 time-saving exercises for "strengthening your marketing muscles," from finding industry mentors to aligning with major marketing associations.
- It provides a website link where helpful templates and sample forms can be found.

So, who am I? As a former major-label, independent, and DIY recording/touring artist, I have over twenty-five years' experience working with the most respected management firms, A&R representatives, music producers, music publishers, equipment manufacturers, songwriters, and journalists. I'm a graduate of Berklee College of Music with a BA in professional music, and a graduate of UCLA Extension with a certificate in instructor development, project management, and marketing. For over a decade I have been teaching a class called DIY Music Marketing at Musicians Institute and UCLA Extension, where I received the Distinguished Instructor of the Year Award. I am also the author of *The Musician's Handbook* (first published by Billboard/Random House in 2003, and now in its third edition), which is used in some of the finest schools around the country. The VP of special events for the American Marketing Association Los Angeles Chapter and the founder of a thriving music consulting company in Hollywood, I speak with literally thousands of artists and music professionals year-round. I can be contacted at www.bobbyborg.com.

What's the best way to use this book? While it's possible to skim the pages and read individual chapters in any order, it's best to read this book from beginning to end so that you don't miss a single word. Before diving into the text, it is recommended that you have a specific business focus in mind (such as becoming a recording/touring musician, a composer of film and TV music, or the owner of a recording studio) so that you can put the information into the right perspective. While it's not immediately necessary, try to fill out the marketing plan templates at the end of each chapter so that you can build a customized plan one step at a time. Or, at the very least, be sure to review the marketing plan samples provided for the band "Rally the Tribes," so you can get a sense of how another DIY company might construct its plan. To get a deeper sense of the materials covered, be sure to regularly utilize the material in the back of this book and review the list of relevant resources and the definitions to important marketing terms. But most of all, just be sure to exercise patience when reading this book. Remember that *marketing is not difficult to understand, but it can be challenging to apply to your own personal situation.* Thus, if you find it less intimidating, you can write a plan for another DIY artist first to get the hang of the principles discussed. Sound good? Cool! So what are you waiting for? Turn the page and *let's do this!*

[Disclaimer: The methods and ideas herein present a systematic approach to marketing that can improve your chances for success, but they do not guarantee "an easy ticket to success." Further, while websites, magazines, and resources suggested in this book are recommended highly, Bobby Borg and his publishers are not responsible for the materials, business practices, and viewpoints of these sources—so exercise caution. Lastly, Bobby Borg and his publishers cannot be held accountable for any third-party licenses or agreements that you enter into—so please, always seek the advice of a personal consultant or attorney in any business matter about which you are unclear.]

THE DIY MARKETING MUSICIAN AT A GLANCE
WHAT DIY MARKETING IS:
A proactive, strategic approach to creating products and services to satisfy fans and make sales.
A way to attract the attention of those who can better help you by first helping yourself.
The process of taking advantage of available and low-budget resources to get the job done.
A realization that no one will care more about your career than you will.
A way to maintain one's true creative vision without letting the "wrong" cooks in the kitchen.
A way to retain a greater share of the profits and leverage better deals.
An "F the establishment" attitude originating from the punk genre and other underground scenes.
WHAT DIY MARKETING IS NOT:
A false shield of empowerment that can cause you to make costly mistakes.
A license to practice music business law.
A degree in shoddy logo making and other graphic arts.
A reason to believe that it can all get "fixed in the mix" down the line.
A reason to believe that you don't need an education because that famous rapper doesn't have one either.
An excuse to pay a publicist you really can't afford just because you're too damn lazy to do it yourself.
A reason not to relinquish some control to leverage creative alliances and favorable deals.

Acknowledgments

Thanks to my dearest Dad; family; closest friends; fellow board members at the American Marketing Association; Musicians Institute and UCLA staff; and John Cerullo, Carol Flannery, Jessica Burr, Joanna Dalin Sexton, and everyone else at Hal Leonard Performing Arts Publishing Group for understanding my vision and making this book possible.

Also a big shout-out to my preliminary feedback team: Katherine Fitzgerald (independent artist, vocalist of Violet UK, Harvard literature graduate), Bianca Philippi (principal and founder of Creative Insights, UCLA Extension distinguished instructor), Patrick Greenough (VP of Technology at American Marketing Association), Ronny Schiff (Ronny Schiff Productions, career counselor and instructor at Musicians Institute), Bob Nirkind (former executive editor at Billboard Books), Gail Hickman (screenplay writer), and the thousands of students and DIY artists who took my classes and attended my seminars.

I'd like to also thank all of my advisors, panelists, and colleagues: Ira S. Kalb (professor of marketing at the Marshall School of Business at University of Southern California; president, Kalb & Associates), Steve Winogradsky (attorney at law, partner at Winogradsky/Sobel), Robert Liljenwall (editor/author of *Marketing at Retail*, MBA, distinguished instructor at UCLA Extension), Nance Rosen (MBA, author of *Speak Up!*, and former marketing executive with the Coca-Cola Company), Jeff Hinkle (certified public accountant at GSO Business Management), Tony van Veen (CEO, CD Baby and Disc Makers), Michael Eames (president, Pen Music Group), Neil Gillis (president, Round Hill Music), Ernie Petito (formerly of Warner/Chappell Music), Andreas Wettstein (digital strategy for Mack Avenue Records), Sydney Alston (product specialist at Disc Makers), John Hartmann (former manager of Crosby, Stills & Nash; America; Poco; Eagles; and others), Robin Frederick (author of *Shortcuts to Hit Songwriting* and *Shortcuts to Songwriting for Film and TV*), Don Grierson (former VP of A&R at Sony/Epic Records, music industry consultant), Fred Croshal (former general manager at Maverick Records; founder of Croshal Entertainment Group, LLC), Blasko (Ozzy Osbourne/Mercenary Management, Inc.), Steven R. Van Hook (president of Educare Research Inc.; faculty at UCLA Extension), Michael Levine (founder of Levine Communications Office, representing Prince, Ozzy Osbourne, and Michael Jackson; and author of *Guerrilla PR*), Michael Laskow (president, TAXI Independent A&R Company), Ted Lowe (president of Choice Tracks), Dave Banta (multiplatinum, award-winning record producer), Chris Fletcher (Coast to Coast), Bryan Farrish (owner, Bryan Farrish Radio Promotion), Bill Zildjian (Sabian), John Pantle (agent at Agency for the Performing Arts), Kether Gallu-Badat (Latchkey Recordings), Bob Fierro (founder of Zebra Marketing), Don Gorder (chair, Music Business/Management Department, Berklee College of Music), Pascale Cohen-Olivar (program director, Entertainment Studies and Performing Arts, UCLA Extension), Nick Casale (graphic arts), and anyone else I missed who was there for me.

I would like to give special thanks to everyone who gave permission to reproduce artwork in this book. This includes Sarah Abdel of Silverback Management, for permission to use the Slightly StOOpid street stencil in chapter 15 (p. 196). I would also like to thank the following for permission to use logos in the chapter 8 graphic "Logo Examples: Independent Artists" (p. 78): Matthew Lindblad (Rebel Revive logo), Alex Quintana (Agruv Studios logo), Rob De Luca (Of Earth logo), Ian Di Leo (IDL Entertainment logo), Shane Quinn (Devil in Drag logo), Drew Petersen (Very Angry Scientists logo), Michelle Filijan (Assuming We Survive logo), Cynda Renae (Cockeyed Optimist logo), Armando Villasenor (Underground Nation logo), Milo Hernandez (Dirty Minds logo), Sabrina Petrini (KingQueen logo), Milo Hernandez (Dirty Minds logo), Gabriel Nava Rodrigues (Walla logo), Alexander Cabral (Clepto logo), Dan Hegarty (Cobra Venom logo), David Palmer (Invisible Poet Kings logo, created by DADABANK), and Shawn Scott (Shawn Scott Music Group logo). The photo of riot police used on pages 99, 241, 269, and 278 is © iStock.com/jon11.

Thanks also to the following for permission to use album cover art in the chapter 9 graphic "Album Art: Independent Artists" (p. 92): Tony Safqi and Oscar Preciado (*Tolerance*, by Reverted), Daniel Beallo (*Ship of the Rising Sun*, by Ship of the Rising Sun), Laura Vall (*Speak to Me*, by the Controversy), James Lawry (*Do Your Part*, by James Lawry), Bill Berends (*Insomnia*, by Mastermind), Colin Reid (*What We Can't Have*, by Colin Reid), Yohannes Skoda (*About Face*, by Mavrik), Eric Baum (*Powerlines*, by Run Rhino), Jens Andersen (*The Great Collapse*, by Immoralis), Gabriel Nava Rodrigues (*Nature*, by Walla; photo by Tercio Guratalo), Eleri Jane (*Play Me*, by Eleri), Bhavana Reddy (*Tangled in Emotions*, by Bhavana Reddy), Craig Costello (*Warning!* Catchy Tune, by Formally Un-named), Demerick Ferm (*All the Wrong Things 2*, by Demrick), and Benjamin M. Lecourt (*Murderology*, by Yard of Blondes).

An Overview of the Complete DIY Marketing Process
Creating and Executing a Plan of Attack in a Nutshell

Marketing is the process of *innovating* products and services to *satisfy customers*, *build awareness*, and *earn market share*. To DIY artists like you, it's the self-starting journey of *creating* music and merchandise to *win over loyal fans*, *entice industry execs*, and *make money*. However you see it, the concepts presented in this chapter (and book) will help you do the following:

- **Become aware of important marketing concepts and terms.**
- **Realize that marketing is an organized system of interrelated steps.**
- **Organize your thoughts into a detailed "Marketing Plan of Attack™."**
- **Understand the importance of being proactive and taking charge. And . . .**
- **Shoot for zero- to low-budget and realistic marketing techniques.**

Oh, and by the way, don't be too surprised when common business terms like *product* are used in place of *music*, *live performances*, and *merch*; when *company* is used in place of *band*, *solo act*, or *studio*; and when *customer* is used in place of *fan*, *audience*, or *following*. While music is an art, it is also a serious business, and you must start thinking about your career from a more professional and businesslike perspective. So get ready to expand your thoughts, learn, and always have a lot of fun.

The following key concepts are introduced briefly to give you a play-by-play look at the entire book. The information is expanded upon fully in subsequent chapters and marketing samples.

Describe Your Company's Vision and Set Your Career on Course

The marketing process typically starts with a "vision"—a declaration that defines that ultimate place you'd like your company to be in about seven to ten years down the road.

Your vision is what gets you out of bed in the morning and gives your life meaning. I'm not talking about some outrageous MTV "Cribs" fantasy, the color of your mansion in the French Riviera, or the remote island you want to own, but rather a vivid musical/business focus that complements your strengths and passions and sets your career on course.

To illustrate, long before Marilyn Manson ever became known to the world, he envisioned himself as being a "pop star who would one day shock the world." Personal sources say that when he was just a student of journalism at a small community college, he actually had drawings of costumes and stage set designs along with other business and creative details. This was Manson's "North Star"—his guiding light. He held true to that vision and projected it into everything his band or "company" did. Several Platinum albums and Top 10 hits later, he succeeded at living his dream.

So then, what are your strengths and passions, and what is your overall musical vision in about seven to ten years?

Do you see yourself playing a style of R&B, rock, folk, hip hop, jazz, or perhaps some new subgenre you aim to create? Do you aspire to be a major recording/touring artist known all over the world, or forever a local independent musician happy to be surviving on your music? Will you sell records, tour, and create merchandise, or will you write and produce? What kind of artist identity will you project to your target fans: wholesome and sweet, gangsta and badass, intellectual and socially conscious, or something else? Do you want people to see you as a role model? Do you want to make people happy and hopeful? Will you be the voice for the oppressed and unfortunate? Or will you stand for certain values in the world that are important to society as a whole?

Look, gang, by determining what's true to your heart and visualizing your higher and greater career and life purpose, you'll be able to more easily chart the course to your desired destination.

Identify Opportunities or "Needs" by Conducting a SWOT Analysis

While keeping your internal strengths, passion, and overall vision at heart, now it's time to examine the "external environment" of your organization more thoroughly and see how your musical vision matches up with people's wants and "needs." By doing this, you can further refine your true musical purpose, and even discover a void in the marketplace that you can fill better than anyone else.

As previously stated, Marilyn Manson had a clear vision of being a pop star who shocked the world. But he also identified and filled a specific societal need and void in the marketplace for an entertaining and horrifically dramatic new stage personality, similar only to what a now-aging Alice Cooper had done 23 years before.

In yet another example, guitarist Pat Metheny always envisioned himself as being an exceptional and forward-moving jazz musician. But he also identified and filled a specific industry need and void in the marketplace for an exciting new artist who could propel traditional jazz into the future using new technologies, such as synthesizers and robotics, unlike any other jazz musician before him.

An extremely valuable tool to help you examine the external and internal environments of the marketplace is called a *SWOT analysis*. SWOT is an acronym that stands for strengths, weaknesses, opportunities, and threats. The purpose of this tool is to:

- Identify a consumer need or opportunity in the marketplace that matches well with your internal strengths.
- Convert any weaknesses you may have into company resources. And . . .
- Minimize or eliminate the threats or risks your company might face.

Primary research methods (surveys, interviews, observation, etc.), as well as *secondary* research techniques (blogs, trade associations, magazines, etc.) can be extremely helpful when conducting your SWOT analysis.

Whether or not this "bigger picture" approach is new to you, be assured that SWOT is a very common tool that has been successfully used in marketing for decades by top companies, and it is one with which you'll soon become even more familiar.

Analyze Your Most Likely Customers and Target Your Market

Now that you have a more refined purpose and clearer idea of the external environment and the market need you will attempt to fill, it's important to identify and thoroughly analyze the most important people in the world: your "most likely" fans. These are people or businesses that share similar characteristics and are most likely to come out to your shows, buy your music, or license your songs. Bottom line: You have to thoroughly understand your target audience. You must know where and how to reach them with consistent marketing messages designed to communicate your company's common-ground beliefs, as well as your products' meaningful and relevant *benefits* (i.e., what your products do for your target customers).

To describe your most likely fans, use any combination of factors you deem relevant and useful, including age range, gender, geographic location, lifestyles (activities, interests, opinions), and behavioral characteristics, such as why they go out to clubs and how often. Should your most likely customers be other businesses, such as when you're a composer serving ad agencies and music libraries, then use factors such as company size, number of employees, and geographic location.

The more narrowly you define or *segment* your customers, the more customized and personalized your products and marketing messages can be to appeal to them. It's one thing to think of your fans simply as "alternative rockers" and another to think of them thoroughly as *male, angst-ridden alternative rockers, aged 21 to 32, with annual incomes of $40K to $60K, who are interested in watching extreme sports, smoking weed, drinking alcohol, and going to clubs once a week to see a high-energy show.*

Once you win over your most likely fans (or primary segment) with customized marketing messages, you can then target your next likely fans (or secondary segment).

To conduct customer research, examine the fans of other bands in your genre or closely related genres, and also by examining the fans you may already have. You can do this by visiting social media sites and reading what fans say, attending concerts and observing the audience, and just speaking with fans to discover what they want and need and *what they may not even know they want or need.*

Don't worry if at first you have trouble creating a fan profile—you'll continually fine-tune and adjust it as you gain more experience as a marketer.

Learn from Your Competitors by Conducting a Competitor Analysis

Differentiation is crucial to your success, so the next step in the marketing process involves conducting a *competitor analysis*. This requires you to thoroughly analyze your competitors' images, products, prices, distribution methods, and promotion strategies. What's that, you say? You don't have any competition? Of course you do! There are many levels of it, but for your purposes, competition could simply be defined as "any artist whom your most likely fan could see as being similar to you." Or more to the point: "any artist who could draw attention away from you."

To conduct a competitor analysis, pick two local artists and two national artists to examine. You can conduct simple research online to determine what works and doesn't work for these artists and, more importantly, to find out what the fans of these artists think! This should provide detailed information to help you set your career apart in a way that's meaningful to your target audience.

To illustrate, after the Police realized that other rock/reggae bands in England had not yet attempted to gain an edge in the United States market, it toured the US relentlessly in vans on a bare-bones budget, won over audiences, and earned the position of being the first band of its kind in America. And as the late talent agent Ian Copeland told me in a personal interview, "The rest is history."

Demo Your Products and Services and Get Invaluable Feedback

The next few steps in the marketing process deals with "research and development." This involves developing, testing, interpreting, and refining your products and services to get invaluable feedback from your target fan. "Feedback is the breakfast of champions," says management expert Ken Blanchard. "It opens your eyes and gives you an opportunity to forecast the future." Without it, you're only creating in a vacuum. And that's risky!

Now consider this:

- The first step in the process involves developing a prototype of your products and services (or just a clear "idea" of them) to gauge the receptivity of your intended audience. This could simply mean writing and recording three to five songs inexpensively, imagining a brand name that captures the personality of your music, and considering a visual identity, such as a logo, that you sketch on a piece of paper.
- The second and third steps are deciding on the method of testing you'll use (surveys, casual observation, interviews, etc.) and then conducting these tests on an audience via your social networks, an informal rehearsal room, or a club performance.
- The fourth and fifth steps involve deciding what your data really means and then determining what changes and/or additional testing (if any) need to be conducted. This might require you to go back and rethink your vision and SWOT analysis and even develop and test more recordings until you can show your idea is something about which people are truly excited.

As Edward McQuarrie explains in *The Market Research Toolbox*, market research can never provide guarantees, but it acts as an "uncertainty reducer." It can help you predict the future and save you a significant amount of time and money, which might otherwise be spent on creating products that simply don't sell. Keep in mind that the key focus of this book is to help musicians like you *turn your art into a more successful business.* It's about creating *music that truly matters to you,* but also *music that gets heard.*

Set Your Marketing Plan Goals by Using the SMART Model

As soon as you feel positive that you have a product/service of which you are proud and that will appeal to your most likely fan, you should set your marketing plan goals for the next year. *Written goals help provide short-term guidance on the path to achieving your long-term vision.*

Goals should be expressed as specific (exact) and measurable (countable) objectives based on the sales and/ or awareness you would like to achieve in the marketplace within one year from executing your plan. For example, your first-year goals might be based on selling X number of units of your six-song debut recording at a specific price, making back X percent of your initial investment of Y dollars, licensing X songs in film and television, or increasing your fan base from X to 5X fans.

Goals should also be established on realistic projections, observations, past successes, and available company resources to ensure they are attainable or "doable." Consider how well your competitors are selling. Think about whether you have sufficient access to personal savings, family loans, and discounted services to meet expenses. And assess whether you have access to band members and fans that can share the workload. These are all important factors.

And finally, goals should include the general strategies you'll use to help you arrive at your desired and specific destination at the end of the year.

In short, goals should follow the "SMART" model (a popular tool revised slightly by me to mean specific, measurable, attainable, road-mapped, and time based). And remember, goals should be high enough to challenge you, but never high enough to beat you.

Find the Right Blend of "Marketing Mix" Strategies to Achieve Your Goals

With your marketing goals firmly in place, you must now develop further the right mix of strategies to help achieve them. These strategies, appropriately called "marketing mix strategies," include the "four P's" of marketing (product, price, place, and promotion) as well as three other important building blocks (company branding, product branding, and measuring). Remember, these strategies will all be expanded upon in subsequent chapters, but they are introduced briefly below:

- **Company Branding:** This involves building a name, logo, slogan, attitude, look, and so forth that together create a unique image in the customers' minds.
- **Product/Service Branding:** This involves creating strong names, packaging, and a personality that are consistent with the overall company brand, yet distinct from your other products/services and those of the competition.
- **Product/Service Development:** This is the process of finalizing your offerings (songs, beats, albums, merchandise, live performances, fan clubs, etc.) for the marketplace, and designing an expert customer service policy to meet the needs of your target fan.
- **Price:** This is the intersection of the amount you are willing to charge for your products/services and the amount your fans are willing to pay for them. Strategies may include keeping the price within consumer boundaries, donation pricing, free pricing, and more.
- **Placement (or Place):** This is the distribution of your products/services to places where your target fans will find them easily, such as specific online sites, live-performance venues or stores, and certain TV shows and video games.
- **Promotion:** This is the process of communicating your products' unique *features* (what they are) and *benefits* (what they do) to stimulate the interest, attention, decision, and action of your target audience. This can be done via the following strategies: Internet, word of mouth, guerrilla marketing, radio promotion, sponsorships, publicity, direct marketing, sales promotions, face-to-face selling, advertising, and more. While there are many promotional methods, the ones you choose will depend on your audience, budget, experience, and careful research. And finally . . .
- **Measuring:** This is the continuous process of collecting, analyzing, and acting on important information collected from the marketplace. This might include feedback about the effectiveness of your marketing efforts and ideas from fans for new products and services. Computer programs like Excel and Access can aid you in organizing data.

Just in case it hasn't yet sunk in—it's not the individual marketing strategies (the parts) themselves that will help you to achieve your marketing goals, but rather the complete "mix" of strategies (the whole) functioning as one complete, integrated system of marketing communication. It's the "right blend in the right amounts" that's required. Thus, careful consideration must be given to how each strategy ultimately affects the others and ultimately affects your target customer.

For instance, if your brand identity strategy calls for promoting your fans' perception of you as the "bad boys of rock," you had better think twice before considering a place strategy including gigs at county fairs between the petting zoo and the cotton candy stand. [*Laughing!*] You get the idea.

As USC professor Ira Kalb puts it, "Marketing strategy planning is a lot like baking a cake—it requires the perfect mix of several ingredients all blended into one to achieve a desired outcome, but also a willingness to get feedback and the patience to carefully adjust the strategies accordingly until you get it right." To which Harvard Business School professor John P. Kotter adds, "The strategy decisions you don't make are just as important to the ones you do make." This might seem like common sense, but as I frequently say, "Common sense is not always so common."

Assemble a Marketing Plan of Attack™ and Present Your Ideas Effectively

Your next step (as if the above steps in the marketing process were not enough!) is to compile all of the information gathered in your research and planning and put it into a standard marketing plan format.

A marketing plan (or as I call it, a Marketing Plan of Attack™) is a written document that serves as a road map for your business idea and marketing campaign, a communicative tool to keep all the members of your organization on track, and even a sales document to attract potential investors, distributors, and others. Yup, you heard right! No matter if you are an artist recording an album to release it to fans or a composer building a studio to deliver tracks to ad agencies, a marketing plan could help you attract investors to fund your career. Marketing plans are tools business people expect, and they include language professionals are used to reading.

While marketing plans can come in all shapes, sizes, and lengths, the ordering and standard elements you'll use for your purposes, as an independent/do-it-yourself artist, are as follows:

- *Front Cover:* A front cover with your photograph or logo, artist name, and website URL.
- *Executive Summary:* A one-page executive summary briefly describing the organization, vision, market need, revenue generators, objectives, general strategies, resources, costs, and the challenges faced.
- *Table of Contents (TOC):* A TOC outlining each section of the plan with page numbers.
- *Vision:* Your company's vision, describing where you want to be in seven to ten years.
- *SWOT Analysis:* An internal and external examination of your company and ideas.
- *Customer Analysis:* A profile of your most likely customer.
- *Competitor Analysis:* A study of your direct competitors.
- *Testing and Feedback:* Results from research tests you've conducted to confirm that your ideas are viable and profitable ones.
- *Goals:* Sales and/or awareness goals that follow the SMART model.
- *Strategies:* Marketing mix strategies explaining how you'll achieve your goals, including company branding, product branding, product, price, place, promotion, and measuring.
- *Costs:* A detailed budget delineating expenses involved in executing your strategies, which for a do-it-yourself artist will be mostly low-budget items.
- *Timeline:* A timeline to help organize the execution of your plan. And finally . . .
- *Appendix:* An appendix containing any detailed charts, graphs, or research findings you'd like to include. (This is optional.)

A Marketing Plan of Attack™ must be clearly written with complete, easily understandable sentences. The information is usually written in one of three ways: first-person plural (we), first-person plural possessive (our), or third person (your company name, or *it* or *they*). Your plan must also be concise (bigger is not necessarily better) and use common, easy-to-read font styles, like Times New Roman at 11- or 12-point size with 1.1 or 1.2 line spacing. A plan should also be paginated well, with consistent headings, subheadings, and bullet-point styles marking each section.

Keep in mind that a marketing plan is "a living, breathing document." In other words, a marketing plan is not something you assemble once and use unchanged for the next year, but rather, it is a fluid tool that is continually revised as you evaluate its performance and observe new marketplace developments on your path to success.

By the way, I call it a Marketing Plan of Attack™ because when it is handled with the extreme detail and care this book outlines, your plan should be analogous to a battle plan—something on which you'd be willing to bet your entire life and the lives of others on your team. After all, your career and success really are that important to you! Right? Music is your heart and soul.

Execute Your Marketing Plan Effectively and Get Results

Doing the aforementioned work and compiling a plan are an essential beginning, but you must now execute your strategies successfully within the framework of your budget and timeline to give them worth. There are several factors that can seriously affect the outcome of your marketing plan (all of which will be discussed in chapter 20 of this book). But here are three things to chew on for now:

- First, you must get together the financing on which you based your marketing plan goals—whether it be *personal income* or *savings*, a *small loan* from family members or friends, personal *credit cards*, customer *dona-*

tions and pledges, or "*barter exchanges*" (which are trade-offs of goods or services with others). Heck, artists like Amanda Palmer even presold her record online and collected as much as one million dollars. Whatever the method you use, now it's time to secure your financing! Remember, you're *not going to get very far if you run out of gas to put into your car.*

- Second, you must take charge of your career and fully embrace the "do-it-yourself" methodology on which this book is based. Or, to think of it another way, you must fully utilize a "do-it-together" methodology toward your business and marketing. One band member can be the website guy, another the fan club and database gal, and another the promotion person. If you're a solo artist, and even if you're in a band, you can create and utilize a street team of your most dedicated hungry fans or friends to help you with all of your marketing tasks. Just remember that you have to take the bull by the horns early, because no one else will. And then, finally . . .
- Third, remember that you must strive to keep your *work ethic* in check over the *long haul*. Marketing is not something you do for just a few weekends. It's a continual process. Like a shark that must keep swimming to take in oxygen, your career dies if you stop marketing and measuring your efforts!

Does this all sound daunting? Look at it this way: your overall strategy can be to attract the attention of those who can help you by first helping yourself! Light as many small fires as you can till people see the smoke and take notice. Create some momentum in your career, and get the managers, producers, publishers, and investors to come to you. And they will come. As Guy Kawasaki, author of *The Art of the Start*, would say, investors are known to "pay attention to when the dogs are eating the dog food." This might take a little time and hard work to make happen, but if you're a "lifer" and not just some wannabe weekend warrior with a rock-star fantasy, sweat and time shouldn't mean a thang!

Keep Learning About Marketing and Strengthen Your Marketing Muscles

And finally, the last step in the marketing process deals with your commitment to learning and staying alert for new techniques and methods that can sharpen your skills. There is so much to learn about this fascinating subject; you should strive to soak it all up.

Read every page that this resource has to offer and then investigate other works, such as *Marketing Management* by the legendary Philip Kotler. While the text is very detailed, you'll be much more prepared for it after reading my book. Classic and more specialized books, such as *Ogilvy on Advertising* by David Ogilvy and *Secrets of Closing the Sale* by Zig Ziglar, are nice supplements.

You should also make sure to read the latest marketing and business news via popular sites and blogs such as *Harvard Business Review*, *Wired*, and *Fast Company*. These are all great reads.

Lastly, be sure to attend seminars and events held by important organizations such as the Direct Marketing Association, the Market Research Association, and the American Marketing Association (for which I sit on the board as VP of Special Events in Los Angeles). If you have any questions whatsoever, visit www.bobbyborg.com or www.musicmarketingforthediymusician.com.

So that's about it, folks: the complete marketing process in a nutshell. But before diving into the heart of this book, take a quick look at a few *general* thoughts on music marketing.

Consider These Overall Thoughts Before Diving into the Text

To ensure that you're really in the right marketing "zone," consider the following points carefully:

- **Be good, because "marketing" won't make you better.** Abraham Lincoln once said, "Whatever you are, just be a good one." If you don't have a great idea or product, you really have nothing at all. Fans do not reward bad songs, poor musicianship, shoddy production quality, and cheap merchandise—they are very discerning and sophisticated today, and there are far too many choices. So do your homework. *Be good first and foremost!* And as they say in marketing lingo, "WOW your customer!"

- ***Don't worry about whether Lil Wayne, Dr. Dre, or anyone else knew this stuff.*** Make no mistake—successful people in all fields apply marketing and business principles to achieve their goals whether they know it or not. The advantage of being consciously aware of these principles upfront is that you don't have to discover them by accident. Rather, you can use them as tools at your own discretion to help you achieve your vision.

- ***Remember that* marketing *is not a bad word.*** Some people think of marketing as sleazy or pushy. This reaction is usually due to bad past experiences with deceptive advertisements or pushy marketing tactics. But as media critic Douglas Rushkoff said in a PBS special entitled *The Persuaders*, "Don't let your marketing show." If you can focus on the creation of products and services that uphold your vision, satisfy fans by giving them what they need, and present your offers in a nonintrusive manner that make fans feel like they are part of the process, people won't even know you're marketing to them. But make no mistake: if you want to *make it*, you have to *market!*

- ***Don't worry if you don't have anything to market right now, or you've already launched.*** Remember that it's never too late, or too early, to learn about music marketing. By understanding the process, you'll know what to do long before starting your next project. And if you've already released your products and services, you'll know what needs fixing and what needs to be left alone.

- ***Don't be afraid to look at yourself under a microscope.*** Finally, the marketing concepts discussed here are not necessarily difficult to understand, but they are certainly challenging to apply. They will push you to ask some very specific questions about yourself and to think long and hard about your music business endeavor. Some of you will be ready to dive into this material and will start using the templates to write a Marketing Plan of Attack™, and others will still need more time to find themselves. In any case, just remember that this material is here to help you, not to hurt you. Be brave, have an open mind, and use what works for you! Okay? Cool!

So, that's pretty much music marketing in a nutshell. I know it was a lot of stuff, but you should now be ready to expand upon each subject and create a solid Marketing Plan of Attack™ utilizing the handy templates and samples at the end of each chapter.

Are you pumped up to do this? I said, *Are you pumped up to do this???* Great! Then read on.

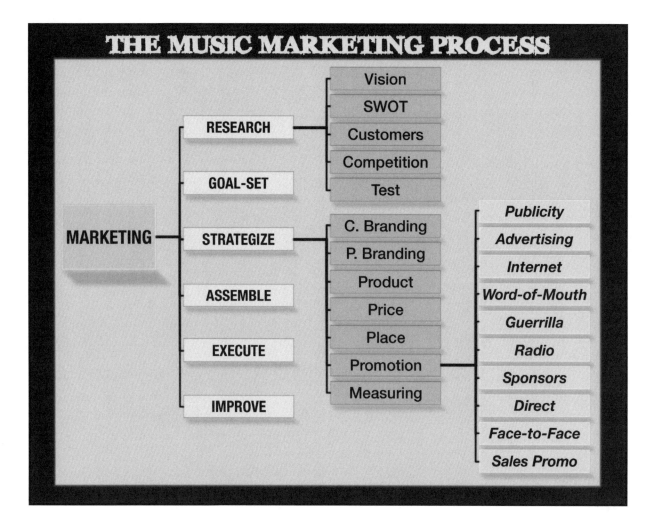

Describe Your Company's Vision

Identifying Your Musical Purpose and Setting Your Career on Course

Describing your vision is the process of reaching down deep into your soul and detailing precisely where you'd like your company to be in the future—say seven to ten years down the road. It's about clearly defining the type of career you'd like to have, the style or genre you'd like to pursue, and the vibe you'd like to project onto the world. Your vision is not contrived or forced. Rather, it's based on that special feeling deep in your heart that inspired you to pursue music in the first place. A vision is the "life" and "purpose" of your career. Your vision is your company's true passion to the core.

Identifying a clear vision can help you to do the following:

- **Pursue profitable marketing opportunities without selling your soul.**
- **Maintain personal integrity when making important business decisions.**
- **Build a career in alignment with your principles, values, and belief systems.**
- **Create a marketing plan with clearly defined short-term goals.**
- **Communicate more effectively with prospective investors and others.**

Without a clear vision to guide you, you'll appear lost in the marketplace, like a tree without roots, reaching out in several different directions but without a firm hold on solid ground. You'll also appear unpredictable—something customers recognize easily and see as a reason to withdraw their allegiance to you, or never pledge their allegiance to you in the first place. What's more, you'll appear undecided to those with whom you desire to work, and thus you'll find it difficult to convince a team of supporters to follow you into battle. As you can see, ladies and gentlemen, it's really no accident that the marketing process begins with identifying a clear vision.

Now, what follows are a few brief sections on how to put your vision into words for the purposes of constructing your Marketing Plan of Attack™. They include:

1. **Identifying the Type of Company You Envision Becoming**
2. **Indicating What Products and Services You'll Provide**
3. **Determining Your Most Likely Genre or Style**
4. **Determining What Level of Success You Wish to Achieve**
5. **Considering What Kind of Industry You're In**
6. **Knowing What You Want to Project onto the Marketplace**
7. **Writing Your Vision Statement Paragraph**

Let's begin.

GOT A COMPANY VISION?

When I was a young boy, I woke up one morning with a vision. It came to me after several years of taking drum lessons and practicing, but it certainly came to me. I saw myself as a professional drummer in a rock 'n' roll band comprised of exceptional musicians: recording albums, touring the world for a major label like Atlantic Records, and playing before large, young, hip audiences. With both my music and presence, I saw myself inspiring people with a positive, uplifting, motivational message that would change their lives and help them get through their tough times. That vision was so burned into my subconscious that I saw it every time I closed my eyes.

Though my career has taken lots of twists and turns since I was twelve years old, and I have adapted to market needs and changing times, that vision has remained constant. I made rock records in varying styles and toured around the world, and now I consult with music professionals and write books. In all cases, I always worked hard to give people a positive, happy, uplifting feeling about their lives and futures. You see, most successful companies really do start from the heart. They have real values and a genuine belief system. They stand for something. They have direction and a sense of purpose. Without this, there is nothing.

Identify the Type of Company You Envision Becoming

Describing your vision starts with identifying the type of company you envision becoming. This is simply the process of asking yourself a few very basic questions: Am I a band? Am I a solo artist? Am I a producer/artist? Am I a songwriter/composer? Am I a contract employee or self-employed performer? Can I be all of them? Clearly, that would require separate marketing plans for each role, so for now, I suggest you stick with one. What follows is a brief description of each company type. If there are any doubts about the career and company you envision, this should help.

Put Together a Band

A band is no different from a professional sports team. It consists of a group of individuals united in the pursuit of a common goal, with each person playing a unique and integral part in achieving a dream. The motto—at least in theory—is "All for one, and one for all." Some of the most celebrated music and idolized musicians originated in bands. But unless strict criteria, like work ethic and tenacity, are employed in forming the band—and unless a proper band membership agreement, including voting methods and percentage splits, is drafted—a band can easily fall apart due to the sometimes large egos of the musicians working alongside each other. Just be sure to check out *The Musician's Handbook* by yours truly for more on this subject.

Be a Solo Artist and Employer

The solo artist is a rare and special breed of musician—an exceptional writer or instrumentalist who plays a melodic instrument, a skilled vocalist who's blessed with undeniable charisma, or a highly motivated individual who possesses the desire to lead. While your name and likeness may be individually displayed on album cover artwork and venue marquees, you'll rarely be working alone. You might employ a group of studio and gigging musicians, and you may even collaborate with skilled songwriters and producers. Solo artists are generally their own bosses and enjoy a larger income than they might in a band, but they also bear the brunt of the hard work, responsibility, and investment risk in time and money.

Envision Yourself as a Songwriter/Composer

The songwriter/composer is a uniquely skilled artist who has devoted an exceptional amount of time to honing the craft of songwriting. She typically writes both the music and lyrics for other artists as well as for a variety of different media—film, television, and radio. She is also capable of writing in a variety of different styles, albeit often excelling in one. For instance, Diane Warren focuses on writing pop songs—for Mary J. Blige, Celine Dion, and the late Whitney Houston—whereas Desmond Childs focuses on rock, for Aerosmith, Bon Jovi, and Weezer.

Songwriters typically write alone, but they are also known to team up with other writers or even artists to cowrite material. Songwriters sometimes serve as their own music publishers, or they are signed to an exclusive songwriter agreement with an outside music publishing company as *staff writers*. Because of various royalties that can be earned, songwriting can be very lucrative. However, competition can make it extremely tough to get songs placed.

Picture Yourself as a Producer/Artist

The producer/artist is typically a talented musician who has recording, beat-making and songwriting skills. While the producer/artist might focus on writing and releasing his own product and promoting his own career, he may also focus on helping other artists with selecting songs to record, arranging compositions, cowriting or composing complete works, and ensuring generally that the artist's work will sound current in the marketplace for years to come. Many producers have their own production companies, recording studios, and even independent labels, which can prove to be extremely lucrative. However, the downside is that with the proliferation of home recording equipment, many DIY artists are learning how to record their own music, thereby diminishing the perceived need for an outside record producer.

Imagine Yourself as a Contract Employee or Self-Employed Performer

The contract employee or self-employed performer is the last type of company to examine. The term *contract employee* refers basically to anyone who agrees to work under a set of conditions, specified by a contract, in a *long-term* or continuing relationship (a talk show band, a concert tour, etc.). A self-employed performer, or independent contractor, refers basically to anyone who makes his or her services available for hire for *shorter-term* relationships (studio work, casuals, etc.).

While the Internal Revenue Service has very strict rules for distinguishing between employed and self-employed workers, the difference is really a matter of how taxes and insurance are handled and who handles them. Besides that, the most important thing to grasp about either position is that you're in the business of *you*! This can provide you a great deal of freedom and flexibility, but you must always stay on the lookout for future work, understand your legal rights, and be extremely clear about the compensation and benefits to which you are entitled as a professional working musician. Check out the American Federation of Musicians (AFM) and SAG-AFTRA for important guidelines and wage minimums for musicians and vocalists.

Indicate What Products and Services You'll Provide

Indicating the products and services your company will offer is the next element of describing your company's vision. It also dovetails with the first section, because if you know what type of company you envision yourself becoming, then it's likely you know what products/services you will be offering. Consider the following:

- *Bands' Products/Services:* If you envision yourself becoming a band or solo artist, then your major revenue sources will likely be recordings, live concert performances, videos, merchandise, sponsorships, fan club memberships, and other revenue generators (acting, modeling, etc.).

- *Songwriters' Products/Services:* If you envision yourself as a songwriter/composer, your main products and services will be your songs, jingles, and film scores.
- *The Products/Services of Producer/Artists:* If you envision yourself as a producer/artist, your products and services will be the beats you produce and the recordings you oversee.
- *Contract or Self-Employed Musicians' Products/Services:* And if you envision yourself as a contract or self-employed musician, your products and services will be your work in studio sessions, on tours, and in lessons and clinics.

Got it?

Keep this section of your vision as simple as possible. There is no need to describe the Subway sandwich franchise you'll own, the tequila you'll invent, or the clothing empire on which you'll make millions. That's all good, but these other businesses will likely stem from your great success as an artist. So for now, it's best to focus on your vision as an artist first and foremost. Make sense? By the way, we'll look further into products and services later in this book.

Determine Your Genre or Style

Now that you've determined what type of company you will be and the products and services you'll offer, it's time to think about the general style of music on which you envision your company focusing. The idea here is to give you a reference point from which to start your marketing journey. Assuming you've already been exposed to music for a good part of your life, and you've put in a few years of practice on your chosen instrument, this shouldn't be difficult to do.

So then, what style do you see your company focusing on? Do you generally envision yourself doing rock, pop, country, R&B, electronica, reggae, jazz, or world? Or maybe you'll envision yourself working in a subgenre style—for instance, alternative rock—or even a substyle of alt rock, such as indie, goth, grunge, emo, or Britpop. Or in the best-case scenario, you'll blend elements of the styles you like best to create a new, innovative sound of your own.

If need be, listen to radio stations to examine what formats they use, look at iTunes to see how they categorize music for consumer sales, and check out websites like Allmusic.com to see how they categorize music. Hopefully, this research will give you a better idea of the general categories of music that exist and where one day you might envision yourself being.

MUSICAL STYLES AND THEIR SUBCATEGORIES

- *Rock Styles:*
  - Alternative (indie, goth, grunge, emo, Britpop)
  - Hard rock (metal, speed metal, goregrind, grindgore, black metal, progressive metal, neoclassical metal, hair metal)
  - Pop (Christian pop, tween pop)
  - Soft rock (singer/songwriter, contemporary)
  - Punk (skate punk, punk-pop, new wave, ska-punk, hardcore, garage band)
  - Roots (rockabilly, blues rock, jazz rock)

- *R&B Styles:*
  - Hip hop (dance hip hop)
  - Urban
  - Rap (gangsta rap, East Coast rap, West Coast rap, political rap)

- Old school
- Go-go
- Drum 'n' bass
- Soul (Chicago soul, Memphis soul, neo soul, retro soul)
- Funk
- Motown

- *Country Styles:*
  - Traditional country (bluegrass, country boogie, square dance, jug band, country gospel)
  - Country pop (Nashville sound, urban cowboy)
  - Alternative country (alternative country rock, Americana)
  - Folk
  - Country rock (new country)
  - Honky tonk (truck-driving honky tonk)
  - Progressive country (rodeo, outlaw)

- *Electronica Styles:*
  - Dance (house, acid, Euro, disco)
  - Electronic (trap, dub step, Dutch house, ambient, techno, trance, trip hop, gabba, experimental dub, downbeat, tribal house, jungle drum 'n' bass, electro)

- *Jazz Styles:*
  - Traditional jazz, smooth jazz, big band (swing, ballroom dance)
  - Bop
  - Fusion
  - Latin jazz (Cuban, Brazilian)
  - New Orleans jazz (ragtime, Dixieland, boogie-woogie)
  - Soul jazz

- *International (World Styles):*
  - African, African folk, Afropop
  - Contemporary flamenco
  - Celtic/British Isles
  - Gypsy

- *And so many more . . .*

[Note: Research conducted on Allmusic (www.allmusic.com).]

Decide What Level of Success You Wish to Achieve

Another important element of defining your vision is to consider seriously just what level of success you see your company achieving. Certainly no one has a crystal ball to tell him or her the future outcome of his or her business efforts, but while the categories I've listed below are simply generalizations, you can at least take a moment to consider whether you are after international, national, or local success.

- *International Success:* International success might mean that you sign with a major-label team and management company where commercial Top 10 hit records are distributed around the world and large-scale tours are scheduled regularly.

- **National Success:** National success might mean that you hook up with a smaller independent label and management team where niche-market recordings and tours are placed primarily in the United States.
- **Local Success:** Local success might mean that you work as an independent contractor on your own terms where you do the majority of your teaching, session work, gigging, and producing in your hometown.

Whatever the level of success you'd like to achieve, go ahead and briefly jot it down. This is truly important. After all, not everyone dreams about world domination, ya' know. [*LOL.*]

Consider What Kind of Industry You're In

The next step in creating a vision statement is to decide precisely what business you are really in. This truly creative and practical approach was developed by Theodore Levitt, a Harvard Business School professor, in his important marketing paper, *Marketing Myopia*. Levitt argues that all companies should ask themselves the question "What business am I in?" They should closely examine their corporate vision and define their businesses broadly to encourage out-of-the-box thinking.

For instance, Exxon can think of itself as being in the business of petroleum, or it can think of itself as being in the business of *energy*. Or Hallmark can think of itself as being in the business of greeting cards, or think of itself as being in the business of *creating memories*. And thus, you might think of yourself as working in the business of music, or think of yourself as being in the *business of entertainment*, the party business, or the business of making people happy.

Jimmy Buffett, an artist who built his career around a Caribbean sea theme or "vacation vibe," once said that he was in the industry of "escapism." He went from writing a song called "Margaritaville" to starting a fan club called the Parrot Heads, developing a line of suntan products, launching a line of barbecue sauces, opening a chain of hotel resorts in remote locations, and creating his own fleet of sea planes to carry passengers to sunny beaches. Wow! Can you see the possibilities Levitt's idea offers? Says Bianca Philippi, a marketing consultant, "This type of thinking can lead to deeper customer understanding/engagement/satisfaction, innovation, and the reinventing of old business models and thinking."

So what business are you in? It's not right or wrong to simply say music, but you may be inspired to get more creative here.

Know What Identity You Want to Project into the Marketplace

Moving on to the final stage of realizing your vision, now take a look at what you want your company to project into the marketplace. This section really gets down to the core of who you are and what type of businessperson you envision yourself becoming. It is essentially the answer to the question "What is your life purpose?" Or, as Bill Chiaravalle asks in his book *Branding*, "What is the important message that you are driven to communicate?"

Is your life's purpose to illuminate political injustices of the world and stand up for human rights like Rage Against the Machine? Is it to make the world a better place and preach peace and hope like U2? Or is it to help gay and lesbian minority groups feel like they have more of a place in the world like Lady Gaga?

The Los Angeles–based indie band KingSize provides a perfect example of a company that has always known what it wants to project onto the marketplace. The members were born into families of philanthropists. Lead singer Jason Gordon's grandfather, Danny Thomas, was a comedian who founded St. Jude Children's Research Hospital, and drummer Andrew Crosby's father, Norm Crosby, was a comedian and longtime ambassador for the City of Hope. The band members agree that they are proudest of their family's humanitarian efforts, and that ultimately this fuels the band's vision and cause-related activities.

At a music industry conference and panel discussion in Austin, Texas, Gordon said:

> Music in general has always been our own way of giving back to people. We use music as the focal point for initiatives we start like the "St. Jude Rock 'n' Roll Hope Show" to benefit special causes around the world, or the "Concert Ticket Surcharge" to be donated to certain causes. Overall, we've always had a strong vision of what our perfect band would be. We want our records to be as strong in people's hearts as it is to their ears.

So what are some of the drives that fuel your big-picture vision? What do you want to project to the world with your music? Whatever it is—put it on paper. This will serve as the true essence of your vision, as well as the cornerstone in building a strong brand image in the minds of your fans.

Write Your Vision Statement Paragraph

Now that you've thought about all of the variables that make up your vision, it's time to write your ideas down in a short vision statement paragraph. Your paragraph is going to project seven to ten years into the future and indicate the following:

- What type of company you see yourself becoming (a band, a solo artist, a songwriter, etc.).
- The products you will most likely release to generate revenue (merch, recordings, fan clubs, etc.).
- The style of music you see yourself writing (rock, jazz, country, etc.).
- The level of success you realistically imagine yourself achieving (international, domestic, local, etc.).
- The industry you'll be in (the music business, the business of making people happy, the party business, etc.). And . . .
- What you see yourself projecting into the world (hope, peace, awareness, etc.).

Your paragraph should be no longer than six lines and sum up accurately the heart and soul of your company. A handy template found at the end of this chapter will help you with your writing.

Now, here's a brief sample of a vision statement paragraph:

In seven to ten years, we envision our company as becoming an internationally known, technologically minded electronic-Latin rave band in the entertainment industry whose main products and services will be digital downloads, live concerts simulcasted on the Web for a fee, interactive games and contests where people pay to be part of our virtual band world, and merchandise (branded computer covers and other tech-geek goodies). Our music and words will be nationally known for raising awareness of important humanitarian issues, and our actions and behavior will be rooted in rallying important charities and causes.

=MARKETING PLAN TEMPLATE=

Be sure to use the template below, or a template like it, to help craft important information that you will use in your Marketing Plan of Attack™. For additional help, refer to the marketing plan example below, the chapter on assembling your plan, and the complete plan provided in the back of this book.

Your Vision Statement Paragraph Template

Answer the questions below to help you form your personal vision statement. Note that in its final form, it is your intention to create a short paragraph by removing the questions and using your answers. This should go into your final Marketing Plan of Attack™. Remember that your vision serves as the starting point from which you will research, modify, and expand your marketing plan.

In seven to ten years, what type of company do you envision yourself becoming (band, solo artist, songwriters, producer, etc.)?

What types of products/services do you envision offering (recordings, merch, tours, etc.)?

What is your musical category, or what do your foresee it being (rock, rap, country, etc.)?

How big a piece of the market do you intend to tackle? (How successful do you realistically see yourself being, given the international, national, and local competition? And do you see yourself ultimately as a major label, indie, or DIY artist?)

What type of "industry" do you see yourself serving broadly (music, entertainment, party, etc.)?

What image do you envision your company and your products/services projecting ultimately onto your public (e.g., an image that is positive, uplifting, or rebellious)?

Vision Statement Paragraph Template: Now you can consider using the information above and the template below to create your very own vision statement paragraph:

In seven to ten years, we envision our company as becoming a _____(locally, nationally, internationally, etc.) known _____(category of music: rap, rock, country, etc.) _____(type of company: band, solo act, studio, etc.) in the _____(type of industry: entertainment, music, media, etc.) business, whose main products/services will be _____(recordings, performances, merch, etc.). Overall, our music, words, and actions will be known for projecting a message of _____(peace, happiness, fun, political awareness, etc.) to our target audience.

=MARKETING PLAN EXAMPLE=

Now here's a marketing plan sample for a mock alternative rock band named Rally the Tribes (RTT). We'll use RTT at the end of each chapter to show you how they might go about laying out their very own marketing plan one step at a time.

COMPANY VISION

In seven to ten years, we envision our organization becoming a nationally known rock/rave band in the business of "music and activism," whose main products/services will be recordings, performances, merch, photographic and poetry books, documentary films, and fan clubs. Twenty percent of the proceeds will be donated to special causes around our nation. Overall, our music, words, and actions will be known for projecting a message of peace, justice, and equality to our target audience and the nation.

Identify Profitable Opportunities or "Needs"
Conducting a SWOT Analysis

After describing your company's vision, it's time to check in with the rest of the world to see how that image matches up with a true marketing opportunity. This is the process of identifying a void, or consumer *need*, in the marketplace, and a unique and profitable concept or approach to filling that need better than anyone else. Artists who can to stay true to themselves, adjust with the marketplace, and push the boundaries of innovation are typically those who are the most successful.

SWOT analysis is a traditional marketing research tool that helps identify true business opportunities and needs. Remember that SWOT is an acronym for strengths, weaknesses, opportunities, and threats. As further described by marketing guru Philip Kotler in *Marketing Management*, it is a process that helps you examine thoroughly both the internal and external environment of your company to help you do the following:

- **Match "external" opportunities with your "internal" strengths.**
- **Overcome internal weaknesses to pursue certain opportunities.**
- **Reduce your vulnerability to external "threats" (things that can get in your way).**

If all this sounds a bit too businesslike, be brave and hang in there! Artists of all genres have used elements of the SWOT analysis, whether they were aware of it or not. Even Tupac Shakur said in the documentary *Uncensored and Uncut*, "My music focuses on raw human *needs* . . . and getting as close to telling the truth and selling records as I can get." You see, identifying a market *need*, and capitalizing on your strengths to fill that need and make a profit, is the essence of SWOT.

What follows is a detailed breakdown of the SWOT process, which, as I have reinvented it, produces something more like an "OSWT" analysis. Sections of this chapter include:

1. **Scanning for Potential Opportunities**
2. **Matching Opportunities with Strengths**
3. **Uncovering Your Weaknesses**
4. **Spotting Potential Threats**
5. **Writing a SWOT (or OSWT) Conclusion**
6. **Hearing It in Their Own Words: Interview with Ira Kalb**

Scan the Marketplace for Potential Opportunities

Conducting your SWOT analysis starts with scanning for a profitable marketing opportunity. As previously stated, a marketing opportunity is a void, or consumer need, in the marketplace, and a unique and profitable concept or approach to filling that need better than anyone else. Put another way, a marketing opportunity is an area of consumer need and interest where there is a high probability you'll succeed. However you see it, here is a brief discussion on identifying opportunities, as well as examining the opportunities on which others have capitalized.

Identify Opportunities

To identify profitable marketing opportunities, you must look into your *external environment*, the realm that is outside of your company and your control. Opportunities can come in many forms: societal trends, technological developments, economic conditions, political-legal regulations, customer markets, competition, distribution channels, and natural causes (such as environmental issues).

Consider the following:

- A company might examine societal trends and identify an opportunity to pursue the next big musical movement and fashionable look.
- The competitive marketing environment may present an opportunity for a company to differentiate its live performances and create a more unique experience.
- A company might scan consumer markets and identify an opportunity to reach an unfilled or neglected market niche.
- A company might keep a watchful eye on technological developments and pursue an opportunity to configure its recorded music in more interesting and interactive formats for consumers.
- Considering all the natural changes in the environment these days, a company might see an opportunity to take a "green" approach in packaging its products and perform live at concerts that promote the green movement.
- A company might follow legal and political developments and use these country and world issues as an opportunity to create subject matter for its songs and titles for its albums.
- Finally, a company might see an opportunity in the current economic landscape to experiment with creative pricing strategies to add value to its offerings.

Examine the Opportunities on Which Others Have Capitalized

While there are numerous examples to illustrate how other artists have found a market need, and an opportunity to fill that need, let's take a look at two classic case studies: Madonna and Nirvana.

Madonna

Madonna, a visionary entertainer who set out to blend music, fashion, and dance into one complete package, is clearly aware of societal and industry trends when she follows new opportunities to reinvent pop music and pop culture. People always *need* fresh music and fashion to stimulate and excite them, and Madonna has always been able to align herself with up-and-coming and elite fashion experts, music producers, and choreographers to innovate new material and deliver quality recordings and tours—from her very first record, *Madonna* (1983), with its dance pop sound and tween pop look, to her seventh release, *Ray of Light* (1998), with its mature sound and goth look, to where she is today. No matter which period of her career you examine, Madonna has remained one step ahead of the pop competition and at the forefront of music and fashion. Remarkably, she continues to be successful into her 50s.

As Robin Frederick, author of the book *Shortcuts to Hit Songwriting*, says, "No one ever really knows for sure where music is going—but make no mistake, it is definitely going!" The challenge is to understand what people are currently listening to, and then to push the boundaries of innovation—not in a way that loses touch with society, but in a way that keeps people fulfilled and interested (and in the best-case scenario, expresses your musical vision and integrity).

To sum this up using the words of the hockey great Wayne Gretzky, "Don't skate where the puck is, skate where the puck is going."

Nirvana

Nirvana, a visionary punk rock band that set out to create real music for real people, was clearly aware of societal shifts and consumer markets (whether consciously or unconsciously) when they followed an opportunity to create a new genre of music called "grunge." Hair metal of the '80s was becoming a cliché of itself, and there was an obvious *need* for change and something new.

As Soundgarden and Audio Slave singer Chris Cornell observed in *GQ* magazine:

> There was a barrage of videos with guys in their late thirties with their supermodel wives doing splits on top of a Jaguar. You would see Motley Crue go from the parking lot to the backstage of a stadium in a helicopter. All of it was saying, "We have a life that you don't have," whereas Nirvana looked like guys you'd go to school with.

Gina Arnold (author of the book *Route 666 on the Road to Nirvana*) also commented:

> I think Nirvana's success has a lot to do with Presidents Reagan and Bush and the end of a repressive twelve-year era. "Teen Spirit" [Nirvana's explosive song on the album *Nevermind*] is not clear at all lyrically, but sonically it's very clear what Nirvana were expressing about culture. It was Grunge's moment in the same way that the Motown era of music in the '60s and '70s expressed something about the joy of civil rights.

Look, no matter how you see it, Nirvana went against the popular flow, appealed to the anti-trendy, and earned their place in rock 'n' roll history. Perhaps you'll be the next artist who follows suit.

IDENTIFY OPPORTUNITIES VIA MARKET RESEARCH

Keep in mind that you don't need huge budgets or sophisticated research techniques to effectively identify a marketing opportunity. Rather, you can just use primary research methods (like surveys and interviews) and readily available secondary sources (like trade magazines and websites).

For instance, you can conduct surveys on your social networks to get a sense of what people really want and need, go out to clubs and observe what other talented bands are doing and not doing, and talk with die-hard fans or "opinion leaders" to learn about new trends or anti-trends.

Additionally, you can read trade magazines for market trends and forecasts, scan popular and fringe blogs for interesting facts, listen to credible podcasts for the latest news, or visit trade associations and government websites to get important statistics. KISS's founding member Gene Simmons actually studied *Billboard* magazine to determine "what the marketplace responds to, what works, and what doesn't work." Hey, if Gene can do it, so can you!

Remember, you just have to open your eyes and ears and investigate what's going on in the world around you. Try to predict where the world may end up in seven to ten years and make sure that your products and services are positioned there first. Surely this is no easy task, but let's face it: anything worth doing is never easy. Got it? Good!

Match Opportunities with Strengths

The next step in conducting your SWOT analysis is to identify your finer strengths, which will qualify you for certain opportunities. Bottom line, you must ask yourself honestly: *Do I have "what it takes" to pursue the opportunities and needs I just discovered?* To make this determination, let's take a quick look at uncovering your strengths and inspecting the strengths of others.

Uncover Your Strengths

Uncovering your finer strengths requires that you look within and assess your "internal environment," which is within your company and your control. Strengths might include company capabilities (your ability to find, train, and delegate the workload to musicians), company resources (your financial assets, professional equipment, relevant skills, and business relationships), company processes (your ability to innovate new material, market it effectively, and get and keep new customers), and geographic factors (your proximity to a music industry epicenter).

Now consider the following:

- Your musical skills and versatility could allow you to take advantage (and stay on top) of a new societal shift and trend in music.
- Your songwriting products and recording skills might meet directors' needs for music in film and television.
- Your financial budget could allow you to take advantage of an opportunity to record with a hip, local producer who has a unique sound and current style.
- Your professional equipment (PA system, transportation, lighting gear, etc.) may help you to capitalize on being a more a distinctive live band in your geographic region.
- Finally, your ability to find/train/manage the best musicians could allow you to take advantage of all the opportunities above simply because you possess the capabilities needed to successfully hold a business together.

Inspect and Evaluate the Strengths of Others

After assessing your strengths and how they benefit you, let's take a look at how other artists have used their internal powers to capitalize on a specific marketing opportunity. What follows is another popular case study: Lady Gaga.

Lady Gaga

Lady Gaga envisioned a career as a powerful young artist who would—in her words—"Revolutionize pop music like Madonna had done 25 years earlier." She understood the societal *need* for people to be completely entertained by "more than just music, but a performance, attitude, and a look" unrivaled by the competition. So, to satisfy this need, she specifically set out to create a unique live show with over-the-top stage antics, catchy songs, and outrageous costumes that pushed the limits of New York City clubs and appealed to those who were different. But what's most important here is that she had the strengths required to take advantage of this opportunity.

Gaga, born Stefani Joanne Angelina Germanotta in the music mecca of New York City, began playing piano at age 4, writing piano ballads at 13, and performing at open mic nights by age 14. She studied acting in high school, excelled academically, and enrolled in New York University's famous Tisch School of the Arts at 17. Lady Gaga had creative and intellectual skills, the financial backing of her father who paid her rent while she pursued her career in music, and an incredible work ethic that enabled her to "eat shit until people would listen." Despite popular belief, Gaga really did have "the goods" and talent to make it! And not surprisingly, in 2010 she topped *Fast Company* magazine's "The 100 Most Creative People in Business" list.

While the examples are limitless, the takeaway is this: *Whatever opportunities you pursue, make sure you truly have the qualifying strengths to achieve them.* And never kid yourself, because the only person you can hurt is *you*!

AFTERTHOUGHT: GET PROFESSIONAL FEEDBACK Sometimes it is difficult to see yourself as you really are. Thus, it may be beneficial to meet with a professional music business consultant or songwriting coach to determine whether you really have what it takes. Ask around for references and expect to pay an hourly fee for these professional services. It will be worth it.

Uncover Your Weaknesses

While it's important to discern whether you have "the goods" to take advantage of opportunities to fill certain needs, now it's equally important to assess whether your company has any weaknesses that might prevent it from doing so. Let's take a look at singling out your weaknesses and then at converting weaknesses into strengths.

Single Out Your Weaknesses

Like company strengths, weaknesses can be found in your internal environment, which is within your company and your control. Weaknesses might include company capabilities (your inability to find, train, and delegate the workload to musicians), company resources (your lack of financial assets, professional equipment, and business relationships), company processes (your inability to innovate new material, market it effectively, and get new customers), and geographic factors (your distance from a music industry epicenter).

Consider the following:

- Your lack of funds, professional equipment, and certain professional skills prevent you from taking advantage of an opportunity to start your own label and release products to a viable niche market.
- Your inability to delegate the workload, hire the right personnel, and rehearse regularly prevents you from taking advantage of just about any opportunity, since these are basic business necessities.
- Your limited writing, recording, marketing, and customer service methods prevent you from releasing new quality material and attracting fans and industry folks who can further your career.
- And finally, an inconvenient geographic location prevents you from fully saturating a desired customer base.

Turn Your Weaknesses into Strengths

What's really important to this discussion is not just that you uncover a company weakness, but that you now decide whether or not a specific weakness is worth turning into a strength, and then strategize accordingly. This really depends on how critical a weakness is to your growth. Fresh Beat Studios provides an interesting case study.

Fresh Beat Studios

Owner Nard Berings of Fresh Beat Studios identified a cultural *need* for American music originating from Los Angeles (an entertainment capital) to be used in the advertising and television industry in his native land of Holland. However, he faced a small weakness: his vocal abilities were less than adequate. Thus, when advertising agencies would contact his mother office in Amsterdam to submit demos for a commercial pitch, he was unable to produce the high-quality, competitive work needed. Berings was wise enough to isolate the problem by seeking honest feedback from his industry relationships and peers whom he trusted.

To convert this vocal weakness into a strength, Berings didn't let his ego get in the way by trying to convince himself and others that he was a decent singer (as many other musicians would have done), but rather he began building a network of top session singers who could be available for hire at a moment's call to get the job done fast. As a result, he was able to convert his company's weakness into a strength, and innovate and produce strong material in a flash. Consequently, Berings quickly developed his company and he now has a successful career creating music for entertainment industries in Amsterdam and the United States.

Hey, reality sometimes sucks, but if you can swallow your pride and see yourself and your weaknesses truthfully for what they are, there are many ways to make up for them and get what you want in the end.

Spot Potential Threats

Moving on to the last letter of the SWOT acronym (T), let's briefly examine the concept of threats. While the word *threat* is used regularly in business, perhaps it sounds a bit doomsdayish and even confusing. So, let's convert the letter *T* to mean: "Things that could prevent you from successfully pursuing certain opportunities." Or, more simply: "Things that could get in your way." Even better, "Things that create risks." In any case, let's take a look at identifying threats, researching threats, and minimizing your threats.

Identify Your Threats

Like opportunities, threats can be found in your external environment, the domain that is outside of your company and your control. Societal trends, technological developments, economic conditions, political-legal regulations, customer markets, competition, distribution channels, and natural causes are all areas where threats can exist.

Consider the following:

- A natural disaster can cripple a region's tourism industry and make it impossible for you to find work.
- A competing local act with greater financial resources and manpower can spot your idea and take it to the next level faster than you can.
- A new law that is being considered by Congress can make it more difficult for you to get a green card or visa to live and work in the United States.
- The latest developments in technology, and society's interaction with it, is making music and its monetization less negotiable and secure.
- A new technology could lower the barrier of entry into the music industry, flooding an increasingly competitive marketplace.
- Finally, a current state of the economy is creating consumer panic, and thus fewer people appear to be going to clubs.

Minimize Your Threats

Whatever potential threats you might spot, just be sure you decide how you can use your strengths to minimize being harmed by them. As you've often heard, "Sometimes the best *defense* is an *offense*." This is important, as illustrated in one local act I've worked with (members wish to remain anonymous). Let's just refer to them as the Vegas Hip Hop Orchestra.

The Vegas Hip Hop Orchestra

Given society's innate and historic *need* to dance and communicate through rhythm, the Vegas Hip Hop Orchestra discovered an opportunity to create an electronic rock/drumcore stage show with multiple percussionists and DJs all dressed in unique costumes. However, a primary threat to the act was competition from rave organizers and theater companies with more experience and resources, which could get wind of their idea before they were able to establish their position as leaders.

To minimize this threat, the act planned to keep the idea as secret as possible by performing select gigs in smaller, private locations, while being especially careful not to leak any materials to magazines and blogs. After polishing the act and getting it impressively tight, they planned to find investors who could fund the size and quality of rave needed to generate extensive media exposure, and thus position the act as the "originals" or "founders." Pretty smart!

Just remember that you can't control external forces and the threats that are all around you, but you can certainly avoid and minimize your damages from them. As spiritual writer Jon Kabat-Zinn wrote, "You may not be able to stop the waves but you can surely learn how to surf." Believe that!

AFTERTHOUGHT: RESEARCH YOUR RISKS Remember that all it takes to conduct research and uncover threats is to open your eyes and ears and observe and investigate the world around you. Trade magazines, credible news broadcasts, popular and fringe blogs, industry conferences, discussions with true music fans and professionals, and a historical analysis of past risks can all help.

Write a SWOT (or OSWT) Conclusion

Finally, after you've considered all of your opportunities, strengths, weaknesses, and threats, it's important to ask yourself just what you have gathered from all this research!

In a brief SWOT conclusion, clearly indicate the most profitable customer need or product/service opportunity you will pursue given your strengths, the weaknesses you might turn into new strengths to better take advantage of a profitable opportunity, and the methods you'll use to minimize your vulnerability to certain threats. This is all very important!

The SWOT analysis is not an easy exercise and there are no guarantees for success, but it has been a proven model for decades for a variety of companies, both big and small. Remember, what's most important is that it can help you further shape your career vision and purpose and even help you identify a void in the marketplace that is perfect for you to fill.

Now here is a brief sample of what your SWOT (or OSWT) conclusion paragraph might look like:

Given our company's vision of becoming a dramatically entertaining act with dance, sound, and visual effects, we monitored the external competitive landscape and identified an opportunity to create an electronic rock/drumcore stage show with multiple percussionists and DJs dressed in unique costumes (all this to meet society's innate and historic need to dance and communicate through rhythm—think "Blue Man Group" and "Taps" gone rave). Our company strengths are well suited to take advantage of this opportunity given our skill set in theater/arts and professional DJ work, as well as our access to professional musicians in the Las Vegas area. Our weaknesses include our limited financial resources, but we will overcome this by selling personal assets and freeing up capital, while also looking for an investor. Our threats include competition from other rave organizers, but to reduce this threat, we plan to keep the idea as secret as possible and perform select gigs in smaller and private locations to gain experience.

In Their Own Words: Q&A with Ira Kalb, Business Consultant

Ira Kalb is a business consultant, trainer, author, speaker, and full-time professor of marketing at USC, where he has already won two Golden Apple Teaching Awards. He is also an artist and woodwind musician who has played with Scott Page (of Pink Floyd), Don Preston (of Mothers of Invention), Grant Geissman (of the Chuck Mangione band), and many others. In this interview, Kalb shares a few tips about identifying market needs and opportunities in the music business.

Q: What would you say to up-and-coming artists who still feel they can create whatever they want and the world will follow?

IK: While this approach can work for some, it can be devastating for most. A more successful approach for your readers is to take the "pulse of the world." This involves looking out into the marketplace to investigate an unfilled niche that they can be passionate about, and then filling it in a way that will be difficult for competitors to duplicate. The more unique they can be the better, but their uniqueness has to be popular enough to have a sufficiently sizable following so they can make money. Remember, if a business is not profitable, then it's not a business, it's a hobby.

Q: Can you share a few examples of artists (well known or otherwise) who spotted a need in the marketplace and fulfilled that need successfully?

IK: Whether they are cognizant of it or not, almost all successful artists pay attention to the competition and what other artists are doing to develop their own sound and style. The Beatles studied Buddy Holly to find a voice of their own. Elvis imitated various R&B artists to find his own niche. And Lady Gaga studied Madonna to take it to another level and create a more modern, musically proficient, and over-the-top persona.

Q: Musicians often believe that examining the needs of the marketplace requires them to "sell out" and only pursue the most profitable and commercially based musical styles. Any thoughts?

IK: Choosing the most profitable commercial market is one way to go, but finding a market where you can still be passionate, authentic, and believable is the best way to go if you want your music to be any good and you want fans who embrace you.

Q: How can an artist determine the potential of a market and whether a specific opportunity will be profitable?

IK: It is hard to know precisely how popular something original will be until you expose audiences to it and get feedback. You can learn a lot about what people like and don't like by just performing and paying attention to what they say. But you have to have a vision that drives you forward and the willingness to improve yourself until you get things right. The Beatles played dives for years until they developed their own unique sound and learned how to be entertaining. Bob Dylan got booed almost everywhere at first, but he maintained his unique vision and sound and eventually became good and entertaining enough to develop a huge following who cheered him on. Vision, research, continual advancement, and more research are all key factors.

Q: Any final points you want to offer regarding the topic of identifying market needs?

IK: Don't be afraid to look outside of yourself to determine what's going on in the world. People want to be entertained in new, exciting, and improved ways, so while remaining true to yourself, identify something that is entertaining, new, and exciting, and pursue it with all your heart.

=MARKETING PLAN TEMPLATE=

Use the template below, or a template like it, to help you craft important information that you will use in your Marketing Plan of Attack™. For additional help, be sure to refer to the marketing plan example below, the chapter on assembling your plan, and the complete plan provided in the back of this book.

Your SWOT (or OSWT) Matrix and Conclusion Template

Use this template to help you craft your SWOT analysis. It's okay to add as many bullet points beneath each SWOT item as you want, but try to be as concise as possible. When formatting your marketing plan, it is not necessary to include the questions with your information. Both a bullet-point analysis and a SWOT paragraph should be included in your Marketing Plan of Attack™.

Opportunities: Identify and explain voids or needs in the *external* competitive, political, societal, technological, economic, distribution-related, industry-specific, and/or consumer marketplace and the opportunities to fill these needs. If possible, provide secondary or primary data that supports your claims and defends your business purpose.

•
•
•

Strengths: List *internal* aspects, like finances, equipment, and skills, that will help fill the above needs.

•
•
•

Weaknesses: List deficiencies in *internal* company resources, finances, skills, company management, and more.

•
•
•

Threats: Identify *external* issues (competitive, political, social, technological, economic, etc.) of which you are not in control and that can get in your way).

•
•
•

SWOT Conclusion Template: Now use your research from the information above to help you write your SWOT paragraph below. Feel free to adjust the template to fit your needs.

Given our company's vision of becoming a _____(type of company, genre, etc.), we monitored the_____(political, societal, legal, technological, natural, economic, distribution, consumer market, industry-related) external landscape and identified an opportunity to _____(what your company will do and the need it will fill). Our company strengths are well suited to take advantage of this opportunity, given our _____(financial resources, equipment, etc.). Our weaknesses are our _____(lack of resources, equipment, etc.), but being that they are/are not critical to growth, we will/will not convert them to strengths by _____. Our threats are_____(competition, legal issues, social changes, etc.), but to reduce these threats, we plan to _____.

=MARKETING PLAN EXAMPLE=

Now here's an abridged marketing plan sample for our alternative rock band Rally the Tribes, to show you how they would put together a SWOT analysis. Remember that this band's vision was to become a nationally known rock/rave band in the business of music and activism.

SWOT (or OSWT) ANALYSIS

a) Opportunities:

★According to data collected by the National Center for Education Statistics, there is a growing interest among young Americans for political news and change, especially since the Obama election of 2008.

★According to the *Billboard* and CMJ charts, there are currently no other bands that fuse rock, rap, and techno rave styles with a strong political undertone.

b) Strengths:

★Intangible Resources: Highly educated band members who are well versed in political issues of the nation and world, have 20-year aggregate training in songwriting and performance, play multiple instruments, and have professional relationships where barter deals can be arranged to reduce certain production costs.

★Tangible Resources: State-of-the-art recording gear, turntables, and a rehearsal facility that has been acquired mostly through donations and professional relationships.

c) Weaknesses:

★Processes: Minimal marketing experience and number of followers.

★Financial Resources: Rely heavily on fan donations and bartering.

d) Threats:

★Censorship from radio stations that prefer not to broadcast our controversial subject matter.

★Public opposition and backlash (over sensitive issues like pro-choice and pro-marijuana viewpoints), and companies' disinterest in associating their brands via sponsorships with a political-minded group.

e) SWOT Conclusion:

Given our company's vision of being a nationally known rock/rave band, we monitored the external political and societal landscape and identified an opportunity to create recordings, performances, and documentaries that give a voice to the political youth movement, fill society's intrinsic need to be part of a bigger cause for change, and provide new and exciting music unlike the competition. Our company strengths are well suited to take advantage of this opportunity, given our academic credentials, musical training, and innovation processes. Our weaknesses are our lack of financial resources and minimal fan base. However, because these are critical to growth, we will convert them to strengths by seeking donations, utilizing limited-budget marketing techniques, and building a database of fans drawn from political rallies, live performances, and social networks. Our most serious threat is backlash and opposition from opposing political groups, but to reduce these threats, we plan to be peaceful and respectful when getting our message out to the people.

4

Analyze Your Customers
Identifying, Segmenting, and Targeting Your Market

Noted marketing consultant and leadership expert Peter Drucker once said: "Without satisfied customers, your business is nothing." This is why analyzing your customers is the next essential step in the marketing process. It involves identifying the people or businesses that are most likely to enjoy your products and services, segmenting them into subgroups based on shared characteristics, and finally, considering your data in a way that will be most profitable for your organization.

This process also helps you do all of the following:

- **Further identify the very specific needs and wants of your most likely fans.**
- **Customize your marketing strategies to effectively satisfy these needs.**
- **Create a more powerful image in fans' minds of what you represent. And . . .**
- **Speak in a tone that resonates powerfully with them.**

Once you begin winning over your most likely customers and building a following, you can then start expanding your market and focusing on your next likely fans, and so on. While you may not understand why you can't mass market to everyone at once, understand that marketing is not a "one size fits all" process. To paraphrase Perreault, Cannon, and McCarthy from the book *Essentials of Marketing*, "It's best to please a select group of people with your marketing strategies extremely well, instead of a lot of people fairly well or not at all."

Companies have successfully used the process of analyzing customers for decades, and it will benefit your company as well. But keep in mind that this is not an exact science. In fact, even after analyzing your fans, you may find yourself going back and adjusting your customer profile if it is not quite working for you or if new markets or opportunities present themselves. This is par for the course. Don't get frustrated.

So now let's take a look at the following sections:

1. **Identifying, Segmenting, and Targeting Your Audience**
2. **Considering Your Data: Writing a Customer Conclusion**
3. **Hearing It in Their Own Words: An Interview with Nance Rosen**

Identify, Segment, and Target Your Audience

If you've been reading this book carefully, then you've already envisioned your musical style or genre, indicated what products and services you'll offer, and identified a specific customer need or void in the marketplace. Now it's time to further identify the customers who are most likely to enjoy your products/services and categorize them more descriptively into smaller, yet still profitable and significant, groups using any number of shared characteristics. It's one thing to think of your market as *metalheads* and another as *male, blue-collar metalheads in Los Angeles, ages 21 to 30, who drink alcohol, like tattoos and piercings, and go out to clubs once a week to get in the mosh pit and blow off steam.*

BRINGING YOUR TARGET AUDIENCE TO LIFE

When analyzing your customers, you might even go as far as creating *visual representations* and actual photographs of your fans to keep close by. This helps you stay focused throughout the entire planning process. It helps you make accurate decisions about merch designs, places to perform, and the tone, look, and feel of social media content and adverts. The end goal is giving fans precisely what they need and want.

Meet Brandon: A male, blue-collar *metalhead* in Los Angeles, between the of ages of 21 and 30, who drinks Jack Daniel's, likes tattoos and piercings, communicates heavily on Facebook to connect with friends and offer recommendations, reads *Thrasher* magazine, and goes out to the Viper Room and King King once a week to get in the mosh pit and blow off steam.

What does Brandon want or need, and how can we best give it to him? Figure this out for your own fans, and thrive!

The characteristics widely used by companies to define their market are called *segmentation dimensions.* These include *demographic, psychographic, technographic, behavioral,* and *geographic* factors, all of which are discussed in the section below. Use as many or as few of these dimensions as you see fit, but remember that the more narrowly you define, profile, and target your market, the more customized and personalized you can make your marketing messages to appeal to it.

Examine Demographic Dimensions

Demographic dimensions represent important categories in our social structure. They include everything from age to social class to religion.

When defining your market, you might decide to use the following:

- *Age: 6–12, 13–19, 20–32, 33–50, 51–62, or other.* Blink-182 targeted the teen market and appropriately dressed young, spoke young, played brightly colored instruments, and sang about teen angst to appeal to it.
- *Education: High school, college, graduate, or doctorate.*
- *Gender: Male, female, or other.* Lady Gaga targeted the transgender and gay communities with the overall supportive message that "it's okay to be different," and won over an extremely loyal group of followers she refers to as "Little Monsters."
- *Income: 12–35K, 35–55K, 55–80K, 80–150K, or other.*
- *Occupation: Blue collar, white collar, military, service, industrial, or other.* Bruce Springsteen targeted blue-collar, all-American working-class folks, and appropriately, he wrote songs that focused on American pride; plus he dressed casually in blue jeans, white T-shirts, and boots to seal the deal.
- *Ethnicity: White, black, Hispanic, Asian, or Native American.*
- *Social class: Lower, middle, upper-middle, or upper class.* Jay-Z targeted the lower social class and those in the projects, but he did it, according to filmmaker Barry Michael Cooper, with songs that focused on the true consequences of doing whatever it takes to get out of the ghetto.
- *Marital status: Single, married or married with children.*
- *Religion: Catholic, Protestant, Christian, Jewish, New Age, Buddhist, Muslim, or Rastafarian.* Bob Marley targeted Rastafarians and those who accepted the important aspects of the religion, and sang songs fittingly about the political issues of Jamaica, peace, and hope.

WHAT'S RELIGION GOT TO DO WITH IT? DISCOVERING THE NEED FOR A HIGHER CAUSE

Unclear of his direction and what "need" he was attempting to fulfill—other than to simply provide music entertainment to anyone who was willing to listen—developing indie folk artist Joe Roff knew he had to get focused. He profiled his small group of unconditional and friendly followers and realized that the majority were Jewish. Not coincidentally, Joe was also a devoted follower.

Enlightened by his market analysis, Joe began developing his offerings (song lyrics and live performances) to meet the needs of Jewish worshipers. He demoed his music inexpensively using his laptop computer, played live in synagogues in his local community, sought feedback from his fans, and even met with performance and songwriting consultants. Soon enough, Joe was able to build a live performance schedule that had him touring synagogues across the country with a professionally produced recording of six songs in hand. Because the Jewish market was not tremendously competitive compared to the indie folk market he had been previously shooting for in Hollywood clubs, Joe was able to create a strong image in his audiences' minds, command fees in the thousands for performances, sell hundreds of records, and gain an incredible amount of experience—all by playing his original music and crafting his marketing communications to center around a religious appeal.

You see, it really does pay to analyze your most likely customers, and to use their special characteristics to craft targeted messages that will strongly appeal to them. Way to go, Joe!

Think About Technographic Dimensions

The next segmentation dimension we'll discuss deals with new technology and people's interaction with it. Technographic segmentation is not necessarily a new concept, but given the amount of time that most people spend on social networks and mobile phones, it is becoming a more widely used dimension to help define and understand customers.

Consider the following:

- **Reasons for Using New Technology:** *To create, review, recommend, complain, share, discover, purchase, network, research, pass time, observe, steal music, or other.*
- **Time Spent Using It:** *Light, medium, or heavy.* DJ Frontalot targeted obsessive computer users by writing songs about video games and other nerdy issues and spearheaded a new genre of music he called "nerdcore."
- **Outlook on Using It:** *Convenient, necessary, expensive, burdensome, or other.*

Look at Psychographic Dimensions

Moving on in our discussion about segmenting your market, now let's take a quick look at psychographic dimensions. This deals with the process of analyzing your customers on the basis of their lifestyles. George and Michael Belch in the book *Advertising and Promotion* explain that analyzing lifestyles helps you better understand the personalities of your consumers, and that this understanding can be gained through an "AIO" assessment (activities, interests, and opinions).

Consider using the following in your customer description:

- **Activities (Things They Do):** *Listening to music, going to shows, playing sports, partying, shopping, going to social events, consuming media (specific books, magazines, television shows, radio programs), or other.*

- **Interests (Things They Like):** *Music, cars, homes, money, sports, sex, food, travel, wine, fashion, health/wellness, or other.*
- **Opinions (Things That Matter):** *Politics, religion, war, education, technology, the environment, the economy, social issues, or other.* Morsoul, an indie alternative rock jam band, targeted environmentally concerned students by writing songs with titles like *Peace Frog*, naming their records with titles like *Sustenance*, performing at Earth Week festivals, arranging "eco-parties" on college campuses, and traveling around the country in a bus fueled by vegetable oil. Yup, you heard right.

TARGETING YOUR MARKET BY LIFESTYLE: THE NEED FOR WEED AND EQUALITY

Dedicated to meeting the needs of those who want more than just your typical hip hop band, Cypress Hill targeted young, harder-edged hip hop fans who were heavily into the marijuana culture. Since their first record in 1991, Cypress Hill has sent out very powerful and direct messages to this target market advocating marijuana, from releasing songs titled "Mr. Green Thumb," to getting banned from *Saturday Night Live* for lighting up a joint on the air, to getting interviewed in magazines like *High Times*. In October 2010, the band organized the Cypress Hill SmokeOut—an event positioned as an "all-day, mind-opening music festival" featuring several high-energy bands, as well as panel discussions advocating for Prop 19 and the legalization of medical marijuana in California. Cypress Hill not only knows and understands their fans, they know how to customize their products/services to appeal powerfully to the market, how to place their products/services where their audience can find them, and how to craft emotionally appealing communications across all media to connect with their audience. With 18 million albums sold worldwide, and 11 million records sold in the US alone, Cypress Hill is hitting their market bull's-eye.

Singer Ani DiFranco is another great case study worth mentioning. Inspired to meet the needs of those who lacked an outlet for expressing their political views, she targeted politically active college students, particularly those of the left wing, who believed in social change and equality for all. Being a very opinionated and openly bisexual person, DiFranco wrote songs about homophobia, racism, and reproductive rights. She also organized her own tour called "Vote Damn it" to urge people to vote for the rights of the oppressed and marginalized. To be sure, she executed one clear and integrated marketing communication across all media channels. Among all of the clutter in the music business and the thousands of other artists she was competing with, DiFranco was able to carve out a clear and distinctive place in her target fans' minds. Among her many other noted successes, DiFranco received the "Woman of Courage Award" at the National Organization for Women Conference and Young Feminist Summit in Albany, New York, and received a Grammy Award for the album *Evolve*.

The above stories are classic examples of how understanding your target market can help you appeal to it, connect with it in an emotional way, make it feel good about itself, give it what it wants, make sales, and win! Perhaps you'll be the next success story. Just be sure to invite me to all of your parties.

Evaluate Behavioral Dimensions

Now let's take a look at possible behavioral dimensions. Richard Czerniawski and Michael Maloney, authors of *Creating Brand Loyalty*, feel that your customers' mind-set is one of the most important things you can understand about them. So let's check out the *attributes sought* in a product by the customer, the *rate* at which the customer uses a product, and the tendency toward customers adopting a product as it moves through its *life-cycle* (introduction, growth, maturity, and decline).

Take a look at the following:

- ***Attributes Sought (What Customers Want):*** *A wide variety of formats (CDs, vinyl, downloads, or download cards), engaging lyric subject matter (heart-felt, political, sexy, or fun), an entertaining live show (mellow, theatrical, energetic, or fantasylike), eye-catching fashion (glamour, street, grunge, or dapper), an appropriate price (free stuff, bargain, midrange, or top-price), a clear brand personality (larger than life, down to earth, humorous, or mysterious), or other.* KISS targeted hard rock fans who wanted a highly visual and explosive concert experience no matter where the show was being viewed from in the arena, even the very back. Needless to say, this paid off big!
- ***Rate of Use (How Often They Go to Shows, Buy CDs, etc.):*** *Heavy, medium, or light.*
- ***Type of Adopter (Tendency to Embrace Innovation):*** *"Innovators" (the first group to adopt a product after it's introduced to the marketplace; a fringe group of music enthusiasts who are interested in taking risks and being first on their block to listen to a band), "early adopter" (the second to adopt; a far hipper and larger group than innovators and more cautious about deciding what will be the next cool and hip thing), the "early majority" (the third to adopt; a large group of people who look to the early adopters to decide what is accepted and hip), the "late majority" (fourth to adopt; a large group of people who follow the early majority just to fit in and be accepted), or "laggards" (the last to adopt a product; a smaller, unhip, and skeptical group of people who accept something only after it is well proven and in the decline stage of its life cycle and going out of style).*

Consider Geographic Dimensions

And finally, let's take a look at one more segmentation dimension that helps pinpoint where your fans live and where your marketing efforts will be concentrated. Personally, I think this is one of the most important dimensions, because, simply put, *the world is not your market.*

When organizing your customers, you might consider the following:

- ***City:*** *Los Angeles, New York, Austin, Nashville, Atlanta, or other.*
- ***Region in the Country:*** *East Coast, West Coast, the South, the Midwest, or other.*
- ***Country:*** *United States, Mexico, Japan, Sweden, or other.*
- ***Region of the World:*** *North America, Europe, Asia, South America, Australia, or Africa.*

TIPS TO TARGET MARKET RESEARCH

So, how do you go about finding detailed information about fans? Utilizing secondary data (information already published) and primary data (information you collect via surveys and other methods) can help. Here are a few tips to get started:

- ***Research "Like" Fans:*** Communicate with the fans of bands you sound most "like" to uncover important information about your target fan. Just by logging into chat rooms and message boards, you can better understand what makes fans tick.
- ***Research Magazines:*** Read the magazines that cater to your type of music and imagine the type of person who reads them. Pay attention to the level of sophistication and the types of ads as well.
- ***View Media Kits:*** The magazines and radio stations that play your type of music outline specific demographic information in the media kits they give potential advertisers. Just call these magazines or stations and ask for the ad department.
- ***Observe Current Fans:*** Post a video clip or digital file of one your songs and observe the people who respond favorably to it. Are there any common characteristics (age, gender, geography) they share?

- *Put Up a Web Questionnaire:* Upload your music online, provide a list of questions (about age, gender, lifestyles, etc.), and ask visitors to fill it out.
- *Survey Your Live Audience:* When playing a show, give your audience a list of basic questions on an index card, and provide an incentive for them (such as a free download) to fill it out and turn it in.
- *Communicate Online with Fans:* If you have a personal e-mail list, use it to communicate with fans and ask them to share personal information about themselves.
- *Use Social Network Tools:* Most social networks, like Facebook and ReverbNation, allow you to view the demographic characteristics of your followers, letting you know their gender, geography, and more.
- *Use the US Census Bureau:* Find the population of any city by ethnicity, gender, education, and income level. Visit www.census.gov and utilize the "State and County Quick Facts" section.
- *Visit the CIA World Fact Book:* This provides information on the history, people, government, economy, geography, communications, transportation, military, and transnational issues for 267 world entities. Visit www.cia.gov.
- *Visit Quant Cast:* This service offers the demographic profiles of the most popular bands. Visit www.quantcast.com.
- *Utilize Arbitron:* With its Scarborough Research Service, Arbitron provides demographic, geographic, psychographic, and behavioral characteristics of the radio listeners of specific stations that cater to your style. Visit www.arbitron.com.
- *Know About the Stanford Research Institute (SRI):* This popular company's VALS (Values and Lifestyles) program profiles customers by personality traits (innovators, thinkers, believers, experiencers, etc.), helps you decide which type is most likely to want your product, and defines where these groups are located geographically. It may be pricy for the DIY artist, but it is still good to know about it. Visit www.sric-bi.com.
- *Visit Nielsen Claritas (PRIZM):* A similar service to SRI, PRIZM names segments (e.g., "Young and Rustic," "Movers and Shakers," "The Grey Generation") and then interprets how this information can be used. Also pricey, but helpful in seeing how profiles are arranged. See www.claritas.com/MyBestSegments/Default.jsp.
- *Visit Your Local Library or Business School:* Your local library might provide atlases, almanacs, and the *Standard Rate and Data Service* [SRDS] *Lifestyle Market Analysis*, which can provide information about local consumers.
- *Call Your Chamber of Commerce:* Your city's chamber of commerce provides detailed information about the city, businesses, people, incomes, demographic makeup, and more. Google it!
- *Use Special Internet Services:* A great site for getting demographic information is ClickZ (www.clickz.com).

Consider Your Data and Write a Customer Conclusion

The final step in conducting your customer analysis is determining just what all your data means. Remember, as previously explained, when putting together your customer profile, you should only use dimensions that help you better understand your customers and how to effectively communicate to them.

Consider the following examples:

- If you defined your customers as being ages 12 to 18, then this should immediately provide clues about where you may need to perform (high school assemblies, youth centers, skateboard parks, etc.).

- If you defined your fans as being into extreme sports and mixed martial arts, then this should spark ideas for creating merchandise (motocross-style long-sleeved shirts, skateboard stickers, wristbands, etc.). And . . .
- If you keyed in on a behavioral characteristic of your target customer, such as "expects a visually impressive and engaging show," then this should inspire designs for promotional posters or ads with explosive graphics (pictures of elaborate stage sets, sexy costumes, talented dance troops, and even attractive audience members having fun, etc.).

Keep in mind that you don't have to nail these strategies down yet, but you definitely want to get your creative juices flowing and generate some ideas as you move forward.

To be sure, your customer conclusion should give meaning to your customer analysis. It should connect customer characteristics with marketing strategies that attract attention, hold interest, and stimulate a buying action. It should also help you speak your customers' language more effectively and ultimately make fans feel good about themselves and about you. Just be sure to use the handy template and marketing plan example at the end of this chapter to aid you in your writing. And that, ladies and gentlemen, is about all I have to say.

Now here's an abridged sample of what a customer profile conclusion may look like:

Given that our most likely customer's <u>demographic</u> profile includes 18- to 27-year-olds, we could focus our promotional campaign on college campuses and getting college radio play. We could also be sure to use a cool, yet not-too-trendy, tone in all of our marketing communications that speak to our audience and not down to them.

Given that our customer's psychographic profile includes extreme-type sports, we could attempt to sell our music at skate and surf shops, seek licensing agreements in FOX Sports–type programming, perform at volleyball and surf competitions in Long Beach, advertise and seek sponsorships with magazines like Thrasher, create merchandising that looks and feels like BMX or Motocross jerseys, and even use action-related graphics and words on album covers and in promotional correspondence.

And given that our customer's behavioral traits (attributes sought) include experiencing an exciting, interactive, and larger-than-life concert performance, we can create a cool light show, use unique instruments, and encourage fans to vote on the songs and make comments via text messaging during the show.

In Their Own Words: Q&A with Nance Rosen, Business Consultant at Sandler Training

Nance Rosen is a former marketing executive for the world's No. 1 most recognized brand: Coca-Cola. She is a consultant at Sandler Training; a world leader in innovative sales, leadership, and management training; and a personal branding and marketing coach for the Screen Actors Guild Foundation. In this article, Nance further clarifies important aspects of target marketing.

Q: What should my readers know about market segmentation?

NR: Rather than try to reach large groups of people with one sweeping marketing communication, you want to focus on fragmented or segmented groups of customers. Segmented groups of customers—or, as I call them, "tribes"—consist of people who act alike, spend their money in a similar fashion, and get their entertainment from the same sources; they are also sizable enough in numbers to produce the revenue a company requires.

While companies with larger budgets might take on a "multisegment approach," where they market to two or more tribes at one time and have separate marketing plans for each of these tribes, DIY bands on a low budget should start with a "single-target market approach" made up of their most likely fans and create one marketing plan to appeal to them. Once they win that group over, they can go after the next logical customer segment or tribe and create a new marketing campaign.

Q: And why is market segmentation important?

NR: Marketing to segments or tribes allows a company to better tailor its communications and get as close to a one-to-one basis as is reasonable. You only want to spend your time and money communicating with people who are very likely to buy from you. Remember that the more tailored your communication, the bigger and faster the remuneration. Bottom line: market segmentation saves time and money.

Q: Is there a certain number of segmentation dimensions you'd recommend?

NR: It takes a combination of dimensions to produce a truly accurate read. Using age, for instance, is not enough, since people who fall into the "20 to 30 year old" range will not all act in the same way. But a combination of dimensions, including age, gender, and behavior, will help you to profile your customer more accurately and customize messages to better appeal to him or her.

Q: What are the segmentation dimensions that one should use if targeting businesses, rather than consumers (such as when a composer or production company is targeting music libraries or advertising agencies)?

NR: Good question. Businesses that target consumers (B2C) use different dimensions than do businesses that target other businesses (B2B).

In a B2B situation, for instance, when you're a songwriter targeting film directors and music placement companies, you can simply segment by company size (number of employees), location (city, state, country), and purchasing criteria (the credentials or experience they expect from you).

Q: Can you share any low-budget and simple research tips for identifying and profiling one's market?

NR: Get out among the various tribes and audiences who are listening to the artists that have similar characteristics as you, even if only slightly similar. See what these audiences are wearing, what they are drinking, and what they are saying (online and on-ground). Then examine the artists themselves. What's their messaging and branding like? Where are they spending marketing time and dollars? You see, by being a voyeur of artists that have already made it—or are, at least, a few steps ahead of you—you get the benefit of all their trial and error. Remember that if you want to be the best, start with someone else's success. Whenever possible, stand on the shoulders of giants.

=MARKETING PLAN TEMPLATE=

Use the template below, or a similar template, to help you craft important information that you will use in your Marketing Plan of Attack™. For additional help, be sure to refer to the marketing plan example below, the chapter on assembling your plan, and the complete plan provided in the back of this book.

Your Customer Profile and Conclusion Template

Use this template to make a brief and handy analysis of your target demographic audience. Use as many, or as few, dimensions as you see fit, and use as many bullet points beneath each dimension as you find necessary. Remember that this is not supposed to be a perfect science, and it is just supposed to offer a perspective on your fans so that you can better market to them. In your final marketing plan, be sure to lay out and retain your customer profile in bullet-point format, followed by a customer conclusion paragraph.

Demographics (Age, Gender, Ethnicity, Etc.):
•
•

Technographics (Online Motivations, Usage, Attitudes):
•
•

Psychographics (Activities, Interests, Opinions):
•
•

Behavioral (Attributes Sought, Rate of Use, Adopter Type):
•
•

Geographics (City, Country, Region of the World, Etc.):
•
•

Who is your next likely customer? [optional] Use a similar layout to the one above if you intend to market to two segments. And remember to only use the segmentation dimensions that you think will be most useful to you.

What is your customer profile conclusion? Now, in a short paragraph, describe how the segmentation dimensions you've chosen might be useful to your marketing strategy decisions. Does it trigger key words or graphics you might use in promotional campaigns? (If so, create a list and description of them.) Does it inspire you to find places to which you might sell your offerings? (If so, name a few places.) Finally, does it give you ideas about slogans you might use to mirror your customers' behavior? (If so, provide an example.) You can write a paragraph for both your most likely and next likely customers. A template like the one below might help. Feel free to modify it to fit your specific needs.

Customer Analysis Template: Fill in the blanks below.

Given that our most likely customers' demographic includes _____ ,we could plan to _____ .

Given that our customers' technographics include _____ ,we could plan to _____ .

Given that our customers' psychographics include _____ ,we could plan to _____ .

> *Given that our customers' behavioral traits include* _____ *, we could plan to* _____ *.*
>
> *And given that our customers' geographic dimensions include* _____ *, we could plan to* _____ *.*

=MARKETING PLAN EXAMPLE=

Now, to help create your own customer analysis, here's an abridged marketing plan example for our case study Rally the Tribes.

CUSTOMER ANALYSIS

a) Demographic:
★Age: 18–28.
★Education: BA and MA: UCLA, Stanford, Berkeley, and so forth.
★Income: $30,000–$70,000.

b) Psychographic:
★Activities: Listening to alternative music, reading literature, attending rallies, volunteering for causes.
★Interests: Photography, documentary films, poetry, social technology, and higher education.
★Opinions: Pro-choice, anti-war, pro–legalization of marijuana.

c) Behavior:
★Attributes Sought: Wanting to feel as though they are part of a larger movement or tribe, wanting to mix and mingle with like-minded intellects and proponents for change, wanting to blow off steam and get in the mosh pit.
★Rate of Use: Attends concerts and raves in clubs and alternate venues on the weekends, purchases music regularly from sites like iTunes, buys at least one piece of merch at shows each month.
★Adopter Type: "Early adopter" who takes ownership and pride in discovering new music and bands early on.

d) Geographic:
★City: Los Angeles and surrounding cities.
★Online Territory: United States.

e) Customer Analysis Conclusion:
Given that our most likely customers' demographic includes 18-to-28-year-olds, we could plan to play college campuses, focus on airplay on college radio stations, and support local college students' campus political groups and movements.

Given that our customers' psychographics include activities revolving around literature and political rallies, we could name our first album War and Police *(as a spinoff on Leo Tolstoy's classic novel* War and Peace*) and design artwork to demonstrate police at war with peaceful protesters.*

Given that our customers' behavioral traits include wanting to be part of a greater and important cause in the world, we could create a slogan that draws on this emotional appeal, such as "Music That Matters," "Advocates for Change," or "We Are Change Agents." We could also run a fan club called Change Agents.

And given that our customers' geographic dimensions include Los Angeles, we could plan to center our promotional campaigns in this area, utilize symbols of LA in our marketing communications, write songs that mention California and its news, and support charities that are localized in the LA community.

5

Learn from Your Competitors
Conducting a Competitor Analysis

Learning from your competitors involves identifying other artists your fans may see as similar to you, analyzing their strengths and weaknesses, and finding a competitive advantage that is both aligned with your vision and relevant to your target fan.

While the word *competitor* can carry a negative connotation, remember that studying competitors can be the key to your success. As Sarah White says in the *Idiot's Guide to Marketing*, "Competitors aren't your enemies, they're your mentors—everything you learn from observing them will help your company to improve."

A process that will help you systematically study and learn from your competitors is called a *competitor analysis*. This organized, thorough approach can help you do the following:

- **Evaluate the strengths and weaknesses of other companies.**
- **Capitalize on areas where competitors are lacking.**
- **Differentiate yourself and earn a unique position in the minds of fans.**

Musicians with inflated egos often believe that they don't have any competitors. While it's true that all artists have a built-in uniqueness just by virtue of being themselves, remember that competitors exist in many forms, both direct and indirect. In fact, competitors can be defined in a broader sense as *any company or product that could draw attention away from you*. This means that artists in different genres, or video games that potential fans decide to play instead of going to one of your shows, can all be considered *indirect* competitors. Seriously!

So grab a highlighter pen and get ready to knock out the following topics:

1. **Identifying Your Competitors**
2. **Analyzing Your Competitors' Strategies**
3. **Interpreting Your Competitor Data and Writing a Conclusion**

You've got your work cut out for you, but your efforts will pay off.

BUT SERIOUSLY, I'M TELLIN' YA' *DUDE*, WE AIN'T GOT NO COMPETITION!

Okay, so you still don't think you have any competition because you're doing something different in your town and you are just so unique. Well, first of all, congratulations for feeling that way. Second, please remember that while you may not have *direct* competition, anyone that can potentially take attention away from you is a competitor. Here's an example using two of my favorite bands, Rage Against the Machine and Tool.

Rage Against the Machine certainly has something unique going for them—their lyrics are politically motivated and delivered in a rap style over heavy guitar riffs and changing tempos. Tool, on the other hand, demonstrates exceptional musicianship using odd time signatures and interesting arrangements.

They are two different bands, but they share some of the same fans. In fact, if both bands were to play on the same night—let's say Rage at the Whisky on the Sunset Strip in Los Angeles, and right next door, Tool at the Roxy Theatre, music lovers would be torn between whether to see Rage or Tool. These days consumers have plenty of alternatives.

As you can see, you might not have direct competitors doing precisely what you're doing (and if you looked hard enough, you'd probably find them), but you have to remember that everyone has indirect competition and is surrounded by a variety of competitive forces. So, just spend a night getting out in your music scene, observing what's going on, and considering what you can learn from it. This shouldn't be too difficult to do—the marketplace is saturated with bands, clubs, and studios. Okay? Note: If you want to learn much more about competition and the many competitive forces that exist, be sure to look up "Porter's Five Forces," a model created by famed Harvard Business School professor Mike Porter. It's some pretty heavy stuff!

Identify Your Competitors

The first step in conducting a competitor analysis is to identify at least two music-related competitors in your geographic market. To help you do this, let's take a look at some of the more important steps you might take. No matter what your company *type* (band, solo artist, DJ, producer, side musician, or composer), most of these methods should apply to you.

Know Who's Getting the Best Bookings

Visit your local clubs and ask the resident bartender which artists are getting the best slots to perform and are drawing the biggest crowds. If you're a producer/composer, ask local musicians which studios are creating the best recordings and beats, and are most popular and trusted. Or if you're a side musician, check your local musicians' union and talk to your local music stores to determine which players are getting hired regularly for the coolest gigs and sessions.

Seek Them Out in the Press

Check out your local music magazines and ask: Who is getting the best music reviews? Who is getting stories written about them? And who is being called the "local hero"? You can even try contacting the magazine itself and talking with staff members to get the inside scoop on who is creating the most hype and essentially drawing attention away from you. While the folks at magazine companies are typically busy, they may offer help.

Hear Them on Local Radio

Get to know your local college radio stations, National Public Radio programs, and "locals only"–type shows on commercial radio stations to see what artists the DJs seem to hype the most.

Discover Who's on Store Shelves

Check out your local indie record/comic/fashion store and see who the clerks are talking about, observe what posters are hanging in the store windows, and find out who is getting shelf space and selling units. You should also read the liner notes of these recordings and pay attention to who produced and played on these recordings, as well as where these albums were recorded. And finally . . .

Locate Them Online

Social networks and blogs are a great place to observe which artists are attracting the most fans, and selling the most merch and music. You should also check out the sites of popular TV shows and music libraries to see if they list the artists with whom they license.

As you can see, there are numerous methods that can help you find your competitors. Sure, it's going to take some work, but as I've said before, anything worth doing is difficult.

HOW HIGH IS TOO HIGH? CAN I JUST COMPETE WITH NATIONAL COMPANIES?

A common problem when identifying competitors is to shoot entirely too high. While it is definitely fair game to compare yourself with those at the top of the charts (because technically these artists are still your competitors), you really have to ask yourself just what there is to gain by comparing yourself *exclusively* with someone at a much higher level than you.

For instance, Jay-Z (one of the most financially successful hip hop artists and entrepreneurs in America) has a net worth of over $500 million, has won 10 Grammy awards, has sold over 40 million records, owns Rocawear clothing, and is co-owner of Roc-a-feller Records. In short, Jay-Z's marketing decisions are based on his having millions of dollars in budgets and on having an expert team of professionals giving him advice—*all things out of your league right now.*

So when identifying your competitors, what may serve you better is to locate two local indie artists who attract your target market, and two major (or national) artists who attract your target market. You'll be conducting a little more research, but you'll have a better mix of some really good information on which to base your competitor analysis. As novelist Benjamin Disraeli once said, "The most successful man in life is the man who has the best information."

Analyze Your Competitors' Strategies

After you've identified your competitors, it's time to assess their individual marketing strategies. Using a "competitor analysis matrix" similar to the one found at the end of this chapter, take note of your competitors' branding, products, pricing, placement (distribution), and promotion strategies. If you can't uncover the competitor information you're looking for, you'll just have to keep digging until you find it, *because it's out there.* Oh, and by the way, you can also analyze your own company alongside your competitors, but if you're just starting out, you naturally won't have much to compare. In any case, let's get started with checking out your competitors.

Examine Your Competitors' Company Branding

Take a good look at your competitors' brand names, logos, slogans, attitudes, fashion sense, musical styles, heritages, and with whom they associate. Are the branding messages clear, consistent, and powerful throughout all of their marketing strategies, or are they confusing and unclear? What are the competitors' fans saying about all of this?

Study Their Product/Service Branding

Assess the creativity of your competitors' product and service brands—from their records, to their songs, to their fan clubs. Look at their names, designs, and packaging. Do your competitors' products and services work seamlessly under the umbrella of their company brand, and with the other products/services they offer? Or are there inconsistencies? What do the fans think?

Look at Their Product Development and Innovation

Look at whether your competitors offer a variety of musical configurations (vinyl, USB flash drives, download cards, etc.), different T-shirt designs, and a variety of live-performance formats (electric set, acoustic set, etc.). Also note the effort they put forth in delivering customer service, interacting and engaging with fans, and making customers happy. To do this, you might even become a customer of your competitor by buying their merch or joining their fan club. Last, consider whether their products have any obvious benefits (such as reasons why people should go to their shows or buy their records). How are the fans responding to their products and services?

Ponder Your Competitors' Pricing

Think about the prices your competitors charge for their products and services, the creative sales strategies they employ, or the free products they distribute to increase awareness and credibility in the marketplace. How do the fans respond to these prices and methods?

Evaluate Their Distribution Methods

Also be sure to observe where your competitors sell their music and merchandise, whether they have an attractive merch booth at their live shows, and in what types of venues (clubs, convention halls, colleges, etc.) they perform their set. Do you think the fans are pleased with where these competitors make their products and services available?

Assess Their Promotional Efforts

Take notice of whether your competitors place ads in local newspapers, conduct interviews on college radio stations, align with various sponsors, work at their online presence and social networks, have a personal website, and send out direct e-mails. On the latter note, you might even join their mailing list to receive regular correspondence so you can study and examine their every move. Would you say that their promotion strategies are unique and interesting? Do the fans seem to respond to these campaigns? And finally . . .

Include Other Relevant Issues

Be sure to also evaluate your competitors' ability to execute their marketing campaigns efficiently, their dedication to continual improvement, and their speed in pumping out new set lists, songs, and ideas. Remember that a company is only as good at its own ability to get things done. And remember, too, that figuring out how to conduct your business more effectively than your competitors can also serve as a true competitive advantage.

Now take a look at the table "Competitor Analysis Example" to give you an idea of how to get started.

	Rage Against the Machine	Rise Against	The Local Rebels	Stand Up and Fight
Company Brand Identity	Alt rap rock. Great musicianship. Cool Image: they wear cool T-shirts with racy statements.	Hardcore punk. Good musicianship. They dress in black T-shirts, and look rather bland.	Heavy alt rock. Fair musicianship. They dress in plain street clothes . . . nothing cool.	Metal/alt rock. Fair musicianship. They dress in black . . . nothing outstanding.
Product Brand	Etc.	Etc.	Etc.	Etc.
Price	Etc.	Etc.	Etc.	Etc.
Place	Etc.	Etc.	Etc.	Etc.
Promotion	Etc.	Etc.	Etc.	Etc.

Interpret Your Competitor Data and Write a Conclusion

Once you've compiled research on your competitors' strategies, you must determine how you'll use this data and then summarize your thoughts into a competitor conclusion paragraph.

Determine How You'll Use the Data

By asking key questions about your competitors' strengths and weakness, you can create a number of distinctive strategies and gain a true competitive advantage in the marketplace. Consider the following:

In What Ways Do Your Competitors Seem Strong?

Is there anything you can you learn from your competitors' marketing strengths? Can you "borrow," and then improve upon, any of their ideas? For instance, if they have a truly strong stage show, could you improve upon your own live performance but only in your own unique way?

In What Ways Do Your Competitors Seem Weak?

Is there anything you can you learn from your competitors' marketing weaknesses? Does this offer insight into where you might focus on filling some unfilled need, or where you might gain a competitive advantage or position that can help differentiate you in the minds of the fans from the rest of the competitors? For instance, if they barely interact with their fans, could you put a lot of effort into creating your own fan club and engaging fans in monthly meetings and other activities?

In What Ways Do You Anticipate Your Competitor Will React to the Decisions You Make?

Keep in mind that every strategy you employ will likely be met with a counterstrategy from your competitor. If you found a unique method of promotion and another band in your area copied that tactic and executed it even better, what would you do? Would you go head-to-head with them? Would you drop your prices? Or would you consider approaching these competitors and joining forces with them to work together on a particular project, like a live performance where you're the coheadliners? You see, it's always important to be thinking two or three steps ahead, much like a player would do in a game of chess. Got it? Good!

Sum Up Your Thoughts in a Competitor Conclusion Paragraph

After answering the key questions above and considering how you'll use the data derived from your research, it's time to sum up all of your thoughts in a competitor conclusion paragraph. Feel free to focus on any aspect of the data you analyzed, but just keep in mind that your objective is to draw useful conclusions about how you can improve your company and ultimately find a true competitive advantage that is aligned with your vision and is relevant to your target fan. To assist you in your writing, a helpful template and marketing plan sample is provided at the end of this chapter.

Now, check out the following short competitor conclusion paragraph below:

Given our other competitors' musical styles and overall watered-down political brand images, we could capitalize by pushing our unique rock/rave sound and the political youth movement message in all of our marketing communications. Overall, our competitive advantage could be as follows: "Real musicianship and thought-provoking lyrics fueled by a tradition for change, to create music that matters, and music that's heard." We anticipate that the competition may respond to this move by adapting a similar political brand identity, so we could push our credibility and family heritage as activists by adopting the slogan "The original change agents" in all of our marketing communications. This may be all we need to remain a step ahead and continue to be a competitive force in our own right.

Just keep in mind that the idea is to create not only "competitive strategies," but rather "sensational strategies." Don't let existing market structures limit your thinking—strive to recreate untapped structures and generate market demand and "temporary monopolies." Check out *Funky Business* by Jonas Ridderstråle and Kjell Nordström for more on competition. The *Blue Ocean Strategy* by W. Chan Kim and Renée Mauborgne is also a good read. Enjoy!

=MARKETING PLAN TEMPLATE=

Use the template below, or a template like it, to help you craft important information that you'll use in your Marketing Plan of Attack™. For additional help, be sure to refer to the marketing plan example below, the chapter on assembling your plan, and the complete plan provided in the back of this book.

Competitors	National Company A	National Company B	Local Company A	Local Company B	Your Company (If Applicable)
Your Competitor Analysis Matrix Template 1 Fill in the blank spaces below to help you assess the unique strengths/benefits, as well as the weaknesses/disadvantages, of your identified competitors. Be sure to include this chart in your Marketing Plan of Attack™.					
Company Brand Identity					
Product Brand Identity					
Products/ Services					
Price					
Place					
Promotion					
Other					

Using the data in your Competitor Analysis Matrix, now fill out the information in the chart below.

Your Competitor Analysis Conclusion Template 2: Interpretation of Data
Use the data you've acquired in your competitor analysis matrix (above) to answer the questions below. Consider your competitors' strengths and weaknesses and how you can improve your own company. Overall, consider how you can differentiate yourself in a way that's relevant to your audience. And remember, whatever decisions you are inspired to make, always think about how your competitors might respond. All of the above information will help you construct a conclusion paragraph (or several paragraphs), which will be used in your marketing plan.

Do your competitors' *branding* strategies (or lack thereof) inspire any ideas about how you might be more unique and competitive? If so, what are these ideas?

Do your competitors' *product* strategies (or lack thereof) inspire any ideas about how you might be more unique and competitive? If so, what are these ideas?

Do your competitors' *price* strategies (or lack thereof) inspire any ideas about how you might be more unique and competitive? If so, what are these ideas?

Do your competitors' *place* strategies (or lack thereof) inspire any ideas about how you might be more unique and competitive? If so, what are these ideas?

Do your competitors' *promotion* strategies (or lack thereof) inspire any ideas about how you might be more unique and competitive? If so, what are these ideas?

Do *any other* competitor elements (or lack thereof) inspire any ideas about how you might be more unique and competitive? If so, what are these ideas?

Overall, how would you sum up your key competitive advantage over the competition?

Competitor Analysis Conclusion Paragraph: Now use the above information and the template below to create a competitor analysis conclusion paragraph (or several paragraphs). Your paragraph should be included in your Marketing Plan of Attack™, together with the competitor analysis matrix you created using Template 1.

Given our competition's _____(brand, product, price, etc.) strategy/strategies, we could capitalize by _____. Overall, we feel our competitive advantage could be as follows: _____. We anticipate that the competition will respond to this move by _____, so we could _____ in order to remain a step ahead and continue to be a competitive force in our own right.

=MARKETING PLAN EXAMPLE=

Now here's an abridged marketing plan sample for our alternative rock band Rally the Tribes, to show you how they would put together a competitor analysis.

COMPETITOR ANALYSIS
a) Competitor Matrix: National and Local Acts:
(Please see the table on the following page.)

	National Act A **Rage Against the Machine**	National Act B **Rise Against**	Local Act A **The Local Rebels**	Local Act B **Stand Up and Fight**
Company Brand Identity	Alt Rap Rock. Great musicianship. They convey a political vibe in everything. Their logo is that of the Zapatista Army. The band regularly wears political statements on shirts and hats and looks cool.	Hardcore punk. Good musicianship. They have a mild political undertone. Their logo is a fist through a heart. The band dresses in black T-shirts and looks rather bland.	Heavy alt rock. Fair musicianship. They have a mild political undertone. Their logo is their name written in IMPACT font. The band is all white, and they dress in plain street clothes (nothing outstanding).	Metal/alt rock. Fair musicianship. They have a mild political undertone. Their logo is a circular lettermark with the acronym SU&P and a lightening bolt in the middle. The band dresses all in black (nothing outstanding).
Product Brand Identity	Album music/artwork/title help convey their strong political brand. The band's live performance opens with air raid sirens, uses searchlights, and displays American flags hanging upside down. Their merch bears cool political slogans.	Album music/artwork/title could hold a more consistent political vibe. Their live performance is cool and highly produced with a lot of lights and smoke. Their merch is dull.	Album music/artwork/title is not consistent with what the company brand identity attempts to project (i.e., rebellion). The live performance is not outstanding in any way. Their merch is dull.	Album music/artwork/title fail to project one seamless message. The live performance is intense in that the band can definitely play, but there is nothing "standout" about the show. Their merch is dull.
Products/ Services	Recordings (CDs, downloads, streams), live performances, placements in movies, and merch (T-shirts, hats, posters, wristbands, cinch bags, bracelets, and bandanas).	Recordings (CDs, downloads, streams, vinyl), live performances, video game placements, and merch (T-shirts, coats, hoodies, posters, bandanas, buttons—strangely, they have a line of kids' shirts).	Recordings (CDs, downloads, streams), live performances, and merch (they only have one offering—a short-sleeved T-shirt with band logo).	Recordings (CDs, downloads, streams), live performances, TV placements in the show *Intervention*, and merch (one short-sleeved T-shirt with logo, and buttons).
Price	T-shirts ($23), hats ($14), posters ($14), wristbands ($5), cinch bag ($14), bracelet ($10), and bandana ($10). Albums ($9.99).	T-shirts ($17.95), posters ($19.95), coat ($44.95), hoodies ($34.95), bandanas ($7.95), button pack ($4.95), messenger pack ($34.99), and photo ($5). Albums ($9.99).	T-shirt ($15). Live performance (pay to play/percentage at door). Albums ($10).	T-shirt ($12) and buttons ($1). Albums ($10).
Place	Etc.	Etc.	Etc.	Etc.
Promotion	Etc.	Etc.	Etc.	Etc.

b) Competitor Analysis Conclusion:

Given that Rage Against the Machine is defunct, and given that our other competitors' musical styles and political brand image is somewhat watered down, we could capitalize by pushing our unique rock/rave sound and the political youth movement message in all of our marketing communications as follows:

1) The brand identity we convey could be centered on our political seriousness and commitment to higher musical and academic educations, and our family heritages and long-lasting tradition in political activism.

2) The songs we release could focus exclusively on important political subject matter, our music videos could have a documentary vibe and key in on failing world economies and other important political/legal topics, and our merchandising (shirts, hats, and bumper stickers) could feature short and daring political slogans.

3) The promotional strategies we implement could focus on charity and benefit concerts to build community goodwill, college and National Public Radio interviews and appearances that focus on music and politics, and a website that features a calendar of political activism events.

Overall, our competitive advantage could be as follows: "Real musicianship and thought-provoking lyrics fueled by a tradition for change, to create music that matters and music that's heard."

We anticipate that the competition may respond to this move by adopting a similar political brand identity, so we could push our credibility and family heritages by adopting the slogan "The Original Change Agents." And for a completely different and more aggressive approach, we could even form a local rock/rave coalition or label, sign competitors, and earn a place in our fans' minds as being these artists' "creators" or "producers."

Demo Your Products and Services
Getting Feedback Before Committing Your Valuable Resources

Demoing your products and services (a.k.a. research and development, or R&D) is the process of getting your offerings into presentable form, testing them out on your most likely fans, and then, finally, making necessary improvements *before* committing your time/effort/money into producing and promoting them. Or, said another way, it's sticking your toe in the water and making sure the temperature is right before going in all the way. While R&D is often overlooked by artists who are overly anxious to get their material produced, protective of their creative ideas, or fearful of rejection, it is a crucial stage in the marketing process that cannot be neglected. Make no mistake, it can save you a great deal of time, money, and effort.

R&D can also help do the following:

- **Efficiently gauge the receptivity of your target audience.**
- **Save the time you'd otherwise waste marketing inferior offerings.**
- **Increase the odds of making profitable decisions.**

Remember that an organization loses momentum when it's unprofitable and unproductive, and that opportunities often dry up after you reach a certain age. Bottom line—your time is valuable and it can't be wasted on an exclusively "build it first and hope they like it later" philosophy. Surely, research is never perfect and people don't always know what they really like or need, but conducting some research is better than conducting none at all.

So, let's take a look at the following topics:

1. **Developing and Demoing Your Products and Services**
2. **Testing Your Products and Services on Your Most Likely Fans**
3. **Interpreting the Data**
4. **Writing Your R&D Conclusion Paragraph**
5. **Hearing It in Their Own Words: Q&A with Bianca Philippi, Founder of Creative Insights**

MARKET RESEARCH IS *REALLY* FOR EVERYONE: FROM MOTOWN TO SLIPKNOT

If you're still someone who believes that market research is not the type of thing artists do, or if you're someone who feels intimidated by it and afraid of potential rejection, you should consider the famous songwriter and record mogul Berry Gordy of Motown Records, the band Slipknot, and others.

According to *Time Entertainment*, Berry Gordy created corporate culture that allowed his artists to experiment creatively, but he also held weekly evaluation sessions modeled after the quality control meetings in Detroit auto plants. In these sessions, in-house staff and guests would rigorously critique music for the purpose of ensuring a consistent sound that listeners would associate with the Motown label.

Gordy's story is not an isolated example by any means. According to a close fan, the metal group Slipknot is known to hold regular meetings with key fans, whom they affectionately call "Maggots," to help them brainstorm new and improved ideas.

And finally, you'd be surprised at the number of artists that conduct research and get feedback without even knowing they're doing it. Yup, that's right! Most artists pay close attention to the number of people who hit the dance floor or mosh pit, the length of applause they get after each song, and whether a set list flows effectively—and then they make adjustments accordingly until they get it right. This is market research, and it works! So do it!

Develop and Demo Your Products and Services

Keeping in mind all the valuable research we've discussed in previous chapters, the first step in the R&D process is to get your products and services into presentable demo form so that you can test them on your audience. This could simply mean putting together a pitch to present your ideas conceptually, or creating a demo/prototype. Whatever the method, let's take a moment to reflect on the following: being patient, being thorough, and being brilliant; deciding on the recipe and how many cooks you really need in the kitchen; and developing and demoing efficiently and doing it effectively.

Be Patient, Be Thorough, and Be Brilliant

Whatever you create (songs, beats, live performances, etc.), take the time to develop the very best products and services you can. Put your heart and soul into your work, and always remain committed to furthering your knowledge and honing the skills necessary for your craft. Consider enlisting the professional advice and training of consultants, schools, and others to set you on track. Be able to say honestly that you've paid some dues and that you are extremely proud of the work that you create. Don't rush the process—this is crucial! As marketing great Philip Kotler has said in *Marketing Management*, "The key to any great marketing campaign starts with great products and services first."

Decide on the Recipe and How Many Cooks You Really Need in the Kitchen

While it's often the chemistry of several musicians working together that generates a brilliant demo, being in a full band or any partnership requires compromise and the juggling of some pretty big egos, all of which can seriously impede productivity. Sometimes things can be far easier when there are fewer "cooks in a kitchen." A guitar, your voice, and a pen may be all you need. Whatever you decide, the real issue is that you create a productive environment that allows you to remain focused on the key tasks at hand—to develop great products and services, get feedback, and make improvements.

Develop and Demo Efficiently and Do It Effectively

Finally, remember that you want to minimize your investment of time and money when developing your products and services. Why? Because you still don't know for sure whether your offerings are viable. Spending a fortune to record your compositions in a professional studio, for instance, can be a major mistake—especially if you come to find out that your material still needs a lot of refinement. So try to utilize creative partnerships and barter relationships with other organizations that can help bring your costs down, or try to utilize your own internal company resources (like your professional equipment, software programs, and more) to get the job done efficiently and effectively.

WITH NO MORE THAN A LAPTOP, SOME SOFTWARE, AND A MIC

While on the topic of being efficient and effective when creating and demoing your products and services, let's take a look specifically at a very common scenario in the music business: the recording process.

Remember that new technology has made it possible (considering you have some skills) to make broadcast-quality recordings in your own living room. Dave Banta, a multi-Platinum, award-winning record producer and author of the series *Home Recording Techniques*, says that you can use a laptop computer these days to make an amazing recording—whether that be a six-song album to sell or a basic demo to get preliminary feedback from customers.

Dave recommends the following basic home recording tools:

• A laptop computer (like a MacBook Pro)
• Music production software (like Reason, which includes drum beats, piano sounds, strings, and more)
• A keyboard with sound cards (like M-Audio with built-in sound cards)
• Recording software (like Logic or ProTools)
• An external microphone (like a Shure SM57)

If that's out of your reach, Andrew Scheps, a noted record producer working with artists like the Red Hot Chili Peppers, feels that musicians can get away with using even simpler recording software like Apple's Garage Band.

To help you learn how to use this gear, there are plenty of recording classes on college campuses, certificate programs in trade schools, and online tutorials. You should definitely look into taking one of these classes. Your investment will pay off big-time in the long run.

Test Your Products and Services Out on Your Most Likely Fans

Once you've invested the necessary effort to get your products and services into presentable demo form, it's time to test them out on your most likely fans and gather feedback. While testing and research can be very scientific when it's necessary to produce accurate results, the process is simplified for our objective of getting a little "doubt reduction." Therefore, your objective here is to get a general sense of whether people like your offerings and why or why not.

So, let's consider the following two test methods: utilizing the Internet and presenting before a controlled audience.

Utilize the Internet

A convenient way to test your products and services on your most likely fans is through personal websites, social networks, and blogs where you can upload a sample of your work.

You can create survey questionnaires using free services like Survey Monkey (www.surveymonkey.com) or Zoomerang (www.zoomerang.com), embed these surveys on your websites, and post hyperlinks on message boards. You can then scour the Internet for relevant websites (such as those of bands that have a similar sound to yours), engage these fans in a two-way conversation to break the ice and form a bond, and then invite them to give you feedback. Of course, you can also ask those whom you may have already befriended via your live gigs and e-mail lists to participate in taking your survey as well.

Just be sure to impose a survey deadline to ensure that you get immediate results, and offer a free song download or some other prize to give people more of an incentive. Sure, all of this will require time and that four-letter word *work*, but it can be done. You must think positively!

CRAFTING SURVEY QUESTIONS: A SAMPLE SURVEY CARD

Survey questions can be open-ended and indirect (like essay questions) or specific and measurable (like multiple-choice questions). The questions you create will depend on your particular situation and what you're trying to measure. But as a rule of thumb, Edward McQuarrie reminds us in *The Market Research Toolbox* to keep your questions simple, clear, easy to read, and complete. You must also phrase questions in language that will be universally understood by your target customers and hold the same meaning for all participants. Oh, and never be afraid to test out your survey questions on a few people before you run your complete test.

The example survey card below demonstrates the use of a number of different questions, including a "Likert scale" (a model that shows how much participants agree or disagree), a dichotomous (yes or no) question, a multiple-choice question, and an open-ended essay question. It was created by a band that wanted to measure their audiences' preferences for their songs, determine what songs should make it on their EP, and discover how people perceive their band brand. It was handed out at a live-performance rehearsal. Check it out.

OUR SIX-SONG MUSIC EP

1) On a scale from 1 to 5, how would you rate each song? (1—It does not immediately appeal to you and you'd prefer not to hear it on our six-song EP, or 5—It appeals to you immediately and you'd love to hear it on our six-song EP.)

   The Turtle:____; No One Else to Blame:____; Socio-pathetic:____; Lost My Mind:____; Say Goodbye:____;

   Sick of It All:____; Nodding Out:____; Out Numbered:____; Read the Writing on the Wall:____; Mother:____

2) Of the songs you liked the best, which one do you think should be our first single, and why?

3) How would you describe our sound? Circle one and explain. A) Alternative B) Metal C) Rock D) Punk E) Other.

4) What do you think is one defining character trait or benefit of our music?

5) What is the top price you'd pay for a physical CD with a four-panel booklet?____ Or for a digital album?____

6) If finances were not an issue, would you purchase a copy today? Circle one: Yes / No / Maybe. Please explain.

Demonstrate Before a Private and Controlled Audience

If testing your products and services on the Internet seems a little impersonal, you can always present them before a controlled live audience. For instance, if you're a singer/songwriter, you could rehearse a few compositions acoustically by yourself or with a partner—or you could work on your material with local musicians with whom you arrange barter deals.

After gathering a sample audience of your most likely fans (for instance, people who may conveniently be part of your gym, student body, workplace, etc.), inviting them to your private rehearsal spot (living room, studio, rehearsal hall, etc.), and then, finally, distributing a survey card like the one presented in the table "Sample Survey Card," you could perform your material while your audience writes their answers.

If surveys seem a little too uncool for you to distribute in person, you could simply observe the audience as they tap (or don't tap) their feet, have someone video record random interviews outside the event as people are leaving, or have an impartial representative conduct something called a "focus group," where he or she asks the audience open-ended questions and observes the participants as they discuss the answers.

Again, just be sure to offer an incentive to those who participate in your research studies. A free song download, a free T-shirt, or a promise to thank them on the liner notes of your recording will normally suffice. *Beer* and *pizza* also work.

I know this all sounds like a lot of work, but it can be done. I should know, I've done it myself! So get motivated and get to work. Market research is important!

AN OVERVIEW OF PRIMARY RESEARCH METHODS

The following processes are known as primary research methods (original research designed to fit your current objectives). Keep in mind that at least two or more methods should be used in any study to maximize accuracy. Consider the following:

- *Survey Questionnaires:* A familiar research technique that can be distributed on websites and blogs, included with record packaging, or conducted in rehearsal rooms or private settings. Survey questionnaires typically consist of a short set of multiple-choice questions with very specific and simple questions and answers, making the data easy to analyze using numbers and percentages. The results offer estimates about the attitudes and preferences of a sample audience and can be used to improve your products and services, your advertising copy, and so much more.

- *Participant Observation:* A method of conducting research where a sample group of a target market is observed (knowingly or unknowingly) as it interacts with various products/services in a more natural setting, such as a live performance. R&B singer Beyoncé said in an interview that before writing her record *Year of 4*, she hung out in clubs to see what music fans were listening to, what new dance steps they were doing, and what clothes they were wearing. She essentially became a fan so she could better craft the direction of her new record.

- *Intercept Interviews:* A research technique designed to get feedback from customers as they are leaving a store, venue, club, or recording studio. This is a useful technique because questions can be more in depth and open ended, and the questions can also be explained to the interviewees if needed. These interviews are usually very short, lasting just a few minutes.

- *Depth Interviews:* A more intense interview method where researchers meet one on one with a participant to ask in-depth and detailed questions to try to get at the heart of their drives and motivations. Bottom line: people don't always know what they know or know how they feel, and getting valuable answers from them requires more time and effort. Depth interviews are usually conducted in more natural settings (clubs, bars, studios, etc.) and can last an hour or more.

- *Focus Groups:* A method whereby a small number of fans (8–12) who fit a particular product's target market are brought together for about two hours in a facility (rehearsal room, recording studio, etc.), asked impartial questions by a moderator, and observed (or even videotaped) while they participate in a discussion about a product. Up to three different focus groups may be conducted about the same product to obtain more accurate results.

- **Experiments:** In *The Market Research Toolbox*, Edward McQuarrie explains that an experiment is a test of two different research conditions (or *treatments*)—such as two different headlines for the same ad. If only 60 percent of a research group likes an ad when it uses headline A, and 90 percent of another research group likes an ad when it uses headline B, it can be said that headline B is better and the condition (the headline) is what caused the outcome.
- **Usability Testing:** A research technique that examines a consumer's interaction with a product as it is taking place. The results are used to facilitate new design ideas and improvements. For instance, before the launch of your new website, a fan might be asked to complete a specific set of tasks (signing up for the fan club, purchasing a song from the Web store, navigating through various links to buy tickets, etc.), and then given the opportunity to express what he or she is feeling as he or she is performing these tasks.
- **Elicitation Techniques:** This is a category of exercises (typically one-on-one) that attempts to draw out deeper subconscious thoughts and feelings about a product or service that people may not even know they have. Common questions may include crazy things like the following: "If our band were to die today, what would you say about it at our funeral?" One method created by Gerald Zaltman of Harvard Business School involves asking participants to bring in photographs of things that remind them of your product or service. The interviewer then attempts to draw out underlying connections or metaphors. The information derived from all of these exercises can provide helpful tips in formalizing your brand, writing advertising copy, and improving your offerings overall. Be sure to check out Gerald Zaltman's creation ZMET (Zaltman metaphor elicitation technique) for further information.

Interpret the Data

After getting your products and services in presentable form and testing them on your most likely audience, you must now focus on interpreting the data you've collected. While the interpretation phase of research can be a very scientific process that is beyond the scope of this book, the following steps should adequately serve your preliminary research needs. These steps include converting your data into readable form and considering the value of your data.

Convert the Data into Readable Form

The first step in interpreting your data is to convert it into readable form. If you created more open-ended or *qualitative* essay questions, which produce answers that can be more broad and in depth, then you must read each answer carefully, look for specific and relevant trends, tabulate them, and draw a meaningful conclusion. For instance, if you asked, "What would you do to make the song better?" then you might look for recurring responses (e.g., "Try to sound more original") and group the data in that way.

If you created direct or *quantitative* multiple-choice questionnaires, which produce numeric answers that can be counted easily, then you can assign percentages to each of the survey questions (for instance, "On a scale from 1 to 5, 56.6 percent of 30 people that were surveyed liked our song and would buy it"). See the graphic "Converting Data into Visual Information."

CONVERTING DATA INTO VISUAL INFORMATION

Did You Like Our Song Enough To Buy It?
(1 = Defintely Not, 5 = Definitely Yes)

1	0%
2	0%
3	3.3%
4	40%
5	56.6%

ANSWERED: 30 / SKIPPED: 0

Consider the Quality of Your Data

The next step in the interpretation process asks you to consider the quality of your data. As stated in the book *Psychology* by Douglas Bernstein, "Researchers can't offer conclusions until they have enough high-quality data to support their claims." But what does the word *quality* really mean? Be sure to consider the following questions:

Was Your Data Really Derived from a "Representative" Sample Group?

Consider the extent to which you reached out to a "convenient sample population" (such as alternative rockers picked from the student body of your college) and the extent to which your *sample frame* (or group of actual research participants) represents an accurate cross section of your population. To simplify by example, just ask yourself, "How well did we announce the research study and give an opportunity for all students to be screened and selected?" And, "Of the students who were selected, how well were they screened before the study?" This is important. Data derived from your closest friends and peers, or data derived only from female students who are mildly into alternative rock—and who haven't bought an alternative rock record in years—would be data derived from a non- (or low-) representative sample group.

Was Your Data Really Derived from a Large Enough Sample Group?

Unless you reached out to a sample group(s) totaling thirty or so people, the optimistic views of just three or four people, for instance, would not "accurately represent" the entire population of your target group. However, if you had trouble gathering up an audience and ended up with only ten people, remember that you can still make some helpful inferences that can prove to be fruitful.

How Reliable Is Your Data?

Remember that the ultimate goal of any researcher is to obtain data that produces consistent, or relatively close, results from one test to the next—*without inadvertently affecting those results*. Thus, you must consider just how meticulous you were in retrieving your feedback.

If you conducted a series of intercept interviews, you should have asked each sample audience member the same questions and in the same order.

If you conducted a series of survey questionnaires, you should have printed all of the survey cards on the same color paper.

And if you used the observation method and invited people out to a series of rehearsal performances, you should have served all of your sample audiences the same refreshments, such as pizza and beer.

Again, your goal is to get consistent, or relatively close, results from one test to another. If any of your methods fluctuated over the course of a study, this is a good sign that you may have unreliable data and more careful testing is needed.

How Valid Is Your Data?

Remember that people often don't know their preferences and therefore are susceptible to certain external forces. For instance, after hearing a six-song record, a participant may be asked the leading question "Which song would you pick to be our first single: song A or song B?" A better, less biased, question might read: "Of the six songs you heard, which one, if any, would you pick to be our first single, and why do you feel that way?" Can you see the difference? Of course you can!

So consider the following about your research:

- Were your questions truly clear and unambiguous?
- Were there any factors that could have led participants to answer a question inaccurately? And . . .
- Did you collect your data with a reasonable amount of care so that it truly addresses what it is you set out to learn with as little bias as possible?

Your answers will help you determine just how confidently you can draw strong and valid conclusions from your data. Okay? Good! And finally . . .

Can Your Data Be Interpreted Meaningfully?

Remember that data that is not fully examined can provide misleading results. To illustrate: a participant in your research study may have answered no to the question "Would you buy my CD?" not because he doesn't like your music, but because he prefers buying *digital downloads* or subscribing to streaming services. As you can see in this example, knowing *why* he wouldn't buy your CD is really what's most important.

AFTERTHOUGHT: BIASED OR NOT? In his book *Survey Research Methods*, Floyd Fowler discusses several factors that can tarnish a research study and lead to inaccurate results, including peer pressure (the very fact that a person knows he or she is being tested), an eager-to-please audience member (like a friend or loved one who thinks you can do no wrong), an involuntary answer from someone who didn't have an answer or opinion, a poorly worded question, and a blank answer from someone who skipped. Also remember that the very fact that something is unfamiliar and new can lead to a biased response in a survey. These biases must be kept in mind when designing studies and analyzing results.

Write Your R&D Conclusion Paragraph

You've come along way, but you are not quite done yet. After developing and demoing your products and services, testing them on your most likely audience, and interpreting the data, now it's time to summarize all your information in a testing and feedback or R&D conclusion paragraph.

Your conclusion paragraph should be no more than eight to ten lines and contain the following:

- What you tested and what you were trying to learn.
- What methods you used to conduct your tests.

- How you gathered your sample audiences.
- How you analyzed the data. And . . .
- What you're going to do next as a result of your findings.

Just remember that your conclusion paragraph should provide verifiable proof to the readers of your marketing plan that your idea is on track and worthy of an investment of time and money. Your paragraph should help you win over potential investors and convince partners that you are truly onto something *big* and *special*! Your paragraph should prove that you're not just talking up a big game; you're backing it up with some hard data too.

To help you write your very own conclusion paragraph, be sure to see the template and sample plan at the end of this chapter.

Now, let's take a look at what a testing and feedback or R&D paragraph might look like:

Given our initial concern about whether or not our target audience would find our music favorable, we conducted research during live rehearsal room performances using survey cards with a Likert scale model from 1 to 5 (1 for "dislike" and 5 for "love"), observational methods by watching people as we performed, and intercept interviews as people left our rehearsal performances. The number of people we used in our surveys was three groups of 30 people that we identified from the student body of the University of Southern California. The data we retrieved from our work shows that our songs get an average rating of 4, that people displayed positive behavior toward our music by dancing to it, and that people thought the music was "hypnotic," "melodic," and very "memorable." As a result of this information and our findings, we feel strongly that the best course of action for our organization is to proceed in the hypnotic/melodic direction and finish writing and recording new material for a full-length recording.

BUT WHAT IF MY TEST RESULTS ARE UNFAVORABLE?

Even after following all of the directions in this book and chapter, some of you may end up with tests results that are disappointing or "unfavorable." You can choose to ignore the hard data and move forward as the true genius you believe you really are. Or, you can get back to the drawing board and invest more time and creative energy to improve your ideas—*before continuing forward with writing your marketing plan and recording that expensive record.* You can also take the following advice to heart:

- ***Don't Get Discouraged, Get Motivated:*** Remember that finding your true creative voice and sound, and finding an audience to whom you appeal strongly, requires a significant amount of time, patience, dedication, motivation, and work flow. It also requires that you do a great deal of experimenting, practicing, training, and creative thinking. Bottom line, it requires that you roll up your sleeves and work hard until you find your right path. This is not meant to intimidate you, but rather to stimulate you. As AC/DC said in their famous song, "It's a long way to the top if you want to rock 'n' roll."
- ***Use Constructive Criticism Wisely:*** According to John Braheny, author of *The Craft and Business of Songwriting*, when the legendary songwriter Diane Warren (Whitney Houston, Faith Hill, Celine Dion) was still honing her craft and sorting out her style, she attended songwriting groups in Los Angeles. Every week following the critique sessions in which she received feedback, she returned with complete revisions of her songs, and she did this with the utmost enthusiasm. She wrote hundreds of songs following this process. That commitment to continuous self-improvement—in addition to pure talent, luck, timing, and planning—was undoubtedly what led to her writing over 50 Top 10 hits and being the first songwriter in the history of the *Billboard* charts to have 7 hits on the singles chart at the same time. Now that's pretty impressive.

- *Be Sure to Concentrate on the Ideas That Have the Most Potential:* Remember that a smart organization puts aside its weaker ideas and concentrates its resources on those that have the most potential. As Scott Austin, former A&R executive of Maverick Records and current VP of Authentik Artists, advises, "Never be afraid to put aside 50 of your compositions to focus on 10 of your very best."
- *Don't Shelve Your Ideas Forever, but Rather Shelve Them for the Future:* Some ideas won't always get the best reviews, but that may be because the marketplace is not right at a particular point in time for that idea. What doesn't work now might work later. Consultant Ira Kalb puts it this way: "One never knows when the opportunity will present itself to go through the vaults of older works."
- *Don't Waste Time:* Don't let the competition beat you to the marketplace while you mope around depressed about the negative feedback you receive or the challenges you face. How many times have you said to yourself, "I could have done that!" or "I thought of that idea first!" Well, you're not going to let that happen again, are you? So what are you waiting for? Get back to work and get it done today!

In Their Own Words: Q&A with Bianca Philippi, Founder of Creative Insights

Bianca Philippi is the founder of Creative Insights, a research-consulting firm providing expertise in marketing. She has worked with firms as diverse as Hugo Boss, the Coca-Cola Company, and Audi, and she is a graduate of Boston University, UCLA, and Harvard University. In this interview, Bianca offers a variety of research resources that can help you save time and money.

Q: What would you say to artists who still feel that conducting research is unimportant or that conducting research is the equivalent to selling out?

BP: Doing customer research doesn't mean you're selling out at all, but creating any kind of product in a vacuum without knowing how the marketplace feels is like shooting in the dark. Unless you do not need customers or care whether or not you sell anything, knowing what your customers think is just smart business.

Q: What are some of the various things you suggest music professionals should test?

BP: Anything they create: songs, band names, logo designs, live-performance concepts, merchandising ideas, website design and functionality, album artwork layouts. You name it.

Q: If the research process sounds too daunting for artists, can they seek outside help from research professionals? How about contacting business faculty at local universities?

BP: Absolutely! Market research or consumer research instructors frequently ask students to conduct research for "real" clients. That being said, artists might want to consider approaching faculty of such business courses and inquire if there are any such opportunities available. Give ample lead time to the faculty, as many of us develop our course syllabi at least a semester in advance.

Q: How about approaching professional organizations to get help with research?

BP: Sure! Artists can most definitely approach representatives of professional membership clubs and associations such as the American Marketing Association, the American Advertising Federation and the Small Business Administration. These organizations usually have a volunteer consulting club or marketing plan/advertising campaign competition. If so, there might be an opportunity to get a talented group of business professionals to take your research project on for free.

Q: Is it feasible to use professional music business consultants or research firms to aid in the research process, or is this help only for companies with big budgets?

BP: Solo practitioners might be between projects or have some down time, and be willing to take on a smaller project at a reduced cost to you.

Larger firms generally will not have the time for a small project, but if you happen to know someone at a marketing or advertising agency, it wouldn't hurt to ask if they could cut you a break.

That being said, artists should never underestimate their ability to conduct market research themselves and gather data that can help them make important inferences about their products. This chapter has given them adequate tools to get the job done; now they just have to be brave and do it.

=MARKETING PLAN TEMPLATE=

Use the template below, or a template like it, to help you craft important information that you will use in your Marketing Plan of Attack™. For additional help, be sure to refer to the marketing plan example below, the chapter on assembling your plan, and the complete plan provided in the back of this book.

Your Demo and Feedback (R&D) Template

Use this template to help give you the information you need to include in your Marketing Plan of Attack™. Even if you do not yet have a prototype of your products/services, you can still test the idea or concept. Do not include the actual questions when formatting your plan, but leave the headers and answers.

Products/Services and/or Ideas Tested: What products/services and/or ideas most significant to your organization did you develop and test (your songs, live-performance sets, studio productions, beats, etc.)?

The Problem (or Issue): What was the problem or issue you were trying to solve with each test (did you want to confirm whether the need and opportunity you are pursuing is truly a viable and potentially profitable one, whether people were receptive to your concepts, etc.)?

Methods: What methods did you use (survey, intercept interviews, observation, focus group, etc.) for each test?

Sample Audience: Who was your sample audience for each test, and how did you gather them?

Example of Tests: Provide a sample of each test (i.e., a sample survey questionnaire, etc.).

Analysis: How did you analyze the data for each test (did you convert it to percentages, look for trends, etc.)? Do you have any charts or graphs you can insert to clearly illustrate your results?

Conclusion: Now write a final conclusion based on both the research findings and your intuition. What did you learn about the issue you were trying to test, and what is the recommended course of action for your company? The resulting paragraph should be included in your Marketing Plan of Attack™.

Conclusion Template: Use this template to conclude your testing and feedback section.

Given our initial concern about _____(what you set out to learn), we conducted research consisting of _____(what type of tests). The number of people we used in our surveys was _____, collected from _____(student body, work, etc.). The data we retrieved from our work showed that _____. As a result of this information and our findings, we feel confident that the best course of action for our company is to _____.

=MARKETING PLAN EXAMPLE=

Now here's a sample for our alternative rock band Rally the Tribes, to show you how they would construct a demo and feedback section in their Marketing Plan of Attack™.

DEMO AND FEEDBACK (R&D)

a) Products/Services and Other Items Tested:
★Products: Songs (fans' opinions of the likability of our musical style and subject matter).
★Other Items: Overall brand identity (fans' interest in politics and important matters of the world).

b) The Problem:
According to secondary data we observed from the National Center for Education Statistics, there is a growing interest among young Americans in political change since the election of Barack Obama. And according to preliminary research we conducted, no one else is mixing rock/rave genres and focusing on important causes. While this data is promising, we wanted to test out our political-minded rock/rave music on our most likely fans to determine the level of receptivity.

c) Methods:
★Surveys: Survey questionnaires were submitted to three separate audiences who attended live rehearsal room performances at our Hollywood rehearsal complex.
★Observation: Participants were observed during the performances, and informal field notes were recorded.
★Depth Interviews: Participants were telephoned and interviewed randomly after the performances.

d) Sample Audience:
★Participants: Sixty persons (20 per performance) were recruited from various college campuses in the Los Angeles area via a qualifying questionnaire. Only fans and recent consumers of rock and rave were chosen.

e) Example of Tests (Survey and Interview Questions):
a) On a scale of 1 to 5, how would you rate our music and why [1 being "don't like it" and 5 being "love it"]?
b) On a scale of 1 to 5, how concerned are you with important events of the world [1 being "not at all" and 5 being "very concerned"]?

f) Analysis:
★Percentages: For questions using a Likert scale, we added up the total scores and divided that number by the total possible scores of 300 (i.e., 60 research persons × 5 possible points = 300 total possible points).
★Trends: We scanned for recurring words and phrases in our surveys and interviews and found the following: "original," "powerful," "master musicians," "amazing to watch," and "music with a message."

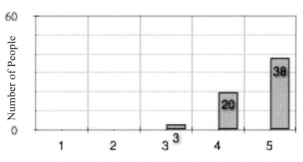

On Closer Examination

From 1-5: How Would You Rate Our Music?

g) Conclusion:

Given our initial concern about whether our target audience would be interested in our rock/rave sound and heavily politically based subject matter, we conducted research during live rehearsal room performances using survey cards with a Likert scale model, observational methods (by having the crowd monitored as we performed), and depth interviews held after the performances. The number of people we used in our surveys was three groups of 20 that we identified from the student body of Los Angeles–area colleges. The data we retrieved from our work shows that people's interest in our music was hot, with a score of 92 percent; people's level of concern about important events and crises of the world was medium high, with a score of 79 percent; and people's interest in attending our shows and supporting our cause was very hot, with a score of 97 percent. The most-recurring comments were: "Amazing to watch," "master musicians and DJs," and "intense performances." As a result of this information and our findings, we feel confident that the best course of action for our organization is to write more material in our chosen style and vibe, move forward with our professional 12-song recording, and capitalize on our raw live energy, musicianship, and visual appeal.

7

Set Your Marketing Plan Goals
Using the SMART Model

After conducting research and getting feedback, you're finally ready to set your marketing plan goals.

Setting goals is the process of dissecting your long-term vision into smaller digestible pieces and answering the question *What needs to get done first?* This allows you to focus all of your marketing efforts on a specific product/service objective that drives your organization over the next year.

A useful goal-setting technique is the SMART model. Remember that SMART is an acronym revised slightly by me for *specific, measurable, attainable, road-mapped*, and *time-based*.

Utilizing the SMART model will help you to:

- **Articulate specifically what needs to get done first.**
- **Find a simple way to measure your progress.**
- **Make sure that your goals are doable and not too far-reaching.**
- **Consider a variety of strategies for achieving your goals.**
- **Provide a one-year deadline on which you can organize your efforts.**

The SMART model was created by management strategists several decades ago, and it continues to be used today by highly successful companies of all types and sizes. Now *you* should use it too.

So, let's start discussing how to set your marketing plan goals by reviewing the following topics:

1. **Making Your Goals Specific**
2. **Making Your Goals Measurable**
3. **Determining Whether Your Goals Are Attainable**
4. **Considering a Road Map for Achieving Your Goals**
5. **Setting Your Goals in the Context of Time**
6. **Completing Your SMART Goals Paragraph**

Sound good? Great! Then let's do this.

Make Your Goals Specific

The SMART goals process begins with focusing in on the specific products and services you intend to release in the next year. These products and services must, of course, represent a logical first step toward achieving the long-term vision you identified in your vision statement paragraph (chapter 2), while also fulfilling the very precise market need you identified in your SWOT conclusion (chapter 3).

To illustrate: Suppose that you are an artist, like the one we've been using in the marketing plan samples at the end of each chapter, who has the creative *vision* to be a nationally known signed rock/rave band with a strong political message. You understand that there is a growing interest among young Americans in political news and change since the Obama elections of 2008, and a *need* for young people to have a voice.

Having read this book, you are wise enough to know that you're not going to accomplish your long-term vision overnight. So, you appropriately set short-term specific goals to independently release a 12-song album titled *War and Police* on your own label, a documentary DVD titled *Occupy World*, a line of T-shirts bearing the political slogan "Voice of the People," and a 12-song live performance set that mirrors a political rally, to be performed in local Los Angeles clubs. This, ladies and gentlemen, is a very specific goal, which is exactly what the *S* in SMART is all about.

Use the above example, as well as the others offered at the end of this chapter, to craft your own specific goal. Okay? Let's move on.

Make Your Goals Measurable (or Countable)

The next step in formulating your SMART goals is to make sure that they contain a countable or measurable element. Remember, it's not enough to say that you're going to release a 12-song album and a live performance set within the next year, you have to indicate realistically just how many albums (physical/digital) you believe you'll sell, streams of your single you aim to get, and/or how many audience members you'll feasibly attract. Why? Consultant Brian Tracy says in his book *Goals*, "If you can measure it, you can manage it." That is, if you can have some sort of measurable element in place that allows you to easily check your progress throughout the months, you can always adjust your efforts one way or another to ensure that you stay on track.

Forecast Your Sales

One way of providing a measurable element of your goals is to forecast your sales. You can do this by using simple observation, speaking with professionals, or using the historical method.

Use Simple Observation

Referring to the competitor analysis you completed in chapter 5, you can get a good feel for how many albums your competitors sell per show and at what prices, how many people they draw into a club and at what door prices, and how many T-shirts or downloads they sell from their personal websites and at what prices. You can also get a lot of answers by observing your local competitors' merch booths at their live performances and even by asking, "How're sales?" Seriously! I've done this plenty of times and it really works. You'd be surprised at how ready artists are to brag about their successes and give you the information. While the figures you discover may not be precise, remember that you're just trying to get a guesstimate number on which you might base your own sales projections. This method is not an exact science. Rather, it's about keeping things simple.

Speak with Professionals

The second method you can use to forecast your sales is to speak with other professionals—like club owners, producers, journalists, disc manufacturers, and print companies—who have a significant amount of experience working with independent artists like you. These professionals have typically been around your scene for a long time and have seen bands "come and conquer" and "burn and fade away." I can tell you from my own personal experiences playing in bands at all levels of the game that if you price your offerings within the boundaries customers expect—and can sell, for instance, 30 recordings and 30 T-shirts on average at each of your gigs (twice monthly)—you're doing better than usual for a do-it-yourself artist. Now factor in another 25 of each item for physical Internet sales, and that's 85 records and 85 T-shirts per month, or 1,020 units of each product per year. If you feel you can shoot for more, and if you have other resources or special industry connections that can facilitate greater sales, then aim for a higher goal. Just be careful not to reach for a number that's too high.

Use the Historical Method

Finally, for those of you who have a little more experience with actually selling your products, you can use the historical method. With this method, you can forecast your sales based on what your company sold last year. So, if you sold 1,020 recordings in the previous year at a midprice of $7 per unit, you have several big performances scheduled in the coming months, and you don't see any sign of economic threats or other things that could get in your way, then you might project a reasonable increase in sales in the coming year of 25 percent (that's another 255 units or a total of 1,305 units). Get the idea? By the way, we'll be talking more about pricing and its effect on demand in chapter 11.

Now let's move on to another way of providing a measurable element to your goals that deals with counting fans, rather than sales dollars or units—an approach that may be more practical for new and evolving artists.

Determine Fan Awareness

Measuring your goals on fan awareness involves making projections about, for example, the average number of devoted followers whom you'd like to attend your shows, and/or the number of followers' addresses you'd like to collect for your e-mail database. You can make as few or as many different projections as you see fit, but the point again is that "if you can measure it, you can manage it." If at the beginning of the year you're only drawing 30 people to your shows on average, and at the end of the year you want to see an average of 100 fans, you can measure the size of your audience at any time and assess whether you're making reasonable progress.

To approximate the number of fans to aim for, you can look to your local competitors and observe the number of people they're drawing to their shows, count the number of fans on other bands' social networks, and/or ask other bands how many people they have on their e-mail/text message lists. You don't have to be overly sophisticated in the way you get your data. Whatever works to help you make a general assumption is fine. Once again, keep it simple. Now let's move on.

AFTERTHOUGHT: WHAT'S MARKET POTENTIAL AND MARKET PENETRATION? University professors typically share several more sophisticated methods for forming measurable goals, such as uncovering the market potential and estimating market penetration. Market potential is the total revenue all competing companies in a market will earn in a given time period (this might be information found only via trade journals, business magazines, and professional consultants). Market penetration is the part (or percentage) of the total market that you think your organization will capture given the competition and other limiting factors. Stick with my methods for now, though. They're easier. :)

Determine Whether Your Goals Are Attainable

Now that we've discussed how to make your goals specific and measurable, the next element of the SMART model is making sure that your goals are realistic and actually attainable or "doable." USC professor Ira Kalb recommends that your goals be challenging enough to push you, but not so challenging that they are impossible to reach. Branding consultant Robert Liljenwall warns that your goals must be believable and not ego based. In his words: "Goals shouldn't bullshit anyone."

Assessing your people power and considering your financial resources are two practical methods that can help in your assessment of your goals. If you recall, these are two things that you may have already assessed as either strengths or weaknesses when conducting your SWOT analysis in chapter 3. In any case, read on.

Assess Your People Power

The people power of your organization is a major factor in determining whether your goals are attainable. Consider the following:

- How many people will you have assisting in your organization? Will it be just you, the solo artist? Or will it be several band members and/or a street team of superfans who join your noble cause and become part of your tribe?
- How good do you think your organization is at getting things done and delegating work responsibility? Does your organization consist of people who possess special strengths that will facilitate the fulfillment of your goal? And finally . . .
- How strong are your professional relationships? Do you have important people in place who can help you get the job done effectively and efficiently?

As I'm sure you can see, all of the above factors weigh heavily on just how attainable your goals really are. They are extremely important issues to consider when forming goals.

Consider Your Available Financial Resources

Your available financial resources also determine largely whether your goals are attainable. Setting goals based on money that you don't have and on money that might only become available after you win the lottery or inherit Uncle Chester's fortune may be a little unreasonable. It's one thing to say you're going to professionally record and film a single track each month, give-away 500 vinyl recordings of your first song, and collect 10,000 new e-mails, and another thing to pay the recording, filming, and marketing expenditures. Bottom line: *you gotta' have the cash to make the dash.*

So then, do you have any of these practical financing methods in your sights: personal savings, small loans from family friends, low-interest personal credit cards, monies from preselling your products and services, fan donations and pledges, barter exchanges (trade-offs of goods or services with others), and/or possible angel investors? If not, who ya' kidding?

Look, gang, you have to remember that this book is about being *proactive*, doing it yourself, and doing it together with people who can help you reach your goals. Dreaming is for sleeping, not for forming *attainable* goals. So wake up! And just make sure that your goals are doable! Okay? Good.

Consider a Road Map for Achieving Your Goals

Now that we've discussed how to make your goals specific, measurable, and attainable, you can start considering a road map for how you're realistically going to attain them. This should get you thinking about strategies (branding, product, price, place, promotion, etc.) introduced briefly in chapters 1 and 5. It should also help you see the path that lies ahead of you more clearly, connect some dots, and make realistic marketing decisions. As legendary big band leader Les Brown once said, "Your goals are the road maps that guide you and show you what is possible for your life." Here are a few things that you might think about:

- **Branding:** What is the overall brand image (attitude, personality, look, level of sophistication, etc.) you'll try to impress on the minds of your most likely fans to meet the goals of your marketing plan? Remember, the more unique you are and the more consistent and clear your message, the better.
- **Product:** What is the overall product/service strategy (e.g., the record configurations, special packaging, or live performance visuals) you'll use to achieve the goals of the plan? For instance, when you get up onstage to perform, are you going to present a live performance "theme" with custom sound and

lights, costumes, interesting instruments, and after-parties unlike your competitors in the area? When releasing recordings, are you going to provide a variety of formats, like CDs, vinyl, USB flash drives, downloads, ringtones, and streaming? When creating merch, are you going to offer a variety of items that are accommodating to your fans, like T-shirts, hats, patches, stickers, jackets, and so forth?

- *Price:* Do you know how your products and services will be priced? For instance, to meet the goals of the marketing plan, you might try a unique tactic to stimulate word-of-mouth buzz, such as when Radiohead offered their recording for a customer-determined "donation price." Or you might use a *disguised pricing* technique, such as when Prince offered a free album with every concert ticket purchased, but jacked up the cost of the tickets. And finally, you might use *free pricing*, such as when you perform and give out your music at no charge to increase awareness of yourself in the marketplace.

- *Place:* What are the distribution channels (e.g., personal websites, live venues, online retailers, film and television networks) you'll use to reach the goals of your plan? For instance, rather than just perform in the same old boring venues, are you going to play alternative venues like tattoo conventions, skateboard parks, or sporting events? And rather than just sell online, are you going to create a really cool merch booth at your live shows with an aggressive and attractive sales force? And finally . . .

- *Promotion:* How will you plan generally to promote your products and services to let people know they exist, educate them about their benefits (what they do), build awareness, and make sales? Will you utilize strategies like Internet marketing to engage fans via your social networks, word-of-mouth marketing to give out free samples, guerrilla marketing to spray chalk messages all over your town's sidewalks, publicity to encourage journalists to write about you, public relations to build goodwill through local charities, and/or any other promotional strategies you can think of?

Just remember that we'll be covering marketing strategy planning in considerable detail later in this book, so for now, do the best you can to provide only a *brief generalization* based loosely on your personal experiences, observations, instincts, and the research about the marketplace and competitors you already conducted in previous chapters. The objective here is not to finalize your complete marketing strategy just yet. Rather, it is to help give you a greater sense of whether or not there is a clear, logical, and realistic path for achieving your goals, and additional confirmation that your goals are truly attainable. Cool?

Now let's move on to adding a time-based element to your goals.

Set Your Goals in the Context of Time

Giving your marketing goals a time frame is the last step in the SMART model. While I've already mentioned that goals are short-term projections of what you want to accomplish in a year, this section is to further emphasize the point.

In his book *Goals*, Brian Tracy asks, "How do you eat an elephant?" The simple answer: "One bite at a time." Similarly, how do you attain your vision of "wanting to be a pop star who shocks the world," like Marilyn Manson did? The answer: one *year* at a time. Goals are the staircase to your vision.

Look, gang, take things in stride: a year is long enough to implement your marketing plan and obtain data from the marketplace about your progress, but not long enough to get you confused or make you feel overwhelmed.

By the way, later in this book, we'll discuss how to further break down your yearly goals *into months, weeks, days and even hours* if necessary, by developing a marketing timeline. Trust me, before you're done reading this book, you're going to have your eyes glued to your clock and schedules more than you ever have before. This is a great thing! You're going to be extra focused on your marketing tasks at hand and dramatically increase the chances of getting the results you want. You're also going to know how to execute those tasks by learning how to delegate work among your partners and your dedicated fans.

To sum things up in the words of Vince Lombardi, the legendary coach for the Green Bay Packers, "Results come only from knowing what you are achieving today and having a clear, specific strategy for closing the gap between today's reality and your vision for tomorrow." Now check out the graphic "The Incremental Goals Model."

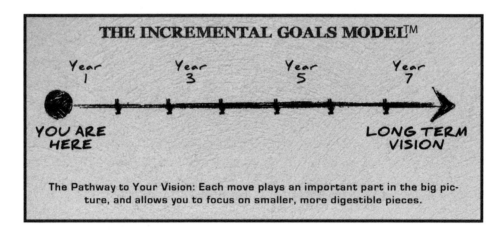

Complete Your SMART Goals Paragraph

Now that you understand all of the elements of the SMART model, you should go ahead and start constructing your very own marketing goals paragraph. For clarity, take each element we discussed in this chapter and create one concise and uniform paragraph that is SMART.

To help you summarize your personal marketing plan goals correctly, there is a template and marketing plan sample provided at the end of this chapter. Some of the questions in the template will simply require you to transfer information you've already provided in previous chapters, and other questions will be new. In any case, don't let the template confine your goal setting in any way—feel free to expand, reduce, or reword any portion of the template to suit your specific marketing needs. This, like all the other templates in this book, is provided to help you, not limit you. Remember that!

Now, here's an example of what your goals may look like:

To fulfill the vision of being a nationally recognized TV/film/commercial composer signed with a major publisher such as Universal, we plan to license three compositions to TV shows like Grey's Anatomy *and to reality shows like* Intervention. *We also plan to compose two complete scores for student documentaries via universities like UCLA, USC, or the Los Angeles Film School, and to compose one complete score for our own documentary about homeless runaways in Hollywood, CA. This all will be primarily accomplished by networking at local film festivals and college film departments, utilizing personal connections and access to high-def cameras, posting video samples of our work on sites like YouTube and Vimeo, entering contests like those on Current TV, utilizing songplugging services like TAXI and Pump Audio, and increasing relationships with music libraries like RipTide Music and Megatrax. The timeline for this goal is 12 months.*

=MARKETING PLAN TEMPLATE=

Use the template below, or a template like it, to help you craft important information that you will use in your Marketing Plan of Attack™. For additional help, be sure to refer to the marketing plan example below, the chapter on assembling your plan, and the complete plan provided in the back of this book.

Your SMART Goals Paragraph Template

Answer the following questions succinctly, and then use the information to write your SMART goals in paragraph form. Do not use the questions in your marketing plan, just the paragraph.

What are your long-term vision and the specific need you plan to fill? (Refer to your vision paragraph and SWOT analysis if needed.)

What are the specific products and/or services you will offer to fulfill this need?

What are your measurable sales forecasts and/or your determined fan awareness numbers for your individual products/services?

Given your manpower and financial resources, is your goal truly attainable?

What are the general strategies (branding, product, price, place, promotion, etc.) that you will use to attain your goals? Do they provide a logical roadmap to success?

What are the start date and the end date for your marketing plan goals? (Remember to work in the context of a year.)

SMART Goals Paragraph Template: Now use the information from the questions you answered above to write a short SMART Goals paragraph. Refer to the examples included in the text above if needed. Note that you can slightly modify this template if necessary.

To work toward our long-term vision of being a _____(type of company, genre, and what you'll project), we plan to offer _____(records, tours, merch, etc.) and sell/gross _____(number of units or amount of money) and/or build fan awareness as indicated by _____(a database of 5,000 names, 1,000 daily hits on our website, etc.). The general strategies to accomplish this goal will consist of _____. This goal will be attained in one year starting approximately _____ to _____.

=MARKETING PLAN EXAMPLE=

Now here's a marketing plan sample, for our alternative rock band Rally the Tribes, to show you how they would put together a SMART goals paragraph.

MARKETING PLAN SMART GOALS

To work toward our long-term vision of becoming a nationally known rock/rave band with a strong political message, we plan to offer a 12-song album tentatively titled War and Police, *a documentary DVD titled* Occupy World, *a line of T-shirts and other merchandising products bearing political slogans, and a 12-song live-performance set. Our goal is to sell 1,000 records (800 CDs, 100 USB flash drives, 100 download albums), sell 500 DVDs, sell out all merch produced, and perform 12 RTT rock/rave performances. We also plan to increase our consumer awareness in Los Angeles, marked by achieving a database of 5,000 fans and an audience attendance of 350 per show. The general strategies to accomplish this goal will consist of Internet (social media, political blogs, and personal websites), word of mouth (giving out samples and targeting key tastemaker fans), guerrilla street-marketing strategies (postcards, stickers, and street stencils), and direct marketing (e-mail and text messaging). This goal will be accomplished within one year from the execution of this plan.*

8

Develop Your Company's Brand Strategy

Creating the Right Identity for Your Company and Its People

After using the SMART model in chapter 7 and setting your marketing plan goals, you can begin to further develop, study, and expand upon your mix of marketing strategies. This begins with *company branding*.

Company branding is the process of presenting clear, unique, relevant, believable, and consistent messages about your *organization* with the intention of exceeding fans' expectations and leaving a long-lasting positive image in their minds—all to help achieve the goals of your marketing plan.

A company brand represents a promise to fans—it's what they come to trust and expect from your organization every time they come in contact with you. Or, explained another way by Jeff Bezos, the founder of Amazon.com, "A brand is what people say about your company when you aren't in the room."

Creating a strong company brand can help do the following:

- **Produce the image you intended in the minds of the fans.**
- **Present fans with a culture that mirrors their own values and customs.**
- **Win over passionate customers who become your brand ambassadors.**
- **Create a special "position" in your fans' minds that is unlike the competition.**
- **Increase company value and equity that can live on far into the future.**

Everything your company does can affect the way customers perceive you—from the identity it puts forth in its musical style, name, logo, and slogans to its personality, look, culture, and associations with other companies.

This chapter contains tools that will help you create a strong company brand, or just polish a brand that you may have already started. Sections include:

1. **Reviewing All Your Research and Goals**
2. **Choosing a Company Brand Name**
3. **Designing a Company Brand Logo That Pops**
4. **Using a Company Slogan or Tagline**
5. **Creating a Company Spokescreature or Mascot**
6. **Considering Your Company's Brand Personality**
7. **Realizing Your Position**

HOW DO YOU BRAND IF YOU DON'T KNOW WHAT YOUR BRAND IS?

While we have been indirectly discussing your brand throughout this book (by finding your vision and what you sound like and stand for, and by identifying a market opportunity and what need you're filling), below are a few more techniques that can further help. I admit that some of these are a stretch, but keep an open mind and they just might help you identify your brand. Consider the following:

- **Write Your Own Eulogy:** As morbid as this may sound, a good way to get to the core of what your brand is about is to write your own company's eulogy (i.e., the speech that praises someone who has just passed away). Would you want people to remember your company for being innovative and trendsetting and/or having a strong personal relationship with customers and fans? Would you want to be thought of as having a high-end, low-end, or middle-of-the-road degree of quality? What would this company be called? How would the employees look and act? What would the company culture or way of life be like? Did this company support any charities? If you're having trouble with this exercise, let someone write this eulogy for you and see what he or she says. Then ask someone else to write it (and so on) until you start to see some common trends. This exercise can prove to be extremely useful.

- **Think About What Animal Your Company Would Be:** Much like the exercise above, thinking about what kind of animal your company could be can help you greatly to discover your brand and create identity tools. If your company is a butterfly, then you might be a beautiful, colorful, and soft singer/songwriter like Mariah Carey (who, by the way, uses a butterfly in her logo). And if your company is a crow, then you might be witty, clever, and have a loud boasting voice like the Black Crowes (who use the black crow in their logo). Sports teams and automobile manufacturers have been using animals for years to help convey what they stand for. In any case, perhaps this technique will help you with your career and brand. Conduct research and find out.

- **Draw a Mind Map:** Finally, another way to discover your brand, and even find a name that reflects it, is to create a mind map. This involves asking a research participant to write a word in the center of a sheet of paper that he or she feels reflects what your company is and then create several branches from that word. For instance, you might use the phrase "rock band," from which several branches are formed. One branch might use the word *loud*, then *powerful*, and end with *guns*. Another branch might use the word *passionate*, then *heartfelt*, and end with *roses*. Put them together and you get the name Guns N' Roses. I think you get the idea of how this could work. Finding your brand is not easy, but perhaps this tip, and the others above, might help.

Review Your Research and Goals and Examine How They Relate to Branding

We've already discussed important research and objective principles in previous chapters of this book, including *vision*, *need*, *customers*, *competition*, *feedback*, and *goals*. If you haven't gotten around to thinking about these issues in detail yet, now would be a really good time to start. Why? You'll see throughout this chapter that they are actually the backbone of branding (as well as product development and many of the other strategies yet to be discussed). So let's go ahead and do a very brief review of your research and goals and examine how they relate to branding.

Don't Lose Sight of Your Vision

In order to be a strong brand, you must have a clear concept of what you want your company to be and do in the future (from its overall musical category to your overall life's purpose and what you want to project onto the marketplace). Strong brands are those that stand for a meaningful idea.

Don't Forget About Your SWOT Analysis: Need and Opportunity

Your company must be focused on filling a specific market need in order to establish a strong brand image in the marketplace. The more unique and *standout* you are, the more memorable your brand image will be in the minds of fans.

Be Sure You Really Know Your Target Audience

Having a thorough understanding of your most likely fans and what's important to them will help your company furnish your customers with marketing messages that are clear and relevant, which are important ingredients in branding.

Reinvestigate Your Competitors

A clear understanding of your competitors allows you to emphasize the unique advantages of your company and stake out a singular position in the minds of fans relative to those competitors.

Reexamine Your Feedback

You must always be aware of what people are saying about your company and clear about what your research truly means. Remember that a major factor in branding and bringing your products to the marketplace is creating customer satisfaction and winning over loyal fans who will depend on you for years to come.

Stick to Your Goals

Having specific short-term goals in place that lead toward your long-term vision allows you to work more thoughtfully toward building a consistent company personality or character from the day you open your doors. Consistency is a crucial ingredient in branding.

So, as you can see, marketing really is an involved, methodical process where many pieces of a puzzle must come together to achieve the desired results. Now let's get started with creating your own brand identity.

Choose a Company Brand Name

Choosing a company brand name is an important first step in creating a strong brand identity. It is what is typically stamped on all of your products and services (recordings, merchandise, performances, etc.) as well as your websites, business cards, stationery, bass drum heads, cases, pens, banners, stickers, car, and even studio door.

Your name, in part, is how people will come to recognize, request, and discuss you among friends, and whenever they hear or see your name, it is what will trigger the series of memories and associations stored in fans' minds about your brand.

Surely there are numerous examples of bands with seemingly meaningless and random names (the Cars, Toad the Wet Sprocket, Limp Bizkit, Strapping Young Lad, etc.) that have nonetheless gone on to achieve great success. But putting your best foot forward and creating a brand name that represents you more clearly than the aforementioned examples will prove to be in your best interest.

Don't just jump at the first name you come up with; give this process some time and formulate a list of several names before settling on one. The following tips will certainly inspire you.

Reflect the Right Mood and Imagery

Kaskade reflects DJ Ryan Raddon's continuous, flowing sounds and powerful textures (much like a waterfall) that he creates in his dance sets. Rage Against the Machine reflects the band's intense and political activist message. NWA makes a strong statement about their gangsta rap style and "F*#^ the man" attitude. And Marilyn Manson hints at the artist's glam look and evil dark metal style. These names are all brilliant and reflect the perfect mood and imagery.

Be Original and in Good Legal Standing

Born David Robert Jones (and known as Davy Jones early in his career), David Bowie's name was created to provide legal distinction from singer Davy Jones of the Monkees. That's right! If your name is too similar to another entertainer—and in some cases, if your name is too similar to another company in a different industry—it's likely you won't be able to use it. If you want to read more about trademark law, be sure to check out the United States Patent and Trademark office (www.uspto.gov).

Invent a Name

The Mighty Mighty BossTones' name was invented by adjusting the name of the city in which the band was formed (Boston, Massachusetts) while saying something about their attitude, horn section, and ska sound. Jamiroquai's name was invented in reference to the band's jam sessions and the front man's empathy for the displaced Indian tribe known as the Iroquois.

Create a Nickname

Jay-Z's real name was Shawn Corey Carter, but he adopted the more appropriate musical nickname "Jazzy" for the stage, which was eventually shortened to Jay-Z. Lil' Kim's real name was Kimberly Denise Jones, but she shortened it and adopted Lil' to reflect her height.

Describe Your Company

The Record Plant, one of the most famous recording studios in the world, describes exactly what it is—a place where records are made. Dave Matthews Band implies that there is one leader, Dave Matthews, but that we can also expect—with some flexibility—the same group or band of musicians working on every recording and performance. These names are simple descriptions and to the point.

Use a Unique Spelling

Korn spells their name with a letter *K*, Three 6 Mafia spells out the word *three* followed by the number *6*, and Boyz II Men uses the letters *yz* and the Roman numeral *II* to create distinctiveness and to be more memorable. Just be careful not to make your spelling too weird, or people will not be able to find you when conducting an online search.

Form an Abbreviation

And finally, LSD's name stands for the drug LSD and for Life, Sex, and Death—perfect for an alternative rock band. And W.A.S.P.'s name was once described by members to mean "We Are Sex Perverts," which is perfect for the debauchery often associated with metal bands.

Design a Company Brand Logo That Pops

Designing an original logo is another important step in creating and projecting a brand identity and, more specifically, communicating your company brand name. As David Aaker says in *Building Strong Brands*, "A strong logo can provide cohesion and structure to an identity and make it much easier to gain recognition and recall."

With a good logo, all it takes is a glance to be reminded of you. In fact, a logo is so important, it may even be a good idea to invest in a professional graphic artist to create one for you.

Now let's take a quick look at the various types of logos that exist so you at least have a clear picture of what works best for your company. There are four basic logo choices: *wordmarks*, *lettermarks*, *brandmarks*, and *combinedmarks*.

Use a Wordmark (Typographic Symbol)

A wordmark features the brand name in a simple and unique typeset and color. Run-DMC's logo is in an impact-type font with red and white colors and the words *RUN* and *DMC* stacked on top of each other. KISS's logo is also in an impact-type font with fire-orange colors and the *S*'s of their name extending downward like lightning bolts. And Pink's logo is in a casual-type font with white and soft pink colors and the *i* in her name turned upside down like an exclamation point. Special attention must be given to choosing a font style and color scheme that evokes your brand. For more on this, be sure to check out the books *Just My Type* by Simon Garfield and *Color Psychology* by Faber Birren.

Consider a Lettermark

A lettermark features the initials of a brand name in simple and unique typesetting and color, and may include the full name spelled out beneath, alongside, or above it. Nine Inch Nails' logo is in a bold font with white letters and the last *N* of NIN turned backward. A lettermark is a great choice when you have a long name that doesn't fit well on merch items, or that, overall, will look and sound better as an abbreviation. In fact, Trent Reznor of NIN denies any deep meaning to the band name, other than that he wanted one that looked cool as an abbreviation on hats.

Try a Brandmark (a.k.a. Symbol)

A brandmark features a graphic symbol (with no words or letters) that, in the best case, reflects your company's personality. For instance, the Rolling Stones' lips and tongue logo in red reflects Mick Jagger's unique mouth and crazy sexual energy, and the Misfits' skull in white reflects the band's heavy punk sound and intense attitude. A brandmark is especially cool, since it conveys the band's character while adding an element of mystery and intrigue. As they say, a picture is worth a thousand words. The challenge, though, is that a brandmark may require extra effort to get people to attach any meaning to it initially, since there are no accompanying words or identification marks attached.

Use a Combinedmark

Finally, a combinedmark is a logo that incorporates two or all three of the above logo types. Wutang Clan's logo is in an Asian-styled font with black letters (a wordmark) and a bat-shaped wing or letter *W* graphic in the background (a brandmark). The Who's logo is in a modern-type font with black letters (a wordmark) and the Royal Air Force's logo with red, white, and blue colors in the background (a brandmark; by the way, notice how the band borrows from the positive emotions of their homeland country of England—all cool stuff). You'll find that brandmarks are the most widely used logo type in music. If you want to check out more information on logos, read *Logo Design Love* by David Airey.

Note: Getting legal permissions to show all of the iconic logos mentioned above is a pain in the butt. Thus, be sure to conduct your own search online using your favorite browser to take a look at each and every logo design mentioned. Also enjoy the graphic herein titled "Logo Examples," which features independent artists just like you.

Create a Company Brand Slogan or Tagline

Choosing a slogan or tagline (the two terms are often used interchangeably) can be another useful step in building your organization's brand identity.

Slogans can provide further information about your brand, communicate an overall philosophy, increase memorability, sell the unique benefits of your offerings, acknowledge your audience, and/or give off a certain personality.

Slogans can be used as part of a short-term campaign, or they can become so important that they are used as part of the company logo and in all advertisements and on all products.

Slogans can also be used apart from the logo when networking and creating short sales pitches (a.k.a. elevator pitches), participating in magazine and radio interviews, using memorable sound bites for an interviewer, and so much more.

Let's take a look at a few tips for creating your own slogan or tagline. Remember that they don't have to be grammatically correct, just short and sweet.

Convey the Right Personality

The indie band Clepto uses the slogan "Thrash Punk Gypsies" in their logo to hint at their Saudi Arabian roots and metal sound and spirit. Punk rocker Henry Rollins uses the tagline "Search and Destroy" (inspired by the

Godfather of Punk, Iggy Pop) to accompany his logo. In fact, Rollins even tattooed the slogan on his back, and he uses it on T-shirts and other merch as well. These are perfect examples!

Appeal to Your Audience

House of Pain uses the slogan "Fine Malt Lyrics" directly in their logo to pay homage to their home city of Boston and the predominantly Irish folks who live there.

Be Believable

Jazz legend Jaco Pastorius used the slogan "The Greatest Bass Player in the World," and the Rolling Stones adopted the line "The Greatest Rock Band in the World." While these slogans were rather bold at the time, both artists could back them up in a big way. Point is: when you're just starting out in the business, using slogans like "the greatest" is just silly. So don't do it! Be real. Be believable.

Offer an Explanation

The classic Southern rock band ZZ Top uses the tagline "That Lil' Ol' Band from Texas" all over their website and on other public relations materials. Billy Joel used "The Piano Man" in all his publicity and even released a record of the same name. These slogans provide more clarity about who these artists are, which is something that can be especially valuable for artists, like you, who are just starting out.

Ask Your Fans What They Think

Finally, ask your most likely fans how they might sum you up in one word or phrase, how they think you're different, and what they feel is most important to them. You could even throw a contest and get your fans to design your slogan for you. You'll not only form a closer bond with your fans by getting them involved, you just might end up with a cool tagline.

SLOGANS AND TAGLINE EXAMPLES: SELF PROCLAIMED AND/OR APPOINTED BY THE PRESS

While the following examples do not represent all of the tips presented above, and while it is unclear whether some of these names are actually self-started or formed in the press and later adopted, let's take a quick look at a few more of the examples that I was able to uncover. These are rather bold claims, but note that these artists truly earned these bragging rights and positions in the marketplace:

- *Ace Drummer Man:* The late, great Gene Krupa adopted this in his advertising and publicity.
- *The King of Blues:* B. B. King uses this on his website and other public relations material.
- *The Prince of Darkness:* Ozzy Osbourne uses this in various public relations matters.
- *The Chairman of the Board:* Frank Sinatra regularly used this in his marketing.
- *The Bad Boys of Rock and Roll:* Aerosmith and Quiet Riot both used this tagline in their promotional efforts.
- *The Queen of Soul:* Aretha Franklin uses this tagline in all of her publicity.
- *The Godfather of Punk:* Iggy Pop regularly uses this line in his press materials.
- *The Fab Four:* The Beatles used this slogan for many years.
- *The Father of Rock and Roll:* Chuck Berry used this in press interviews.

- *If It's a Hit, It's a Miracle:* This slogan was used by Motown Records.
- *The World's Most Flexible Record Label:* Stiff Records in London used this slogan.

[For more information on slogans, check out the books *Kiss and Sell* by Robert Sawyer, *Integrated Marketing Communications* by Robyn Blakeman, and *Ogilvy on Advertising* by David Oglivy.]

Create a Company Brand Spokescreature or Mascot

Creating a "spokescreature" or mascot that represents something memorable, relatable, and relevant to your personality (or the personality of your target market) is yet another tool you can use to communicate your brand's identity. As David Aaker says in his book *Building Strong Brands*, the advantages of using a spokescreature or mascot are that they reinforce your personality and they can be updated to reflect current changes or styles in your industry.

Companies of all musical styles utilize spokescreatures or mascots on their Internet sites, record artwork, live-performance backdrops, and T-shirts. Consider what these following bands use:

- Iron Maiden features their evil skeleton mascot named "Eddie the Head" (also known as "Edward the Great" or "Evil Eddie") on their album cover artwork, patches, stickers, T-shirts, and concert stage backdrops, and even as an enormous mechanical stage prop that blows smoke and moves about while the band plays. Eddie is a perfect representation of the band's heavy metal music and personality.
- Kanye West features his mascot named "Dropout Bear"—a cool, collegiate-looking teddy bear—on the cover of three of his albums and in music videos. Perhaps this mascot alludes to his mother's academic background as a college professor in Chicago and the fact that Kanye dropped out of college and achieved great success in music.
- The Gorillaz feature four animated mascots, which really take on more of the persona of the actual band members themselves, as part of a fictional universe on the band's website, music videos, and live stage performances. This high-tech presentation is quite amazing and also a reflection of the band's incredible musicianship and more serious demeanor. And finally . . .
- Sublime featured a mellow mascot named Lou Dog—their pet dalmatian—on album covers and T-shirts. Lou Dog was quite an appropriate mascot for Sublime's laid-back style and chill personality, but sadly, the dog passed away a few years back. RIP Lou.

Note: Once again, getting legal permissions is a pain. To view all of the mascots discussed above, conduct your own search online. Also be sure to check out the mascots used by Deadmau5, Motörhead, Megadeth, and other great artists.

Consider Your Company's Brand Personality

Moving along in our discussion about company branding, let's take a look at your personality (or character). This can be reflected in your attitude and vibe, look, and associations with established brands.

Identify Your Brand Attitude and Vibe

A company brand's attitude and vibe relates to the overall posturing it chooses to project to its public. It can be described by personality types and adjectives like *bad boy, bad girl, gangsta, ghetto, intelligent, all-American wholesome, down to earth, over the top, unpredictable, fun, flirtatious, serious, provocative, confident, powerful, sexy, slutty, diva, obnoxious, lush, intellectual, sophisticated,* and many others words and phrases.

No matter what brand attitude and vibe your company chooses to project to its public, just be sure that it is consistent with your company's long-term vision, in line with your products and services, and appropriate for your target market. Otherwise, you will appear fake and unbelievable.

By identifying the attitude and vibe that fits your brand at its core, you can project this personality strongly at every point of contact with your public—from what you convey in your photographs, to how you present yourself onstage, to how you conduct yourself in interviews with the press, to how you interact with fans. Your public will begin to identify and understand what to expect from you, which helps them develop a clear image of you in their minds.

If you're still unsure of what attitude and vibe you want your company to project, you can conduct research through your social networks and ask your target audience what they expect. Okay?

Consider the Look of Your Brand

The look or visual style that your company projects is also crucial in building a strong brand personality. I'm not suggesting that you adopt some outlandish or over-the-top look, but just one that remains consistent with your brand's overall vision.

Artists, however, can feel uncomfortable about fashion. They feel that their look (their hair, clothes, etc.) should be kept separate from their art and music. While I truly understand this temperament, consider the following question: if your brand was a classy restaurant, wouldn't it make sense to locate it in a classy building, dress the tables with fancy tablecloths, and have fancy menus and well-groomed waiters? Since the clientele would expect this, it would only make good sense to present a consistent experience. So then, it's really no different than your musical brand. Make no mistake, the look of your brand is crucial to the branding process and to projecting a very identifiable, consistent personality and character. Impressions really do matter. So whether you dress up or you dress down, if you haven't given it some thought already, get to work now!

AFTERTHOUGHT: CAN INDIVIDUAL PEOPLE WITHIN A COMPANY BE A BRAND? KISS branded each of their representatives to look like comic book characters and take on a very specific persona. The Spice Girls also adopted very distinct names, looks, and personalities for each member of the band. And Led Zeppelin used four abstract and seemingly random symbols that represented each member of the band when they released their fourth album. Needless to say, this gives fans so much more to identify with and also a greater reason to fall in love with a band.

Associate with Other Brands

Finally, by associating your company with other brands that already convey strong emotions in your target fans' minds, you can "build" (or, as consultant Philip Kotler says, "borrow") brand value to further shape your personality and character. As it has been said, "You can recognize a man's true character by the people he surrounds himself with."

The guest musicians you hire in the studio, the producers you use on your recordings, the successful songs you cover, the bands you form alliances with and open for, the equipment you play onstage, the clubs you choose to play in, and the magazines you get to review you can all build your company's brand personality and an image in the minds of your audience. Additionally, the industry people who offer you quotes of endorsement, the journalists who write your band's biography, the music teachers you study with, the prestigious schools you graduate from, the charities you choose to support, the companies you establish sponsorships with, and even the city or neighborhood in which you live and identify with can also be brand builders.

By associating your company's brand with a more well-known and identifiable one, fans will begin to think of them both simultaneously. In the psychological world, this is what's called Pavlovian Association—named after Ivan Pavlov and his pioneering theories about classical conditioning. In fact, these associations might be the very thing that gives people a reason to buy from you (come out to your shows, download your music, etc.). In their eyes, it is what makes you more credible, and it is what conveys the right emotional appeal.

Now, if this all makes sense to you, take a brief moment and consider just how using associations can help shape your brand image.

GOOD BEHAVIOR HELPS BUILD STRONG BRANDS: DEALING WITH BRAND CONTACTS

Watching your brand's behavior and its interactions with its fans, the press, business associates, the community, and others is another important part of the branding process that is often overlooked by many young bands. As branding consultant Robert Liljenwall warns, "Brands are never rewarded for bad behavior."

- *Relate to Your Fans:* When dealing with its fans, a brand must consider the commitment it will make to building solid relationships and making its fans feel as though they're part of the brand's success. Marketing consultant Philip Kotler says that getting close to customers is what is known as "relationship marketing." The members of Metallica were known early in their career to wait in front of the stage after every show and shake hands with every fan. KISS even created a fan club they called the KISS Army where fans were given opportunities to win special prizes, chances to hang out with the band, and even opportunities to interact with the band's product/service decisions like creating set lists and naming albums. This level of relationship marketing and good behavior toward fans equates to a very positive brand image, and also to building loyal fans who become personal ambassadors of your company— from wearing your T-shirts, to telling all of their friends about you, to even becoming a brand of their own (fans of Jimmy Buffett are called "Parrot Heads," and fans of Nicki Minaj are called "Barbies"). This all helps build an emotional bond that can last for years.

- *Interact with the Press and Other Professionals Accordingly:* The manner in which your brand behaves when dealing with the press and other professionals (such as club promoters, sound men, and lighting technicians) is also extremely important when building your brand's image. *A band brand must be entirely clear that the world does not revolve around it and that it is owed absolutely nothing.* Be sure to thank press people who write about you in local magazines, club owners who give you an opportunity to perform, and lighting and sound crews in clubs who make you look and sound better. Don't become known as the difficult, ungrateful, flakey, and self-centered company or artist. Rather, build a strong brand image by being aware of the professionals around you. Everything you do matters.

- *Build Character Through Community Relations:* The behavior and concern you demonstrate for others in your community can greatly affect the brand image you'll create for yourself. Will you be seen as a leader who reaches out to charities and throws benefit performances? Will you be a role model to others coming up in the world? Will you support any special causes or organizations? As Lynn Upshaw says in his book *Building Brand Identity*, customers tend to feel closer to brands they respect and with whom they share the same set of values. In fact, this is the very thing that often commands the attention of press people and other industry folks who might have otherwise overlooked a certain artist.

Realize Your Position: Know Your Point of Differentiation and Plan to Exploit It

To finish up our discussion on company branding, let's talk about one final and very important branding tool—*positioning*. While we have already discussed it indirectly in covering the SWOT analysis (and finding a specific need or void in the marketplace), market segmentation (and targeting a very specific group of fans who all behave in a certain way), and the competitor analysis (and finding your own unique competitive edge), it's time to turn our attention to positioning itself.

Positioning is *the process of getting your target audience to see your company in a way that is unique from your competitors.* Put another way, positioning helps identify that one unique benefit about your entire organization that you want your fans to remember, and that helps them remember you. Overall, positioning is about exploiting your uniqueness and earning a place in your fans' minds.

By identifying and exploiting your position, you won't be just one of thousands of female pop R&B singers; you'll be the *female pop/R&B singer with a five-octave vocal range* (Mariah Carey). You won't be just one of thousands of alternative rock bands; you'll be the *hard-edged rap/rock alternative band with politically fueled lyrics* (Rage Against the Machine). And you won't be just any punk band; you'll be the *high-energy punk band that strongly fuses traditional Irish roots with their punk sound* (Flogging Molly). These artists are all unique, and they promoted this uniqueness in everything they did.

So, will we be able to recognize you with as little as one word or phrase, as demonstrated by the artists above? What piece of the "puzzle" among millions of competing messages will you present to fit neatly into the minds of your fans? Think about it.

Define Your Company's Position and Exploit It

Now that you have a basic idea of what positioning is, let's move on to defining your own position in the marketplace. While there are numerous techniques you can use and detailed books you can read, you'll find the following four tips useful.

Position Yourself Based on Your Identified Need and on Being First

Chuck Berry is positioned as being the "Father of Rock and Roll." According to historians, he was the first to fulfill society's need for new and exciting music and performances by taking the music popular with white folks (country and western), fusing it with his own unique electric guitar riffs and outlandish stage antics, and playing it for black audiences. Though blacks thought Berry was crazy, they quickly accepted his music because it was still danceable. Shortly after, white folks followed suit.

Berry sang the words, "Hail hail rock and roll, deliver me from the days of old," and that's precisely what happened. Berry earned the unique position in fans' minds as being an innovator of rock 'n' roll and the precise title "The Father of Rock and Roll." Though others have argued that they were the originators, Berry nonetheless used the slogan in interviews, bios, and other promotional activities consistently throughout the years, and his organization still uses it on his website today. Berry sought to be unique and he promoted this uniqueness, thereby earning a strong place in music history.

AFTERTHOUGHT: IS POSITIONING JUST FOR BIG ARTISTS? Indie artist Jonathan Coulton (who made over $500,000 in one year without a label) is clearly positioned in the marketplace as follows: *An Ivy League computer geek known for his quirky, witty lyrics about science fiction and technology.* This message is pushed out all over the Internet, on NPR radio stations, and in science magazines. If other indie artists can find a strong position and earn a place in fans' minds, so can you! Even if it is just the slightest of things that is unique about you, figure it out and promote it.

Position Yourself Based on Specific Characteristics of Your Target Audience

Cypress Hill is essentially positioned as being the "pot smokers' hard-edged rap band." From releasing songs titled "Mr. Green Thumb," to getting interviewed in magazines like *High Times*, to organizing the Cypress Hill SmokeOut festival, Cypress Hill successfully identified a rebellious need in their most likely fan, filled that need, and positioned themselves in fans' minds as being more than just your average rap band. Whether we agree with this position or not, Cypress Hill created a company culture that mirrors the history, beliefs, customs, habits, values, and social behavior of their audience and gave fans something to identify with. Among all of the other rap bands out there, they own a very specific place in the minds of fans. To paraphrase authors Jack Trout and Al Ries in the book *Positioning: The Battle for Your Mind*, Cypress Hill "earned a window in their prospects' minds."

Position Yourself as Being the Direct Opposite of the Competition

In a classic example circa 1991, Los Angeles–based Ugly Kid Joe purposely positioned themselves as "ugly comic/metal rockers," while the leading Sunset Strip band of the time, Pretty Boy Floyd, pushed their androgynous glam-rock metal style. As if that move weren't enough to distinguished itself in the marketplace, Ugly Kid Joe also created a logo that featured a cartoon character of an ugly kid sporting a backward baseball cap and raised middle finger, dressed down in jeans and T-shirts, and presented a "who cares, f*#% you attitude" in everything they did in public. Furthermore, the band named their first album *America's Least Wanted* and released a single titled "As ugly as they want to be"—which made it to the *Billboard* Top 10 charts. Now that's pretty damn impressive!

But note that Ugly Kid Joe's success was not just the result of going against the grain and doing the exact opposite of what was big at the time. More importantly, the band identified a societal need for something new musically among the sea of cookie cutter hair metal bands in Los Angeles that dressed up like women and wore bad makeup on stage. In fact, groups like Nirvana, Pearl Jam, and Soundgarden quickly took over the charts. Androgynous hair metal was now dead!

AFTERTHOUGHT: ASK THE FANS Another way to find your position is to ask the fans. Simply asking "What is the one thing that stands out about us that you think is cool or important?" can yield a point of distinction you can then exploit. Be prepared for the unexpected—fans will often identify things that you may not think are important to them. Don't be resistant. Take the time to examine this feedback. You'll be glad you did.

Position Yourself Based on a Strength and Unique Benefit

The last method you can use to find your position is to focus on a company strength. What's your strongest attribute? What's that one, unique benefit you offer? And what general solutions to people's problems can you offer?

Is it, for instance, that you create music for ravers who like to hear short, well-crafted songs rather than just ten minutes of beats and atmosphere? Is it that you have 12 years' experience spinning records in Amsterdam clubs and earned a degree in songwriting from Berklee College of Music? Is it that you are the only three-time winner of a local artist-of-the year achievement award or some other note of honor? Is it that your audience will feel raved out, funked up, or superhigh after dancing and singing along to your music? Is it that they'll feel deeply satisfied, powerful, and important after listening to the profoundly spiritual and positive messages in your lyrics? Will they feel happy? Romantic? Angry?

As you can see, the questions could go on and on and on. And each of these could unearth a truly valuable position for you that is difficult for your competitors to copy.

Finding a position is not an easy task, but as consultant Ira Kalb says, "Every company has a built-in uniqueness at varying levels. Some are very unique and impossible to copy, which is the best case; some are difficult to copy; and some are easy to copy. You just have to be willing to find your uniqueness, exploit it, and remain open to refocusing it, if needed, as times and trends change."

=MARKETING PLAN TEMPLATE=

Use the template below, or a template like it, to help you craft important information that you will use in your Marketing Plan of Attack™. For additional help, be sure to refer to the marketing plan example below, the chapter on assembling your plan, and the complete plan provided in the back of this book.

Your Company Brand Identity Template

Company Name: What is your company name?

Description of Name: What does your name mean and/or what emotions does it convey?

Logo: Describe your brand logo (include a draft if possible).

Slogan: Do you have a brand slogan or tagline? What is it?

Mascot: Have you created a mascot or spokescreature?

Personality: What is your brand's overall personality or character (attitude, dress, and associations)?

Enhancement Methods: How will you use the various identity tools you created above to enhance your brand image? (Will you include your name and logo on websites, blogs, social networks, T-shirts, cards, stationery, pens, condoms, car wraps, rolling paper, lighters, bookmarks, the front of your drummer's bass drum heads, banners, stickers, or any other appropriate item that specifically caters to your audience?)

Positioning: Finally, what is your company's position? That is, how do you want your customers to think about your company in a way that is unique from your competition? Can you create a short positioning phrase that sums it all up?

=MARKETING PLAN EXAMPLE=

Now here's our marketing plan example, for the band Rally the Tribes, to help you to put together your own company brand strategy.

COMPANY BRAND STRATEGY

a) Company Band Name: Rally the Tribes.

b) Description of Name: The name represents our vision of bringing together people of many cultures via our music to fight for important causes of the world.

c) Logo: The logo is a circular shape (perfect for patches and stickers) with a shadow of a man holding his fist in the air, similar to a victory salute. At the top of the circle, the name Rally the Tribes is presented in the upper arc. At the bottom of the circle, the band's home city of Los Angeles is presented in the lower arc. The logo also features the Knights of Malta Cross—not only does founder Robert Jr. have family roots in Malta, but the Knights were a valiant group founded to protect the sick, poor, and needy no matter what religion or race, and they are known for winning the Great Siege of Malta against all odds in the 1500s. The logo's font is PortagoITC TT to project a military or battle theme. The colors are mostly black, which represents honor.

d) Slogans: "Music with a Mission," "Music That Matters," and "The Original Change Agents."

e) Mascot: N/A.

f) Personality:
★Attitude: Politically motivated, serious, angry, and determined to cause change.
★Dress: Our look is that of fashion-trendy, collegiate jocks with mohawks, rugby shirts, track jackets, baseball and soccer jerseys, tattoos, piercings, skinny jeans, and Nike footwear.
★Associations: Public relations activities will include our associations with the Coalition for Humane Immigrant Rights of Los Angeles and the Los Angeles Coalition to End Hunger and Homelessness.

g) Enhancement Methods: We will use the name, logo, and slogans on websites, blogs, social networks, the drummer's bass drum head, live-performance banners, equipment cases, T-shirts, stickers, street stencils, and more.

h) Positioning: "A politically minded rave/rock band fueled by a tradition for change, to create music that matters and music that's heard."

[Note: Founder Kennedy Robert Jr. on vocals and K. Luther Martin will also have a side project called RTT Digital, performing their DJ set in select dance clubs when Rally the Tribes is not performing. This, of course, will also promote RTT.]

9

Develop a Brand Strategy for Your Products/Services

Achieving the Desired Image for Your Tours, Records, Merch, and More

Product/service branding is the process of presenting clear, unique, relevant, believable, and consistent messages about your offerings with the intention of exceeding fans' expectations and leaving a long-lasting positive image in their minds—all to help achieve the goals of your marketing plan. If this definition sounds familiar, it's because the ideas presented in the previous chapter on developing a company brand strategy also apply largely to the branding of your products/services. That's right! Branding consultant Robert Liljenwall explains that an album can be a brand (the Beatles' *White Album*), a song and lyric can be a brand (Jimmy Buffett's "Margaritaville"), a tour can be a brand (Ozzy Osbourne's Ozzfest), and even a piece of merch can be a brand (Mastadon's "Asstadon" shorts . . . ha ha, but seriously). Just remember that in today's crowded marketplace, where people are inundated with thousands of marketing messages every day, good branding cuts through the clutter and helps customers form a distinct image of your products/services in their minds.

When done successfully, product/service branding also helps you do the following:

- **Produce the right image in the minds of the fans.**
- **Distinguish your offerings from each other (and from those of competitors).**
- **Win over loyal customers who will spread the word of mouth happily.**
- **Increase your company's value and equity, which can last far into the future.**

So then, what follows is a brief introduction to building (or polishing) your product/service brand strategy that includes the following topics:

1. **Deciding on Your Brand Structure**
2. **Envisioning the Best Names/Titles**
3. **Using a Product/Service Brand Slogan or Tagline**
4. **Conceptualizing the Right Design/Look/Mood**
5. **Defining Your Product's Position and Exploiting It**
6. **Hearing It in Their Own Words: Q&A with Robert Liljenwall, Owner of the Liljenwall Group**

Important note: Remember that right now you are creating a "conceptual" product/service brand identity that you will soon use to finalize your offerings and place them in the marketplace. While these product/service brand ideas are subject to change as you move further along in your creative and marketing processes, it is necessary to think through all of the elements (e.g., album names, song titles, cover designs, and more) in advance so that your concepts can help guide you. I know that it's not always easy to think about things like the color of your album cover before you've even completed writing all your compositions. However, doing so can be extremely useful and can help keep your brand on track. Sound good? Awesome. Then let's get started.

AFTERTHOUGHT: REVIEW YOUR RESEARCH Before diving into this chapter on product branding, take another minute to review your vision, market needs, customer profile, customer feedback, SMART goals, and company branding, and think about how they can all affect your product/service brand decisions. Everything in marketing is interrelated.

Decide on Your Brand Structure

A discussion on product branding begins with *brand structure* (a.k.a. *brand architecture*). Brand structure describes the various ways a company brand and a company product brand relate to each other. Bill Chiaravalle describes the levels of brand structure in the book *Branding* as *company dominant*, *company endorsed*, and *company silent*. While the company dominant structure is the most applicable to the DIY artist on a limited budget, and while the latter two structures are more applicable to advanced artists whose businesses have already grown and expanded, nonetheless, let's take a brief look at all three structures.

Choose a Company Dominant (or Combined) Brand Structure

A company dominant (or combined) brand structure is a type of brand architecture in which the identity of the company supports the overall image of all of its products and services. In other words, a band may create several albums, types of merchandise, live performance sets, tours, sponsorship activities, and videos that each carries its own individual name/title, look, and attitude, yet they still all bear the "stamp" of the parent company brand.

To be sure, a company dominant brand structure is one that is consistent and seamless. By virtue of combining the company name with the product, the equity and good reputation of the company translates to all of the products and services, and vice versa. A combined approach requires less energy, and it typically requires less of a financial investment. Numerous entertainment companies incorporate this approach, and this will be the focus of this chapter and book as well.

AFTERTHOUGHT: CAN YOU SEE THE DIFFERENCE? Many people can't see the difference between company branding and product branding because in their eyes, the artist (the company) is also the product (the talent). But are all of Dr. Dre's records simply called *Dr. Dre*? Are all of Dr. Dre's songs called "Dr. Dre"? And are all of Dr. Dre's tours and videos simply called Dr. Dre? No. Each product and service employs additional and different branding elements to bring it to life and provide distinction, while remaining consistent and fitting under the umbrella of the Dr. Dre brand. Make no mistake: company branding and product branding are different.

Employ the Company Endorsed Brand Structure

A company endorsed brand structure, also called *cobranding*, is a type of brand architecture in which the company uses its identity to support the image of products and services outside the realm of its usual line of products and services. As pointed out in the *Harvard Business Review on Brand Management*, the endorsing company may even be used temporarily as a way to help another brand build credibility and take roots before the endorsing company name is separated.

An example of a company endorsed brand includes Christina Aguilera, who endorses her own perfume line called Royal Desire (the packaging reads "Christina Aguilera/Royal Desire").

Another example is Ludacris, who endorsed his own version of the TAG body spray called Get Yours (the packaging read "Ludacris/TAG Signature Series/Get Yours").

And even this book's author designed a drum stick model in cooperation with Dean Markley musical equipment manufacturers named Bobby Borg (the stick read "Bobby Borg/Dean Markley").

Once again, the company endorsed brand structure is perhaps atypical for most independent artists, but who knows—if you are truly creative, you too might form your own extended and relatable brands and endorse them with your company brand name.

Apply the Company Silent (or Separated) Brand Structure

Lastly, a company silent (or separated) brand is a type of brand architecture in which the identity of the company is separated from the various products and services it provides so that the image of one product/service can't affect the image of another product/service. In other words, the parent company name is *not* used on the product or service so as to prevent potential confusion in the marketplace.

For instance, an original band—while climbing their way to the top and in need of extra money to pay their bills—may want to perform covers for weddings under a completely different company name so as not to dilute or tarnish the image of the original company brand name.

Further, an original band—while still developing and in need of live-performance experience—may want to secretly perform their music under a temporary alias name, so that any damage they incur early on can be avoided when launching their intended long-term brand (the Foo Fighters did this when starting out).

And finally, an actor—who also has a strong reputation as being a gangster rapper named 50 Cent—may want to go by the name Curtis Jackson to make a statement to directors and casting agents that he can play more than the drug dealer role in films and on TV. Makes sense, right?

But note that because of the additional resources required to build equity in an entirely new and separate company brand, a company silent (or separated) brand structure can be a rather daunting endeavor for the music professional who is just starting out. Thus, once again (yes, I know I've said this before), the focus of this chapter and book is on using the company dominant (or combined) brand structure for each of your products/services. To be absolutely clear, your company name *will be* used on all of your products and services. Okay? Cool!

So now let's move on to envisioning the best names/titles for your products/services.

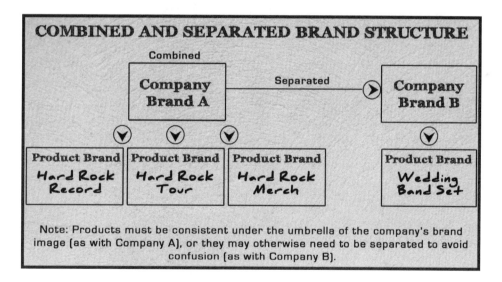

Envision the Best Names/Titles

Now that you have a strong understanding of brand structure, let's discuss naming your products and services. Like your organization, your products and services must be given names and titles that resonate strongly with your target fans.

Since the general ideas we discussed in the previous chapter for naming your company brand can essentially be applied to your products/services as well, there's really no need to go into great detail here. Just remember you can reflect on the mood, describe the product, invent a name, be original, and more.

Check out the examples below:

- The Red Hot Chili Peppers' album title *Californication* is a unique invention combining the words *California* and *fornication*, and a great representation of the Chilis' West Coast brand.
- Radiohead's song title "Creep" definitely reflects the song's disturbing mood and the band's overall ethereal vibe.
- Velvet Revolver's tour name The Rock N' Fucking Roll Tour clearly describes their rebellious live performance and persona.
- Lady Gaga's fan club name "Little Monsters" is definitely original (let's face it, she didn't call it "The Lady Gaga Fan Club") and mirrors her common-ground beliefs and identity.
- Mastadon's name for a pair of shorts, "Asstadon," is perfect for this band's heavy-metal decadent attitude and style.

UNIFORM BRANDING: FROM THE COMPANY TO THE PRODUCTS/SERVICES

It's so important that your names and titles work seamlessly under the umbrella of the company brand structure, and with the other products/services that you offer. Notice the consistency in the following examples:

- *Company Brand: Guns N' Roses:*
  - *Inferred Company Brand Image:* Sex, drugs, and rock 'n' roll.
  - *Album Name: Appetite for Destruction.*
  - *Song Titles:* "Night Train," "Mr. Brownstone" and "Anything Goes."

- *Company Brand: NWA (Niggaz wit Attitude):*
  - *Inferred Company Brand Image:* Angry civil rights rappers.
  - *Album Name: Straight Outta Compton.*
  - *Song Titles:* "Fuck tha Police," "Gangsta Gangsta," "Parental Discretion Iz Advised."

- *Company Brand: Public Enemy:*
  - *Inferred Company Brand Image:* Pro-black, anti–"The Man," gangsta rappers.
  - *Album Name: Fear of a Black Planet.*
  - *Song Titles:* "Fight the Power," "Anti-N****r Machine," "Revolutionary Generation."

- *Company Brand: Nine Inch Nails:*
  - *Inferred Company Brand Image:* Edgy, dark, industrial artist.
  - *Album Name: The Downward Spiral.*
  - *Song Titles:* "Mr. Self-Destruct," "I Don't Want This," "Hurt."

Use a Product/Service Brand Slogan or Tagline

After considering the best name/title for your products/services, you are now ready to consider a slogan. As with company branding, a good product/service slogan or tagline is one that provides more information than what the product/service name offers and is one that sells the benefits of the product/service to the customer. Here are just a few examples:

- Cypress Hill branded their festival performances Cypress Hill SmokeOut, and used the tagline "An All-Day, Mind-Opening Music Festival." Clearly, this slogan provides additional useful information.

- Apple branded its first-generation portable music player Apple iPod, and used the slogan "1,000 Songs in Your Pocket" to sell the benefit of having digital storage for your personal music collection that you can take anywhere and everywhere you want.
- Bring Me the Horizon (a British metalcore outfit) branded their sophomore album release *Bring Me the Horizon/Suicide Season* and utilized the advertising slogan "A Perfect Soundtrack to a Life Spent on the Edge." This slogan definitely helps sell the attitude of the band to the fans. Who knows, creating a similar product/service slogan might also work for you.

Conceptualize the Right Design/Look/Mood

The look and mood (colors, fonts, graphics, materials, design, etc.) of each of your products/services must also be thought out carefully so that they create the desired image in the minds of the fans. Remember that in a company dominant brand structure, the identity of the company is projected on the identity of the products/services, so everything must be consistent. Oftentimes a skilled designer (discussed more in the next chapter) may be needed to help you make design choices. In any case, the following few tips might offer some inspiration and direction. Just remember that you can always test these on your target market before making any final decisions.

Consider the Appropriate Colors

Be sure to consider the colors you'll use to represent your products/services, and be ready to explain why you've made those choices.

Jay-Z, one of the most successful hip hop entrepreneurs and known for his smooth and cleverly flowing style, appropriately used the color black and the name *The Black Album* for one of his releases. According to psychologists, black is the color of authority, power, and honor.

The Beatles, a group that established themselves as a clever, experimental pop-rock group, appropriately used the color white and also the name *The White Album* for their ninth release. Richard Hamilton, the designer for *The White Album*, said that he intended it to resemble the look of conceptual art and elegance, which was quite appropriate for what the Beatles' music represented at the time.

And Weezer, known for their light-hearted, big-harmony, alternative geek-rock style, used the color red for *The Red Album*, blue for *The Blue Album*, and green for *The Green Album*—all of which are known to produce happy, calm, and upbeat emotions that are perfect for the band's style.

To be sure, the importance of color does not just apply to album artwork, but also to merch products, stage design, and any other revenue-generating products/services you manufacture.

AFTERTHOUGHT: BRANDING IS PSYCHOLOGICAL—TRIGGER THE HUMAN BRAIN A great method for discovering what branding choices you should make is to first decide what feelings you want to convey in your products and services, and then ask your target audience to tell you what images, colors, sounds, words, tastes, and smells they associate with those specific feelings. You might also want to conduct some secondary research on the Web to understand the psychology behind colors. This will give you ideas about the communications you can use to trigger your target markets' brains and get them to feel the way you'd like them to feel every time they come in contact with your brand. Pretty heavy stuff!

Think About Which Fonts You'll Use

Aside from incorporating your company brand logo onto all of your products/services, you are also going to include other typesetting and information (subtitles, lyrics, song titles, slogans, website information, ad copy, etc.) and this requires careful branding as well. Different fonts produce different emotions, and thus choosing those fonts that convey the right vibe for your products/services is crucial. Sometimes the font used is precisely the same as the one that your logo carries, but more typically it will be slightly different and carry the same mood, as with Nirvana's *Nevermind* and the Clash's *London Calling*, to name just two. In any case, be sure to look through books about typesetting and fonts, such as one by David Carter called the *Big Book of 5,000 Fonts*. You can also check out the website DaFont (www.dafont.com), which lists hundreds of very cool fonts available for free downloading.

Use the Right Graphics

Moving on in our discussion about product/service brand design, you must also think about the general graphics that you'll use—assuming that you'll be using graphics at all (hey, the Beatles didn't use graphics on their *White Album*). Again, your decisions must be consistent with your company brand and must also convey the right attitude.

I remember once seeing a graphic on an independent artist's album cover of a truck spinning out on a dirt road with the colors of fire, as if all hell were breaking loose (the album was titled *The Hell with the Devil*). This graphic would have been perfect if it were for a metal band, but it turns out it was for a Christian band. You see, the problem here is that there is an element of confusion, and anytime there is confusion, you run the risk of a potential fan passing you by.

So, give careful thought to the graphics you'll use on your album covers, website, T-shirts, video packaging, and all other revenue-generating products/services you create. Conduct a search on the Internet for terms like "best album covers" or "best T-shirt designs" and you'll find hundreds of examples to review. You can also see the graphic "Album Art: Independent Artists," which displays independent artists just like you. Just be ready to describe the graphics you intend to use for all your products/services in your marketing plan, and be sure to provide valid reasons for your decisions.

Use the Right Materials

The materials you use for your products and services can also help brand you and your company. A trend in a number of industries right now is to make and package products with materials that are environmentally safe—or, to use the buzzword, "green." While this certainly can be a good approach to take for your products/services, "it has to be in line with your company brand image and vision or it means nothing," as we are reminded in *Brandweek* magazine by Andrew Benett and Greg Welch.

In the entertainment industry, a number of music companies began releasing albums using the Digipak (cardboard CD packaging) in lieu of the plastic jewel case covers, and a number of bands are making T-shirts using hemp material (which flourishes without the use of harmful pesticides) instead of using cotton. All this just might send a message to your fans that you really do care about the environment and the world around you.

Overall, consumers like it when artists stand for something. So use the "right" materials and be sure to write your decisions into your marketing plan.

Create Unique Designs

And finally, design applies to all your products/services—from the concepts you use for your videos to the look and slogans you use on your T-shirts, to even the presentation of your live performances—and you should always strive to be as unique and creative as possible in all cases. Let's consider your live performances as an example.

While you might have little flexibility as an indie artist in terms of what you can get away with up onstage due to time and space constraints, you should still think about what you want your shows to look like and how you can spice up your live performances to make them more entertaining and unique. Doing this, of course, can help create a certain mood and attitude that strengthens your brand identity and the image your fans form of you in their minds.

I remember that when the rock band Extreme was coming up in the city of Boston, their presentation was always several levels above the majority of other local bands. They used special laser and strobe lighting, smoke machines, video tape, audio recordings of special effects between songs, impressive equipment (special drum risers and amplifiers), banners with their brand logo, go-go dancers, and so much more. Of course, all of this befit the "larger than life" rock 'n' roll identity that they were trying to convey. All good stuff! So what will you do?

THE BRANDING OF YOUR RECORDINGS: EVERYTHING HELPS SET THE TONE

Everything your company conceptualizes about its products and services can help form the right brand image in the minds of its fans, especially with the recordings you're planning to create. Let's take a brief look at just a few of the decisions that can be made. Just remember to include all your ideas into your Marketing Plan of Attack™.

- *Formats:*
  - *CDs:* While there is a lot of speculation in the industry about whether CDs will stay around, given the digital and online world we live in, they are still a necessary tool for the DIY artist to sell at live shows and on the street, and to send to radio and other promotional mediums. From a branding perspective, CDs are essentially status quo, and if anything, manufacturing them sends out the image that you're just conducting "business as usual."
  - *Enhanced CDs:* These are audio CDs that contain video, images, downloadable screensavers, lyrics, press clippings, and more. From a branding perspective, enhanced CDs provide added value, and they send a message that you care about forming more personal relationships with the fans.

- **CD & DVD (or Blu-ray) Combo:** CDs with music and DVDs (or Blu-ray discs) with video footage can be packaged together in a dual case. From a branding perspective, this also provides more value for your fans, and sends a message that you care about getting more intimate with them and sharing your story.
- **Digital Downloads:** Making your music available in digital format for download on various Internet sites has become an industry must these days. From a branding perspective, this makes the statement that you are up with the times and ready for the next change that's brewing on the horizon.
- **Streaming Music:** Like downloads, this makes the statement that you are a forward-moving artist.
- **Vinyl:** Refers to the 12- and 7-inch vinyl plastic analog storage mediums sold in big cardboard sleeves that were once the most popular medium. While many people do not own the proper equipment (a turntable) to play vinyl, vinyl maintains a loyal following with collectors as well as enthusiastic fans of electronic dance, alternative, hard core, and even pop music. For this reason, vinyl can help reinforce a brand statement of integrity, authenticity, and nostalgia.
- **USB Flash Drives:** These are small portable computer storage devices that hold all types of data (music, video, pictures, etc.) that can be uploaded onto several devices. They come in a variety of designs, from the more professional "swing drives" to more casual-looking bracelets. From a branding perspective, this might help say something about how technologically savvy or current your brand is.
- **Download Cards:** These are the credit-card-sized cards that typically include a picture of your band and your name together with a code that allows users to visit a website whenever they'd like to download your music. Once again, from a branding perspective, this might reinforce that you are technology savvy and trying to remain current.

- **CD/DVD Packaging (Specific Elements):**
  - **Cases:** Will you use a plastic jewel case (which is the industry standard and what most consumers expect), Digipak casing (which contains less plastic, is environmentally friendly, and is also an industry norm), or eco-wallets (which contain no plastic, are environmentally friendly, are typically flatter, and can include a spine for industry standards)?
  - **Panel Inserts:** Will you use two-panel inserts, four/six-panel inserts, or eight-panel inserts? (Obviously the more panels you use, the more of a branding statement you can make when using professionally photographed pictures, lyrics, poetry, bios, information, and more.)
  - **Color Printing:** This deals with the number of colors you intend to use on the packaging. The more colors you use, the bigger the statement of quality you make and the more professional your products can look.
  - **On-Disc Printing:** The amount of printing you do on the actual CDs or DVDs (or Blu-ray discs) will also have a lot to say to your audience about quality and the mood you are trying to project.

[More ideas can be obtained by going to www.discmakers.com.]

Define Your Product's Position and Exploit It

Next up in our discussion about product and service branding is the topic of positioning. Czerniawski and Maloney's say in *Creating Brand Loyalty* that "Positioning is the way we want customers to perceive, think, and feel about our [products/services] *relative to the competitors*. It's that special—and in the best case, unique—place we want to earn in the hearts and minds of fans."

While we've essentially been discussing the backbone of what positioning is throughout this book (when identifying a market need, finding a competitive advantage, and putting forth your company identity), positioning is the final step in the branding process to ensure that your fans will notice you. Or, as Sarah White says in the book *Marketing*, "Branding is like the graham cracker, and positioning is like the milk that makes it go down."

What follows is a review of key positioning points specific to your products/services and new positioning ideas as well. Just remember that when defining your position, strive to find one that sets your offerings apart from those of outside companies, as well as those within your own organization so as to avoid *cannibalization* (competition among your own products/services).

Position Your Product/Service Based on Your Identified Need (or Unfilled Need)

When jazz guitarist Pat Metheny introduced his *Pat Metheny/Orchestrion* album and concert tour on a CBS news feature, he positioned them as a *first and never-to-be-done-again technological project intended to push new limits, and awe and entertain audiences.* The best thing about taking on this position is that Metheny had the goods to back up this statement. Not only was Metheny's new concept unique from all of the other albums and tours out there (it featured Metheny as a one-man band triggering a spectacular wall of musical robots), it distinctly set Metheny's *Orchestrion* album and tour apart from all of his other products and services. And remember, it's not enough just to make a positioning statement about, for instance, being technologically advanced—you have to embody that in every marketing message you put forth (from deciding what price to charge, which venues to play, or which media outlets to target).

Position Your Product/Service Based on Its Target Audience

When AC/DC released their eighth studio recording, entitled *For Those About to Rock*, they also released a single and video by the same name, showing the band saluting their audience as they sang, "For those about to rock, we salute you!" While the band explained that a book about brave Roman gladiators inspired the title, it also served as something of a tribute to AC/DC's most devoted and loyal fans who were rock 'n' roll warriors. AC/DC's album was positioned essentially to be exclusively for "those about to rock."

Position Yourself Based on a Competitive Advantage

When hip hop artist Nas introduced his *Nas/Life Is Good* album on an MTV interview blog, he positioned it as being "unlike most of the music in [the] genre, which tends to dwell on the darker side of life," and as being music specifically intended to "give people hope and to encourage their appreciation for the finer blessings of life." This indirect statement about hip hop music in general seemed to work fairly well for Nas because it essentially focused on a competitive advantage and benefit to the fans. But as George and Michael Belch of the book *Advertising* remind us, just be careful not to directly attack any one competitor when positioning. This reduces credibility, leads to competitor counterattacks, and often insults other fans.

AFTERTHOUGHT: POSITIONED ON STYLE Pink Martini is a DIY success story with an interesting and unique position: "Music of the world, without being world music." Apparently this works. With a founding member who attended Harvard, this thirteen-member band has it together, selling millions of records on their own label called Heinz Records and selling out venues as large as the Hollywood Bowl.

Position Yourself Based on a Strength and Unique Benefit You Can Offer

And finally, when guitarist Slash released his solo album simply entitled *Slash*, he utilized his personal connections and reputation in the industry to assemble an A-list of guest performers and positioned his record in adverts, blogs, and interviews as "Slash and friends: with everyone from Ozzy to Fergie." Of course, the added relevant benefit to fans was that they could be entertained by hearing many of their favorite entertainers together in a never-heard-before collaboration for the price of just one record.

Yes, I do realize that you could never get Ozzy Osbourne, Chris Cornell (of Soundgarden), Dave Grohl (of the Foo Fighters), Lemmy Kilmister (of Motörhead), and Fergie (of the Black Eyed Peas) to play on your record. But perhaps you could actually get all the local independent heroes from your hometown together to present some kind of unique collaboration.

Look, the point is that if an established artist needs to find new and creative ways to release material that is uniquely positioned from his own body of work and from that of competitors, then you had better be doing the same. Just be patient and find what works best for you.

ADDITIONAL POINTS ABOUT POSITIONING

Here are a few extra points echoed throughout the books of these marketing masters: Lynn Upshaw (*Building Brand Identity*), David Aaker (*Building Strong Brands*), Ira Kalb (*The Nuts and Bolts of Marketing*), Philip Kotler (*Marketing Management*), and Bill Chiaravalle (*Branding*). For further information, be sure to check out all of these great books.

- Don't use a position that's different just because it's different.
- Your position must be relevant and important to your fans.
- Your position must be believable and not based on hype.
- Your position should be as unique as possible, not just any position.
- Uniqueness comes at many levels (impossible, difficult, and easy to copy). Shoot for impossible.
- Don't bullshit: if you truly can't live up to it, it's not a viable position.
- Your position should not copy someone else's position.
- Your position should not brag—don't say you're the best.
- Don't position based on having a lower price: that can be challenged easily.
- Position on quality and value.
- You might position yourself on what you're not. (7-Up said it was the "un-cola.")
- You might position yourself based on a weakness. (Avis said "We're not No. 1, but we try harder.")
- A position can be based on how it will transform your audience or make it feel.
- Find a problem and offer a better solution than others have.
- Be open to changing your position to adapt with changing times.

In Their Own Words: Q&A with Robert Liljenwall, Owner of the Liljenwall Group

Robert Liljenwall, owner of the Liljenwall Group, is a senior marketing consultant who teaches branding and marketing as a distinguished instructor at the University of Redlands Graduate School of Business and UCLA Extension. In this interview, Robert reinforces important aspects of both company and product/service branding—from *what they are* to *how to achieve them*.

Q: Would you share three introductory tips that artists might use to begin branding their companies and their products and services?

RL: Sure, I'll offer three tips:

1) Create great music. The most critical part of any band's brand is their music and performance, which must reflect the highest quality. Fans do not reward poor musicianship—they are very discerning and sophisticated today and there are far too many choices. So, therefore, a band must have a clear vision of what their "act" is all about—you can't jump all over the creative landscape and expect fans to follow you down one dark alley after another. A band's products must be creative yet consistent.

2) Always find out what your fans think. Create fan clubs, give fans a voice, and listen to what they say. Perhaps the most effective research is just watching sales, because fans vote with their wallets, but it's also important to dig much deeper. You should get fans' opinions and get them involved in voting on all types of issues, like product choices, album names, song titles, slogans, and product designs and colors, etcetera. This type of research is gold, and it also makes the fans feel like they have ownership pride in your brand.

3) Strive to be different. In the cutthroat and competitive music world of today, a group must strive to differentiate both itself and its products/services, or die. Oh, one can always make a living as a cover band imitating other creative work, but to be truly successful, one must carve a creative niche. A band must then know how to explore this niche in order to keep its fan base interested over time, but it must do this without wandering off too far from its core and confusing fans. If the latter happens, then a brand is in big trouble. Only a handful of bands last over 10 years.

Q: To expand on your last point, what must a musical act do over the years if it wants to stay current and hip as new musical trends come in and old trends go out?

RL: You must always be aware of the external environment around you and be able to adapt successfully to it as it shifts and changes—the SWOT analysis is a handy tool to help with this. Staying aware and being flexible requires discipline, tenacity, and a deep understanding of how to push yourself in both a business and creative sense to be your very best. It can be a painful process, but your true passion and integrity will ultimately drive you forward through the valleys and over the hills to newer limits of innovation. Good luck.

=MARKETING PLAN TEMPLATE=

Use the template below, or a template like it, to help you craft important information that you will use in your Marketing Plan of Attack™. For additional help, be sure to refer to the marketing plan example below, the chapter on assembling your plan, and the complete plan provided in the back of this book.

Your Product/Service Brand Identity Template

Use this template to craft your product/service brand identity strategy ideas. When formatting your marketing plan, you can remove the questions and keep the headers and your answers. Remember that before making your final decisions, all of your product and service branding ideas can be tested on your market. *Just be clear that a strategy must be created for each product (e.g., one for your recordings, one for your merch, etc.), but note that not all of the questions will always be applicable to all of your products/services.*

Product or Service: What is the product or service for which you are creating a product brand strategy (album, merch item, live-performance set, etc.)?

Brand Structure: What is the brand structure you will be using for the product/service?

Name/Title: What is the product/service's name/title (e.g., the album name, song titles, video name, merch title, or tour name)? You can also list the general vibe that the title is intended to convey or explain the meaning behind the name.

Slogan/Tagline: Do you have a specific tagline for the product/service (e.g., for a particular album or tour)?

Colors/Fonts/Graphics: Are there any specific colors, fonts, and graphics you have in mind to use for the product/service?

Design Concept: What design ideas (or look) are you considering for the product/service?

Materials/Formats/Packaging: Are there any special materials you'll use for your product/service (for instance, what will the product packaging consist of)? How about the format in which your product will be delivered (CD, vinyl, USB flash drive, download, streaming, etc.)?

Positioning: What is the unique position, or positioning statement, you'll use for the product/service? That is, how do you want your customers to think about a specific product in a way that is unique from your competition? Can you create a short positioning phrase that sums it all up?

[Note: This section should include a visual representation of all of your ideas to increase the effectiveness of your Marketing Plan of Attack™. This includes pictures of record covers, T-shirts, stage designs, and more. Artists like Marilyn Manson were even known to have drawings of costumes early on.]

=MARKETING PLAN EXAMPLE=

Now here's an abridged marketing plan example for the band Rally the Tribes, to help you put together your own product/service brand strategy. Notice how several product offerings are addressed here. Just be sure to include all of your products/services in your plan.

PRODUCT/SERVICE BRAND STRATEGY

a) 12-Song Album

★Brand Structure: Combined.

★Album Title: *War and Police* (a spin-off on Leo Tolstoy's classic novel *War and Peace*).

★Song Titles: "Petty Thieves Hang, Big Ones Get Elected," and more in the works.

★Slogan/Taglines: The slogan "Music That Matters" will be used in promotional campaigns.

★Colors/Fonts/Graphics: A black-and-white cover will give an editorial vibe. PortagoITC TT fonts will project a military vibe. The graphic will be a picture of police and protesters.

★Design Concepts: To make a political statement about misuse of power and project quality, our CDs will include a six-panel insert featuring photographs of world injustices.

★Materials/Formats/Packaging: CDs will be packaged in Digipaks, which are better for the environment. We will also manufacture USB flash drives and offer digital downloads and streams to project a current and technologically savvy vibe.

★Positioning: "Political-minded rock/rave music powered by jock punks and guest DJs."

b) Merchandising Line

★Brand Structure: Combined.

★Names/Titles: Change Agent Hoodie, RTT Jock/Rock Jersey with George Cross, Rally the Tribes Military Hat, RTT "Man Not Mouse" Pad, "Petty Thieves Hang, Big Ones Get Elected" T-shirt, and Rugby Rally with Logo.

★Slogans/Taglines: The slogan "Merch That Matters" will be used in promotional campaigns.

★Colors/Fonts/Graphics: Mostly black and white with splashes of red and yellow using PortagoITC TT font. The graphics used will include RTT's logo, fan club name, and song lyrics.

★Design Concepts: We will project our politically based brand and jock/rock vibe. Baseball jerseys and rugby shirts with our logo will help project the collegiate element of RTT's brand.

★Materials: T-shirts will be made from hemp to help make a statement about the environment.

★Positioning: "Merch That Matters: 20 Percent Donated to Local Charities."

c) Live-Performance Set and Production

★Brand Structure: Combined.

★Names/Titles: Rock/Rave.

★Slogans/Taglines: The tagline "Gathering at the . . ." will be used to help convey the rally or protest vibe.

★Stage Design Concepts: Overall, the design of the show will be captivating visually, ominous, and intense. The idea is to emulate a protest march. It will open with a recording of air raid sirens and police lights on each side of the stage to add to the effect. RTT's drummer will face backward to the audience with a three-panel reflecting mirror set up in front of him so that the audience can see both what he is playing and his facial expressions. In between songs, RTT's singer will regularly speak into a bullhorn, similar to what an organizer might do at a rally.

★Positioning: A "Rock/Rave Gathering" or "Rave/Mosh Rally."

10

Finalize Your Products and Services for the Marketplace

Delivering on the Promise of Your Brand

Finalizing your products and services for the marketplace is the process of taking your offerings from brand *concept* to *reality* with the intention of satisfying fans and achieving your marketing plan goals. This includes making decisions about how to merge your brand names, packaging, look, and feel (discussed in chapters 8 and 9) with manufacturing methods, quantity decisions, and customer service policies for your recordings, videos, tours, merch, and more.

Finalizing your products and services for the marketplace can help you do the following:

- **Realize an exceptional brand image that exceeds fans' expectations.**
- **Service customers effectively and earn their loyalty.**
- **Provide a meaningful solution and benefit to customers.**
- **Generate income that you can reinvest back into your brand.**
- **Build a reputation on which new products/services can be anticipated by fans.**

Keep in mind that while the word *finalize* is being used for your products and services throughout this chapter, you must always remain open to improving your offerings over time, if feedback from your target audience indicates the need.

Also note that while this chapter discusses the planning process involved in taking your products and services from brand concept to reality, you'll still need to make further considerations (including price, place, promotion, and measuring) before your offerings can be fully ready for release to consumers. These considerations will all be covered in following chapters.

Now, let's get to finalizing your products and services for the marketplace by looking at the following topics:

1. **Creating a Product and Service Development Plan**
2. **Finalizing a Customer Service Policy**
3. **Analyzing the Features and Benefits of Your Products and Services**

PRODUCT INNOVATION AND CREATIVITY

Your products and services (whether they be your recordings, tours, merch, or more) are the "stars of the show." They are what generate revenue and keep your business afloat. This is why it is so important to push the boundaries of innovation and creativity and find a variety of ways to satisfy your audience and make sales.

Take a song, for instance. It can be recorded and simply released as a single, but that's not all.

- If you remix it and take the lyrics away, it is now an instrumental version that can be licensed to film and TV.
- If you re-record it live, it can now be the "live version" and re-released as the live single.
- If you re-record it acoustically, it can now be the "unplugged version."
- If you sing it in another language, it is now a "translation" suitable for new markets.
- If you remix it with a guest DJ, it can now be the "electronic dance version."
- If you compile it with 6 or 10 other songs on an album, it can be an "album track." And . . .
- If you offer the recorded stems (individual tracks), it can be an "interactive product" where fans can create new mixes and share them with each other.

    Furthermore . . .

- If you allow the song to be experienced (heard, critiqued) in real time during the writing and production phase, it can be an "exclusive content perk" to paying fan club members.
- If you take the words from the song's chorus and place them on T-shirts and hats, it can be a cool accessory or "merchandising product."
- If you create a video of the song being performed and/or acted out, it can be part of a DVD "collection of video singles" and/or used as a tool to generate advertising revenue on video sites.
- If you film yourself while writing and recording the song, it can be part of your "the making of" home video.
- If you transcribe the music into printed form, it can be a piece of "sheet music."
- If you keep the broken drumsticks, skins, picks, and other tools that were used during the recording of the song, they can be sold as "collectors' items." And . . .
- If you pile a number of the items discussed above into a classy box, it can be a cool "limited gift set" that your fans might find as a great value and "must have" item.

The point is that from one product you can create a variety of extensions. This shouldn't suggest that the more products you offer, the better (in fact, that could create buyer confusion). Rather, the point is that if you can keep the juices of creativity and innovation always flowing by being open minded and observing what's around you at all times, you can better satisfy the needs of your target customers and serve others you may not be reaching currently with quality offerings. And thus, you can generate even more income for your company. Just remember that the purpose of your company is to make a healthy profit. If it's not profitable, it's not a business; it's a hobby.

Create a Product and Service Development Plan

No matter what products and services you intend to offer, the first step in finalizing them for the marketplace is to create a "product and service development plan." This requires making important decisions about how to realize your desired brand image and level of quality while keeping your production and manufacturing costs as low as possible. Let's take a look at finalizing everything from your music to your merch.

Decide on How You'll Finalize Your Music

Your music is one of the most important assets for your company and it is the foundation on which many other products and services are created. There are essentially three methods to get your music finalized for the marketplace: completing it internally, using an outside cowriter or consultant, and using outside songs or beats.

Complete It Internally

Completing it internally involves finalizing your music by yourself or with your regular partners within your organization. The advantages of writing exclusively within your organization is that you may preserve any "magic" (vibe, allure, panache, excitement, unique recipe, etc.) you might possess, which could otherwise be diluted by the influence of an outside writer. Of course, there are also the financial benefits of writing within your own organization, since you'll hold onto a greater share of the copyrights and profits. All this is a very personal choice you have to weigh honestly and objectively.

Use an Outside Cowriter or Consultant

This approach usually involves bringing in someone outside of your organization who has a more proven track record and expertise in honing and polishing songs.

Professionals could include a talented artist from a local band who is getting airplay, a composer with a number of tracks placed in film and TV, or a music producer with a number of records under his or her belt.

The advantages of using an outside professional is that you get some much-needed help from someone who is not as close to your work as you are, as well as the *brand equity* you can borrow by cobranding your work with other music professionals. As Robin Frederick, author of *Shortcuts to Hit Songwriting*, says, "An outside writer or consultant has the ability to see you more clearly than you see yourself, and the credibility that goes with that skill."

AFTERTHOUGHT: MORE COWRITING THAN YOU THINK You'd be surprised at the number of young acts who use cowriters and outside songs. The key writers of Beggars & Thieves (my former band) were talented enough to write by themselves, but wise enough to utilize their networking skills and convince hit songwriter Desmond Childs to cowrite with them. This move helped land a deal with Atlantic Records. Perhaps *you* can also find credible people to work with.

Use Outside Songs or Beats

And finally, using outside songs or beats is yet another way to finalize your music for the marketplace. This involves licensing completed songs or beats, or previously released "cover songs," from more established music publishers than yourself. In very simple terms, you could do this by contacting the author/owner or his or her representatives and paying a fee.

The advantages of using an outside song or beat are that you might find something completely unique and polished that fits your identity. Furthermore, you can cobrand yourself with that writer's credibility and even benefit from his or her success and visibility. For instance, Alien Ant Farm used Michael Jackson's "Smooth Criminal" to score a No. 1 hit on *Billboard*'s Modern Rock Tracks at the beginning of their career when they were completely unknown. There are so many more examples. Perhaps you'll be the next.

For more information on music publishing issues, you can check out *The Musician's Handbook* by yours truly, or *Music, Money, and Success* by Jeff and Todd Brabec. Now let's discuss finalizing your recorded product.

Determine How You'll Prepare Recorded Product

Whether you intend to release your music as singles or complete albums, license it to film and TV, or get other artists to use your songs, preparing your music for the marketplace almost always involves getting it recorded. But you'll have to make some important decisions that ultimately can affect the quality. These include deciding whether to record it at home or to rent a studio/producer/engineer.

Record It at Home

Utilizing new technology to record in the comfort of your own living rooms *whenever* you want and for *as long* as you want, is the essence of recording music at home.

As previously described in chapter 6, you can set up your studio easily with as little as a laptop computer, music production software, a keyboard with sound cards, recording software, and an external microphone. The best part is that you can record a competitive-sounding album for as little as $5,000, depending on your skill set. Better yet, if you're really talented, you might even be able to utilize your gear to record other artists and make a few bucks as well. Can't beat that!

Rent a Studio/Engineer/Producer

If you're looking for more than what recording it at home might offer, then you may be ready to rent a studio/engineer/producer. Tom Weir of Studio City Sound in Studio City, California, says that considering an outside location with pro gear and staff typically broadens your options to include the following:

- A variety of room sizes that can capture a "larger" drum sound.
- An assortment of unique musical instruments, including grand pianos.
- A choice of analog or digital recording gear.
- An array of sound processing gear.
- A variety of expensive microphones.
- Isolation from the distractions of your everyday life at home. And . . .
- Access to a professional who can provide recording and budgeting advice.

All of the above factors can greatly affect the quality of your finished recording, but this can also come at a cost: about $35 to $75 per hour on the low end, and $100 to $500 on the high end.

To find recording studios with competent engineers and producers, try typing a few keywords into your favorite search engine, utilizing a music industry directory, or asking other indie artists in your area you trust for recommendations.

AFTERTHOUGHT: AT-HOME AND IN-THE-STUDIO COMBINED You might wonder whether you can use a combination of home and outside studio. Of course! Some people might record guitars and vocals at home, record the drum tracks in a larger room in an outside studio, and then do the mixing and mastering in an outside studio with a producer/engineer. There are number of different scenarios that can exist. Choose what works for you, and write these specific decisions into your marketing plan.

Determine How You'll Produce Video Product

Moving on to video products, another important decision you may need to make is how you'll record your video footage for eventual release to the marketplace. No matter what type of video product you choose to create (live performance, documentary, or a collection of single music videos), you must decide whether to produce the videos yourself or to hire a professional videographer. Let's take a look.

Produce the Videos Yourself

Producing the videos yourself involves taking advantage of new technology to capture raw and spontaneous video footage of live performances, rehearsals, backstage antics, and more. This might require purchasing or borrowing video equipment, deciding on a theme, planning and directing the shots, deciding on the style of the video (black and white or color), capturing the right footage, editing the material, and adding effects for release.

To help you get the job done, you can use affordable high-def digital video cameras that have jacks for external microphones (such as the ones offered by Sony and Canon) and editing software (such as Final Cut

Pro for Macs and Sony Vegas Pro for PCs). You might even think about licensing stock video clips (like that of the Hollywood sign or some awesome ski footage) that you can edit into your video (check out sites like Videoblocks [www.videoblocks.com]). Finally, you might even use certain online services (like Animoto [http://animoto.com]) that help you produce quality videos from your photos and video clips in a flash.

Just remember that producing your own videos requires some know-how and patience if you expect to create something that represents your desired professional image. Bottom line: you gotta have some skills.

Hire a Videographer

Hiring a videographer means renting the skill set, experience, and equipment of an outside video professional. The multiple cameras, professional lighting, sound equipment, editing expertise, soundstage, makeup artists, and fashion consultants that professionals use could make a big difference. Professional videographers can range from a senior student at a local film school who has access to great equipment (which could cost you nothing or a few hundred dollars) to a more experienced professional who makes documentaries and videos for a living (which could cost you from $3,000 to $35,000 or more). Your decisions will be determined greatly by the level of quality video product you wish to create, the brand image you want to project, and your company resources.

AFTERTHOUGHT: HIRING STUDENT FILMMAKERS Los Angeles indie artist Jodie Whiteside says that making his video was practically effortless. In Jodie's words, "Students at the Santa Barbara Film School in California, who needed to turn in a final project to graduate, shot the video. They used two student actors, supplied all the camera gear, shot in a public park, did all the editing, and gave me a master recording. This cost me as little as $50 and change—the amount it cost me to buy them a bunch of Subway sandwiches and Cokes. The final product looked great."

Choose How You'll Manufacture Your Albums and Video Products

After you get your music and videos in recorded form you'll need to get them manufactured. Depending on the desired configuration (CDs, vinyl, download cards, digital downloads, DVDs, or streaming music), you can either manufacture them yourself or use an outside manufacturer.

Manufacture Them Yourself

Using a number of available home tools, you can easily "duplicate" and package a limited run of CDs and DVDs by yourself.

This means using software programs like Adobe Photoshop or Illustrator to create your own artwork and labeling, licensing stock photography from sites like iStockphoto (www.istockphoto.com) and others to incorporate into your artwork, printing and cutting inserts to fit them into cases, and using a bulk duplication machine like the Disc Makers Reflex Series to burn your music and label the discs' surfaces. This will definitely require a lot of your time and hard work, but with some know-how and a lot of patience, the results can turn out well.

Manufacturing your albums and video products yourself can also help brand you in the minds of fans as a true independent do-it-yourself artist. Take Rob Danson of the Los Angeles band Death to Anders, for instance, who went as far as creating his own unique packaging for literally every record (every unit) he sold at his live shows. This is a serious commitment to customization. While some might feel that this could create brand confusion, Danson stated it created scarcity: "There was only one of each design, and people felt they were getting a true collector's item." A very good reason. Way to go, Rob!

Use an Outside Manufacturer

Another option to get your albums and videos finalized for the marketplace is to use an outside manufacturer. This involves using the services of a company that has the equipment and personnel to "replicate" high-quality/

quantity CDs and DVDs, as well as to manufacture flash drives, download cards, and vinyl, and prepare music for digital distribution and streaming sites.

Using an outside manufacturer can also mean trusting a representative to master your music and get it sonically ready for release (raise levels and add highs, bass, compression, and metadata), get your packaging design and labeling up to professional standards (add bar codes, copyright notices, and publishing company names), and make sure your products arrive safely on your front doorstep ready for sale.

While there are a number of professional manufacturers you can use, Disc Makers, Oasis, and Rainbo are great places to start.

MANUFACTURING PRODUCT: DO CDS, USB FLASH DRIVES, VINYL, AND DOWNLOAD CARDS STILL MATTER?

At the time of this writing, there has been a lot of talk about whether an independent artist should incur the extra costs to manufacture CDs and other physical products like download cards, vinyl, or USB flash drives containing music. In the digital world in which we live, why bother with the expense and hassle? Why not cut costs and increase the potential profit margin by releasing digital downloads or streaming music? Do people even care about physical records anymore? What about the future?

According to Sydney Alston, a representative at Disc Makers, physical products make for a nice memento for fans at your band's concert and provide an opportunity for bands to brand themselves via creative packaging and artwork. Furthermore, they are still useful for certain promotional avenues, like submitting to college radio (a format that still prefers submissions by CD).

Michael Eames of PEN Music Group, a songplugging company, says that there is still a need for both physical and digital copies when it comes to submitting music to music supervisors and advertising agencies. It depends on each person's preference.

The independent band Clepto, a group known for living out of their van for years on the road, said that if it wasn't for having a 6- or 10-song physical album on hand to sell after their performances, they might not have had enough money for gas or food. In their words, "Physical product is a face-to-face immediate cash transaction."

And finally, Brian Perera of Cleopatra Records says that physical product allows for companies to create some really cool branded box sets, which could include a vinyl record, CD, button, and sticker. The sets can even be numbered and manufactured in limited quantities to make fans feel they are getting something extra special and exclusive. On that note, Perera even knew one band that sold raw cassette recordings of their rehearsals. Okay, so cassettes might be going a little too far, but you get the point.

So in conclusion, does physical product matter? Answer: it's probably a good idea to cover all bases and have all formats of your music available. Keep this in mind when writing your marketing plan.

Determine How You'll Get Your Act (Live Show) Together

Moving right along in our discussion about finalizing your products and services for the marketplace is your live performances—my favorite topic.

To help you get your act together, let's take a look at two different approaches: taking a minimalist inside approach and using outside personnel and bigger production. I'm aware that each method depends greatly on several factors (such as the type of company you are and the style of music you play), so focus on the method that fits your situation best.

Take a Minimalist "Inside" Approach

Taking a minimalist inside approach is the decision to keep your company's personnel and stage production as simple—and within your control—as possible.

This might include performing with as few people on stage as you can, using self-controlled loop pedals, and utilizing taped backing tracks and samples. It might also include using minimal sound and lights, and few or no special visual effects.

Taking a minimalist approach allows the true magic of your performances and songs to shine through. A raw, stripped-down, or more intimate vibe often allows for more direct, one-to-one communication with the audience, which can help build a strong bond with fans. It also keeps you more mobile and able to perform in a variety of places without the restrictions and hassles that can come with a larger production and concert setting.

Use Outside Personnel and Bigger Production

Using outside personnel and bigger production is another approach you can use to create a more full and produced sound, as well as a better thought-out and larger-than-life image onstage.

This approach could involve hiring freelance ensemble players to support your solo career, or hiring accessory musicians (percussionists, horns, backing singers, etc.) to enhance your company's pre-established group. It could also involve hiring a sound engineer, lighting technician, dancers, choreographers, and musical directors who can assist in rehearsing your band.

Using outside personnel and bigger production might also involve bringing in extra sound and lighting equipment, attempting to play in larger venues, and even putting together a package deal with other artists to create a festival-themed event or rave for the evening.

If all this sounds expensive and out of reach for the independent musician, think again. Remember that there are more creative ways to pay people for their services than just with money. For one, don't forget you could "barter" your services with other companies to make a fair and even trade. Hey, this really works. I know, because I've done it myself.

KEEPING YOUR LIVE PERFORMANCE SIMPLE, BUT NOT REALLY!

Independent artist singer/songwriter Robbie Fitzsimmons is just one example of a man who keeps the production of his live performances extremely simple, yet he creates an impressive wall of sound that is in no way basic. Robbie uses loop pedals, keytars, and the power of his remarkable voice to create beautifully rich textures and sounds. This approach also provides him with more flexibility to pick up and hit the road and play a variety of venues and festivals both large and small.

In another example, Australian artist JP stays mobile by recording drum loops he creates by banging his guitar, playing bass lines with his thumb, playing chords with his fingers, and singing. On the show *Australia's Got Talent* (the equivalent of *American Idol*), JP wowed the judges with a cover of Men at Work's hit song "Down Under," received a standing ovation from the crowd, and advanced to the finals. Keeping his act stripped down allowed JP to showcase his musical talents in a variety of venues and draw attention to his highly original abilities. Pretty raw and impressive.

And finally, for a completely different example of keeping your live performance simple, here's a band that went from massive to minimal: the heavy metal band Megadeth toned down their enormous stage production and created a set of their songs in a folk acoustic format. I can still see the band clearly in my mind all sitting on stools with tambourines and acoustic guitars. It was actually really cool. By using the same songs, the band essentially created two different products: it was like *Megadeth Electric* and *Megadeth Unplugged*. Perhaps you might consider a similar approach. Hey, if the idea tests well with your fans and conveys the right brand image, why not?

Think About How You'll Develop Your Web Real Estate

The next-to-last product and service we'll examine in our discussion on finalizing your offerings for the marketplace is your Web real estate. In the technological age in which we live, creating a personal Web destination and making sure people can find it is crucial for most companies, and it can also become a significant revenue generator when selling products to fans and ad space to other companies.

Let's take a peek at developing a site yourself and/or using a Web developer.

Develop It Yourself

Taking advantage of low-cost computer programs, free Web services, and content management systems (which enable you to update information) is what developing it yourself is all about.

You can use easy-to-build software programs (such as Adobe Dreamweaver), prebuilt or template sites and services (such as HostBaby or Bandzoogle), or a number of free service destinations online (such as WordPress, Virb, and Flavors Me).

A variety of Web tools or widgets can be embedded onto your site, allowing visitors to download music, order merchandise, buy tickets, join your fan clubs, view pictures, and more (check out Bandcamp, Topspin, and FanBridge for starters).

Any number of affordable hosting companies (such as GoDaddy) can be used to launch your site on the Web, register a Web address and top-level domain (.com, .net, .org—and even more personalized TLDs; stay tuned), and provide search engine optimization to make sure that people can find your site.

Your decision to develop your Web real estate yourself will depend on your company's internal skills and budget, as well as your desired brand image. Developing it yourself is an economical way to get the job done, and it also affords you the direct control necessary to upload materials quickly and regularly, which helps you cultivate and maintain a more personal and effective one-to-one communication with your fans. Perhaps this approach works for you.

If more info is needed on finalizing your website for the marketplace, check out Sue Jenkins's *Web Design All-in-One for Dummies*, which highlights everything you have to know about building and maintaining a site yourself.

Use a Web Developer

As an alternative to doing-it-yourself, you might consider using a professional Web developer who can bring years of experience to the table and help you keep current on the extremely fast and ever-changing world of the Web.

A developer's specific role might include the following:

- Polishing up your personal website design.
- Building Web pages.
- Scrutinizing traffic and other statistical data.
- Making sure people can find you on the Web.
- Uploading new content that you provide.
- Dealing with companies who wish to advertise on your pages. And . . .
- Replying to user comments and questions on your behalf.

To find a Web developer, you can ask for referrals, contact art schools for *competent* graduating students, or post notices online and have people bid for the job. The decision to use a developer depends on your financial resources, the level of one-to-one interaction you desire to maintain with your fan base personally, and of course, the brand image you so desire. Weigh the choices wisely.

For further information, be sure to check out *Online Marketing Heroes* by Michael Miller. Also note that websites will be discussed further in subsequent chapters of this book. Okay? Cool!

So now let's move on to the last, but not least, product you'll finalize for the marketplace: merch.

Decide on How You'll Manufacture Your Merch

Your merch is yet another product that must be considered in your Marketing Plan of Attack™. Standard merchandising items (such as T-shirts, hoodies, hats, patches, bandanas, and autographed pictures) and more specialized items (such as rolling papers, lighters, water bottles, mouse pads, jewelry, and even condoms) can provide a great source of revenue for your company, while also helping to advertise and establish your brand image.

Depending on which products you want to manufacture and to fit your brand, you can either do it at home or use a screen printing company.

Do It at Home

Doing it at home means making the decision to use a number of home tools to create merchandising items limited to mostly T-shirts.

This can include preparing your design ideas via computer programs like Adobe Photoshop, buying T-shirts like Hanes or American Apparel brand, and printing your designs on iron-on heat transfer paper and applying them to your shirts with a hot iron.

Doing it at home can also include tie-dying your T-shirts by folding them into patterns, binding them with string or rubber bands, and applying special reactive dyes and sodium carbonate, which can be found in local hardware stores. Beads, studs, and other materials found at craft stores can add a special touch.

Whatever methods you use, the great thing about creating your own T-shirts is that it provides you with the opportunity to make limited-quantity runs, gives you a certain level of personalization and control, and truly conveys the independent artist spirit that fans love.

AFTERTHOUGHT: MERCH ON DEMAND If you don't want to make your own merch, but you're worried about the cost of using an outside screen printing company, check out companies that offer "print on demand" services (they'll literally manufacture the merch as it's ordered with no upfront costs to you). While the quality of the merch and the design options are often limited, be sure to check out companies such as CafePress and Zazzle.

Use a Screen Printing Company

Rather than creating merch yourself and limiting production to just T-shirts, you might decide to use a professional screen printing company to manufacture a variety of products ranging from the basics (T-shirts, hoodies, hats) to the more specialized items (condoms, rolling papers, and lighters).

When using a professional printing company, you have a variety of other cool options. Consider this:

- You can either produce artwork using online design templates provided on the company's website, or you can utilize the company's design staff.
- You can choose between various materials, like plastisol ink (to produce a common everyday look), mixed specialty inks (to produce a more interesting mirror or glitter effect), and beads, studs, and threads (to produce an embroidered look).
- You can choose between various fabrics, like polyester, preshrunk cotton, hemp, and cotton/polyester mixed.
- You can choose between various printing methods, like screen printing (the most common and high-quality option for quantity orders), digital printing (a quality solution for smaller orders), or iron-on heat printing (a very low-quality solution suitable for small orders and one-offs).
- And finally, you can also benefit from bulk printing services, quick turn-around time, and nationwide shipping.

All of the above elements will affect the final quality and look of the merch. Your decision to use a printer should be based on your budget, the products you intend to create, and your desired image.

To find reputable and experienced companies, Bob Fierro of Zebra Marketing in Los Angeles recommends using a simple Web search with keywords like "screen printing" and "promotional items," or to ask other local indie bands for recommendations.

KEY CRITERIA FOR HIRING OUTSIDE HELP (A.K.A. OUTSOURCING)

Should you decide to use an outside company (a process called *outsourcing*) to bring your products and services to the marketplace, you'll find the following criteria to be of great help:

- *Hired Musicians and Songwriters:*
  - *Musician Prices:* Will they agree to play under a *work-for-hire* relationship? (This would be the best case.)
  - *Songwriter Splits:* Will contributors agree in writing to a copyright share proportionate to their contribution?
  - *Dependability:* Are they known for showing up on time?
  - *Reputation:* Are they known for delivering quality work?
  - *Equipment:* Do they have well-maintained instruments?
  - *Experience:* What have they done professionally, and for how long? (The more experience they have, the better.)
  - *Ability:* Can they play well in a variety of different styles and with a variety of different musicians?
  - *Personality:* Are they fun to be around during long sessions or tours?
  - *Look:* Do they fit your visual brand image?

- *Recording Studios:*
  - *Price:* Do they have affordable pricing?
  - *Reputation:* Are they known for delivering broadcast quality work?
  - *Equipment:* Do they have a wide collection of mics, assortment of instruments, and choice of gear?
  - *Facility:* Do they have the right atmosphere and vibe?
  - *Personnel:* Do they have quality engineers and producers on staff?
  - *Availability:* Does their schedule permit you to finish your project on time?

- *Producer:*
  - *Price:* Does he have a fair fee structure? (A flat fee is preferred, with no royalty sharing.)
  - *Copyright Issues:* Can he do the job on a work-for-hire basis? (This would be the best case.)
  - *Reputation:* Is he known for creating work that fits your brand?
  - *Work Habits:* Are you compatible (you and he both like to work at night or early morning, etc.)?
  - *Methods:* Does he fit your preference? (He tracks with or without click, he records basic tracks as a band or individually, etc.)
  - *Availability:* Can he complete the project without large periods of interruption?
  - *Personality:* Does it appear he will be compatible with you under stressful and long hours?

- *Videographer:*
  - *Price:* Is she within your budget?
  - *Portfolio:* Does her previous work demonstrate the ability to fulfill your brand vision?
  - *Equipment:* Does she have access to modern equipment, multiple cameras, and lighting?
  - *Locations:* Does she have a professional studio or great location ideas?

- *Manufacturers/Merchandisers:*
  - *Price:* Are they willing upfront to quote all costs (tax, shipping, set-up fees, etc.)?
  - *Economies of Scale:* Does the per-unit pricing get lower when the quantity of your order gets larger?
  - *Turnaround Time:* Can they guarantee a delivery date that is accommodating to your schedule?
  - *Payment Options:* Will they conveniently accept a deposit upfront and the balance of the order at completion?
  - *Manufacturing:* Make sure they produce onsite and that they are not just a broker middleman.
  - *Customer Service Policies:* Make sure they promise to deliver excellence and they guarantee it.
  - *Additional Services:* Do they offer promotional tips or online distribution? (This would be a plus.)

- *Web Developer:*
  - *Price:* Is she within your budget?
  - *Payment Options:* Make sure she takes a deposit upfront with final payment due upon delivery.
  - *Turnaround Time:* Make sure she can get the work done within your desired time period.
  - *Copyright:* Make sure the ownership of copyright is in your name.
  - *Passwords:* Is she willing to provide you with all passwords and important site information?
  - *Approvals:* During the construction stage, be sure she implements quality control checkpoints.
  - *Reputation:* Be sure that she has a portfolio befitting your brand image.
  - *After Service:* Make sure she offers adequate hosting options and updating services.

- *Lights and Production:*
  - *Fees:* Do they offer affordable rental fees?
  - *Terms:* Make sure they provide adequate time to return the gear.
  - *Equipment:* Make sure they have up-to-date and well-maintained gear.
  - *Safety:* Do they have safe and easy-to-use gear?
  - *Delivery:* Do they have trucks that can deliver, unload, and set up gear if needed?
  - *Personnel:* Make sure they have a knowledgeable crew that can run gear and troubleshoot.
  - *Experience:* Make sure they have a long history in the concert production business.

[You get the idea! And don't forget to use intuition. Does the situation feel right? Do you get the right vibe? Always trust your gut. Good luck.]

Finalize a Customer Service Policy: The "Other" Part of Product

As if creating a product/service development plan above were not enough to think about, the next phase in the finalization of your offerings for the marketplace is to create a customer service policy.

Customer service is the level of care that's provided to your target fans at every stage of the relationship—from the moment they hear about your brand to long after they become fans. In other words, a product or service is not confined to just "what it is" or "how it is built," but also to the attention the customer receives *before*, *during*, and *after* the sale.

The better the customer service you provide and the more unique you can make the experience, the happier your customer will be. In fact, according to a poll by Opinion Research in Princeton, New Jersey (my birth city), companies that provide great customer service tend to be *more profitable.* Seriously!

So let's take a closer look at finalizing your very own customer service plan. From deciding on your commitment to quality to determining a database management plan, be sure to write some (or all) of the following ideas into your very own Marketing Plan of Attack™.

Decide on Your Commitment to Quality

Deciding on your commitment to quality is typically the first of many things you want to consider when putting together a customer service strategy. Remember, your commitment to producing top-quality work in everything you do, *every time you do it*, is a major part of what great customer service really is.

So are you going to strive to create the best products and services you possibly can? Will you work with a songwriting consultant and get feedback from your target audience before rushing off and recording your next album? Will you replay or re-record your parts as many times as needed until you get that perfect track? And will you give it your all each and every night that you perform no matter how bad your day may have sucked?

Keep in mind that there is something called *customer lifetime value*. This is the amount that customers are worth to you in sales, considering that they keep on buying from you—and it can be pretty substantial. As Tony van Veen, President of Disc Makers and CD Baby, says: "If you offer high-quality work at a great price, customers will keep on coming back. But if you offer subpar work, they'll fade away."

Again, I know this is a lot to consider, but it's crucial. Be sure to write your thoughts into your plan.

Think About How Much Effort You'll Put Forth

The next step in putting together a customer service policy deals with the degree of effort you'll put forth with your fans. Going out of your way for them can really pay off in the long run. This is precisely why Philip Kotler advises in *Marketing Management*, " Always give customers a little more."

Thus, are you going to sign autographs, shake hands with each and every fan, and respond to every single e-mail message or social network posting? Are you going to collect fans' birthday dates and send them birthday cards? And are you going to follow up with thank-you notes after a customer hires you to create a beat or track? You better think about it!

Consider a Delivery Commitment

In our high-tech, fast-paced world, people want immediate gratification. They don't want to wait around for anything! Considering a delivery commitment is, thus, the next step in finalizing a customer service policy.

When someone orders your record from your site, how fast are you going to get to your local branch of the United States Postal Service (USPS) or some other mail service to ship it (even if all you have is *one* order)? If you're providing production services to a client, will you give up some of your personal and family time, if necessary, to complete the job? Figure it out!

Determine How Accessible You'll Be

Your availability when people need you can make a big difference in how people perceive you and whether or not they buy from you. I'm not suggesting that you become so available that you lose an element of mystique or importance as an artist and businessperson. Rather, I'm suggesting you make a small effort to be somewhat available by, for instance, including an 800 number or instant messaging contact on your website. Should someone have a question about an order they'd like to make, you and your team can offer assistance. It's often the smallest conveniences that make fans the most happy.

Simplify the Buyer's Experience

The value that a customer places on a product and service is not only an issue of money, but also of the *time* and *effort* they have to put into getting it. By reducing the time and effort necessary to buy your products, and by making the buying experience a more pleasant one from the very first moment they come in touch with your brand to long after the sale, you can increase the perceived value in the customers' minds.

Given the above thoughts, will you make it extra easy for your fans to purchase products from your Web store by providing them with clear instructions and giving them a safe method to use their credit cards? Will you make it easy for them to come out to your events by offering downloadable maps or even physical transportation (e.g., a "party bus")? Let's face it, this level of customer service can make a big difference.

Contemplate a Satisfaction Guarantee

Nothing can validate your belief in your offerings better than putting your money where your mouth is.

Will you guarantee complete customer satisfaction for your products and services? Will you print your guarantee clearly on your packaging or website and then live up to it every time? Jot down your thoughts now.

Draw Up a Problem Resolution Strategy

Coming to the halfway point in our discussion on finalizing a customer service policy, it's a good time to mention *problem resolution*. Studies show that effective conflict resolution can strengthen customer relationships and cultivate even more customer loyalty.

Thus, should any type of complaint be made, will you treat the customer in a calm and empathetic manner, apologize for the problem, and/or take care of the issue immediately?

Having a plan for how to deal with unhappy customers (promoters, fans, music production houses, etc.) is crucial. In the digital age in which we live, remember that negative news travels twice as fast as positive news.

Contemplate a Monitoring and Measuring Strategy

While on the topic of problem resolution, it's also important to think about how you'll spot any problems. Did you know that only about 4 percent of dissatisfied customers complain to a company, and the other 96 percent who don't bother to complain spread the negative word of mouth to 9 or 10 other people within a week? Yup! According to the *Wall Street Journal*, it's true!

Given the above data, will you regularly monitor your social networking feeds to see what people are saying about you and then strive to fix any problems you might uncover?

After the owner of the Roxy Theater in Los Angeles spotted a social network post from a girl who had just complained about a drink, he immediately located her in the club (by observing her profile picture) and gave her a new drink—*all in real time.* Her response: "I'd recommend this place to friends in a heartbeat." Now that's what I call turning things around.

Can you think of similar strategies you can use to spot unhappy customers and nip the problem in the bud before it grows to be worse? Give it some thought. You'll be glad you did.

Determine Your Commitment to Company Training

Determining your commitment to company training is the next and major part of creating a strong customer service policy. It includes ensuring that everyone in your organization participates in providing excellent customer service (from your singer, to your bass player, to the girl behind the merch table, to the roadies who move your musical equipment).

Will you regularly bring up your customer service policies during band meetings and make sure to verbalize them to new employees whom you might hire onto your team? And will you continually strive to improve your policies over the long term? You should!

Commit to a Level of Customer Personalization

Another big score for the customer service department of your company deals with personalization. Remember, if you can't take the time to address the fans personally, they just might feel that they don't have the time to come out to your shows. Case in point: even when my name is *Bobby* and I live in *Los Angeles*, I get e-mails all the time that say things like, "Hey *gang*, come out to my show in *Brooklyn!*" And this pisses me off!

Consequently, when you correspond with your customers, are you going to address them in a personal and more intimate manner? For instance, are you going to take the time to personalize each e-mail message and isolate fans by city and state? You should give this some serious thought. Personalization is one of the most important considerations and steps in finalizing your very own customer service plan.

Consider Whether You'll Put Your Best Fans First

Remember the rule that *20 percent of your customers will provide 80 percent of your business.* In fact, these loyal fans may be all you need to maintain your business.

In an article in *Wired* magazine, author Kevin Kelly essentially calls this the "True Fan Theory." If you can nurture and retain at least 1,000 true fans who will spend at least $100 a year on you (buying merch, recordings, and tickets), that is a total of $100,000. I know that this is easier said than done, but I'm just trying to put it into perspective that not all fans are equal, and that you don't need millions of fans to make a living.

Therefore, are you going to give your "true fans" more attention than the other customers? Will you give them access to special perks before anyone else? Will you spend a little extra time communicating with them on your social networks? And will you get these folks invites to those backstage parties? You better!

Reflect on How You'll Create Customer "Loyalty" Through "Ownership"

Getting close to the end of our discussion on customer service, you should know that loyal and long-lasting fans can be cultivated by giving them a sense of pride and ownership in your brand. Ownership can be developed by providing opportunities for fans to get involved in making important business decisions (a technique known as *crowd sourcing*).

So are you going to ask fans to vote on the songs that make it on your album, create T-shirt designs you sell on your website, decide on set lists for your live performances, and attend monthly brainstorming sessions where they offer new ideas for your band to execute in the coming months? Make no mistake: all these activities go a long way.

Determine How You'll Build a Customer Culture or Community

The next-to-last customer service consideration deals with building a community around your company and putting forth the effort to make your customers feel like they are part of one big happy family. In fact, Trent Reznor of Nine Inch Nails has executed some unique strategies to engage fans and help them engage each other.

For instance, Reznor encourages fans to take videos and pictures of themselves, which he then compiles on his own website for all to see. He also released a free iPhone app that allowed fans to locate and communicate with each other and share photos and videos. Pretty epic stuff!

So what will you do to make your customers feel like they are a part of a big family or tribe? How will you get fans to engage each other? Whatever you decide, be sure to write it into your Marketing Plan of Attack™.

Create a Database Management Plan

And finally, the last consideration you might make when preparing your customer service policy for the marketplace is to think about your level of commitment to updating your database. The better and more up-to-date your lists are, the better the level of customer service you can provide.

So, will you put forth the effort to delete returned e-mails, remove people who ask to be unsubscribed, and even utilize a professional e-mail service to help you manage your lists? There are a number of services that can help. Check out Constant Contact, MailChimp, and Bronto for starters. Okay? Cool!

Well, that's about all on customer service, folks! Hope you found this section helpful. Now let's move on to the last phase in finalizing your products and service for the marketplace: analyzing features and benefits.

WHAT'S THE RITZ-CARLTON GOT TO DO WITH IT?

The next time you perform in a Ritz-Carlton Hotel or have the chance to stay in one when on the road, check out their customer service—they are known for being really great at it.

They have an incredible database that tracks everything about a customer. They know who you are when you pull up, because they know your license plate, and they know what kind of amenities you like in your room (flowers, cookies, etc.) and will often leave them for their more frequent customers. They also have discretionary money on hand to solve problems on the spot without having to consult upper management. Pretty cool.

The classic metal rock band Slaughter serves as another relevant example. It used to announce fans' birthdays on stage and do shout-outs to various fans in different cities. They even visited the homes of their best fans, had meals with them, and performed private shows. Wow! This is definitely what made this band a success.

So think about how you can make a comparable show of dedication in your own company.

Analyze the Features and Benefits of Your Products and Services

The final section in our discussion on finalizing your products and services for the marketplace involves features and benefits. These are extremely important concepts in product development as well as in promotion, which will be discussed in subsequent chapters.

For now, let's just review the difference between features and benefits and then look at formatting a *product features and benefits* (PFB) *chart.*

Be Clear on the Difference Between Features and Benefits

The difference between a product's feature and its benefit is rather subtle, but extremely significant.

Product Features

A *feature* is what a product or service is and what it is composed of. A laptop computer, for instance, might include a *Core 2 Duo Processor.*

Product Benefits

A *benefit* is what a product or service feature specifically does for the customer, and the level of convenience it provides. While a computer may have a Core 2 Duo Processor, what's more important is that the processor allows the customer to *multitask several recording programs without losing speed*. See the difference? Of course you do. Again, this is what customers are really interested in.

A popular saying in marketing is that you should never sell a quarter-inch drill (the product feature), but sell the quarter-inch hole it makes (the customer benefit). Believe that!

Format Your Product Features and Benefits (PFB) Chart

When finalizing your products and services for the marketplace, a handy tool to assess the features and benefits of a product is called a product features and benefits chart (PFB chart). Your PFB chart, which can be created in a Microsoft Excel or Apple Pages document, should include the following:

- Columns with three headers: 1) Products/Services, 2) Features, and 3) Benefits.
- Rows with the names of all your products and services: albums, songs, merchandise, live performances, and even your customer service policies.
- Cells (where the columns and rows meet) that include the product feature and benefits information that you fill in appropriately.

Remember that if you have trouble identifying the features and benefits of your offerings, you can always conduct research and ask your fans what they think, just like we did in chapter 6's testing and feedback. For now, just be sure to study the table "Products and Features Benefits Chart" to give you ideas about how to fill in your own table, and about how to be as unique as possible. Okay? Good luck.

RALLY THE TRIBES (RTT) PRODUCTS AND FEATURES BENEFITS CHART		
Products/Services	Feature(s) of Product/Service	Benefit(s) Important to Audience
a) Merchandising Line by Rally the Tribes	Features a full line of shirts, hoodies, military hat, and accessories bearing interesting slogans. Made from hemp materials.	Perfect for the fan who wants to make a strong political statement, feel good about not harming the environment, and make a positive change in the world (20 percent of the price goes to special charities). Products shipped from the RTT website are guaranteed.
b) Customer Service Policy	A declaration of the level of care provided to our target fans at every stage of the relationship.	Products sold online will arrive within just three days to those who order in the US, guaranteed. To reduce the customer's anxiety about ordering online, RTT will call every fan prior to mailing products to ensure them of the fullest satisfaction. Fans will be made to feel like they are more than fans, but rather part of a close family.
Etc.	Etc.	Etc.

=MARKETING PLAN TEMPLATE=

Use the template below, or a template like it, to help you craft important information that you will use in your Marketing Plan of Attack™. For additional help, be sure to refer to the marketing plan example below, the chapter on assembling your plan, and the complete plan provided in the back of this book.

Your Product and Service Strategy Template

Use this template to guide you with information needed in your marketing plan. Be sure not to include the actual questions when formatting your plan, and just use the answers and headers. *Just be clear that a strategy must be created for each product (e.g., one for your recordings, one for your merch, etc.).*

Product/Service: What is the product and service you plan to bring to the marketplace (album, merch item, live-performance set, etc.)?

Production: How will you create and prepare the product and service for the marketplace? Will you do it in-house or outsource? (This includes writing and recording songs and creating graphic arts materials.)

Manufacturing: How do you plan to reproduce your products or services? Will you reproduce them in-house or outsource?

Companies: What are the specific companies (if any) that you will use to bring the product or service to the marketplace? (Go as far as listing people, company names, addresses, and contacts.)

Quantities/Frequency: How many copies will you manufacture of the product? And how often might you make your service, such as your live performance, available in a given year? (Remember that you considered this in part when formulating your SMART goals and estimating sales and awareness in chapter 7.)

Explanation of Choices: Be sure to describe why you chose all of the above methods, personnel, and companies. Was it because of their reputation, experience, location, or low cost?

Customer Service Strategy: What is the customer service strategy that you will you provide for the product/service (i.e., will you make a commitment to professionalism, guarantee quality, etc.)?

Product Features and Benefits Chart: Create a product features and benefits (PFB) chart. What are, or will be, the features and benefits of your products/services? Remember that a feature is what a product is, and a benefit is what it does for the customer.

=MARKETING PLAN EXAMPLE=

Now here's an abridged marketing plan example for our alternative rock band Rally the Tribes, to help you put together your own place strategy. Note that only some of the band's offerings are addressed here, but you'll have to list all your products and services when writing your plan.

PRODUCT/SERVICE STRATEGY

a) 12-Song Album: *War and Police*

★Production: In-house and outsourced. Founders Kennedy Robert Jr. and K. Luther Martin will compose the album material while consulting with an outside professional. RTT's album artwork will be created in-house utilizing graphic arts software such as Adobe Illustrator. RTT will also record their music in-house utilizing their home recording gear, consisting of MacBook Pro laptop computers, Logic recording software, Reason software, keyboards with sound cards, and external microphones like Shure SM57s. Utilizing their professional relationships to arrange barter deals, they will also outsource certain production needs, such as the recording of the drums, mixing, and mastering. RTT will also outsource their regular musicians and guest DJs.

★Manufacturing: The manufacturing of records (both CDs and USB flash drives) will be outsourced. We will also consider outsourcing a limited run of vinyl, should the demand justify this decision.

★Companies: RTT will outsource Berklee songwriting coach Brian Wilston. RTT's outsourced recording needs will be handled by LA producer Bob Sloan and Sloan Productions. RTT will use musicians Ace Lincoln, Robbie Roosevelt, and Churchill Preston. Records will be manufactured using Disc Makers in Pennsauken, New Jersey.

★Quantities: RTT will manufacture 1,000 CDs and 100 USB flash drives. They will also release their records as a digital download and in a streamed format, utilizing CD Baby.

★Explanation of Choices: RTT's founders have extensive graphic arts experience using Adobe Illustrator, as well as recording experience using Logic and other home recording gear. Producer Bob Sloan is known for his work with electronic music in Amsterdam and will enhance RTT's rock/rave direction and brand. He has also agreed to do all the work on spec until RTT gets a deal. Musicians Ace Lincoln, Robbie Roosevelt, and Churchill Preston are some of the best in Los Angeles and are already known for their work in the popular punk band the Crooked Presidents. They have agreed to barter their services. Disc Makers is the leading company in disc manufacturing for independent artists and offers fair prices: approximately $1,200 for 1,000 CDs, $745 for 100 wristband flash drives, and minimal charges for digital distribution. This will all help keep quality up and profits high.

★Customer Service Strategy: All customers who purchase the album, whether live or online, will receive a thank-you card in the mail. RTT will also feature each customer's profile picture on the RTT site. At the end of the month, RTT will call each person who purchased the record and ask for feedback. All customers will also receive a birthday card.

b) RTT Fan Club

★Production: In-House/Outsource: We will utilize free online services, and the design skills of John Interpoll, to create an online fan club.

★Companies and Methods: WordPress, FanBridge, and John Interpoll.

★Explanation of Choices: Both WordPress and FanBridge provide free and easy-to-use content management systems. John Interpoll is a friend and recent graduate of a local art school who is willing to donate his time.

★Customer Service Strategy: Each fan that joins will be privy to special news and updates around Los Angeles, private BBQs and parties, and private brainstorming sessions with the band.

Etc.

Product Features and Benefits Chart (PFB Chart)		
Products/Services	Feature(s) of Product/Service	Benefit(s) Important to Audience
a) Album: *War and Police*	Twelve songs featuring four intellectual and highly skilled musicians creating music that can only be described as Skrillex meets Tupac meets Rage Against the Machine. Recorded in one of LA's top studios. Available in CD, flash drive, digital, and streaming formats.	This album's unique blend of rock and rave will grab the listener by both his throat and mind and pull him onto the dance floor turned mosh pit for 60 minutes of entertaining music that really matters. Fans will feel like they are contributing to an important cause (20 percent of the price goes to special charities, such as the Los Angeles Coalition to End Homelessness).
★Track 1 from *War and Police*: "Petty Thieves Hang, Big Ones Get Elected" (Lead Track from the Album)	A mid-tempo rock/rave song featuring the thought-provoking lyrical rhymes of Kennedy Robert Jr.	This three-minute power-packed song empowers the listener with the idea that everyone can make a positive change in this world. It could also be perfect for music in a video game like *Call of Duty*. Being that it is written by one owner/author, licensing the track for any music supervisor is simple and quick.
b) The Change Agents Fan Club	A group of like-minded fans, followers, and change makers privy to special news and updates around Los Angeles, private BBQs and parties, and private brainstorming sessions with the band.	This group provides "change agents" all around LA and the world to be part of a bigger and more important cause. Fans will feel like part of an important family that comes together to make a real difference in the community.
Etc.	Etc.	Etc.

Devise a Pricing Strategy
Reinforcing Your Brand Image and Generating Revenue and Awareness

Determining the amount that your target customer is willing to spend for your products and services, and the amount that you are willing to charge, is what devising a pricing strategy is all about. A pricing strategy should represent a good value to your customers—while at the same time create profits for, and awareness of, your company. In short, a pricing strategy should represent a win-win proposition. This is why devising an effective pricing plan is so important.

An effective pricing strategy can help you do the following:

- **Reinforce your desired brand image.**
- **Attract attention to your offerings and get people to check you out.**
- **Help create distinction from competing products and services.**
- **Generate revenue to cover costs and to reinvest back into your company.**
- **Help you gauge the motivations and demands of your target fans.**

This chapter is *not* just about pricing your *music*! It is about pricing any one of your products and services—including your physical and digital recordings, T-shirts, hats, stickers, fan club memberships, and more. Several pricing strategies from which you can choose are covered here, but note that there will be many professional instances when you'll have a limited say (or no say at all) in choosing your own price; this is due to industry standards, union regulations, and statutory laws and rates. Also, keep in mind that a discussion on pricing could venture deeply into matters of accounting, finance, and economics; however, this chapter keeps things as simple as possible.

So then, the pricing concepts and strategies in this chapter include:

1. **Knowing How Your Research, Goals and Other Strategies are Connected to Price**
2. **Choosing the Pricing Strategies That Are Right For You**
3. **Hearing It in Their Own Words: Interview with Jeff Hinkle, Business Manager**

SOME CREATIVE SALES STRATEGIES: FROM FREE, TO BOX SET, TO UNIQUE AND ENGAGING

The digital revolution has allowed anyone with online access to hear music for free, and thus artists and record labels are getting more creative about how they price and sell music. In fact, there is a lot of talk about whether anyone should even bother making a profit on recordings, and whether music should just be given away for free to promote the sale of other products and services like box sets, concerts, and T-shirts.

Trent Reznor of Nine Inch Nails offered his recording titled *The Slip* for free in exchange for an e-mail address, but on the same day, he also announced his next Nine Inch Nails tour at a top price. The tour sold out quickly.

Reznor, on the release of another recording, charged a hefty $300, but this was specifically for a limited box set that included the songs on high-quality vinyl together with attractive print images—all personally signed by Reznor. As there were only 2,500 copies manufactured as part of a special sales promotion, the sets quickly sold out.

And finally, Prince cut a deal with a British tabloid, allowing it to exclusively distribute free coupons for his new album *Planet Earth*. Prince was paid a flat fee by the tabloid, the tabloid made money from all the advertisers that wanted to be included in its Sunday edition, and the fans got a free CD. Everybody won. Pretty clever.

Examine How Your Research, Goals, and Other Strategies Are Connected to Price

To determine the optimum price for your own products and services, let's begin by taking a quick look at how everything from your SWOT analysis to your SMART goals to your product and service strategy relates to price.

Reflect on Your SWOT Analysis

The market *need* you identified in your SWOT analysis can play a major part in helping you determine your pricing strategies. Remember that the more unique you are, the more flexibility you may have in setting your prices.

Review Your Target Customer's Profile

Customer demographics (age, income level, and social status) as well customer psychographics (activities, interests, and opinions) can provide important clues about how much your fans can afford to pay and what you should charge. Clearly, selling a $30 T-shirt at a youth center concert full of 12-to-17-year-olds with no income is out of boundaries.

Take a Look at Your Competitor Analysis

An analysis of what your competitors are charging and whether these prices are effective can be extremely useful for setting your own price strategies. Remember that by logging onto your competitors' websites, you'll be able to view all, or most, of their pricing strategies.

Revisit Important Testing/Feedback Data

The feedback that you collect from your target audience can be extremely valuable to your decisions about pricing. While people are not always certain about *how they feel or what they need*, they can still provide valuable insights. If you haven't asked your target customers what they'd be willing to pay for your products and services, now is a good time to ask.

Reference Your SMART Goals

The sales you want to make and the market awareness you want to build are paramount to pricing. For instance, if your goals were focused more on building market awareness than on making a profit, your pricing strategies should logically reflect this choice.

Consider What Type of Branding and Positioning You Are Putting Forth

Make no mistake: image and price go hand in hand. If you're presenting a "high end" identity at a "low end" price, people get skeptical, and vice-versa, when you're presenting a more casual identity at a higher price. Furthermore, did you know that people often judge the worthiness of a new product based on the price that is being charged? That's right, folks. *The price can validate the brand.* This is important information to think about when pricing your products and services!

Revisit Your Product and Service Strategies

Look closely at the costs you incurred to finalize your products and services for the marketplace; remember that a product can't be priced at an amount lower than it costs (unless it's for short-term promotional purposes), or you won't stay in business very long.

Oh, and while on the topic of product, don't forget to consider your customer service strategy. Keep in mind that the greater the customer service you provide, the greater the price you can charge. Customers appreciate great customer service and see this as an extra value.

Consider Other Strategies

Last, but not least, be sure to consider strategies like *place* (or distribution) when pricing your products and services. Place is discussed in detail in the next chapter, but it is important to mention now briefly, as these middle-person distributors will come at an additional cost to you. When pricing your products and considering the profits that you want to make, you must keep this issue in mind.

Choose the Pricing Strategies That Are Right for You

Now that you've had a chance to consider how your research, goals, and marketing mix strategies interact with pricing, it's time to choose the pricing strategies that are right for you. Let's take a look at a variety of methods, including pricing within consumer boundaries, pricing it for free, utilizing donation pricing, utilizing bundle pricing, and so much more.

ECONOMICS 101: FIND THE ECONOMIC PRICE— WHERE SUPPLY AND DEMAND INTERSECT

While I promised that this chapter wouldn't go too deep into complex financial matters, understanding a little bit about something called the *economic price*, as well as that phrase you certainly heard in school, *supply and demand*, is certainly useful in a chapter about pricing.

To keep things simple: the magic point (the perfect price at which supply and demand intersect) is called the economic price.

In theory, if you were to raise the price of your T-shirts above the economic price, people wouldn't buy (the demand would go down) and you'd start noticing extra boxes of T-shirts (the "extra supply") piling up around your apartment.

On the other hand, if you were to lower the price of your T-shirts below the economic price, people would theoretically buy more of your goods (the demand would go up), and you'd start sending more and more fans away from your merch table without the shirts (due to the shortage in supply).

So, what does this all mean for you and your pricing strategies? According to our lovely friends the economists, and according to the most basic economic principles, if a surplus of product exists, you should lower the price to increase demand, and if a shortage of product exists, you should raise the price to lower the demand and even it out with the supply. Finding this balance, or economic price, is often a matter of precise and detailed research, but for many companies, simple observation and trial and error can suffice. Just something to think about.

Price Within Consumer Boundaries

The first, and most practical, pricing strategy to consider for your marketing plan begins with pricing within consumer boundaries. This involves finding the *boundaries* (a top, middle, and low price) that your target customer is *willing* to pay for a particular product/service category, and then choosing the price that is most in line with your goals.

For example, suppose that after surveying your target customers to determine what they'd pay for a 10-song recording, your data shows that they'd dish out $10 on the top end, $5 on the low end, and $7 in between.

You might use a *top-market price* if you wanted to recover your production costs as quickly as possible and/ or capitalize on the excitement and demand that accompanies a new release. You might use a *low-market price* if you wanted to *stimulate trial* (get people to check you out) and increase your awareness in the marketplace when no one knows who you are. And you might use a *mid-market price* if you wanted to take a more conservative "business as usual" approach, after your recording has been released and sales are going well.

In any case, understanding your customers' boundaries and pricing within this range is an important concept to understand. If this sounds useful to you, be sure to conduct the appropriate research and write a top, middle, or low price into your plan.

Consider Your Bottom-Line Cost, and Profit and Loss

While we just illustrated how important it is to know the range of prices your customer is willing to pay, understanding the bottom-line unit costs (a.k.a. *cost of sales*) of each of your products and services is also significant.

To illustrate, suppose that your recording and mastering costs for a 10-song, low-budget indie recording are $6,000, and your manufacturing cost to make 1,000 units is $1,000. This brings your total costs to $7,000 and your bottom-line cost per unit to $7 ($7,000 ÷ 1,000 = $7).

So, if you charge a top-market price of $10 for your recording, you'll yield an approximate profit of $3 per unit ($10 − $7 = $3). If you charge a mid-market price of $7, you'll break even on each unit ($7 − $7 = 0). And if you charge a low-market price of $5, you'll take a loss of $2 per unit ($5 − $7 = −$2).

As you can see, your bottom-line costs can determine your profit and loss, which can ultimately help determine the pricing strategies you choose. Some people will want to make the highest profit possible on their work. Other people will be happy to just make back their money. And still other people (perhaps independent artists like you) will be fine with losing money on each recording as long as it gets their company's name into the marketplace where they can eventually turn a healthy profit. Choose what makes sense to you. Be sure to check out the table "Bottom-Line Costs, and Profits and Loss."

BOTTOM-LINE COSTS AND PROFIT AND LOSS Example: Recordings: One-Year Indie Artist Projection: 1,000 Units			
	Ex 1: Low-Budget Indie Recording	Ex 2: Mid-Budget Indie Recording	Ex 3: Larger-Budget Indie Recording
Recording/Mastering	$6,000	$9,000	$14,000
Manufacturing	$1,000	$1,000	$1,000
Total Costs	$7,000	$10,000	$15,000
Bottom-Line Unit Cost	$7	$10	$15
Approximate Profit/Loss per Unit at Top Market Price: $10	$3	$0	−$5
Approximate Profit/Loss per Unit at Mid-Market Price: $7	$0	−$3	−$8
Approximate Profit/Loss per Unit at Low Market Price: $5	−$2	−$5	−$10
Note: While it is sometimes impossible, try not to make a product that's so expensive that you'll either have to lose money on each unit or be faced with needing to sell more units than even possible before breaking even (example 3, above, represents this). Remember that your goal should be to make the best product at the lowest possible cost.			

Price Your Products and Services for Free

While it certainly would be nice to break even or make a few bucks on the sale of your products using one of the pricing strategies discussed thus far, there will be times when independent artists must simply *price it for free*, which brings us to our next strategy.

Pricing it for free is based on the idea that the easier it is for people to experience your company's offerings, and the more that people start to talk about your offerings, the sooner people will want to pay for all of your company's offerings (whether it be your albums, DVDs, concerts, T-shirts, beats, etc.). In other words, while you may take a loss initially, pricing it for free offers the possibility that *if you sacrifice today, you'll capitalize tomorrow.*

When using a free strategy, just be sure to do the following:

- Tell customers that your offerings are "at no cost to them," as opposed to just being free.
- Always plug your products' "value" (e.g., the expensive studio and producer you used).
- Explain your true business intentions (e.g., that the price is only a "new artist price" intended to stimulate awareness in the marketplace). And . . .
- Ask customers for an e-mail address and permission to follow up and get feedback (i.e., show them how important and valuable your products and services really are to you).

Just keep in mind that failure to use the above points can cause a negative outcome. You see, the prices of your products and services create a perception of value. If you simply lay out your recording, for instance, on your merch table with a sign that says "Take one, it's free," you just might find that some people will view your offerings as disposable. Should this be the case, you've accomplished absolutely nothing.

So again, take the aforementioned tips above very seriously. You'll be really glad you did!

Allow Donation Pricing

If you don't want to offer your products and services for free, and if you're more immediately concerned with increasing awareness about your products and services than you are with making up your costs or making a profit, then you might consider using a donation pricing strategy.

If you use a donation pricing strategy, you'll tell your fans that they can pay whatever they can or wish. Or, you may set a very low "suggested" starting donation price (let's say $1) for a limited time (let's say one month).

Whatever the specifics, you'll find that donation pricing can really win over fans and that some fans will even be willing to pay more than what you would have otherwise charged.

One independent artist I know received a hundred-dollar bill for a ten-song recording just because a fan really wanted to support the band and loved the fact that he felt trusted to name the price on his own. Wow—f***** epic!

By the way, independent artists and start-up companies are not the only organizations that use donation pricing. Even major-selling bands have executed this strategy.

Prior to the official release of their recording *In Rainbows*, the alternative rock band Radiohead offered their music for a donation price for a limited time and stimulated quite a buzz in the process.

Perhaps you'll also give a donation strategy a try.

Try Disguised Pricing (Make It Feel Free)

Another alternative strategy for pricing your products and services for free is disguised pricing. It cleverly involves hiding the price of one product into the price of another to generate sales.

For instance, to keep out potential deadbeats who have no intention of buying drinks at the bar, the Rainbow Bar and Grill on the famous Sunset Strip in Los Angeles charges a door price of $10 and then gives out two drink tickets at no extra cost to the customer. While the club owners see this as simply guaranteeing revenue at the bar, customers see this as getting an added value of two "free" drinks. This strategy has worked for the Rainbow for years.

Here's how you might apply this pricing strategy to your career: If you're playing a club that doesn't enforce a cover charge on a particular night, you could speak with the owner long in advance about charging a cover charge of $7 at the door that goes into your pocket. To justify that price in the minds of customers, you could include a free recording or T-shirt for each paying customer. You see, what this really guarantees is that you're generating revenue at your merch table from *everyone* who walks through the door. Just be sure to announce the "fee and free" offering all over your posters and in your e-mail announcements, so that people aren't surprised by the charge at the door. Okay?

Consider Pledge Pricing

Moving on to a completely different pricing strategy than the ones mentioned above, many bands these days are creating a variety of project proposals at various prices and asking fans to make a pledge.

To demonstrate how this works, suppose your company wanted to raise $2,000 in one month to help pay for the mixing and manufacturing of your recording. For $1, a pledger might be promised a copy of your recording when it is finished. For $25, a pledger might be promised your finished recording, an autographed poster, and a free pass to the record release party, where food and drinks will be served. And for as much as $1,000, a pledger might be promised a lunch date with the lead singer, a copy of your finished recording, and the kitchen sink. You get the point.

To ensure that a pledge pricing strategy goes off without a hitch and important issues are worked out in advanced (such as what happens if you don't raise enough money and your recording is never completed), you should consider using a professional online pledge pricing service. While there are many services out there, PledgeMusic (www.pledgemusic.com) and Kickstarter (www.kickstarter.com) are good places to start. Check them out.

Utilize Bundle Pricing

When you have a variety of different products or services that can be gathered up in one package for sale, another useful strategy to consider is called *bundle pricing*. Bundle pricing provides a lower aggregate price to customers than if they were to buy each product individually, yet it helps you move more inventory and still makes you a profit as well.

To demonstrate, suppose your were to offer your recording for $10, a T-shirt for $16, and a sticker for $2 (that would be a total of $28). Now, suppose you were to offer all three items together in a package for a bundle price of $20 (that would be a savings of $8 to the fans). Assuming the bundle price still covers your costs, makes you a profit, and encourages fans to buy more and save, then everyone wins!

Whatever bundle price you come up with, be creative and devise the system that works best for you and your customers. Now examine the table "Bundle Price Example."

BUNDLE PRICE EXAMPLE			
	Your Unit Cost	**Individual Selling Price**	**Bundle Price**
CD	$5.00	$10.00	$7.00
T-Shirt	$8.00	$16.00	$12.00
Sticker	$0.50	$2.00	$1.00
TOTAL	**$13.50**	**$28.00**	**$20.00**

Price Above the Competition

Getting to the halfway point in our discussion about choosing the right pricing strategies for you, let's take a look at setting your prices intentionally above what your competitors are charging and focusing on your products' quality.

To demonstrate, suppose that you're performing at a festival where there are several other bands selling shirts at their merch booths. If all of the other merch booths have T-shirts at a low price of $7, you may immediately feel it's necessary to follow this strategy in order to be "competitive" and go along with the flow.

While there is certainly a time and place for everything, a better strategy may be to intentionally charge $12 per T-shirt and focus on how much more the customer will get for just a difference of $5. It may be that your shirts hold their color better, they don't shrink, and/or they are made of a fabric that is much safer for the environment. So long as that higher price is still one that is within a comfortable range for your target audience, and you can back up your claims of quality, then *pricing above the competition*, rather than *matching the competition*, is usually a better plan.

So be sure to keep this strategy in mind the next time you're feeling the "heat in the kitchen" from competitors. Don't forget!

Use a Percent Occupancy Method

Another pricing strategy you can use is the *percent occupancy method*, which establishes an early lower price for customers when the available occupancy in a venue is high, and a subsequently higher price for customers as the venue fills up and the available occupancy space is low. The airlines use this strategy all the time, and you might be able to utilize it too.

Suppose you are a DJ/producer who established his own Halloween rave and is selling tickets. You might put the tickets on sale for $10 one month before the party, $20 two weeks before the party, and $25 one week before the party, as the number of available tickets steadily decreases.

Whatever the situation, the general idea behind the percent occupancy method is to get people to act sooner rather than later—a technique known in the sales world as an *urgency close*. If this is a strategy that works well with your particular marketing plan goals, perhaps you'll consider using the percent occupancy method too. It really works!

Consider the "End in 9 or 5" Psychological Approach

Setting prices that end in a 9 or a 5 is a common psychological technique that you may also want to consider using in your Marketing Plan of Attack™. Rather than pricing something at $10, you price it at $9.99 or $9.95. Studies have actually shown that people react better to prices that end in 9 or 5 because they appear to be much lower—seriously!

While setting prices that end in 9 or a 5 might work, keep in mind that it can have a reverse effect when considering your brand image. If, for instance, you wanted to project a higher-end image as a studio owner but you sold your services for $199.99 per hour, clients might feel that this actually cheapens the image of your company rather than strengthening it with a better-sounding deal. A price of $200 per hour might actually sound better and classier to your target customers. Bottom line: there is a time and a place for everything.

Offer Quantity, Cash, and Special-Event Discounts

Special short-term discount prices of your offerings can also be utilized as an effective pricing strategy. While this is really a promotional strategy, it works hand in hand with price and fits right in with the discussion here.

To provide a few examples of how discount pricing works, you might have a quantity discount or two-for-the-price-of-one deals on your T-shirts for fans who buy more than one unit (to encourage them to buy for a friend or family member), a cash discount (to reward customers for eliminating your burden of dealing with checks and credit card processing), and a live-performance discount (to get fans to buy your products right before/during/after one of your shows).

If all of the above ideas sound too salespersonlike, think of it this way: you are providing your fans with exceptional offerings of which you are extremely proud, that are of exceptional value, and that the fans will greatly enjoy. Manipulating prices simply helps them make the right decision.

AFTERTHOUGHT: CHANGE THE PRICE, CHANGE THE PRODUCT/SERVICE Validate all price increases with an improvement in the product or service; otherwise, people will feel ripped off. The same works in reverse: validate all price decreases with a promotional discount or reduction in service time, or people will think something is wrong with the product or that there is a catch. Get it? Good.

Use Loss Leader Pricing

Coming close to end of our discussion on pricing, it's important to discuss loss leader pricing. This is a strategy whereby you mark down one product to draw customers into your store to buy the more expensive product.

To illustrate, at your live performance, you might announce that you have cool patches marked down from $3 to $1 (below your cost) in order to draw fans over to your merch table, where you have more expensive items that can make up the profits. This really works. If you've ever been enticed into a Best Buy store to purchase the advertised recording for a ridiculously low price, and then walked out of the store with a new digital camera or game console that you've been meaning to buy, then you have already experienced the power of loss leader pricing.

If loss leader pricing sounds like a strategy that's right for you, be sure to write it into your plan.

Offer a Money-Back Guarantee Price

The next strategy you might consider is one whereby you charge a slightly higher price for your products and services, and then justify that price by offering a money-back guarantee.

For instance, you might charge a $20 cover charge for a party you organize where you perform or spin records, and tell people they'll get their money back if they express any dissatisfaction within a certain time frame. Or you might sell a T-shirt for $25, and tell people that they'll get their money back if it fades within one month of purchase. You get the idea.

Essentially, offering a money-back guarantee is like putting your money where your mouth is. Sure this can create all kinds of logistical problems, but if you can work out the details, perhaps this idea is right for you.

Use Zone Pricing (for Shipping/Handling)

A discussion on pricing would not be complete without mentioning the costs of shipping and handling for sales of physical products from your websites. But because these costs can vary greatly, you might consider devising a per-region (or *zone*) price.

Zone pricing can be established easily by asking the post office for the shipping costs to select cities where you expect the most sales and then averaging these costs out. If it costs $3.00 to ship a T-shirt from your home to Nashville, $3.50 to Chicago, and $4.00 to New York (a total of $10.50), your zone pricing for shipping in the United States would be $3.50 ($10.50 ÷ 3 = $3.50). You can do the same thing for the territories of Canada, Europe, and other "zones" as well.

Of course, you might also want to tack a handling charge on top of your shipping costs for the time it takes to drive to the post office and wait in line, but that's more difficult to calculate accurately. So, sticking with our above example, you might charge an additional $1.50 and then list one flat shipping/handling rate of $5.00 ($3.50 + $1.50) for all sales in the US for every order that is generated.

Whatever you arrange, just be sure to list, clearly where they can see them, all of the customer's additional costs. If there's one thing people hate, it's being hit up with additional charges at the very last step of the transaction. You know what I mean? Right? Good! Then let's move on.

Price over the Product's Life

Another important consideration to make when setting prices for your products and services is how you'll handle the various life stages. Consider the following:

- *Introduction:* In the early stages of your career when no one really knows that you have a new recording out, you might offer an *introductory* or *free* price.
- *Growth:* As the buzz gets out about you and the demand increases, you might raise the prices, try to make up your costs, and even make a profit.
- *Maturity:* After some time passes, when it appears that the hype is starting to die down, you might offer short-term sales promotions or giveaways to encourage the *late majority* to make a purchase. And finally . . .
- *Decline:* When it appears that sales are at a minimum, you might keep prices really low to encourage all the *laggards* to make a purchase.

Look, while the above might seem like common sense, just remember that common sense isn't always so common. Believe that!

Flow with the Establishment: Retailing, Booking, Publishing, and More

Winding down to a final thought on pricing, be clear that there will be many instances when independent artists like you will have a limited say (or no say at all) in choosing pricing methods and strategies because of certain industry practices, laws, and more. Let's examine online sales restrictions, the rules of the road, and film and TV laws and practices.

Online Sales Restrictions

The online retailer iTunes, one of the largest sellers of music, dictates the price points at which digital downloads and albums must sell. While there is some variation for major-label artists and artists that iTunes picks at its discretion, independent artists typically have no choice at all in determining their price. What's more, you have no say in how much of a percentage share it takes from your sales either. Check "iTunes royalties per song" on your search engine for the current royalty rate.

The Rules of the Road

Another area where you may have no control over setting your prices is at your live performances. Some promoters will have a *pay-to-play* policy (where you must pay them a fee to perform in their venues), *play for free* policy (where you are offered to play in return for the exposure and experience you may gain), or a "play for a percentage of the cover charge we say" policy (where you are offered a percentage of the fees taken in at the door). All of the above may sound disappointing and like you'll have a lot of dues to pay. However, remember that after building demand in the marketplace, you'll have the leverage to negotiate more advantageous methods of payment. So hang in there. For more on live performances, see *How to Be Your Own Booking Agent* by Jeri Goldstein.

Film and TV Laws and Practices

Finally, in the film and TV licensing world, there are often set rates by law and certain ordinary industry practices that will determine the pricing (or fees) that you will receive for licensing your music. Further, there are often budget constraints (such as the ones that independent filmmakers and fledgling game developers often experience) that will determine the fees certain music professionals and upstart companies can pay, if they can pay anything at all. Just be very careful about every business decision you sign (an experienced music publishing attorney may be needed), and think of all the aforementioned situations as par for the course and as an opportunity to hone your craft, gain exposure, and establish a fan base. Of course, this could all add to more pricing leverage down the line. Check out *Music, Money, and Success* by Jeff and Todd Brabec for more information.

So that's pretty much all I have to say on pricing, folks. Now here's an extremely comprehensive interview with Jeff Hinkle, business manager, with more advanced information about pricing your products and services. You won't want to miss this!

AFTERTHOUGHT: GOT BOOKS ON PRICING? If you're someone who wants to check out two books that are completely focused on the topic of pricing, be sure to read *Pricing Strategy* by Morris Engelson and *The Strategy and Tactics of Pricing* by Thomas Nagle and John Hogan. Enjoy.

In Their Own Words: Q&A with Jeff Hinkle, Business Manager at GSO Business Management

Jeff Hinkle is a certified public accountant (CPA) with GSO Business Management, one of the largest business management firms in the San Fernando Valley, representing a diverse group of legendary entertainment and touring clients. In this interview, Jeff explains some of the more complex issues concerning pricing, sales tax, and so much more. This may make your head spin, but it's important info. So be brave!

Q: *Gross profit margin*, *return on investment*, and *markup* are additional and very common pricing strategies used in the business world. Please explain each.

JH: These are formulas and potential pricing strategies that all say something different. Gross profit margin (GPM) tells you *the percentage of the price, given your costs, that you can keep as gross profit*. It can be found using the following equation: (price – cost) ÷ price. To demonstrate, if an independent artist targeted a top market price of $10 for her 10-song album, and her bottom-line costs were $7 per unit, she would earn a GPM of 30 percent. Put another way: $(10 - 7) \div 10 = 0.30$.

Return on investment (ROI) tells you *by what percent your initial investment (or risk) on a specific product or service should grow*. The following equation is used for ROI: (price – cost) ÷ cost. To demonstrate, if an independent artist targeted a top market price of $10 for his 10-song album, and his bottom-line costs were $7, he would earn a return on his investment of 42 percent. Put another way: $(10 - 7) \div 7 = 0.42$.

And finally, markup is *what you do to the cost to find a price*. It can be found using the following equation: cost + markup = price. To demonstrate, if an independent artist's bottom-line costs to record and manufacture her 10-song album were $7 per unit, and she used a target markup of 43 percent, she would arrive at a top market price of $10. Put another way: $7 \times 1.43 = 10$.

A company may use any one of these formulas and strive to stay within a certain percentage range or use a certain markup, based on its individual goals and industry *best-case benchmarks*. For instance, a GPM of 50 percent, a ROI of 100 percent, and a markup of 100 percent would all be superb goals. But of course, in reality, a company's ability to meet these goals all depends on how low it can keep its manufacturing costs and how high it can price its products within consumer boundaries. Just be sure to refer to the table "Advanced Pricing Methods in Review."

ADVANCED PRICING METHODS IN REVIEW		
Gross Profit Margin	**Return on Investment (ROI)**	**Mark-Up**
(price – cost) ÷ price	(price – cost) ÷ cost	cost + markup = price
A percentage of the price, after costs, that is left over.	A percentage by which your initial investment grows.	A percentage by which you mark up costs to get a price.

Q: As demonstrated above, costs (or, as accountants would say, *cost of sales*) plays a major factor in setting prices. That being said, what really counts as costs of sales for both a product and a service?

JH: Cost of sales includes all costs directly associated with bringing a product or service to market.

For a product, like a recording, all costs to get the music into a saleable condition should be included, such as recording costs (studio time, engineers, rehearsal time, mastering, etc.) and any recording gear or equipment purchased by the artist to make the recording. Packaging the music (insert artwork and manufacturing) should also be included.

For a service, like a live performance, all costs or expenses related to the performance could be included as your cost of sales, such as travel, gas, parking, production costs, fees paid to musicians, etc.

Q: Are ideas like *fixed costs* and *variable costs* worthy of mention in a discussion on setting price?

JH: Yes. Being aware of fixed and variable costs is helpful in any business endeavor. In theory, a company must set its prices high enough to cover its fixed costs (costs that don't change no matter how many units are manufactured and sold) and its variable costs (costs that fluctuate up and down depending on the number of units that are manufactured and sold).

In the table "Fixed and Variable Expenses" [see table], the cost of recording and mastering an album is $14,000, and it is unchanged no matter how many units are produced. This is called a fixed cost. On the other hand, the cost of manufacturing and selling 1,000 recordings is $1.19 per unit, the cost of 1,500 recordings is $1.05 per unit, and the cost of 2,000 recordings is $0.96 per unit. These are called variable costs.

Once again, the idea in theory is that a company must keep a watchful eye on its fixed expenses and on its variable expenses (which fluctuate) to ensure that it always makes up for both these costs (if possible) in the prices that it sets.

FIXED AND VARIABLE EXPENSES: LARGER-BUDGET INDIE RECORDING			
Costs	**Example 1**	**Example 2**	**Example 3**
Fixed Costs (Don't Change)	$14,000.00 Recording/Mastering	$14,000.00 Recording/Mastering	$14,000.00 Recording/Mastering
Variable Costs (Vary)	$1,119.00 Manufacturing 1,000 Units ($1.19 each)	$1,578.00 Manufacturing 1,500 Units ($1.05 each)	$1,919.00 Manufacturing 2,000 Units ($0.96 each)
Total Costs	$15,119.00	$15,578.00	$15,919.00
Per-Unit Bottom-Line Costs	$15.11	$10.30	$7.95

Q: What happens if your costs are too high to allow you to make a profit and stay within a fair consumer price? Is conducting a *break-even analysis* useful here? Please elaborate.

JH: Absolutely. Given a specific price, break-even analysis will let you know how many units you will need to sell before recovering all of your costs (both fixed and variable). A simple formula to find the break-even point is as follows: fixed costs ÷ (price – variable costs) = your break-even point.

Using information from the table "Fixed and Variable Expenses" (see example 1 in the second column from left), if you decided to sell your recording for $10, your break-even point would be 1,589 units. Put another way, $14,000 (fixed costs) ÷ $10 (price) – $1.19 (variable costs) = 1,589 units. But this presents some problems: First, you realistically may not be able to sell 1,589 units. Second, you don't have 1,589 units; you only manufactured 1,000. Third, most manufacturing companies base their price quotes only on even-number quantities of say 1,000, 1,500, and 2,000. And fourth, additional units mean additional variable costs, for which you may not have the extra funds.

But if you decided to make the extra units needed (see example 3 of the box above where 2,000 units are manufactured), and you were selling your recording for $10, your break-even point would now be 1,548 units. That's $14,000 (fixed costs) ÷ by $10 (price) – $0.96 (variable costs) = 1,548 units. Now, for the remaining 452 units of the 2,000 you manufactured, you could continue to sell them at $10 a pop to make a profit of $4,520, or you could just plan to give them away and chalk it all up to promotion.

I hope your readers' heads are not spinning too badly. If they can get this stuff, more power to them! Understanding the concept of break-even analysis is pretty important.

Q: Is there anything besides the cost of sales [discussed above] that could ultimately cut into the net profits for independent musicians?

JH: Sure, essentially, anyone in the distribution channel that agrees to sell your products for you will want a piece of the pie. For instance, if you sell your physical recording on consignment at a record store or through an online distributor (like CD Baby), they might want as much as a few dollars out of the sale price, which could certainly lower your profits. But this is all the cost of doing business.

Q: Finally, when setting prices, must independent artists remember to ask for an additional amount to cover sales tax?

JH: Here's how sales tax works: The state in which you conduct your business will typically charge you a sales tax for the tangible goods you sell.

When you're on tour, this means that you are technically liable for sales tax in every state where you sell your merchandise. Though, as a practical matter, multistate sales tax compliance usually doesn't happen at the indie artist level. Be sure to speak with your accountant for advice.

When selling from your website store, you are supposed to charge sales tax to customers who specifically live in the state where you are "based."

Taxes can be rather complex and certainly not what this chapter is about. But if your readers have further interest in this area, I suggest that they speak with a certified public accountant (CPA) who has a significant amount of music industry experience, and who can answer questions based on a person's individual situation. To find a CPA, ask for references from fellow musicians you trust. Good luck.

= MARKETING PLAN TEMPLATE=

Use the template below, or a template like it, to help you craft important information that you will use in your Marketing Plan of Attack™. For additional help, be sure to refer to the marketing plan example below, the chapter on assembling your plan, and the complete plan provided in the back of this book.

Your Pricing Strategy Template

Use this template to help you organize information that you'll need in your marketing plan. Be sure not to include the actual questions when formatting your plan and to just use the answers. Organize the information any way you'd like, but a matrix (such as the one in the example below) may come in handy. *Just be clear that a strategy must be created for each product (e.g., one for your recordings, one for your merch, etc.).*

Product or Service: What is the name of the product or service for which you are creating a price strategy (album, merch item, live-performance set, etc.)?

Initial Pricing Strategies: What is the "name" of the pricing strategy you will be using (top-line price, free price, etc.)?

Price: What is the actual price (the amount) associated with the strategy you chose above ($10.00, $14.99, etc.)? Note: You may also want to include additional information, such as the gross profit margin that each price will yield your company. Remember that gross profit is found by the following equation: (price − cost) ÷ price.

Units: Is there any specific number of units for which you will set the price? For instance, you might offer a "top-line price" on your recording of $10 for 800 units and a "free price" on the remaining 200 albums.

Initial Time Period: Are there any initial time frames during which you will be offering the above price? For instance, you might make your recording free for the first three months following its release and then change to a $10 fee.

Alternate Price Strategies: Are there any alternate pricing strategies for the products and services you offer? Will you consider other pricing strategies (such as loss leader and donation pricing)? If so, on how many units will you be offering this price, and/or for what initial time period?

Shipping/Handling Strategy: Will you use a shipping/handling charge as part of your pricing strategy? If so, what will you charge for purchases through your online stores? For instance, if you sell recordings or T-shirts online, what is the amount you'll add for mailing them to the client?

=MARKETING PLAN EXAMPLE=

Now here's an abridged marketing plan example for our band Rally the Tribes, to help you put together your own pricing strategy. Note that only some of the band's offerings are addressed here, but you'll have to list all of your products and services when writing your plan.

a) 12-Song Album: *War and Police*

CD Pricing for Album Titled *War and Police*		
Strategy Names (Initial and Alternate)	**Prices/Amounts**	**Units and Time Periods**
Top-Line Price for Recordings	$10.00 (Note: Manufacturing cost per unit is $1.20. Estimated GPM is 88 percent.)	On 800 units (of a 1,000 unit pressing). Term of one year.
Free Price	$0 (Note: Manufacturing cost per unit is $1.20. Will take a loss.)	On 200 units (of a 1,000 pressing). Term starting at least one month prior to the official release date and continuing until all units are distributed.
Money-Back Guarantee Price Offer	$10.00 full refund with shipping/handling will be mailed back to the customer.	On all paid units sold online. One year.
Zone Pricing (On Shipping and Handling from Web Sales)	$3.00 (US and Canada orders) added to price. $5.00 (other zones) added to price.	On all paid units sold online. One year.

b) RTT Merchandising Line

The Rugby Rally and the RTT Jock/Rock Jersey		
Strategy Names (Initial and Alternate)	**Prices/Amounts**	**Units & Time Periods**
Top-Line Price/Psychological End-in-9 Price for Rugby and Jersey Shirts	$19.99 (Note: Manufacturing cost per unit is $6.00. Estimated GPM is 70 percent.)	On all units (of an initial printing of 36 units)—less those used in special sales promotions. Term of one year.
Money-Back Guarantee Price Offer	$19.99 full refund with shipping/handling will be mailed back to the customer.	On all paid units sold online. One year.
Zone Pricing (On Shipping and Handling from Web Sales)	$5.00 (US and Canada orders) added to price. $7.00 (other zones) added to price.	On all paid units sold online. One year.
Special Event Discount Price (Buy Rugby or Jersey and Get Military Hat for Free)	$19.99 (Note: Manufacturing cost per shirt is $6.00. Cost per hat is $5.00. Estimated GPM is 44 percent.)	Term: Short event sales promotions planned throughout the marketing year.

c) Live-Performance Set

Regular Club, College, and Other Performances		
Strategy Names (Initial and Alternate)	**Prices/Amounts**	**Units and Time Periods**
Establishment Price	Pay-to-play/free/guarantees up to $1,000 and more per show.	Each show is subject to a different policy. Term of one year.

Etc.

12

Establish a Place Strategy, Part 1
Booking Live-Performance Sets and Distributing Records

Creating a place strategy is the process of making *all* of your products and services *convenient* for users to find, buy, book and/or license—all to achieve the goals of your marketing plan and beyond.

The products and services for which you'll create a plan can include your recordings, live performance sets, merch, songs, beats, production services and more. This chapter, part 1, will focus on your live-performance sets and recordings and offer a combination of distribution methods for each. In the next chapter, part 2, we'll focus on your merch and musical compositions.

A well thought-out place strategy can help your company do the following:

- **Establish and publicize your products/services in the marketplace.**
- **Remain profitable and stay in business.**
- **Serve markets that competitors aren't reaching.**
- **Give customers what they need and want, when they need and want it.**

Your place strategy can take an *indirect* route—starting with creators (like you), moving through intermediary companies (like retailers, bookers, and songpluggers), and finally arriving in the hands of end users (like fans and other music-related businesses). Your place strategy can also take a more *direct* route, starting with creators like you and flowing straight through to fans.

Whatever the method used, remember that everyone involved in the placement process or *channel of distribution* provides a different value-added function and convenience to the other at a price.

For instance, creators have the skills to record, perform, and directly market products and services for end users to enjoy. Intermediary companies generally have warehouses and/or bandwidth to handle a variety of products in varying quantities, agreements with retailers to offer promotional opportunities, and software systems for effectively processing and fulfilling orders. And end users want, demand, need, buy, and license products and services. (See the graphic "The Place Process.")

Be clear that *placement* is not necessarily the same thing as *promotion*. While placement does provide visibility in the marketplace, it takes a promotion strategy (discussed in subsequent chapters) to educate people about the features and benefits you offer. Remember, it's not enough to just put a product on a shelf and hope people stumble upon it; you have to entice them to buy it.

Now let's create an effective place plan of your own by looking at the following key topics:

1. **Reviewing Your Research, Goals, and Other Marketing Strategies**
2. **Creating a Live-Performance Place Strategy**
3. **Developing a Place Strategy for Selling Your Recordings**

Sound good? Then read on.

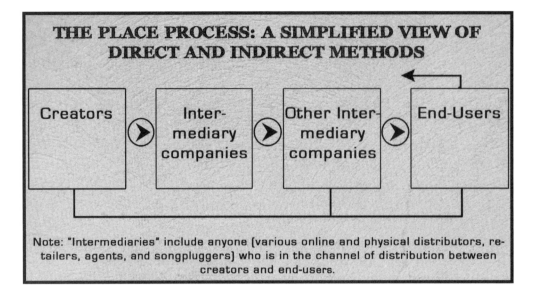

Consider How Distribution, Research, and Other Strategies Are Related

Before creating a place strategy and making decisions about where and how to place your products and services for sale and/or licensing, it is important to review your research and other marketing mix strategies once again to understand how they relate to distribution. To be sure, all the research methods, goals, and marketing mix strategies that you've already considered and selected should influence strongly the distribution channels that you ultimately choose. So let's take a look at everything from your strengths and weaknesses to your pricing strategies.

Revisit Your SWOT Analysis and Consider Your Strengths and Weaknesses

A strong understanding of your company's SWOT analysis and its strengths and weaknesses will play a big part in your place strategy decisions. If your company is lacking in professional accomplishments, financial resources, and customer demand in the marketplace, certain methods of placement involving intermediaries (agents, traditional distributors, record companies, etc.) will not be an option, because they will not be interested in working with you. Thus, your company will need to focus on more realistic and direct methods of placement (utilizing personal websites, street marketing methods, smaller local clubs, etc.) until you are able to build leverage and attract the attention of others who are willing to help.

Consider Your Customer Analysis

Considering the lifestyles of your target fans (where they hang, shop, entertain themselves, etc.) will help you make creative decisions about where to place your products and services so that they can be conveniently found and sold. If you are an alternative rock band and your fans tend to have tattoos and piercings, you can perform at tattoo conventions, sell your recordings on consignment at tattoo parlors, and strive to get placements in reality shows that document the lifestyles of tattoo artists. This is not to imply that you should rule out other channels like your typical club or record store, but rather it's to inspire ideas about how to reach your market in unique places.

Analyze the Competition

Reviewing your competitor analysis can help you to make decisions about whether to perform/sell/license your music in the same places that your competitors do—and even better, in places where they do not. On the latter note, if you can reach a market that is underserved or not served at all, you can gain a true competitive advantage. For instance, don't just look to perform your music in places where music is already being performed; seek out that cool new restaurant or hotel lounge that doesn't have entertainment, speak with management, sell the benefits, and help make arrangements. As Ralph Waldo Emerson said, "Do instead where there is no path and leave a trail."

Execute Consistent Branding

Having a clear sense of your branding strategy and what you want to convey to the public is paramount in making place decisions. Bottom line: your branding and distribution channels must be in synch. For instance, if you want to present yourself as an ultrahip and cool band but choose to play at the state fair between the cotton candy stand and the petting zoo, something is out of synch. A downtown underground party or rave might be a more selective channel. Makes sense, right? Yet you'd be surprised at the number of independent artists who make these kinds of mistakes.

Consider Product and Service "Life Cycles"

While this book generally discusses your current career strategies and "breaking into" the marketplace, having a strong understanding of your products and services over the full course of their life cycle (from introduction and growth to maturity and sales decline) can influence your decisions about place.

In the introductory stage, you will most likely be concerned with getting a significant amount of exposure in as many places as appropriate. However, further down the life cycle of your products and services, you may want to back off a bit so as to not to oversaturate the marketplace or compete with one of the newer products you release.

Match Your Place and Pricing Strategies

Finally, you must consider how your place decisions will match with the prices you intend to charge. If you're planning to open a higher-end studio and charge $200 an hour, it might make sense to open it in a more upscale part of town where people can afford those fees and feel safe when parking out front.

It is also important to keep your desired gross profit margin (the amount of revenue from a sale that actually goes in your pocket) in mind. Remember that when you involve an intermediary company in getting your products and services to end users, typically you'll have to pay a fee for their services. This isn't to say that you should avoid using these people or that your only goal in placing your music should be to make the biggest profit possible. Rather, it is to make you fully aware of the trade-offs, pros, and cons of every distribution decision you make, and to get you to think about the most effective and efficient methods for your situation.

Create a Live-Performance Place Strategy

Now that you've reexamined all your research and other strategies, it's time to create an effective and efficient place strategy for your first, and perhaps most important, product and service we'll discuss: your live-performance sets (a.k.a. your concerts, jams, shows, or whatever you want to call them).

A live-performance set is the most direct way to take your music to the marketplace. Essentially, it creates a platform for one-on-one sales.

Armed with no more than your voice, guitar, and the songs you write, you can receive payment for your performance, win over new audiences, and build a strong legion of fans (not to mention, you can have a whole hell of a lot of fun in the process—I know, I've spent years doing it myself!) This is why it is so important to have a realistic and well-thought-out live-performance place strategy.

So let's take a look at targeting local bars and clubs, considering alternative venues/events, thinking about touring, and looking ahead to hiring a talent agent.

Target Local Bars and Clubs

One of the most obvious and cost-effective channels for placing your music before a live audience is through local bars and clubs. You can promote your shows via nearby radio stations, retail stores, and local magazines, and you can motivate your friends, family members, and schoolmates to attend your gigs and help build your buzz. Using these resources effectively, you can slowly but surely win over local promoters, who will then be motivated to offer you better and bigger gigs. Yes, yes, we'll talk about touring in a minute. But to be sure, starting in your local market, building a following, and then expanding your geographic region outward is the way to go.

To conduct research for local bars and clubs near you, type something like "local live music venues" into your favorite search engine, speak with similar local bands to see where they are performing, browse your local music newspaper to get a sense of the different clubs that exist, and refer to booking resources like the Musician's Atlas (www.musiciansatlas.com) and *Billboard Musician's Guide to Touring and Promotion* (www.musiciansguide. com). Be sure to gather important information such as the bookers' names, addresses, e-mail contacts, website URLs, phone numbers, and submission procedures.

Los Angeles booker Sean Healy adds the following words of wisdom:

> When putting together your target list, just be sure to focus on venues that are consistent with your genre of music and with the number of people that you can draw reasonably. And don't be disappointed about having to play for free or starting in smaller clubs, because if you can pack smaller venues, you'll earn the respect of larger venues that will offer better nights and opening slots. You might even be able to move into paying situations much sooner. Be patient and be willing to pay your dues first.

THE FREQUENCY RULE: PERFORM ONCE PER MONTH (WITH SOME EXCEPTIONS)

So how many times should you perform per month? While there are no hard and fast rules, most people would agree that you should perform one time per month in your local market and make each gig an explosive night to remember. *Quality before quantity.* However, there may be a few exceptions to this rule that are worth examining.

- *Club Residencies:* In a club residency, a promoter will give a new band an opportunity to perform as often as four times per month (once weekly) in his venue with hopes that it can generate word-of-mouth promotion and build up local demand. But if an artist fails to promote effectively and attract a crowd, the club residency can quickly be terminated and the relationship with the promoter forever damaged.
- *Alternate Format Performances:* This is a situation where you perform two or three times monthly, but you do it using noncompeting formats of your music. For instance, an indie artist might play one territory with her full electric band the first week and then do a more intimate acoustic solo performance

in the same territory on the third week. This can be a pretty cool way to get fans to keep you at the top of their minds. However, you must monitor your audience to be absolutely sure that you're not creating competition between your own sets.

- **Dual Territory Performances:** This is a situation where you play once a month, for instance, in each of two (or more) separate and defined territories. For example, an artist in Southern California might play in Hollywood during week 1 and in Long Beach during week 3. The result is that he is playing two times monthly, and once monthly in each territory. However, to pull this off successfully, you have to promote your ass off and build up a following in two separate territories. Needless to say, this can be extremely difficult and require a lot of time, money, and energy. And finally . . .
- **Tours:** Tours are typically booked with enough distance between each venue so that there is little competition between markets. Thus, when touring, you typically play several nights in a row, and as much as 25 times per month. But remember that touring is usually not something you would do until you've built up some demand first in the local marketplace and you are at a more advanced level to expand outward.

Consider Alternative Venues and Events

Another method for placing your music before the public is to use alternative venues and events (those that are not your typical club or concert setting). Depending on the profile of your target fan and the brand identity you want to project, alternative venues can include the following: bookstores, independent record shops, art galleries, skateboard parks, military bases, conventions, and even corporate parties. All of these places are typically less competitive than your average club, and they can provide a faster route to building awareness in your local marketplace. Note the following example.

While attending the Berklee College of Music in Boston, my very own rock group rented a small house that we named the "Rock House of Waltham," built a small stage in the cellar, and threw our own wild parties that we promoted at all of the local colleges in the area. Because students perceived these events to be more private and exclusive than clubs, hundreds of people showed up. Eventually we moved this crowd into the clubs and bypassed the typical "Sunday night at 7:00 p.m." booking slot that most bands have to endure. We accomplished this by using a less competitive channel of distribution and by proving, on our own terms, that we had a following.

So, whether it is coffee shops, wineries, or some other alternative place to play, be sure to write alternative venues into your very own Marketing Plan of Attack™. You'll be really glad you did.

WHO WANTS TO GO BACK TO COLLEGE? ANSWER: YOU DO!

Colleges are a great place to perform your music, make new fans, collect e-mail addresses, sell merch, and make a few bucks in the process. Here's what you need to do: Get an updated phone list for colleges in your area (you can conduct an online search or ask another local band that might be willing to share its list with you). Phone the colleges and ask to be directed to the student activities department, and from there, the student in charge of music programming. Tell this student that you would like to be considered as part of their weekly entertainment concerts or *nooners* (colleges often have regular noontime concerts). If they like your music, you're in. Adds Chris Fletcher of Coast to Coast Booking: "And the best part about all of this is that colleges usually have budgets ranging from $150 to $750 for new music every week—which means you get paid! Can't beat that!"

Another way to break into the college circuit is through NACA, which stands for National Association for Campus Activities (www.naca.org). NACA is an organization that holds regional and national events—perfect for getting you connected with college regional bookers (and nationwide bookers too). "But while NACA's conferences are great," says Fletcher, "they can also be costly—from $1,000 to $1,500 to attend. This is not always practical for independent artists on a budget, but a few bands might team up together and split the costs. Where there is a will there is a way."

Think About Touring: Consider "Viable Places" to Perform

Yet another method for placing your music before live audiences is to consider touring. When the demand warrants it, the road can be a distribution channel of its own, connecting one location to the next. But still, some places and events will be more "viable" to play than others. What are viable places, you ask? Let's take a look.

Consider Venues Within a Short Drive

Territories and venues that are a short drive (about one to two hours away) from your hometown can certainly be viable places to perform. You'll incur minimal travel expenses and be close enough for your most dedicated fans to make the drive themselves, or jump on that "party bus" you hire.

Evaluate Places Where You Lived, Worked, Went to School

Viable places to perform could also include nearby cities and venues where band members have lived formerly, went to school, or worked, and still know a lot of people. This makes it far easier to promote the show and get people to attend.

Focus on Venues Where You Can Gig Swap

Viable places to perform could also include areas and venues where you have befriended other bands that are willing to *gig swap* with you (they invite you to play on a show and expose you to their fans and territory, and vice versa). The built-in audiences associated with bands with which you gig swap provide you with an advantage when traveling outside of your comfort zone, where drawing fans is more difficult.

Try Venues in the Proximity of Where You're Getting Some "Love"

Venues in the proximity of stores that are selling your recordings, stations that are broadcasting your music, and/or publications that are writing about your act are also viable places to perform. You can draw a healthy crowd more easily by getting your connections to hang posters in their stores, giving away tickets on their radio shows, and mentioning you in the "events" sections of their papers.

Consider Places That Are Part of Anchor Events

Viable places to perform could also include those situations located in and around *anchor events* (i.e., established, preexisting "happenings" that already attract large numbers of industry people and enthusiasts from around the world, such as the South by Southwest (a.k.a. SXSW) music convention in Austin, Texas.

Mayfield, a Los Angeles independent band, drove from Los Angeles to the popular Sundance Film Festival in Park City, Utah, to perform an industry showcase. While at the festival, they also played at a number of hotel parties for various film directors and music supervisors, and they picked up a few more gigs for entertainment-based companies in attendance as well. This eventually landed the band a placement in an internationally released film with a major star. Pretty cool!

Think About Venues That Are Part of Festival Tours

Finally, promoters of major festivals like Bonnaroo (www.bonnaroo.com), Vans Warped Tour (www.warpedtour.com), Voodoo Music Festival (www.voodoomusicfest.com), and the Sasquatch Festival (www.sasquatchfestival.com) may offer deserving local bands a shot at playing secondary stages and even opening slots on the main stages. The indie band Ghostland Observatory went from playing small clubs in Austin to performing at several of these festivals in just two years.

If you think you're ready, you can send the promoters of these events a press kit (physical or electronic) and show them you are generating demand. You might also encourage your fans to get on the festivals' websites and spread some love in the forums. Another way to get on the bill of a festival is to check out the websites of certain sponsors of the event to see if they are holding a competition. One such sponsor, the string manufacturer Ernie Ball (www.ernieball.com), hosts an impressive battle of the bands and awards the winner with a week of dates on the Vans Warped Tour.

And when the above methods don't get you on a festival tour, musician-turned-manager Rob "Blasko" Nicholson says *you should tour any way you can.* That's right! He suggests that you load up in your van, follow the tour, and play out in the parking lots (acoustically, or whatever you can arrange) as the fans are heading into the venue. But just be sure that your musicians have what it takes (i.e., the balls) to fully execute a grueling strategy such as the one previously mentioned. The last thing you'll want to deal with are wimpy musicians who can't hang on the road.

AFTERTHOUGHT: TOURING DECISIONS AND COSTS Transportation, trailers, equipment cases, gas, tolls, hotels, insurance, food, tips, personnel, and miscellaneous expenses are all important items to include in a *tour budget* when planning to hit the road. Weigh these decisions and expenses against your profits or losses, and see if hitting the road makes sense. Hey, sometimes you just gotta get in the van and make it work in any way you can, but by first creating a budget you'll at least know what you're up against.

Look Ahead Toward Hiring a Talent Agent

And finally, talent agents are yet another source of distribution that is instrumental in getting your live performances in front of an audience. An agent sells your act to venue promoters, negotiates fees, collects deposits, routes the direction of a tour, and helps decide for whom you should open.

But most professional talent agents of national caliber won't work with you until you prove you can book your own gigs and generate "healthy" fees. Why? Agents get paid a commission based on the money taken in at your gigs. As the late Ian Copeland told me in an interview for *The Musician's Handbook,* "No fees for the band and no commission for the agent equals no agent!" In any case, it's still wise to know about agents and research with whom you'd like to work one day.

To conduct research, ask successful bands in your area for recommendations, and jot these names down. Browse resources like *The Booking Agency Directory* (www.pollstar.com) and *International Talent and Touring Guide* (www.billboard.com) to read up on companies that represent new bands in your genre. Also, be sure to prepare the proper "tools" to pitch yourself to an agency by keeping detailed logs related to all your performances. These logs should contain the names of the venues at which you perform, the number of fans you draw, and the amounts you're paid.

That's pretty much all you can do for right now in regard to placing your live performances. So let's turn our attention to placing your recorded albums (CDs, vinyl, USB flash drives, download cards, digital downloads, streams, and more).

SEVEN TIPS TO BOOKING YOUR OWN GIGS IN CLUBS

Keep in mind that the best way to get gigs is often to pick up the phone and do it yourself. Consider the following:

1. Put together a list of your target venues. Find the name of the booker, number, e-mail, and best time to make contact. You can use a program like Microsoft Excel to create an organized database.

2. Call or e-mail the club or promoter with a clear idea of your style, the bands you sound like, and the dates you'd like to perform. Promoters are busy people, but don't be too afraid—they're people! Be patient and pleasantly persistent; just don't be a pain in the butt.

3. Keep good records of all correspondence, including the date and time you called and what the promoter said. You don't want to call the club back in a week when he asked you to call in a month.

4. Be prepared to send a press kit containing a disc with three of your best songs. Also include a bio that outlines the clubs at which you've already performed (if you've already performed) and your average nightly draw. Also, establish a personal website or social networking account where promoters can get all the information they need about you in one click. You might also consider utilizing a service like Sonicbids (www.sonicbids.com) to establish an *electronic press kit* (EPK).

5. Let the promoter know that you're available at a moment's notice to fill in for cancellations. It might also help to have at least two sets worth of music prepared, just in case you're asked to perform longer. (Learning a few cover songs could help.)

6. Be sure to work out the logistical aspects of performing live, such as how you'll move your gear. Be sure to have sturdy cases that allow you to carry your equipment conveniently. Also visit some of the van and truck rental places in your area and ask them about the requirements to rent from them.

7. Remember that moving up in the club circuit and expanding your territory into touring is not only about how good you are, but how many people you can draw. Promote your asses off and make every show an "event" not to be missed. Create hype, throw amazing after-parties, invite tons of beautiful people, and involve a charity that you and your audience care about. Just be amazing and people will keep on coming back for more.

Develop a Place Strategy for Selling Your Recorded Albums

Moving on from placing your live performance sets, now let's create a distribution strategy for your recorded albums (CDs, vinyl, USB flash drives, downloads, download cards, streaming music, or DVDs). Distribution channels might include live-performance venues, "the streets," the Internet, brick-and-mortar retailers, and alternative stores. Let's look at each.

Distribute Your Recorded Music via Live-Performance Venues

Live-performance venues might be the most *direct* and *effective* place for DIY artists to sell their recorded albums and build local awareness. Whether you perform in clubs, in bookstores, or at conventions, the thrill and excitement associated with live-performance venues can help generate more album sales than any other place. Thus, it is essential that you be prepared to take the following three steps:

1. **Set Up Your Booth:** To set up an attractive sales booth, get a sturdy, large table where your records and other products can be displayed neatly. You might design a vinyl sales banner featuring your band name to hang from the front of your table, utilize attractive lighting such as LED lights and lava lamps, and hang glow-in-the-dark posters that announce your products and prices. You might also lay out your MacBook computer with headphones so that your fans can "try before they buy." And finally, you can even utilize a "mobile merch booth" by walking around the club with a carrying case similar to what vendors use at baseball games. Yeah, I know the latter idea is a crazy one. But crazy things usually get crazy good results.

2. **Accept Payment:** To accommodate every consumer, be ready to accept several different forms of payment. For a convenient and reasonable method for processing credit cards, the independent distributor CD Baby (www.cdbaby.com) offers a credit card swiper program that enables you to process cards anywhere and at any time, for a small fee. Or you can use convenient devices by companies like Square Inc. (squareup.com) or PayPal (www.paypal.com) that plug right into your own smartphone. As for processing checks, be sure to get the customer's driver's license, address, and current phone number in case the check bounces and you have to contact him or her. And while on the topic of payment, it may also be a good idea to buy a receipt book at a local office supply store so that you can provide a copy of the sale to your customer and keep one for your own records. I've found books providing carbon copies to be the best.

3. **Hire a Staff:** Finally, you'll have to hire a crew to manage your booth and make sales. Some prospects will want to buy your products automatically after your show, and others will need more convincing. Seek out a cute or handsome friend or fan with the retail experience and conversational skills that can lead to plentiful sales. I know one LA band that hires beautiful fashion and hair models from a local arts school to entice sales. I know another artist who has his salespeople dress up in scary masks to attract attention. And finally, I know another artist, a rapper, who jumps behind his sales table after every show to sell his recordings, sign autographs, and collect e-mail addresses. If you think this is selling out, I call it *buying in*! You can't be afraid to sell yourself.

AFTERTHOUGHT: PAY A HALL FEE TO A CLUB? Remember that in the distribution channel, everyone provides a value-added function at a cost. Club promoters, for instance, provide the space, location, security, parking, and liquor licenses. Thus, promoters will often ask for a *hall fee* of up to 35 percent of sales (less state sales taxes) for letting you sell your products under their roof. Just be sure to ask the venue owner/booker about this in advance of performing your next gig.

Place Your Recorded Music Guerrilla Marketing Style via the Streets

The next method we'll discuss for selling your recorded music is hitting the streets! I've seen artists join the ranks of street performers, place their products at flea markets, and even walk the city streets to distribute their music. Let's take a look at each of these methods.

Join the Ranks of Street Performers

Street performers are essentially street retailers. With guitars firmly in hand and records proudly displayed on city sidewalks, they make healthy sales. In Boston, Massachusetts, artists perform in Harvard Square. In Santa Monica, California, artists perform on the Third Street Promenade. And in Stockholm, Sweden, they perform in Old Town Square. These street performers stimulate curiosity, draw large crowds, and excite fans. Los Angeles–based street performer John West even progressed to signing a major label deal. Pretty cool! Just be sure to check with your local police department or city hall. Performing on the streets and making noise typically requires a small yearly fee and license. As I said before, everyone in the distribution channel provides a function at a cost.

Place Your Products at Flea Markets

Flea markets, outdoor locations where sellers converge to sell their goods, can be another channel for placing your recordings and making sales. Flea markets are everywhere, in every city and every town, and they are held on the weekends when people are less stressed and spending time with friends and family. As long as you feel your target fan frequents these types of events, flea markets are a smart move. For a small fee you can set up a table, lay out your products, and jam your music through your laptop computer. One student of mine said he made a killing doing this. In his words, "We became the soundtrack of the flea market." Be sure to check out a flea market near you. And finally . . .

Walk the City Streets

Walking the city streets with a box of your recordings and an iPod player is our last guerrilla strategy. You can jot down several key locations in your area (sporting venues, shopping malls, main streets) and get face-to-face with your target fans. In Hollywood, hip hop artists literally walk up and down Hollywood Boulevard and sell to tourists and other folks. Rapper Master P once sold records successfully at service stations.

But I have to stress that in order to be successful with street sales, you must focus on selling to your target audience. Selling your rap record to an old couple who are more annoyed by you than anything else might put a few bucks in your pocket, but it's not going to help you get your name out there and build a following. Rather, your record will most likely be thrown in the trash. So be smart!

Get Your Recorded Music Online

Moving away from offline distribution methods to the second-to-last placement method we'll discuss in this chapter, the Internet is perhaps the most *convenient* channel for independent artists like you to place recorded music, both in physical and digital format. With little more than a computer, Internet connection, Web hosting service and Web address, artists can make their recordings, videos, and other products available in personal Web stores, on mobile devices, on social networks, and with online DIY friendly distributors. Let's take a look.

Use Your Personal Website to Distribute Directly to Fans

Remember that you can use your personal website as a storefront to directly distribute your products and services and make sales to your target audience. We discussed building a personal website in chapter 10, but recapping and adding some new information specifically focused on distribution is definitely important in this chapter. Just be sure your site is uniquely branded and conveniently laid out as follows:

- *News and Social Networking Links:* With performance schedules, press updates, and current gossip to help get your visitors' attention to your store.
- *About:* Including your company's history, product reviews, company policies, shipping information, and money-back guarantees to build sales credibility.
- *Media:* With music samples, videos clips, and product graphics to hold their interest and entice them to buy.
- *Contact:* Including an e-mail address and phone number to eliminate ordering concerns and help customers make a decision to buy.
- *Links:* Including more established online retailers to provide alternative places to make sales.

- *Mailing List:* With fields to capture e-mails and other personal information to facilitate ongoing communications and customer service. And most importantly . . .
- *Store:* To offer your records securely in both physical and digital formats, and provide detailed ordering, processing, and logistical information to get customers to take action.

On the latter note, remember that a number of services and application software or "Web widgets" (such as Bandcamp and Topspin Media) can make it easy for you to create a store and sell your recordings online. E-commerce services (such as PayPal) and customized "shopping carts" (such as osCSS and OpenCart) can help you process credit cards and make sales. You can also easily allow your customers to pay by check or money order by providing your mailing address and allowing them to connect with you the old-fashioned way—by snail mail.

For more information on e-commerce, check out Janice Reynolds's *The Complete E-commerce Book: Design, Build and Maintain a Successful Web-Based Business.* By the way, we'll discuss websites more in subsequent chapters when we discuss promotion.

AFTERTHOUGHT: GET A MOBILE SITE Remember that distribution is all about providing convenience for your target audience. That being said, you might also consider getting your website optimized for viewing on small mobile devices. This will help make viewing and ordering your products from your site far easier for your target customers on the go. For further details, investigate services like GoDaddy's dotMobi feature (www. godaddy.com) and mobiSiteGalore (www.mobisitegalore.com).

Get Your Own Mobile Phone App Built

Another method for placing your recorded music online is to get your own mobile app. Since nearly everyone accesses the Internet with mobile phones and tablet computers these days, an app can serve as an efficient form of distribution.

An *app* is a computer software application meant to give customers direct and easy access to your company. As long as you can get your fans to download it, your app can serve as a direct reminder that your Web store and promotional information are just a touch a way.

Says Kether Gallu-Badat of Latchkey Recordings, "Even when you think your band is just starting out and no one cares, a cool app can set you apart from other artists. You can either sell your app or just give it away for free. Decide if an app is right for you and write it into your plan."

To get your very own app built, check out companies like Mobile Roadie (www.mobileroadie.com) that offer free trials and rates starting at $99 monthly. Pretty cool stuff.

Sell from Social Networks

While social networks are typically seen as promotional tools to draw fans to your personal website, they can also be used as your primary website and yet another place to sell your recorded music online. You can usually embed or paste Web widgets that enable you to sell music (such as the ones provided by Disc Makers, BandPage, and others), or you can simply post links on your social networks to other services where you sell your music online, such as iTunes or CD Baby. For a detailed list of social networking sites, search Wikipedia (www. wikipedia.com) for its "list of social networking sites."

AFTERTHOUGHT: SELL FROM SUBSCRIPTION SERVICES Bob Moczydlowsky of Topspin Media says that his company is investigating methods for selling music directly from social networks and music subscription services. In other words, as music is being streamed, consumers can simply click and buy the song (and other band products) instantly without going anywhere else. Just keep your eyes open for new developments happening online every day.

Use an Online "DIY Friendly" Distributor

A final method of online distribution we'll discuss is the DIY-friendly distributor (e.g., CD Baby, TuneCore, The Orchard). These are companies that have been approved to place independent artists of all levels on popular digital download and streaming sites (like iTunes, Rhapsody, and Spotify). In some cases, DIY-friendly distributors can get you into the databases of retail stores across the country too—but that's another issue).

In return for a small share of the sales and/or a small fee for their services, these online-friendly distributors will help prepare your digital files to meet the varying specs of the many stores that exist online, will help you get both an ISRC Code (International Standard Recording Code) and a bar code, necessary for identifying singles and albums and tracking royalty payments, and may offer other promotional opportunities and services. You can choose any of the number of existing companies, but you should always start with the more popular distributors with strong sales and fulfillment services, solid reputations for paying royalties when due, and highly trafficked websites (such as the ones mentioned previously).

Just keep in mind that DIY-friendly distributors typically request the *exclusive digital distribution rights* of your recordings, since no two DIY-friendly distributors can digitally distribute the same recordings on the same download sites. To decide which company will work the best for you, be sure to ask your network of friends and local artists for their recommendations. And *before* signing any agreement, always be prepared to ask the proper business professional, such as a consultant, manager, or attorney, for advice.

So that's it for online distribution. Now, moving on to the last placement method in this chapter, let's discuss the placement of your recordings in physical stores.

Place Your Recorded Music with "Brick and Mortar" Retailers

The last method we'll discuss for placing your recorded music (and for placing video content too, such as live concert DVDs) are brick-and-mortar retailers. For our purposes, a brick-and-mortar retailer is any walk-in store on the street, including record shops (which are becoming extinct) and alternative shops (like sports stores, gift stores, and clothing outlets, which are alive and well).

To place your recorded albums in brick-and-mortar stores, you can set up retail consignments, consider a large traditional independent distributor, or think about creating a deal with an independent record company. These are all discussed briefly below. Hang in there, we're almost done.

Set Up Retail Consignments

You can distribute your recorded music through select retail stores in your area by setting up *consignment agreements*. Consignments facilitate the process of leaving your records in stores and collecting payment after they sell.

While consignment may provide a means for you to sell a few units, don't expect to sell hundreds. Rather, view consignments as a means to build relationships with local store owners who may also be willing to hang up your flyers in their stores, play your music over their sound systems, allow you to do in-store live performances, and recommend you to customers.

To set up consignment agreements in your area, Randall Kennedy, a former marketing representative for Warner Bros. Records, advises that you should visit the larger indie record stores like Amoeba ((www.amoeba. com) and Newbury Comics (www.newburycomics.com) but also focus on smaller boutiques or "mom and pop" stores in your area. Notes Kennedy, "Smaller stores will feel more beholden to support local artists."

You can also consign your recorded music, videos, and other products in non-record stores. These stores include bookstores, coffee shops, sporting good outlets, fine and folk art galleries, and more. Derek Sivers, founder of CD Baby (a successful online retailer), suggests that you set up non-record store consignment agreements directly with your fans or other like bands in your area that draw a similar audience to you.

Just don't set up more consignment agreements than you can effectively promote. Remember that if your records go unsold for several months, you'll likely be asked by the consignors to pick them up, and your deals will be terminated. And you don't want this to happen to you! Right? So be conservative.

EIGHT STEPS TO CONSIGNING YOUR CDS, VINYL, DVDS, AND MORE

1. Compile a list of local stores by typing words like "independent record stores" or "skateboard shops" into your Internet browser and by asking similar bands in your area for referrals.
2. Call each store, get the manager's name, and ask about their consignment policies.
3. Put together a press kit (with a biography, news clippings, and press release) that shows you're "attracting attention" in your community and that your music is in demand. The greater the demand, the bigger the benefit to the store.
4. Visit with each store's manager and be prepared to sell yourself. Bring your press kit, recordings, posters, and an attractive display box that holds your recordings. Also bring an iPod or smartphone with full foam headphones (not the ones you stick "inside" your ears) so that the manager can listen to your music on the spot.
5. Don't be pushy, but if the manager is really impressed with your band, you might convince him or her to buy a few records outright, place your music in *discretionary listening posts* (where consumers can sample your music), and book you for an *in-store performance*.
6. Put together a simple consignment agreement that indicates the number of records you're leaving, the date you're leaving them, and the price *per unit* you want to receive. Then get the manager's signature. Note that sample agreements can be found at www.bobbyborg.com or by searching on the Web.
7. Tell your fans to visit the stores and buy your record. You can even hand out postcards and provide links on your website to these stores. Let the stores' managers know about your promotional efforts.
8. Finally, check back every few weeks with each store and speak with the manager. Don't bother sales representatives, who will typically be unfamiliar with your agreement. Be persistent, but be pleasant. So that's about it for consignments. Good luck!

Seek a Large "Traditional" Independent Distributor

Depending on the demand for your music in the marketplace, traditional independent distributors just might provide another channel for placing your recordings into brick-and-mortar retail stores (and other places too). For decades, their general purpose was to get records into smaller record and alternative stores, but their function has now expanded to include online distribution and even placement in film/TV/videogames.

Traditional independent distributors typically buy product in large quantities and then sell it in smaller amounts to various stores. They provide a warehouse function for storing recordings or DVDs around the country, fulfill orders, handle accounting functions, prepare digital file formats for the varying needs of online retailers, and even set up retail marketing programs (listening booths and product positioning in stores).

Nail and Redeye are good examples of reputable independent distributors. Some of the larger independent distributors (which, by the way, are owned by major record labels) include Alternative Distribution Alliance (Warner), Red (Sony/BMG), and Fontana (Universal).

While getting a traditional independent distributor may be on your radar, just remember that closing a deal with one is more difficult than you think. Distributors work mostly with multi-artist labels that are more established. In fact, to get with a larger traditional independent distributor, you might need the following:

- Verifiable sales data (such as tax returns, credit card slips, and other reports) to show that you're already making substantial sales.
- Press samples to show that your company has garnered a strong buzz.
- Finances to buy into special marketing programs arranged by the distributors.
- Experienced industry representation (like a consultant, attorney, or manager) to show that you're well guided. And . . .
- A realistic and professional marketing plan (like the one you're learning to write by reading this book) to show distributors that you really know your business!

Without some, or all, of the above things, seeking a large traditional distributor may not even be an option for you. Sorry folks, but that's just the cold hard facts. But hey, look at the bright side: getting one of these distributors can surely be something you work toward down the road. Right? Good! Now let's move on.

AFTERTHOUGHT: BAR CODES, RETAIL STORES, AND PROVING SALES When selling your album in retail stores, you'll need a UPC bar code placed on your packaging to identify, track, and share information. The most prudent approach is to obtain a *unique company prefix number* from GS1US (www.gs1us.org) and create an *item number* and bar code. But since this is not the most affordable approach, you can contact a company like Disc Makers (www.discmakers.com) that can use its own company prefix number to issue you an item number and bar code at a small charge. To receive sales and other data about an album as it passes through scanners in retail stores, you must then register that album's bar code (and your company) with Nielsen SoundScan (www.nielsen.com). SoundScan can be quite expensive, so be sure to ask about affordable subscriber packages for indie artists.

Think About a Deal with an Independent Label

Finally, while this book focuses essentially on independent and do-it-yourself musicians, it's worth discussing a few of the ways that the more advanced artists reading this book can contract with an indie label to help place recordings into brick-and-mortar stores—and, for that matter, everywhere else too.

Indie labels can come in all shapes and sizes—from smaller labels run out of a garage with a sole proprietor and a few employees, to a larger label (even owned by a major) run out of a fancy office and with a large staff. Most relevant here, established independent labels typically have relationships with regional or national traditional independent distributors that can place your recording in all types of stores.

An indie label might sign an artist to a recording deal (where they provide full financing for recordings, tours, and videos for several years), a pressing and distribution agreement (whereby they license your already finished masters to manufacture, distribute, and provide some marketing), or a *pass through agreement* (where the label simply distributes your recorded product for you.)

But as previously stated, these deals are for more advanced artists who have already generated a great deal of momentum on their own. This means they have already sold thousands of records, built an e-mail list of thousands of fans, created an impressive Internet presence, and received a modest amount of press and radio play. Without these accomplishments under your belt, *you're a long ways off from a label deal*. But don't let that get you down: with all the advice offered in this book, you're sure to attract label attention one day. Just keep the faith and keep pushing forward. And remember this reassuring proverb: "The mighty oak tree was once a small nut that held its ground." Good luck!

=MARKETING PLAN TEMPLATE=

Use the template below, or a template like it, to help you craft important information that you will use in your Marketing Plan of Attack™. For additional help, be sure to refer to the marketing plan example below, the chapter on assembling your plan, and the complete plan provided in the back of this book.

Your Company Place Strategy Template (Part 1)

Use this template to craft your product/service place strategy ideas. When formatting your marketing plan, you can remove the questions and just keep the headers and your answers. Be thorough! Don't just answer the questions below. Be sure to review the chapter to get specific ideas for a variety of placement methods. Utilize the points below that best apply to you.

Live-Performance Sets: Where will you perform (in clubs, alternative venues, or other)? What are the specific names of these places? Do you have any tour plans (anchor events, gig swapping, etc.)? Will you use an agent? If so, who? Note: Just be sure to label each strategy (clubs, anchor events, etc.) clearly, as I have done in the marketing plan sample below.

Recordings (CDs, USB Flash Drives, Vinyl, Etc.): Do you intend to sell recordings at your live performances? If so, how? Will you set up consignment agreements in stores? If so, which stores? Will you sell from your personal website and/or indie-friendly distributors? Many methods were discussed in the chapter, so which will you use? And remember, wherever you place your recordings, label each strategy clearly.

Videos: Will you distribute your DVD videos via your live performances, set up consignment deals at local stores, or sell them from your Internet site or social network? These are just a few of the things that you can do. Label your ideas carefully.

=MARKETING PLAN EXAMPLE=

Now here's an abridged marketing plan example for our band Rally the Tribes, to help you put together your own place strategy. Note that only some of the band's offerings are addressed here, but you'll have to list all products and services when writing your plan.

PLACE STRATEGY
a) Live-Performance Set
★Clubs: RTT will perform at local LA clubs like the Key Club and specifically attempt to set up a monthly residency with this club.
★Alternative Venue Performances: RTT will perform at college frat parties at UCLA and USC, small film festivals (such as the Silver Lake Film Festival and the Temecula Valley Film Festival), and at corporate holiday parties (such as Vortex Skate Shop in Hollywood and Truth Clothing on Melrose).
★Anchor Events: RTT's founders will invest in attending and performing at SXSW, Sundance Film Festival, and Winter Music Festival in Miami. They will also play at select anchor gigs and local clubs and raves.

[Note: Between RTT gigs, founders Kennedy Robert Jr. and K. Luther Martin will also make select appearances as "RTT Digital" in DJ and rave clubs (like Vanguard and LAX) to spin a short set and promote RTT shows.]

b) 12-Song Album: *War and Police*

★ Live-Performance Venues: We will create a merch booth and sell product at live performances at clubs, political rallies, and other places we play. We'll accept cash, check, and credit card (using Square on our smartphones).

★ Online Personal Website: We will build a Web store at www.rallythetribes.com, where physical records will be sold utilizing the e-commerce services of PayPal and the US Postal Service. We will also provide a link to iTunes where *War and Police* will be available for digital download.

★ Online DIY-Friendly Distributor: RTT will utilize CD Baby to get on sites like iTunes, Rhapsody, and Spotify.

★ Brick-and-Mortar (Record Store) Consignments: RTT will set up a consignment agreement with Amoeba Music in Hollywood, California.

★ Brick-and-Mortar (Non–Record Store) Consignments: RTT will set up consignments with local college bookstores (like UCLA, USC, and Loyola), as well as hip fashion boutiques on Melrose, like Truth Clothing and others.

c) DVD Soundtrack-Umentary™: *Occupy World*

★ Live-Performance Venues: Using their merch booth, RTT will sell their DVD film at live performances; they will accept cash, checks, and credit cards (using Square on their smartphones).

★ Online Personal Website: Using our store at www.rallythetribes.com, we will sell our DVD by accepting checks and payments through PayPal, and by mailing physical product via the United States Postal Service.

Etc.

13

Establish a Place Strategy, Part 2

Distributing Your Merch and Songs Effectively for Sale and/or License

You already know from reading chapter 12 that creating a place strategy is the process of making your products and services *convenient* for users to find, buy, and/or license. You focused on placing two key revenue generators: your live performances and recordings. Now in this chapter, let's focus on creating a place strategy for your merch and songs—all to achieve the goals of your marketing plan and beyond!

A well-thought-out place strategy can help you do the following:

- **Establish and familiarize your merch and songs in the marketplace.**
- **Give customers what they need and want, when they need and want it.**
- **Serve markets that competitors aren't reaching.**
- **Generate healthy profits and stay in business.**

Remember that your place strategy can take an *indirect* route utilizing the resources of intermediary distributors and/or a more *direct* route flowing straight through to fans. In either case, the marketing mix strategies and research techniques you've already considered and selected should influence your decisions. For instance, your pricing strategy and desired *gross profit margin* should help determine the various intermediaries with whom you'll arrange distribution agreements for your albums. And your customer research and *psychographic data* should offer ideas about where you'll place and sell directly your merch. You see, as I've said before and will say again, *everything in marketing really is interrelated.*

So now let's build upon your place strategy by examining these key topics:

1. **Placing Your Merch Effectively for Healthy Sales**
2. **Placing Your Songs and Instrumentals in Film/TV/Games and More**

Sound cool? Then let's get started with creating a place strategy for your merch.

Place Your Merch Effectively for Healthy Sales

Merch includes the T-shirts, hats, stickers, programs, posters, pictures, bags, hoodies, and other goods that bear your company's name, likeness, and logo. When placed effectively, merch can be the most immediate and reliable source of revenue, especially early on in your career when you must give away records and perform for free to build awareness.

The three most common places for distributing your merch are your live performances, personal website stores, and a traditional merchandising company.

Distribute Merch at Your Live Performances

Placing your merch at your live shows is an effective method for making sales. You can lay out all of your merch products on a sturdy table or tack them up on a tall, attractive standing display. The more attractive you make your merch booth, and the more variety in payment options you offer, the better.

While I've already mentioned the process of distribution at your live performances (when placing recordings), one thing you must specifically remember when distributing merch is to make sure to know how much product to have on hand in the venue. This is more challenging than handling recordings, because typically you'll have a variety of merch styles and sizes to consider.

Bob Fierro of Zebra Marketing says you want to have enough variety on hand (including designs, sizes, and colors) to meet the demands of your target audience, but not so much that you're hauling box after box in and out of the venue. The space allocated to you in most venues is limited, and you don't want product to get lost, stolen, or mixed up with the merch of other bands selling on the same night. Make sure to hire a competent sales rep who knows how to keep track of merchandise, count inventory into and out of the venue, and make healthy sales each night. You'll be glad you did.

Distribute Your Merch Online

The next best channel for distributing your merch is your personal website. You can include attractive graphics showing off your products, detailed information outlining your money-back guarantees, and e-commerce systems that provide secure methods of payment for your customers. Just be sure to have a variety of different products in stock and ready to ship as soon as your fans request them. And remember to think carefully about what your target fans really want and need, so you don't end up with boxes of unsold product gathering dust around your apartment.

Another way to distribute your merch online and reduce your costs and inventory is to use *print on demand* companies. These are online businesses that will literally manufacture and ship your products for you as your fans order them. In fact, they will even host a Web page for you on their server where your fans can view graphics of your offerings and place orders. While some people may feel that the quality of the products are subpar, and the percentage that the artist is charged from each sale is rather high, print-on-demand companies definitely offer a nice solution to the DIY artist on a low budget. Bottom line: you can have a complete line of merch products for sale within minutes without any upfront costs. A few companies you should check out are CafePress (www.cafepress.com), Spreadshirt (www.spreadshirt.com), and Zazzle (www.zazzle.com).

AFTERTHOUGHT: IRON-ON SOLUTIONS When selling your merch online, you might provide a high-resolution file of your company's logo on your site and suggest that fans download it onto special transfer paper that allows them to iron it on their own shirts. This is definitely a low-budget merch solution, but it works really well. Why not give it a try?

Contract with a Traditional Merchandising Company

The last method we'll discuss for distributing your merch is to contract with a merchandising company.

Merchandising companies (or merchandisers) typically offer advances and royalties in return for the rights to manufacture and sell your products at stores and performances. Merchandisers work most typically with extremely successful artists or soon-to-be-signed up-and-coming acts that are preparing to release a recording and embark on a major tour.

If you don't fit either of the above descriptions, you should at least study the current players—because you'll one day be ready for a deal. Bob Fierro of Zebra Marketing suggests that you start your research by looking at major merchandisers (like Signatures Network), midlevel merchandisers (like Zebra and Band Merch), and smaller Internet-based companies that seem to "pop up" far too fast to even keep track of.

Well, folks, that's all I have to say about merch. Now let's take a look at placing your music in film/TV/games and more.

Place Your Songs and Instrumentals in Film/TV/Games and More

With all of the developments in digital technology and home recording gear today, musicians are empowered to record high-quality recordings of their original songs (with training, of course) and pitch them for placement in film, television, video games, and other mediums of distribution. A few placements in a film or TV show can get things rolling for your career, help build your band's story, and even generate more income than trying to sell a thousand downloaded albums.

There are numerous methods that can be used for placing your music. What follows are several of these methods, including shooting for placements in student films, placing your music with music libraries, utilizing a music placement service—and so much more. Let's take a look.

AFTERTHOUGHT: INDIE SUCCESS STORY When Staten Island indie artist Ingrid Michaelson got a placement on the television show *Grey's Anatomy*, her career took off. Her songs have been used in a substantial number of successful shows, such as *One Tree Hill*, *Scrubs*, and *90210*, and she's even been asked to visit talk shows like *Ellen* and *The Tonight Show*. Perhaps you'll be the next success story.

Shoot for Placements in Student Films and Video Games

A great place to begin your search for music placements is at your local college. Budding student film directors and game developers have access to expensive equipment, knowledgeable and connected staff, and other useful resources. All students have final projects they must turn in and all students need music for these projects. While they often have access to royalty-free music made accessible through their colleges, many students want to use authentic local bands.

In Los Angeles, I literally walked my entire UCLA class of DIY musicians over to the film school during an open lecture and introduced them to the film students by simply asking, "Who needs music for their films?" Everyone in the film school raised their hand and exchanged numbers with my class. Many of my students went on to contribute music for documentaries and small films that, in fact, went on to be shown in popular film festivals. You can't beat that.

To seek placements in student films and games, you can simply type in the keywords "[your city] + film school" or "[your city] + game schools" into your Internet search engine and make a list of the institutions that have film/design/art/animation departments. In the Los Angeles area, you'll find the Los Angeles Film School (www.lafilm.com), USC School of Cinematic Arts (cinema.usc.edu), and UCLA School of Theater, Film and Television (www.tft.ucla.edu). In New York you'll find NYU's Tisch School of the Arts (about. tisch.nyu.edu), and in Nashville you'll find Watkins College of Art, Design, and Film (www.watkins.edu). Give these schools and the institutions like them in your area a call, and ask to speak with the program director. Then offer your original songs at no cost for use in their students' projects. You'll build a résumé of placements—and, more importantly, you'll nurture valuable relationships that will one day lead to paying gigs.

AFTERTHOUGHT: READ ABOUT IT IN THE PAPERS Jeff Gray, director at Fox Sports, says that you might also consider checking out sites like Craigslist (www.craigslist.com), where often you can find advertisements from student and indie directors looking for music.

Place Directly with Directors and Producers by Networking at Festivals

Attending film festivals and game conventions to network with industry professionals is another possible method for getting placements in film, television, and games. You really never know what film director, music supervisor, or game developer will be attending these events.

Just be ready to describe the vibe and mood of your music in as few words as possible and to understand specifically which television shows, films, or games—as well as what types of moods (love, high-energy car chase, etc.)—are best suited for your music. Remember that getting film and TV placements are all about how your music can fulfill a *need*, and how your music can *fit* the film or show, *not how the show can fit your music.* This is confirmed by the words of Mason Cooper, a music supervisor and soundtrack consultant, who said, "I'm in the film business, not the music business."

To find a list of festivals and conferences to attend, simply conduct a search on the Internet. In Los Angeles, you'll find the American Film Institute Festival (www.afi.com) and the Temecula Valley International Film and Music Festival (www.tviff.com). Both hold annual events at affordable costs, and if you're on a tight budget, they provide volunteer opportunities too.

You can also look into attending the bigger film festivals, such as the Sundance Film Festival (www.sundance.org/festival/) in Park City, Utah, and others like it, but of course, this requires a bigger investment of time and money.

Finally, a great place to network with game developers from around the world is at the E3 Expo (www.e3expo.com). The E3 Expo website states that it is the world's most important annual gathering for "everything that is interactive entertainment—it's where business gets done, connections are made, and the future of the industry is revealed." Sounds awesome! Now be sure to check out other game conventions too by first conducting a search online.

AFTERTHOUGHT: LOOK FOR POSTED OPPORTUNITIES TO GET INTO GAMES At the time of this writing, one famous game, Rock Band, allows indie artists to upload their songs to the Xbox Live Marketplace, set a price (from $.50 to $3.00), and earn a royalty on sales. It requires some production work, such as making MIDI charts for each instrument in the song, but their software shows you how. Visit *Rock Band*'s website, and look for placement opportunities with other games as well.

Think "Outside the Box" and Uncover Alternative Placement Opportunities

Possible methods for placing your music will also come from just getting creative and thinking outside the box. There are literally thousands of places where music is used and needed. Just don't be afraid to pursue the less obvious and indirect channels you might identify. Here are few examples:

- *Example 1: Actors' Reels:* One student of mine at UCLA understood that his demographic audience consisted of actors. With further research, he also discovered that actors use demonstration reels featuring personal footage and that these reels included music. Digging even deeper, my student realized that when actors auditioned for upcoming parts (in films and shows) and they submitted their reels to industry professionals (casting agents and directors), his music would get further exposed and even licensed. As it turns out, my student licensed his music to actors at a small fee and licensed a few songs in low-budget documentary films. Pretty clever.

- *Example 2: MMA Events:* Another student of mine knew that his fans enjoyed both World Wrestling Association and Mixed Martial Arts events. Thus, he decided to reach out directly to these organizations to uncover possible placement opportunities. As it turned out, the MMA was putting together a compilation of fights to be aired on cable TV and then sold in a DVD, and it was looking for hard rock music. Bingo! Needless to say, my student got placed. Now that's putting yourself out there and getting the job done!

- *Example 3: European Advertising Agencies:* In another "outside the box" story, a friend of mine who immigrated to the United States from Holland decided to pitch ad agencies in his homeland. He did this by positioning his company as creating sounds of California featuring the best Los Angeles musicians. Working out of Venice Beach and corresponding with his brother in Amsterdam, the team was able to set up appointments with ad agencies in Holland, sell their American brand appeal, and land some pretty big gigs, ranging from car to beer commercials. While I made this sound simple, you should know that the team spent seven years building up their catalogue of songs and honing their sound before their business started gaining traction. But what's most important is that they identified a great idea and succeeded, and so can you!

- *Example 4: Wedding Videos:* Finally, another independent female singer/songwriter knew that her music appealed to young professionals 21 to 35. She also realized that there are literally thousands of people within this age group around the United States each week that get married. She discovered that these people typically have their ceremonies videotaped and create productions to distribute to family and friends. She then realized that these productions need the right kind of music and mood, as well as music that is licensed legally. Putting all of this research together, she set up booths at wedding conventions and met with videographers and couples who wanted to license her music. She also turned the idea into a business and started representing other indie artists as well. This demonstrates another great idea. It's all about being proactive, having an entrepreneurial spirit, and looking out for creative opportunities to make placements.

AFTERTHOUGHT: COWRITE WITH OTHER ARTISTS Independent artist Johanna Petree suggests that if you want to get music placed in television and film, try to cowrite with people who are already placing their music in these markets. These folks are not necessarily untouchable, so just think out of the box and start making things happen.

Get Local Businesses to Use Your Music in Advertisements and Jingles

Another proactive method for placing your music is to go directly to small businesses yourself and pitch your music for commercials. Small businesses in your hometown often advertise on cable television to reach customers. Surely you've seen those late-night ads for local restaurants, record stores, and skate shops. Many of these businesses are on low budgets and usually can't spend a whole lot of money on music—*and this is where you come in.* The business gets to use your music for free or a small fee, and you build your résumé and experience in the TV placement business.

To get started, make a list of the small businesses in your area that sell the same kinds of products that are associated with your target fan. If you are an alternative rock band, you might approach a small tattoo shop. Visit the store, ask to speak with the proprietor, and pitch him or her on the benefits of cable advertising and using your music. I know this sounds like a totally grassroots, long-shot strategy, but I am living proof that it works. When in I was in Boston and attending Berklee College of Music, my buddies and I went as far as writing and recording a jingle for our favorite package store. The owner loved it so much, he decided to use it in a radio commercial! Bingo! *You can do the same!*

Allow Others to Use Your Music via Creative Commons

Making your music available for licensing at Creative Commons is yet another grassroots method that can lead to interesting placement opportunities. Creative Commons provides a simple way to license your music for free while letting it be known precisely how your music can and cannot be used. You always retain the copyrights to your music, and you are attributed credit at all times.

On the Creative Commons website, Jonathan Coulton, a successful DIY musician, says that "with Creative Commons, the act of creation becomes not the end, but the beginning of a creative process that links complete strangers together in collaboration." By making his music available at no cost to the customer via the Creative Commons site, and posting the Creative Commons banner ads on his own Web page, Coulton eventually had his work placed in a videographer's series of war documentaries that received millions of views of various cable television stations. As Coulton says, "This is very good for someone who has a marketing budget of zero dollars. This type of exposure leads to further placements and paid work."

To understand more about how Creative Commons can help you, be sure to check out the Creative Commons website (www.creativecommons.org).

AFTERTHOUGHT: GET IT ON MTV MTV is known to license songs from DIY artists for use in many of its cable broadcasts. Though the licenses are free, you'll get some exposure and build your résumé. Contact MTV's music and media licensing department for further information. Also see MTV's site (www.soundtrack.MTV.com).

Try to Place Your Music in Trailers via Trailer Houses

Trailer houses produce short advertisements (or *trailers*) for production and film companies, and they just might provide another channel for your music to get placed and exposed as well. In Los Angeles alone, there are over 50 "houses," and while many work exclusively with more experienced writers, there are some people and companies, such as Art Ford and pigFACTORY, that are more open to working with indie artists like you. As Ford explains, "Emerging artists have a better chance of getting their music in a trailer for a major film than they do for getting placements in the film itself."

According to Ford, trailer houses look for music that captures the right energy and vibe of a particular film to be released, and subsequently gets the viewer excited about seeing the film. Sometimes the trailer consists of the same music found in the film, but often that music just isn't right for a trailer and they need outside sources. Since trailer houses often lack the large budgets needed to pay for the hottest popular acts, and since DIY artists may be interested in licensing material to build their résumés at a low price or for no money at all, there could be a match.

The best way to get in touch with trailer houses is to conduct a Google search, pick up the phone, and start dialing.

So, as you've heard me say before, *what are you waiting for?*

Utilize a Music Placement Service or Songplugger

As if the above suggestions for placing your music were not enough, placement services and songpluggers are yet another channel for getting your music distributed in film, TV, and more.

Some of these placement companies will provide you with lists of opportunities and allow you to submit your music (physically or electronically) for a chance to get placed, some will screen your music and provide feedback so that you can improve your songwriting skills, some will upload your music into a large database of songs and make your music available to music supervisors, and finally, some will enter into a formal agreement with you to pitch your songs and collect income in return for a share in the copyright.

While many placement services and songpluggers are very selective and will only work with artists that meet certain requirements and levels of expertise, others are open to the public and will work for an annual membership fee.

On the latter note, you must be very careful of the more aggressive companies out there that will actually surf the Web and send upcoming artists (no matter what their talent level) a very flattering e-mail just to get a membership fee out of them. What happens next, of course, is *nothing*—the company never gets placements for the artist because the artist wasn't ready yet. So be careful, be realistic, conduct research, and watch for the sharks.

Note: Two companies that seem to get very favorable reviews and have been around for a long time include TAXI and Pump Audio—check them out. For a more exclusive company, try PEN Music.

AFTERTHOUGHT: USE SOCIAL NETWORKS Ritch Esra of the Music Business Registry suggests that you utilize social networking sites as a way to network with songpluggers and other folks and get your music placed. For instance, at the time of this writing, sites like LinkedIn have certain "groups" you can join, such as Music Supervision Exchange, Synch Music Professionals, and TV/Film Music Opportunities. Why not check these out? They're free.

Place Your Music via a Music Library

Getting close to the end of our discussion on placements in film/TV/games, let's talk briefly about music libraries. Music libraries provide yet another channel for getting your music placed in a variety of mediums.

Music libraries are businesses that make a wide variety of songs and instrumentals available to users who are looking for music.

Music users (e.g., advertising agencies, film directors, television supervisors, corporations, and game companies) look to music libraries in hopes of finding "that perfect piece of music" for a specific job or need—*but the music and recordings have to be* really good *and comparable to what is already being used professionally in the marketplace!*

If you truly feel you're ready to approach music libraries, check out Opus1MusicLibrary, RipTide Music, and Killer Tracks for starters. If you log onto any of these companies' sites, you should find submission policies and other useful information. When getting in touch, remember to be professional and to the point, and be ready to provide each representative with a link to a site where he or she can immediately listen to your music.

So that's pretty much all for music libraries. Let's move on.

RESEARCH THE "HOLLYWOOD" WAY

If you want to place music into film and television programming, you've got to do the research to understand what projects are in production, what each project needs, and whether your music is right for such projects.

LA-based songwriter Leslie Waller suggests that one of the best methods for doing this is to utilize the Tuesday print edition of the *Hollywood Reporter* (www.hollywoodreporter.com). This issue not only lists all the films and TV shows that are currently in production, but oftentimes the name and contact of the music supervisor, producer, and production company as well. You might also be able to find contact information by using the *Film and Television Music Guide* (www.musicregistry.com) or the Internet Movie Database Pro (www.imdb.com). If you're able to get through to "Joe Placement," be professional, concise, and to the point. If he allows you to send your music, be sure to remind him of what it is, who you are, and what it's for.

Ted Lowe of Choicetracks suggests that if you're making an introduction to a supervisor, send a link where he or she can preview your music online. Says Lowe, "It speeds up the whole process, and if they hear something they like or can use, they'll ask you for a high-quality file or CD."

Sign with an Established Music Publishing Company

The last method we'll discuss for getting your music in film, TV, games, and more, is to sign with an established music publisher. Music publishers are in the business of *songs*. They do everything from plugging your songs to offering advances and collecting generated incomes—*but publishing deals do not grow on trees.*

The larger companies (such as Warner/Chappell Music, Universal Music Publishing Group, and Sony/ATV Music) generally look for artists with a lot "going for them." Says Ernie Petito, formerly of Warner/Chappell, "Unless your music is being solicited by a well-established attorney or personal manager, one of your biggest challenges will be getting past the receptionist."

Smaller independent music publishers, however, may be more accessible to independent musicians who are starting to create some "noise" in their hometowns. Jon Rosner, formerly of Bicycle Music Group, says: "A smaller independent publisher might look at a smaller group and that one licensing opportunity for $5,000, while a larger music publisher will see that as a waste of their time."

All things said, it couldn't hurt to look ahead toward getting a music publishing deal one day, particularly with the smaller companies. Get to know more about the various publishers that exist, and decide on which ones might be suitable for you. Pay attention to the types of artists certain publishers are signing, and see if you can discover the reasons why.

For a complete listing of music publishers, see the *Film and Television Music Guide* (www.musicregistry.com). It's updated three times a year and is available in physical and electronic form.

15 TIPS FOR PREPARING AND SUBMITTING YOUR MUSIC FOR FILM/TV/GAMES

1. Understand that you must own your own masters and publishing. If you don't know what this means, you had better read my book *The Musician's Handbook* and Jeff and Todd Brabec's book *Music, Money and Success*. And be sure to never sign any agreement that you do not understand. Contact the appropriate professional.
2. Make sure your music evokes a lot of feeling and is loaded with memorable and interesting hooks. Your lyrical subject matter should be clear and applicable to a variety of scenes and moods. Note that specific lyrical subjects using names and places are harder to place.
3. Make sure your songs are professionally recorded and mastered and that they sound current. Talk to a local producer with film and TV experience, if needed.
4. Be sure your performances are supertight (no flat or sharp vocals, fluctuating meter, or wrong notes).
5. Make sure to have instrumental and "clean" versions (without profanity) of your music ready.
6. Make sure not to have unauthorized samples of other artists' music.
7. Have a variety of different mixes available. For instance, veteran music placement specialist Cindy Badell-Slaughter suggests that you have "vocal down" mixes. These are mixes where the vocals are mixed extremely low so that they do not get in the way of the film dialogue.
8. Know what works. Go to the movies, and notice who did the music and why it worked. "Listen" to videogames, and listen to the television. Check out sites like TV Show Music (www.tvshowmusic.com) for further research.

9. Have important information ready about your songs, such as (if applicable) the names of cowriters, the percentages of the songs each writer owns, the publishing company name and affiliated performing rights society, and any union affiliations (such as the AFM or SAG-AFTRA). Note that the easier your material is to license, the better the chance at licensing it.

10. You should have high-quality song files uploaded on your website or social networks for industry professionals to hear. Michael Eames of PEN Music suggests you should also use a cloud-based service like Dropbox (www.dropbox.com) and Hightail (www.hightail.com).

11. If sending your music by regular mail, make a clean, professional presentation, but avoid fancy packaging and press kits. Says Jon Rosner, formerly of Bicycle Music Group, "Your songs are always what matter the most."

12. Be sure that the track names and other information for your digital recordings are included, so that when people attempt to play your record in their computers, your song data (metadata) will show up. To do this, open your iTunes application on your computer, select the recorded track, choose File, then Get Info, and enter the data. (You might want to register your tracks with Gracenote's media database as well. Be sure to check out their site at www.gracenote.com.)

13. Do your research (know everything about the company) before getting in touch.

14. When speaking with companies, be eloquent and sound knowledgeable.

15. Be patient and don't give up. Film/TV/games are important distribution channels. Good luck!

=MARKETING PLAN TEMPLATE=

Use the template below, or a template like it, to help you craft important information that you will use in your Marketing Plan of Attack™. For additional help, be sure to refer to the marketing plan example below, the chapter on assembling your plan, and the complete plan provided in the back of this book.

Your Company Place Strategy Template (Part 2)

Use this template to craft your product/service place strategy ideas. When formatting your marketing plan, you can remove the questions and just keep the headers and your answers. Be thorough! Don't just answer the questions below. Be sure to review the chapter to get specific ideas for a variety of placement methods. Only create strategies for the products that relate to you.

Merch: What are the various methods you'll use to sell your merch (T-shirts, hats, stickers, lunchboxes, etc.)? Will you sell them at your live performances? Will you sell them from your personal Internet site? Will you try to get a small merchandising company? Remember to review the chapter if necessary. And be sure to label each strategy (personal website, venues, etc.) as I have done in the marketing plan example below.

Songs: How will you get your music in film/TV/games? Will you use a music publisher, music library, or song placement service or songplugger? Will you get songs in student films, go direct to music supervisors by networking at conventions, or try to create deals with local businesses that advertise on cable? Be sure to think about all the methods discussed in the chapter.

Other: Are there other products you created? If so, list your place strategies here.

=MARKETING PLAN EXAMPLE=

Now here's an abridged marketing plan example for our band Rally the Tribes, to help you put together your own place strategy. Note that only some of the band's offerings are addressed here, but you'll have to list all products and services when writing your plan.

PLACE STRATEGY

a) RTT Merchandising Line

★Online Personal Website: Utilizing their web store at www.rallythetribes.com, RTT will sell their line of merch products, and they will include a link to www.cafepress.com, where they will sell their "Man Not Mouse Pad" and the "Change Agent Hoodie." For products sold on their website, RTT will accept payment utilizing PayPal and personal check, and will send product using the United States Postal Service.

★Live-Performance Venues: Utilizing their merch booth at live performances, RTT will proudly display their line of merch products. They will accept cash, checks, and credit cards (using Square on their smartphones).

b) RTT Songs (Licensing Opportunities)

★College Films: Songs like "Petty Thieves Hang, Big Ones Get Elected," "LAPD—Treat 'Em Like a King," and "Protest/Anti-Test" will be used in the student documentary film produced by RTT called *Occupy World.*

★Creative Commons Website: RTT will load their music at www.creativecommons.org and allow student game developers and student independent documentarians to use the music in their student projects and film festivals.

★Songplugger: PEN Music Group, personal friends of RTT, will strive to plug songs in television shows similar to *SouthLand* and *Intervention*.

★ Out-of-the-Box and Local Business Licensing: RTT will pitch their music to local activist and cause groups (like PETA) who do cable advertising and video blogging.

Etc.

14

Formulate a Promotion Strategy, Part 1
Winning Over Fans via Publicity and Paid Advertising

According to marketing expert Philip Kotler, people are bombarded with over 3,000 commercial messages and numerous product and service choices daily. Thus, it's not enough to just create and distribute amazing music and expect people to stumble upon it. You have to promote your ass off long before your product hits the marketplace, and then continue to promote your ass off in various waves and levels of intensity throughout your product's life. *Promotion can never stop, or your career dies.*

Promotion is the process of effectively communicating the unique *features* and *benefits* of your offerings in order to generate an eventual purchase and achieve your marketing plan goals. Remember that a feature is part of what a product actually *is*, and a benefit is what a product *does* for the intended audience.

Experienced marketers often use the AIDA model in planning a promotional strategy. AIDA is an acronym for attention, interest, decision, and action. It can be more thoroughly described as a sequence of promotional steps with the following objectives:

- **Grab the attention of your target audience and increase awareness.**
- **Maintain their interest in your company and offerings.**
- **Help them decide to buy your products and services.**
- **Lead prospects to take action, make a purchase, and become fans.**

Fully discussing just one of the many types of promotion could easily fill the pages of a book. But for our purposes, we'll tackle the subject in four chapters, starting with publicity and advertising in part 1; Internet, word-of-mouth, and guerrilla marketing in part 2; radio promotion and sponsorships in part 3; and direct marketing, face-to-face selling, and sales promotions in part 4. Your challenge is to deliver a "mix" of several of these strategies functioning as one complete promotional campaign (also known as an *integrated marketing communications program*, or IMC). You've got your work cut out for ya, but I've got faith in you.

So now let's take a closer look at:

1. **Creating a Publicity and Public Relations Plan**
2. **Developing a Paid Advertising Campaign**

Be sure to grab a yellow highlighter—you won't want to miss any of this.

KNOW HOW YOUR RESEARCH, GOALS, AND OTHER STRATEGIES RELATE TO PROMOTION

Before putting together your promotional plan, be sure to review all of the research and marketing strategies, as we've been doing throughout this book, to see how they relate to promotion.

- *Reexamine Your SWOT Analysis:* Be sure to reexamine chapter 3 and the market need you identified and are trying to fill. If you are merging technology and music to create a "never done before" entertaining live performance (such as when guitarist Pat Metheny created a full stage of robots triggered by switches), then this unique selling point should obviously be communicated and stressed in the concert posters you design and the announcements you put on your websites.

- *Study Your Target Customer's Profile:* Knowing your audience's *lifestyle* will help you determine the types of magazines you should target for publicity. Knowing about your audience's *behavior* will help you create effective posters, including words, graphics, slogans, and themes that best resonate with them. And knowing where your fans *live and spend their time* will help you to remain focused on promoting in your target territories. This is all important stuff.

- *Revisit Your Competitor Analysis:* Remember that people don't just want to hear about your products and services; they want to know how your products and services differ from those of competitors. They want to know why, for instance, they should take music lessons from you as opposed to another teacher. So, be clear on what differentiates you from your competitors, and promote the heck out of it.

- *Know Your Brand:* The brand you wish to convey must be delivered consistently in all promotional materials—from your publicity pictures, to your poster designs, to your website and social media profiles. Consistent colors, fonts, and tone of voice must be used. If you are still unsure what your brand is all about, now is the time to figure it out.

- *Know Your Products' Unique Features and Benefits:* The unique features and benefits of your products and services (sometimes called your *unique selling proposition*, or USP) set the tone for all of your promotional communications. Review the product features and benefits chart you created in chapter 10, and incorporate this information into all of your promotional correspondence.

- *Revisit Your Price Strategy and Know How to Promote It:* Remember that price is a big factor in people's decisions to buy. Be sure that you understand the finer details of how pricing works and the various ways you can manipulate numbers to trigger a buying response in your customers. Price really does go hand in hand with promotion. And finally . . .

- *Promote the Places in Which Your Products Can Be Found:* Communicating where people can find your products is key. Remember that it's not enough to *get* your music on iTunes or Spotify, you have to *promote* that your music is on iTunes or Spotify. Otherwise, people won't know it's there and you'll end up with zero sales.

[IMPORTANT NOTE: Budgeting and Allocating Expenses: Companies often wonder how much they should spend on their promotion. Some base it on 1) a percentage (5–15 percent) of last years' sales, 2) what they think their competitors spend, or 3) what they believe needs to get done. For the purposes of this book, remember that DIY artists on a low budget to no budget, like yourself, must try to utilize as many free methods as possible, invest small amounts in the media channels where they think they'll have the most success, and utilize their personal relationships with people who can offer discounts or barter services with them. Got it? Good! Now you're ready to learn more about promotion.]

Create a Publicity and Public Relations Plan and Stimulate Free Promotion

The first strategy we'll discuss writing into your marketing plan is publicity and public relations.

Publicity (a.k.a. *earned media*) refers to the unsolicited comments, reviews, and stories about your company made by journalists that are *not paid for, or directly controlled by*, your company.

Public relations (PR) specifically refers to the various activities a company does to help promote and protect its brand image in the eyes of the public.

Submitting press kits, sending press releases, organizing charity events, and networking at important functions are just a few of the things you might implement in your own publicity and PR campaigns. What follows will help you decide on the strategies that work best for you.

Prepare a Press Kit (Physical and Electronic) for Submission

A press kit includes important information about your career and is used to build awareness among journalists, editors, bloggers, and others. While I've mentioned press kits throughout this book, now it's time to get into the juicy details.

There are two types of press kits: *physical* and *electronic*.

Physical Press Kits

Typically a physical press kit contains the following:

- **Folder:** A nine-by-twelve-inch two-pocket presentation folder with a solid color and glossy finish can be purchased at most office supply stores. You can then affix a sticker bearing your company name and logo that you make through websites like StickerJunkie (www.stickerjunkie.com), or for an even more professional look, you can utilize a company like Vistaprint (www.vistaprint.com) or Pocketfolder.com (www.pocketfolder.com) to design and print your own customized folders.

- **Business Card:** A business card could include your company name, logo, career title, URL, social network, QR code, and phone number. You can also include a company slogan describing what you do, for whom you do it, and why you're different. To design a card, you can easily use software like Photoshop by Adobe and then print your design at a local office supply store such as FedEx Office. Or you can use a service like Vistaprint that makes business cards for free. Also be sure to consider services like Moo (www.moo.com) or Tinyprints (www.tinyprints.com), which create uniquely sized plastic cards, and Zazzle (www.zazzle.com) that even offers cards with 3-D printing.

- **Biography:** Your biography should be written in the third person and void of fancy or overly colorful adjectives. You should include the date your company formed, the city in which you reside, your name, style of music, and like bands. Aim to engage people with an interesting story (or *hook*) about your company, list your professional accomplishments, and describe your future goals. If possible, include testimonials you've collected from club owners, radio DJs, or industry pros. To make an even greater impression, consider hiring someone of note in your area to write your bio for you (such as a local radio personality). Sample bios can be found at www.bobbyborg.com.

- **Photograph:** Though independent publicist Lisa Pardini says that an eight-by-ten-inch glossy photo print is no longer required in your press kit, you should still consider shooting with a professional photographer who can capture your image using proper lighting, high-quality equipment, and talented stylists. You can then merge that photo into your bio. If a larger/higher-resolution photo is needed by a media source, you can either provide it on a disk or simply provide a link where people can go online to obtain it when needed.

- **One-Sheet:** A one-sheet (see the graphic "Rally the Tribes") presents information on a single sheet of paper in a way that can be assimilated in just a glance. A one-sheet features your picture and/or album cover, a very brief bio that includes your name and musical style, a bullet-point list of your accomplishments, a bar code associated with your record (optional), and your contact information. To view more samples of one-sheets, see www.bobbyborg.com.
- **Recording:** Finally, your best bet is to include a *professionally mastered* CD that is packaged in a plastic jewel or Digipak case (but having other formats on hand, like USB flash drives, is also a good idea). To be clear: Do not send a burned CD with your name written in Magic Marker on the front. This only sends the message that you're still a bunch of kids rehearsing in your mom's cellar and don't have your shit together yet. Okay? Let's move on.

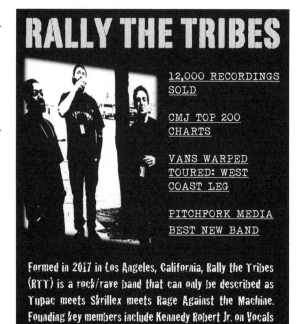

Electronic Press Kits (EPKs)

Now that you have a good idea about what fits into a physical press kit, you must consider specifically looking into building an *electronic press kit* (EPK).

Just like a physical press kit, an electronic press kit contains a bio, one-sheet, picture, music, and more, but it it's presented in digital format and can be e-mailed and hosted online. This will likely be the format of the future, but for now, you should probably have both a physical and electronic press kit to accommodate the needs of all your recipients.

A number of marketing companies specialize in creating EPKs and, as part of their services, offer opportunities for you to submit your press materials to a variety of different partners (bookers, sponsors, etc.). Typically these marketing companies charge a small monthly fee to build EPKs but offer free trials. Be sure to check out Sonicbids, ReverbNation, and ArtistEcard.

QUICK WORDS OF WISDOM: CREATE A "LOCAL" MEDIA LIST: FORGET ABOUT *ROLLING STONE* MAGAZINE AND OTHER LARGE PUBLICATIONS

To ensure that you don't send out your press kit and other promotional materials to the wrong sources, independent publicist Lisa Pardini says, "When it comes to print media, forget about targeting the bigger print publications and national outlets, because *you're probably not ready for them*. Understand that national publications focus on bands making national news, and unless you're one of these bands, the cover of *Rolling Stone* magazine or *Billboard* might be a long way off for you."

Stick with local newspapers, magazines, and fanzines that publish both off- and online. Build a media list by noting which publications are carried in local newsstands, getting referrals from other like artists, and using media resource guides such as The Musician's Atlas, *The Indie Bible*, and Standard Rate and Data Service (SRDS).

Next, jot down the contact information, important personnel, and a few notes on the general attitude or tone that a particular outlet exudes. Also be sure to make note of the publication schedules of each media source, since most of them (especially monthly publications) decide on what will be covered in each issue several months in advance.

Finally, compile this information into a spreadsheet program like Microsoft Excel or Apple Numbers, and update it regularly. In time, you'll have generated enough contacts and local press clippings to begin expanding into other territories and diversifying your media outlets.

Strengthen Media Relationships with an Outreach Strategy

While many artists are anxious to send out their press materials to their contacts as soon as possible, you might consider establishing an *outreach strategy*. This entails building strong relationships with editors, writers, and other folks in the media.

To execute an outreach strategy, you might study the important media professionals in your area and get to know their work (their style of writing and the articles they publish) and then congratulate them on a recent piece they wrote. As a relationship forms, you might even send out holiday greetings and birthday cards. Eventually, you might submit a press kit and invite them out to one of your gigs. And when these folks finally write something nice about you, you might send a personal thank-you card and even chocolates or flowers.

Bottom line, the purpose of an outreach strategy of this type is to show that you're interested in building a long-lasting relationship with your local media people and that you're not just another company overly consumed with *itself* and desperate for exposure! This approach will be well received by media folks, I assure you!

Decide on Your Press Objectives and Prepare for Them

Another important part of contacting the media is to be clear first about why you're specifically approaching them. Is it to get a *feature story*, an *interview*, or a *review of your recording or live gig?*

If you're going for a feature story, then prepare an interesting hook about your band and show how the publication's subscribers can benefit from reading it. If you're going for an interview, then prepare a list of "suggested questions" and have witty answers, sound bites, and anecdotes in mind. And if it's a live review you're seeking, then make sure your band is well rehearsed and ready to knock the socks off of the reviewer who comes out to see you.

Says publicist Lisa Pardini, "Whatever it is you're going for, just *be super prepared*. You simply cannot afford to blow a great opportunity to win over a press person because you were *all go and no show*. Remember that first impressions are truly everything, especially in the media!"

AFTERTHOUGHT: GOT MEDIA TRAINING? You should! Prepare to be interviewed on video, pose for pictures, and speak effectively. Think about body language, know your perfect pose or angle, repeat the interviewer's questions in your answers, reply with colorful and insightful sound bites, and refrain from getting mad when asked uncomfortable questions. *Interview Tactics* by Gayl Murphy is a good read. Check it out.

Submit Press Releases

Aside from sending your press kit to various targeted media sources in an attempt to generate exposure, you can also furnish them with *press releases* that contain *current and newsworthy* bits of information.

Write and Format Your Release

Press releases come in all shapes and sizes, but you should focus on the following three pointers when writing and formatting your own releases:

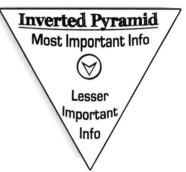

1. *The Headline and Lead:* Press releases typically start with a catchy headline caption in capital letters that sums up your news and draws readers in. If possible, try to use "the five W's" (*who, what, where, when,* and *why*) and use colorful active verbs and keywords that your target customer may use when conducting an online search. For instance, a terrific caption might read something like this: "LOS ANGELES-BASED ARTIST JOHN DOE SELLS 15,000 RECORDS FROM THE TRUNK OF HIS CAR AND SECURES WEST COAST LEG OF VANS WARPED TOUR." You might also try to tie in certain aspects of your career with special holidays or other current events to create newsworthy hooks. For instance, "JOHN DOE SINGS SONGS ABOUT PEACE AT A TIME OF WAR." You get the idea. Just be creative and always be truthful.

2. *The Body:* The body of your press release should begin with the date and city from which the release is being distributed (e.g., June 1, 2018: Beverly Hills, CA). Next, include the most important information first (which oftentimes means repeating the headline) and lesser important information as your writing progresses (this is often referred to as an *inverted pyramid* style of writing—see the graphic). Just try to eliminate unneeded words. Use short sentences. And keep your release at a length of about one to one and a half pages, tops.

3. *Other Notables:* Finally, the words "For Immediate Release" should appear at the top of the press release page, and a brief summary and the contact information of the organization that is releasing the news should appear at the bottom. To indicate the end of a page, use the symbol -###-. If needed, be sure to check out *The Associated Press Guide to News Writing* by René J. Cappon.

Get the Most Out of Your Press Release

It's not enough to just a write and format a press release; now you need to know what to do with it. One thing's for sure: blasting out mass press releases and expecting results is extremely unrealistic and old-school marketing. Try to target specific media folks and outlets the best you can. For instance, you can submit press releases to your own business contacts, post them on your blog, send them to your fans, ask other like bands to send them out on their lists, or look into *newswires* (such as the very popular *PR Newswire* [www.prnewswire.com] and *PRWeb* [www.prweb]). Whichever channels you choose, think of press releases as just one of the many things you'll do to generate publicity and positive PR.

Now check out a sample on the next page that was written a while back about one of my first books.

Submit Photo Stories and Impromptu Photos

Photo stories and impromptu photos are additional tools you can use to generate publicity and positive PR about your company. Let's take a look at both.

Photo Stories

Photo stories are photo-documented proof of a "newsworthy" event in your career, which can lead to exposure.

To demonstrate, say you secure a spot on the second stage at the Vans Warped Tour, and while traveling cross-country, you take pictures with all of the headlining acts. After returning from the road, you submit these photos to local media outlets with a couple of sentences that sum up your experience and inform others about how you got the gig. Since you are providing value to the magazine's target audience, you just might get published.

SAMPLE PRESS RELEASE

Contact Watson-Guptill
770 Broadway, New York, NY 10003
www.watsonguptill.com

For Immediate Release:

INTERNATIONAL RECORDING AND TOURING ROCK DRUMMER, TURNED AUTHOR AND ARTIST
ADVOCATE, DELIVERS THE FACTS ABOUT THE MUSIC INDUSTRY—NOT THE FAIRYTALES!

June 1, 2015: Beverly Hills, CA: Former international major-label recording artist Bobby Borg has released a revision of the best-selling industry book *The Musician's Handbook: A Practical Guide to Understanding the Music Business*, with a message that's loud and clear: *Music is an art, making money from it is a serious business!* Originally published in 2003, the book offers comprehensive coverage of each of the four types of business relationships musicians may encounter, the five key players an artist needs to succeed, and the four major sources of music revenue, as well as a list of 35 steps necessary to pursue a successful career in the new music business. *The Musician's Handbook* gets down to basics and provides a solid introduction to the business of music in an easy-to-read style that allows musicians to quickly study up and then get back to doing what they love most: CREATING MUSIC. Available on Amazon.com, BobbyBorg.com, or at a store near you.

The Musician's Handbook:
A Practical Guide to Understanding the Music Business
Author: Bobby Borg
New Release: Billboard Books
ISBN: 978-0-8230-8357-8
Paperback $19.95

Contact: Watson-Guptill Billboard Books/Random House
770 Broadway, New York, NY 10003
www.watsonguptill.com

Watson-Guptill is an American publisher of instructional books in the arts. The company was founded in 1937 by Ernest Watson and Arthur L. Guptill. Billboard Publications acquired Watson-Guptill in 1962. The Dutch publisher VNU (later renamed the Nielsen Company) acquired Billboard in 1993. Random House acquired Watson-Guptill from Nielsen in 2008.

-# # #-

A photo story doesn't have to be "life on the road"; it could be pictures of you in the recording studio with a notable producer, or it could be pictures of you throwing a charitable event in your community.

However you approach it, submitting photo stories can certainly lead to exposure.

Impromptu Photos

Impromptu photos, those spontaneous pictures of interesting people or events that unfold before you, can also lead to exposure. With camera phone technology today, there's no excuse to not be prepared.

Says booker/promoter Chris Fletcher of Coast to Coast, "Mick Jagger of the Rolling Stones came into a club where one of my bands was performing and allowed me to snap a photo of him and my lead singer. We used this photo everywhere (from our website to gig announcements). The caption read: "STARS ARE COMING OUT TO THE SMALLEST OF CLUBS TO SEE THIS BAND!" Furthermore, we sent the photo to local magazines with hopes it would run, and it did! Pretty cool.

Bottom line: you always have to be thinking "out of the box" for ways to get exposure, and be looking for opportunities on which to capitalize.

Know Where to Network and Generate PR

We've already discussed a number of tips on generating publicity and PR, but no marketing book would be complete without talking about networking at key events. As I have always told my clients and students, *if you want to be part of the press that covers your scene, you have to be part of the scene your press covers.*

Live performances, annual award shows, charitable events, magazine-sponsored showcases, industry parties, film festivals, and nightclub openings are all great places to connect with folks in the media and even jump into free impromptu photos with them as well. Since music conferences are a central meeting point for industry folks in your territory (and folks all over the world), you should also consider attending popular events like SXSW in Texas, West Coast Songwriter's Conference in California, and the Durango Song Expo in Colorado.

Wherever you decide to hang, be sure to write these key events into your Marketing Plan of Attack™. And don't forget to create a system for organizing your business contacts and following up with them as well. Remember that a drawer full of business cards from media folks and others is worthless unless you do something with them. So what are you waiting for? *Get working at networking.*

Design Publicity Stunts

Janet Jackson exposed her breast during the Super Bowl Half-Time Celebration, and Madonna kissed Britney Spears during a televised awards program. As long as *publicity stunts* like these are consistent with the image you want to project, you might also consider designing a few stunts yourself to generate publicity.

While I am not advocating the following examples in any way, shape, or form, here are three that I've seen indie artists pull off to great effect in the last few years:

- *Example 1: Ringling Bros. Revolt:* One indie singer/songwriter in Los Angeles protested Ringling Bros. and Barnum & Bailey Circus on behalf of PETA (People for the Ethical Treatment of Animals). Half nude and painted like a tiger, she sat in a cage on Hollywood Boulevard and held a sign that read, "Their abuse, your entertainment." Local press that covered the story also discussed the artist's band in great detail, and they included it in a two-page spread in the *LA Weekly*.
- *Example 2: Michael Jackson Crash Jam:* When Michael Jackson was being brought to trial for allegedly having sex with a minor, one indie alternative rock group actually dressed up in diapers, quickly unloaded their equipment in front of news crews standing by the courtroom, and performed an original tribute to Jackson while waving a sign that read, "Free Michael." The band made it to both the national and international news!

- ***Example 3: City Council Shutdown:*** And for an even crazier publicity stunt, the Florida metal band Hell on Earth, which claimed to support assisted suicides, announced that it was throwing a concert in a local club where a terminally ill fan was going to end his life on stage. While most people are sure it was a publicity stunt, the city council of St. Petersburg could not take the chance and thus put pressure on the theater to shut the show down. This created great controversy and brought national attention to the band in magazine articles, blog postings, radio programs, and television news reports.

Okay, okay, okay—I know what you're thinking: shouldn't my career be all about the music? Well, yes and no. Music comes first, but make no mistake: publicity stunts are a big part of the entertainment business and have been used for decades as a way to build awareness in the marketplace. If done creatively and within the boundaries of your brand identity and the law, publicity stunts can work magic. Disclaimer: I'm not responsible for anything crazy you do. [*LOL.*]

PREPARE A CRISIS MANAGEMENT PLAN

The saying "All publicity is good publicity" is not always true. A company must be prepared to deal *immediately* with certain rumors and factual events that may unfold and tarnish its brand image. Good news travels fast, but bad news travels faster. Consultant Ira Kalb offers some excellent tips on the subject.

- ***When a Rumor Circulates:***
  - Do not publicize the rumor by repeating it.
  - Promote the exact opposite of the rumor by reminding people of all the good you do—but again, without mentioning the rumor.
  - Deal with the person(s) who started the rumor by letting them know you are upset and that you will even take legal action if necessary.

- ***When a Factual Mishap Occurs:***
  - Admit to the problem and apologize.
  - Limit the scope of the problem by putting it into perspective (e.g., "In several years of working as a professional musician, this is the only time something like this has ever happened").
  - Outline a solution that shows you're taking responsibility (e.g., "There is nothing that we can do to make up for the problem, but we will investigate how something like this could have happened, and we'll work to ensure it will never happen again").

[Note: For more information on crisis management, be sure to read up on the general topic of public relations, brand management, and crisis management. For starters, see *Harvard Business Review on Crisis Management* by Harvard Business Press.]

Plan a Record Release Party or Press Conference

Next up in our discussion about publicity and PR is the record release party and press conference.

Record Release Party

This is an event where you book a private hall (club, studio, etc.), arrange for catering and open bar, invite people in the media to attend, and perform a live concert (or you can just broadcast your recording via a public address system). The fact that the word *party* is attached to the event is often enough to whet the appetites of curious journalists and motivate them to attend the event and write about you. This is also a great way to get fans excited about your career and even get them to start spreading the word about you. So perhaps you'll consider writing a record release party into your plan.

Press Conference

Similar to the record release party, but even more private and exclusive, is the press conference. If you've ever watched the news where journalists are sitting in one room before a sports team and all scrambling to get their chance to ask a question, then you've seen a press conference. Of course, as an independent artist, it isn't easy to attract extensive media attention. However, as soon as you build up a little momentum in your career, you might consider inviting a few members of the local media out to lunch or dinner and furnishing them with updates about your career. Try this; it works!

Organize a Charity Event

Another great way to generate positive PR about your company (and do some real good in the world too) is to organize a charity event. Whether it is for a children's hospital, an environmental organization, a disaster relief program, or a cancer or heart disease center, you'll find that media in your community will rally around important causes and be more willing to support you.

Decide on the Charity Arrangement

There are many different ways that you can arrange a charity event.

For instance, you can focus it around a live performance, sell tickets, and give an organization a portion of the money you raise. On a similar note, you might make the event performance free and merely ask people to make a cash or item donation (such as a can of food, a toy, or old clothes). Another interesting possibility is to ask sponsors to get involved by donating products to be raffled off during the performance to raise money.

Whatever your approach, just be organized, be professional, and be sure to keep in constant communication with the charity for which you are throwing the event. This will help ensure that your event goes off without a hitch.

Get the Most Out of Your Charity Event

To get the word out about your event, remember to alert the media by issuing press releases and sending out postcards via direct snail mail or e-mail. You might also want to contact your local radio stations and ask them whether they'd be interested in doing a *public service announcement* (PSA). In addition, you can call your local television news stations to see whether they'd be interested in covering the event, or you might video the event yourself, create a short clip, and send it to a local television news station. Often times, "morning shows" on various networks are looking for content.

Finally, you can ask the charity organization how they intend to generate publicity for the event. Will they be mentioning the event on their website? Will they be sending out a press release to their contacts? Will a representative be attending the event and shooting pictures for their newsletter? Will a representative be setting up a table in the venue or hanging up a banner? These activities can all be helpful.

For more information, and types of charities that exist, be sure to check out Charity Navigator (www.charitynavigator.org), which provides information on over 5,000 charities.

Prepare to Expand into New Territories That Make Sense

Looking into territories in which you are connected, or will be connected, is yet another way to generate publicity for your company and maximize your marketing efforts.

You might consider approaching media in the cities where you have previously lived, attended school, or were born—especially if you built up a name for yourself when you were there. This strategy is known as the "hometown boy does good" angle, and it's quite effective. You see, papers are always happy to write about one of their former community members who went on to be successful.

Also consider reaching out to media outlets located in cities where you're planning to play live, sell records, or get radio play. The more places that people see and hear your name, the more likely they'll be to take an interest and even purchase your offerings and come to your shows. This is basic knowledge, but the basics are the first things that are often overlooked.

Consider Hiring a Professional Publicist, or Not!

And finally, for the last thought about generating publicity and PR for your company, let's consider the possibility of hiring a professional publicist, *but for only a moment.*

A publicist is a person whose job it is to give information about your career to various media outlets. They can range from the self-starting and well-meaning enthusiast who sends out packages and EPKs on behalf of local artists, to the educated communications expert at a large firm who exposes established artists to his or her incredible list of professional contacts. Prices can range anywhere from $300 to a $7,000 a month (and much more), with a suggested term of several months to achieve optimum results.

But since most young artists can't afford much more than their monthly rehearsal room expenses, and they can accomplish many of the same things that an entry-level (and even mid-level) publicist can, the prospect of hiring a publicist is probably a long way off for you. However, I had to bring up the idea anyway for those of you who are still trying to buy your way out of doing the dirty work.

So roll up your sleeves, get pumped up, and create a killer publicity and PR plan that will *attract the attention of those that can help you by first helping yourself.* In the process, you'll form tight bonds with your fans and industry types as well. And remember, "The harder and smarter you work, the luckier you'll get." So as Nike says, *just do it.*

Well, that's about all I have to say about "earned" publicity and PR. Now let's move on to another form of promotion that is commonly discussed in contrast to publicity: paid advertising. While I know I've already presented a lot of ideas, hang in there folks—you're already long past the halfway point in this chapter. We're almost done.

Develop a Paid Advertising Campaign

Moving away from the publicity that you *earn* from various media sources, *paid advertising* refers to the marketing communications you *direct* other companies to publish at a *cost to you.* In case that didn't sink in, advertising is about paying magazines, newspapers, radio stations, and other media to say/do precisely what you want them to say/do. For this reason, paid advertising does not carry the same credibility with customers as unsolicited publicity, but it's still extremely effective for those companies that are willing to make the needed investment.

So then, let's briefly examine three major forms of paid advertising: Internet, print, and broadcast. Since most of you are on a limited budget, I promise that I will keep this section brief.

Use Internet Advertising

Search results page ads and website ads are two affordable, targeted, and popular forms of paid Internet advertising. Let's briefly examine each.

Search Results Page Ads

Small classified-style text ads can be placed on the results pages of a specific keyword search made by a target consumer.

Based on the amount you "bid" for that specific keyword, your ad (consisting of a highlighted link and brief description of your company) will show up toward the top of the search page or to the right of the page, while other *organic* (or unpaid) search results, will show up further down the page (see the graphic that features Google Adwords, a registered trademark of Google, used by permission). Since you can decide on the amount you want to spend for keywords, pay only when someone clicks on your ad, and access data on the number of people who actually clicked through to your website, this is an attractive form of online advertising.

One of the first companies to offer search engine advertising was Google Adwords sponsored by Google. Another provider to check out is Yahoo! Search Marketing by Yahoo!

Website Ads

Ads on the websites and social media pages of other companies that fit your brand can also be a great method to attract attention and get your target audience to take action. Ads can come in different types and sizes using text and/or graphics. These include:

- **Banner Ads:** Ads that are placed on website pages in the following sizes: Rectangle (180 × 150 pixels), horizontal leader-board (728 × 90 pixels), and vertical skyscraper (160 × 600 pixels).
- **Pop-Up and Pop-Under Ads:** Ads that come in similar shapes and sizes as banner ads, but that pop up over and under the Web page.
- **Interactive Ads:** Ads that include short videos and small games (which are also called *advertgaming*).

Website ads can be placed by contacting popular social networks (Facebook, etc.) or search engine companies (Google, Yahoo!, etc.). Company servers then deliver your ad to a number of different participating websites that contain content relevant to your ad, or they are delivered to participating websites based on the viewing behavior and habits of a specific Web user. When a user clicks on the ad, you are charged. Note that ads may also be placed by contacting the owners of the sites personally and asking about rates.

Utilize Print Media Advertising

Moving away from online advertising, print media is the next form of advertising that you might consider writing into your marketing plan. While its future fate is uncertain given digital technology, print is still a widely used source. Magazines, newspapers, and yellow pages/directories are discussed below.

Magazines

Magazines are divided generally into two major categories: consumer magazines (*Thrasher, High Times* magazine, etc.) geared toward nonbusiness personal use, and trade magazines (*Billboard, Entrepreneur*, etc.) focused on specific industry professionals.

The most common form of magazine advertising is the *display ad*, which consists of text and graphics divided into various measurements of a page (full page, half-page, quarter-page, one-eighth page, etc.).

The advantage of using magazines is that they:

- Cater to a specific audience.
- Allow you to connect with your fans via a specific interest (sports, music, etc.).
- Allow a wide degree of creativity when choosing colors, design, and layout. And . . .
- Have a long lifespan when left out in recording studios, music schools, and tattoo shops.

The disadvantages of using magazines is that they:

- Can be relatively expensive for most advertisers like you.
- Are rather inflexible regarding the lead time required to place an ad (it must be done 30 to 90 days in advance of publication). And . . .
- Are typically cluttered with ads from many other advertisers competing for readers' attention.

Overall, magazine ads can be effective if you have the budget to place repeated ads in targeted publications, but they can otherwise produce "questionable" results if your ads are infrequent. The choice is yours.

Two magazines that might be a good place for indie artists to place their ads are *Music Connection* magazine and *Alternative Press*. Give them a call about rates.

AFTERTHOUGHT: KNOW ABOUT CO-OP ADVERTISING When placing your ads, consider partnering with local bands that might be performing on the same night and in the same club as you. It's not difficult to see that an ad paid for by four individual bands is more affordable for all. This idea can work in partnerships with local businesses as well.

Newspapers

Newspapers are the second type of print media advertising we'll discuss in this section. There are three major categories of newspapers: *daily/weekly* papers that focus on local news, *daily papers* that focus on national news, and *weekly specialty newspapers* that focus on more specific categories (such as entertainment).

The most common form of newspaper advertising is the display ad (see the graphic "Want to Get Paid to Play?"), which can include both text and pictures and comes in a variety of sizes (full, half, quarter-page, etc.). Also popular is the classified ad, which includes two to three lines of text placed under categories like "Instruments for Sale" at the back of the paper. You know what I'm talking about.

WANT TO GET PAID TO PLAY?
BASS PLAYER WANTED!

Blues Guitarist With Investor and Pro Management Auditioning
Text 4521 to 2794 by June 1
Reference: "LA Weekly Display AD"

The advantage of newspapers is that they:

- Reach a large variety of people.
- Are viewed by people as a trusted source for concert, club, movie, and restaurant listings.
- Allow you to place ads up to a few hours before the publication deadline (in fact, newspapers often offer last-minute discounts on unsold ad space).

The disadvantage of newspapers is that they:

- Have a lack of focus (generally they have too broad a reach, with the exception of specialty newspapers).
- Have poor reproduction quality and limited colors.

• Have a short life span and are discarded immediately. And . . .
• Are cluttered with other ads.

So, all things considered, weekly specialty papers that focus on a specific category (like entertainment) are probably your best choice for newspaper advertising. Check out *LA Weekly*, *The Village Voice*, and *The Nashville Scene* for starters.

Yellow Pages and Directories

That last form of print advertising we'll discuss is yellow pages and directories.

Yellow pages are those big ol' thick books on your counter that contain the addresses of thousands of businesses in your area.

Directories are those *more specialized* resources that list the contacts of recording studios and musical instructors.

The most common ads in these sources are red, regular, and bold-face text ads listed by category and alphabetical order, as well as display ads that allow for pictures and text.

The advantage of advertising in yellow pages and directories is that they:

• Are highly available and seemingly everywhere.
• Provide low-cost advertising.
• Are nonintrusive (people typically use them as a resource after they've already decided what they need).

The disadvantages are that they:

• Are printed yearly, and all ads must be submitted long in advance.
• Are sometimes viewed as a dated source, since businesses regularly change their information.
• Are extremely cluttered.

In closing, yellow pages and directories are still used by many companies (especially since they have become available online) and they just might be a good method of promotion for you as well. For starters, be sure to check out two highly used directories in the music business: *Music Business Registries* and *The Indie Bible*. Search for many more online.

WHAT'S IN A GOOD PRINT AD?

It's not enough to just place an ad—you have to place a great ad! While there are so many techniques from which to choose, here are a few ideas that can help you be more effective in everything from ads to posters and fliers:

• *Headline:* Headlines usually appear as a simple, short phrase at the top of the page and are intended to grab the attention of a particular audience. Headlines can be either direct or indirect. *Direct headlines* are complete, straightforward, and informative (offering the company/product name, the unique benefits, and/or a promise), while *indirect headlines* are vague and meant to lure the viewer into reading the ad (perhaps by using a question, command, or time-sensitive offer). Often headlines include attention-grabbing words and phrases, like *introducing*, *new*, *quick*, *easy*, "save time/money," "how to," or "[number] reasons why you should . . ." In either case, just remember that the headline is the most important and most-read part of an ad. According to advertising legend David Ogilvy, "If the headline doesn't grab the reader, chances are that they will not read anything else."

• *Subhead:* Subheads usually appear below the headlines and provide additional information and product benefits to hold the reader's interest.

- **Body:** The body usually appears midway down the page and contains finer product/service details, testimonials, and even pricing to help the reader make a decision. This is usually presented in smaller type size and short sentences.
- **Graphic:** The graphic usually appears midway down the page and ties in nicely with the headline. It is extremely important in selling the product. As they say, "A picture is worth a thousand words." Graphics in advertising are typically intended to show what a product looks like, what its features and benefits are, and/or its actual scale of size. Sometimes a graphic shows a product in use to get customers to imagine themselves using it. And of course, sometimes a graphic is used to just convey a mood or attitude, or to amuse or shock the audience. As stated by Robert Sawyer in *Kiss and Sell*, advertisers might even go as far as using a graphic with no written copy at all.
- **Call to Action and a QR Code:** A *call to action* appears at the bottom part of a page and should tie into your headline and cause the reader to take the next step (e.g., "To experience over 30 world-class DJs spinning for 3 nights of incredible fun and dancing, reserve your tickets now"). This is also where contact information (URL, phone number, e-mail), logo, and brand slogan or tagline can be provided. A *QR code* (Quick Response bar code) can also be added so viewers, using their mobile phones and a special scanning app, can be directed immediately to a website where more information and even e-commerce systems can be accessed. To get your very own QR code and/or learn more about how they work, check out QRStuff (www.qrstuff.com).
- **Market Information System Code:** Finally, a market information code should also be included at the bottom of the page (e.g., "Use the promotion code 1234 when placing your order"). This will help you monitor the effectiveness of your ad.

[Note: To learn more about writing ad copy for print (as well as radio, television, and electronic media), read books like *Kiss and Sell* by Robert Sawyer, keep your own notebook of effective ads that you've noticed, and check out resources like *Brandweek*, *AdWeek*, and *Advertising Age*.]

Know About Broadcast Media Advertising

And finally, the last, but certainly not the least, source of paid advertising we'll discuss in this chapter is broadcast media, which includes radio and television. The most affordable option for indie artists are *spot buys* on select local stations. Sales departments at various broadcast companies are more than ready to speak about getting you the best rates, purchasing bundle time, and running advertisements into the late night. So, let's take a quick look at both cable and radio media outlets.

Local Cable Spot Buys

Given the number of specialty cable programs that exist (sports, music, and more), local cable advertising provides the opportunity to reach a select and captive audience with a creative audio/visual message.

Yes, I agree that cable is still greatly overshadowed by major networks and direct broadcast satellite services, but occasionally you hear of an independent-artist success story that gives cable advertising a glimmer of hope for all of us.

According to journalist Bernard Baur of *Music Connection Magazine*, an indie act by the name of Dig Jelly bought time from a local cable provider to promote an important upcoming showcase. The spots, which ran on MTV and VH1 for ten days, cost about $2,000 total. (Note that the 30-second commercial they produced was free—thanks to a friend's video service.)

As it turns out, Dig Jelly's show was a big success. The showcase was packed, and it cost the band about as much as two full-page print ads. Not bad!

Perhaps for an extremely important event, such as your record release party or industry showcase, you'll also give cable advertising a try.

Local Radio Spot Buys

Given the emotional relationship listeners often form with local radio stations and personalities, the selectivity that specific radio formats offer, and the fact that ads can be purchased just hours before they air, local radio stations can also be a useful form of advertising.

Okay, I know that radio lacks visual appeal, listeners often tune out stations during ads, and there's a lot of competition from commercial-free satellite radio, but the following indie success story might shed a different light for you on using radio.

The small indie label Lizard Sun Entertainment (now Loco Entertainment) signed Jim Morrison's alleged son, Cliff, and arranged a performance at the NAMM convention in Anaheim, California. The label bought 15-second commercial radio spots on the local station KLOS to promote the show.

After only four days, Cliff and his camp received urgent phone calls from both NAMM and hotel reps. They indicated that the number of people inquiring about the show was overwhelming (almost 10,000 e-mails and phone calls), and that they were afraid that they could not handle the overflow without hiring extra security. They then requested the label stop all ads.

Though Lizard Sun was forced to comply immediately, Cliff's show nonetheless attracted one of the biggest crowds that NAMM had seen in years. Pretty cool!

Perhaps radio advertising can work for you too. If so, be sure to write it into your plan.

So that's about it for paid advertising and for this chapter as well. If there seem to be too many difficult decisions to make, you can always contact a local advertising agency to provide objective and experienced advice. Some agencies offer low rates for small businesses just like your own. Conduct a search online and see what you find in your area. Good luck.

WAIT! GOT OTHER TYPES OF ADVERTISING?

Advertising is a multibillion dollar business! While there are many different types that probably won't apply to you (like *product placement*, as when you see MacBook computers in TV shows and movies; or *infomercials*, when you see people on TV at 1:30 a.m. trying to sell you a juicer), here are just two more forms of advertising that you might consider:

- *Out of Home (OOH):* This refers to *outdoor* promotional ads such as billboards, bus stop benches, subway station walls, and aerial advertising. While most out-of-home advertising may be "out of reach" for the independent artist on a low budget, you might consider a *vehicle wrap*. Vehicle wraps are advertisements (logos, company names, etc.) that are wrapped around your car, truck, or van. Wraps cost about $700 and can generate as many as 10 million up-close and effective impressions every year! Check out Buswraps.com (www.buswraps.com), or just type "vehicle wrap" into any search engine.
- *Specialty Advertising (a.k.a. Promotional Merch):* This refers to the everyday items your company pays to have manufactured with the sole purpose of giving them away. Key chains, calendars, flash drives, and pens that bear your name and logo are all examples of specialty advertising. The idea is to get your name in the minds of your customers and keep it there for as long as you possibly can. Check out services like Branders.com to get a variety of specialty advertising items made for you.

=MARKETING PLAN TEMPLATE=

Use the template below, or a template like it, to help you craft important information that you will use in your Marketing Plan of Attack™. For additional help, be sure to refer to the marketing plan example below, the chapter on assembling your plan, and the complete plan provided in the back of this book.

Your Company Promotion Strategy Template (Part 1)

Use this template to craft your promotion strategy. When formatting your marketing plan, you can remove the questions and just keep the headers and your answers. Utilize the points below that best apply to you. Be thorough! Don't just answer the questions; be sure to review the chapter to get specific ideas for a variety of promotion methods.

Publicity and Public Relations Plan: Will you create a physical and electronic press kit? What is your target list of local media? How do you plan to develop relationships with journalists and other media folks? Do you have any particular networking events that you plan to attend to generate publicity? Will you use publicity stunts? Will you build PR through charity events? Are there any other areas outside your local region where you can generate publicity? Be sure to label each strategy as I have done in the Marketing Plan Example below.

Paid Advertising Strategy: Will you advertise on the Internet? Will you advertise using magazines, newspapers, or the Yellow Pages? How about broadcast advertising—will you place ads on radio or television? How about outdoor advertising? Whatever you come up with, be sure it is the best fit for your customers, your budget, and your time.

=MARKETING PLAN EXAMPLE=

Now here's an abridged marketing plan example for the band Rally the Tribes, to help you put together your own promotional strategy.

PROMOTIONAL MIX STRATEGY
a) Publicity and Public Relations Plan
★Press Kit: RTT will create a 9″ × 12″ two-pocket customized presentation folder with RTT logo, business card, one-sheet, and bio. We will have the folders and cards made at Vistaprint and pay local writer Bob X of *Music Connection* magazine to write the bio (a move that will help build a stronger relationship with the magazine). We will also build an electronic press kit utilizing the services of Sonicbids.

★Target List of Local Media: To stimulate reviews and mentions, RTT will submit to local music magazines such as *Music Connection*, *Skinnie*, *Alternative Press*, *Campus Circle*, and *Rock City News*. RTT will also submit to student and lifestyle papers and magazines, like *Daily Bruin*, *Thrasher* skateboard magazine, and *Tattoo* magazine.

★Charity Events: RTT will promote their live-performance charity events for local LA organizations like the Coalition for Humane Immigrant Rights of Los Angeles and the Los Angeles Coalition to End Hunger and Homelessness. Local magazines and citizen bloggers will be invited to these events and furnished with official press releases. RTT will also participate in events to help feed the hungry during the holiday season (such as Thanksgiving and Christmas/Chanukah) and take photos of these events to be posted on their websites and social media profiles.

★Publicity Stunts: RTT will arrange "imitation police" to raid their record release party on March 1 and drag the band away. RTT will also play "commando raids," where they perform on the street (in front of City Hall and other government offices, college campuses, etc.) in protest of certain important issues. At these "raids," RTT will motivate fans to attend via their social networks, and ask fans to create their own personally designed picket signs.

b) Paid Advertising Strategy

★Search Results Page Advertising: RTT will utilize the services of Google Adwords. Since RTT can decide on the amount they want to spend for keywords, pay only when someone clicks on their ad, and access data on the number of people who actually clicked through to their website, this is an attractive form of online advertising. Estimated bid per key word is $0.20 per click with a capped expense of $1,000. Keywords might include "RTT," "Rally the Tribes," "LA Bands," "Music That Matters," and "Political Rallies."

Etc.

15

Formulate a Promotion Strategy, Part 2

Using Internet, Word-of-Mouth, and Guerrilla Marketing to Get Customers

Promotion is the process of repeatedly communicating the unique *features* and *benefits* of your offerings in order to generate a *buying action* and achieve your marketing plan goals. Sound familiar? Yup, the definition is no different than in chapter 14, only now we're going to look into other forms of promotion, like Internet, word-of-mouth, and guerrilla marketing.

Just remember that the objective of this is to:

- **Grab the attention of your target audience offline and online.**
- **Hold their interest in your company and its offerings.**
- **Help them decide to buy your products and services.**
- **Lead prospects to take action, make a purchase, and become a fan.**

Be sure to keep all of your research and marketing strategies in mind, just as you did in the previous chapter. Review your customers' profiles to help you make important decisions about *where and how to communicate* effectively with them. Think about how you are *unique from competitors* to help you clearly position your products and services in fans' minds. And consider how your products and services can *benefit* your target audience and help answer the important customer question "What's in it for me?"

So let's jump right into the heart of the following topics:

1. **Putting Together an Online Marketing Plan**
2. **Using Word-of-Mouth Marketing**
3. **Utilizing Guerrilla Tactics**

As always, we'll focus on lower-budget promotional options that are available to independent musicians like you. Find the mix of these strategies that makes the most sense, and write them into your own plan.

Put Together an Online Marketing Plan

Online marketing is one of the newest, most affordable, and most exciting methods of promotion for the do-it-yourself artist. By definition, it is *the art and science of using the Internet to communicate your message and get people to take action.* It's about using a variety of online tools to engage fans, and get them to spread the positive word about your brand and make recommendations to friends.

As long as you can plan out your day effectively and avoid becoming overwhelmed by the arduous process required, *online marketing is a godsend.* And the best part is that many online marketing activities are low budget and even free!

Take a look at some of the online methods you might consider to help achieve the overall goals of your marketing plan, from using a professional website as your hub to creating social media profiles.

THE ZERO MOMENT OF TRUTH

Given the development of new technologies, consumers have changed the way they make decisions. To move from "undecided" to "decided," they specifically look online at a number of different sources to read reviews, talk with friends, look for samples, and compare other products—and they do this right in the store or at home as they shop. Thus, you must embrace this "new step" in consumer behavior and have a variety of systems in place (Internet sites, blogs, social networks, positive reviews, mobile phone apps, QR codes on product packaging, etc.) to help educate your consumers and guide them through the process of taking action. Google calls this step the *Zero Moment of Truth* (ZMOT). For helpful business concepts, see Google at www.thinkwithgoogle.com.

Use a Personal Website as an Effective Promotional Hub

We've discussed getting your site built in chapter 10 and using it as a direct channel of distribution in chapter 12, but now let's discuss how it relates specifically to promotion.

Many Internet experts agree that a personal website is your most important destination on the Web. It's that special place where you want to direct and draw in potential customers to capture their addresses and eventually get them to make purchases. But unless your target customers can find your website easily and they are enticed to stick around once they do find it, your site is essentially dead. This brings us to these important issues:

- **Content:** Rutherford D. Rogers, a Yale University librarian, once said, "We are drowning in information and starving for knowledge." Bottom line: your site must be updated regularly with concise, informative, entertaining, and relevant product and service information that fulfills your target customers' needs and reminds them why they should be excited about being your fan. Songs, lyrics, pictures, podcasts, videos, quizzes, surveys, games, contests, testimonials, fan profiles, press releases, and tour dates can all help you draw customers to your site and keep them coming back for more. Remember, the challenge is to present a content-rich website without it looking cluttered and confusing. For more advice on creating promotional content for the Web, check out *The Copywriter's Handbook* by Robert Bly and *The Idea Writers* by Teressa Iezzi.

- **Optimization:** Besides posting your website link literally everywhere (on social networks, blogs, and other relevant websites that are linked back to you), you must dedicate your time to doing so much more to ensure that your target fans will find you—a process called *optimization*. Be sure to regularly identify keywords that people might use to search for the type of things you offer ("Music in LA," "Local Bands in Austin," etc.), strategically incorporate these words into the text of your site, and then tag your site with these keywords into various search engines. If all this stuff sounds foreign to you, then make sure to seek recommendations for a Web developer, consultant, or service provider who can help. The boxed information titled "Eight Introductory Tips to Search Engine Optimization" will also offer you a few helpful tips for now.

EIGHT INTRODUCTORY TIPS TO SEARCH ENGINE OPTIMIZATION (SEO)

If you want your site to show up with high-ranking search results in search engines like Google (www. google.com), you better take search engine optimization (SEO) and the following tips seriously:

1. Be sure to have a clear idea of your intended market and specifically what they want and need. This is a crucial first step in attracting people to your site.
2. Find out the specific words people use when trying to find sites like yours. You can take a poll among your fans, use the service Wordtracker (www.wordtracker.com), or go to your competitors' sites and use the Reveal Source button on your browser to see what relevant keywords they use. Be sure that these relevant words, or *meta tags*, are used in the titles and in the body text of your site as often, but as naturally, as possible. Again, check out *The Copywriter's Handbook* by Robert W. Bly for more information on writing for the Web.
3. Log on to search engines like Google and register your URL to their databases; just look for "Submit your site" or something similar, and it will ask for your URL and "meta description."
4. Get linked to other relevant sites, and get them linked to you. One way to do this is to simply contact various websites and propose a link exchange. Another way is to pay a small fee to a Web owner for the privilege of advertising *your* link on his or her site, and then posting *his or her* link on your site. Finally, you might want to look into *Web rings* that allow you to join or start your own Web community of people all linked together. Check out WebRing (dir.webring.com/rw).
5. Ask your site's visitors to bookmark your URL and get them to "tell a friend," too. This will help spread the word and hopefully keep them coming back. The more people who hit your site, the higher you will rank in search engines. Just be sure to keep your site current with relevant and engaging content.
6. Avoid building a site that uses a lot of flash animation or moving text and graphics. While flash can look cool, sites that utilize it are less likely to show up in search engines. Simply put, the software (called spiders) that search engines use to find and index Web pages typically do not read flash.
7. Hire a professional Web consultant to increase your SEO. Ask for referrals from people that you trust. And finally . . .
8. Read books like *SEO: Search Engine Optimization Bible* by Jerri Ledford, and check out sites like Search Engine Watch (www.searchenginewatch.com) and Search Engine Land (www. searchengineland.com). The information on the topic of SEO is plentiful.

Create Your Own Personal Blog

A blog is a distinctive website that organizes posts in chronological order, gives visitors an opportunity to leave comments, and utilizes a format called RSS (Really Simple Syndication) that alerts subscribers of all updates.

A blog is meant to educate people about who you are, what you do, and what you think about a particular topic. It can include text, pictures, videos, and links to other relevant content and social media destinations and services. The material is usually fresh, interesting, and concise (and often includes the "read times" for each post [e.g., 45 seconds] to help engage easily distracted and multitasked visitors).

Overall, blogs are meant for building relationships with readers, drawing them to your personal site, and making sales.

Dave Jackson of the website The Musician's Cooler (www.musicianscooler.com), notes: "Fans seem to flock to blogs—especially those that are updated with tales from the road and wild happenings backstage—since they are less static than most personal websites. Better yet, search engines also love blogs, because blogs are seen as 'authority sites' where valuable and current info can be found. And the best part about blogs is that all of them are built on a platform that can be maintained easily by a novice Web user. Some people even build their entire website on a blog platform."

To get started with your blog, check out WordPress (www.wordpress.com), Blogger (www.blogger.com), Tumblr (www.tumblr.com), and Typepad (www.typepad.com). Also be sure to check David Meerman Scott's book *The New Rules of PR*, which covers blogging extensively.

Create Profiles on Social Networks to Attract Fans

Creating profiles on social networks and paying attention to the profiles of other companies similar to yours allows you to share your personal story about your brand, read what people are saying, and engage with fans in a nonintrusive way.

Social networks are a place where you can be the real thing, build trust, and form solid relationships over long periods of time.

But most importantly, social networks are also places from which you can patiently direct traffic to your own personal website, entice fans to make a purchase, and ultimately collect their e-mails for your database.

While there are many things social networks can do for you, there's one thing they cannot offer: a place to *push* your messages on people and spam them with annoying requests. That's a big no-no in the social networking community.

As Shama Kabani says in *The Zen of Social Media Marketing*, "Social media is *not* just about YOU. It's about what your customers have to say, and then using their collective interest in you as social proof to attract even more fans. Social networks are about word-of-mouth!"

To utilize your time on social networks most effectively, pick the top three most popular sites for your target audience, and then be sure to automate them so that you can upload data on multiple platforms from one main site (to help you do this, be sure to check out the tools available on each social network). You must also create a social media agenda for yourself and schedule the frequency with which you will upload content, and even plan out the type of content and exact times of the day and week that you will post. The more organized you are with your time on social networks, the better.

For a detailed list of social networking sites, remember to search Wikipedia (www.wikipedia.com) for its "list of social networking sites," and don't forget to check out the detailed resource guide found in the back of this book.

SOCIAL RULES OF ENGAGEMENT FOR BUSINESS

As defined in *The Power of Real-Time Social Media Marketing* by Beverly Macy and Teri Thompson, "Your behavior on a social media site should really be no different than your behavior would be at a cocktail party." In any case, here are a few rules of engagement you might want to consider:

- *Use Your Personal Name:* It feels more authentic to people when they know they are talking to a person rather than a company.
- *Create an Attractive Profile:* Use attractive profile pictures and provide thorough and interesting profile information.

- *Use an Open-Enrollment Policy:* Have an open-enrollment policy, but quickly delete anyone who spams you or makes inappropriate posts or comments.
- *Have a Plan:* Have a precise strategy, and limit the time you will devote to each social network. For instance, you might just place an update, check messages, and respond for a total of 30 minutes per day. Be consistent so that people know what to expect.
- *Remember It's Not Just About Numbers:* Having *thousands* of people on your social networks is good, but having *hundreds* of people with whom you communicate and form relationships is better.
- *Engage People:* Engage people in conversation and read carefully what they have to say, rather than just forcing your own messages down people's throats.
- *Create Social Events:* Create events on your social network that draw traffic. For instance, you might announce that you're signing photographs digitally and e-mailing them to anyone that joins the conversation.
- *Give Up Some Control:* Get people to interact with each other, and then sit back and see where the conversation goes. Don't always feel as if you have to interject every other minute and control the conversation.
- *Be Transparent:* Be transparent by letting people see that you are a fallible and real person. Let them in on more casual information that does not cross any professional boundaries. Just be careful not to leak personal information that could jeopardize your safety and cause you harm. There are some real nuts out there.
- *Strive to Build Trust:* Social networking is about getting to know people and forming tighter bonds.
- *Provide Great Content:* Post quality, relevant, and current content that people want to share. Try to avoid multiple posts about the fact that you just drank a glass of water. Ask enticing questions, make an intriguing statement, conduct polls, initiate contests that draw people to your site, share interesting photos and videos, and post links to interesting articles. And be sure to use keywords that are pertinent to your company in these posts as well for purposes of building search results.
- *Go Beyond Networks:* Engage your social network community both on and offline. Reach out to specific people directly on the phone and even by mail.
- *Learn from Your Posts:* Take note of the people who seem to correspond with you most and get to know more about them. What is it about your posts to which they seem most drawn?
- *Do-It-Yourself:* Outsourcing people to answer your social networks for you defeats the whole purpose of transparency and building a strong community. Social networking should be done by your company, not someone pretending to be you.
- *Build a Community:* Make people feel as if they are part of a bigger cause or family by being involved with your social network. Perhaps you can create a general name for them, similar to the way Lady Gaga refers to her fans as Little Monsters or KISS refers to their fans as the KISS Army. Whatever you do, think of your network as family.
- *Personalize Your Social Network Address:* For a professional look, you can personalize your URL (e.g., YourName.com), *forward* it to your social network, and *mask* it so that your personalized URL still shows up as the destination address. Ask your hosting service for more information about forwarding and masking.
- *Don't Argue:* Do not allow yourself to be drawn into arguments with people.
- *Be Careful:* Remember that word of mouth travels fast on social networks. You will be held accountable for everything your company does and doesn't do. So think before you act.

- *Follow the Conversation in "Real Time":* See what people are talking about on other social networking feeds, monitor their conversations just as they are happening, and then quietly post your feelings in a nonintrusive way.
- *Drive Traffic to Your Personal Website:* Social networks can come and go, and so will all of your contacts and data. Thus, remember to build a personal website that will serve as the hub for all of your online marketing.
- *Use Other Promotional Platforms:* Remember that social networking is only one part of your promotional strategy. Remember to use an integrated mix of a variety of different strategies—both online and offline.
- *Be Ethical:* The Word of Mouth Marketing Association posts online rules of ethics at womma.org/ethics/code/. Use them!

Generate Online Publicity via E-zines, Blogs, and More

E-zines, blogs, and other online media that review independent artists and publish interesting stories are yet another great place to attract attention to your career and make sales. These sources are typically viewed as authorities on what's new and cool in the music industry and have large and loyal groups of followers made up of both fans and industry professionals.

Create a database of various sites to pursue by conducting a keyword search with terms like "indie music reviews" or "indie music blogs." You can also investigate where your competition is generating publicity and pursue those options.

Once you find a few online media outlets, familiarize yourself with the editors' names and the tone of the various sites and their submission policies. You'll be required to e-mail a link to your website where your accomplishments, pictures, and music samples can be found, or e-mail similar information in an electronic press kit (EPK), which lays out your information attractively in the body of the e-mail. Should you entice an editor of a successful blog to write about you, you could earn a significant deal of exposure.

AFTERTHOUGHT: GOT PRESS LEADS? Be sure to check out PitchFork Media (www.pitchforkmedia.com), Cokemachineglow (www.cokemachineglow.com), and Stereogum (www.stereogum.com), which are known for writing great reviews. Also be sure to use the blog search tool Technorati (www.technorati.com/blogs/directory) to generate helpful leads.

Post Content on Video Sharing Sites

Creating and posting video content on blogs, social networks, personal websites, and video sharing sites is another great way to attract attention, stimulate interest, and make sales. These days, shooting and editing video content has never been easier.

One independent artist in Southern California used the camera on his Apple laptop along with iMovie editing tools to record a quality clip of his band. He uploaded it online to advertise his next show and started getting hits in 30 minutes' time.

Another artist used a Sony Handycam and a lavaliere microphone plugged into an external jack on the camera to record a quality clip of him playing a Bach piece on his bass guitar. He got 500,000 hits in just a few weeks.

And did you know that hip hop artist Mac Miller built up a very respectable buzz via quality video posts and other social media content and quickly transitioned to selling out shows across the world? That's pretty kick-ass, wouldn't you say?

To increase the number of viewings and get the most out of your videos, Gene Smith of nForm, and author of the book *Tagging*, suggests the following tips:

- Keep your content short and concise (30-second snippets to 3-minute pieces).
- Create a variety of content (music, interviews, teaser videos to promote your single).
- Include a lot of cuts to keep people engaged and interested.
- Include your URL to draw fans to your site.
- Use interesting words in your title (such as "leaked" video or "exclusive release").
- Use relevant *tags* (keywords and descriptions) so that search engines will find you. And . . .
- Take advantage of special tools (like YouTube "annotations") offered by each site.

That's about it. To start posting your own videos online, check out popular video sharing sites such as YouTube (www.youtube.com), Vimeo (www.vimeo.com), DailyMotion (www.dailymotion.com/us), and more. You might even consider a multichannel network like Fullscreen (www.fullscreen.com) that can help you with a number of services such as growing your audience and earning ad revenue. And finally, you might consider live video streaming sites such as Ustream (www.ustream.tv) and StageIt (www.stageit.com) to present "real time" video interaction with fans, and conduct a keyword search for other, more obscure sites as well.

CREATE OUT-OF-THE-BOX "VIRAL" VIDEO PRODUCTIONS

Guitarist Shawn Owen of Stolen Element said that he uses a variety of "out of the box" video concepts in an effort to attract fans, get them to share content with friends, and stimulate word-of-mouth buzz. These include lifestyle videos, stupid videos, cover videos, fan-generated videos, outrageous videos, and lyric videos. Take a look:

- *Lifestyle Videos:* Lifestyle videos work well, especially for alternative and punk bands. Says Owen, "We conceptualized our video to feature bits and pieces of my band's live performance with a focus on self-produced extreme sports footage. Our target fan enjoys biking, snowboarding, and surfing. Since I have a lot of close friends who are into that stuff too, I was able to get some great action footage. We mixed that with small clips of us playing live and used our music as background throughout. Besides posting it on sites like YouTube and Vimeo, we sold it as a complete DVD at skate shops and got it aired on cable stations like Fuel TV ([now Fox Sports (www.msn.foxsports.com)]."
- *Stupid Videos:* Stupid video footage is also a really cool way to promote your band. Humor is a huge factor in generating hits. Says Owen, "With all the wacky websites out there like StupidVideos (www.stupidvideos.com), eBaums World (www.ebaumsworld.com), and Break (www.break.com), we produced some 'crank video clips' of our band in action and then uploaded them on various sites. Stupid stuff, like secretly pointing the smoke machines at our drummer and then smoking him out during a performance, can get a lot of hits. It worked for us."
- *Cover Videos:* Cover videos, where you film yourself playing a popular cover, are a great technique to get exposure, since you will have a built-in audience that is already looking for that song. However, says attorney Steve Winogradsky, many people do it without obtaining proper licenses (thus infringing others' copyrights), which could lead to a *take-down notice* from the host of the video site, or even a letter from the song owner's attorney. Be sure to contact the publisher of the song for permission, check out multichannel networks (like Fullscreen—fullscreen.net/creators) that facilitate licensing, and just stay tuned for developing laws and advertising policies regarding this issue.
- *Fan-Generated Videos:* Fan-generated videos are also helpful in attracting attention. Owen says, "We held a contest among our fans for the best lip-synched video of our single. This helped us to engage our fans and create that little extra spark of excitement about our new recording."

- **Outrageous Videos:** Rapper Tyler the Creator released a video that features him eating a Madagascar cockroach, throwing up on himself, and then hanging himself, all in order to pitch his record and hip hop collective. He received nearly 75 million hits. Sure, this may not work for you if you're in a Christian country band, but I think you get the idea. Outrageous videos work!
- **Lyric Videos:** Finally, lyrical videos provide a quick and easy solution to creating content. Typically, lyric videos have a plain solid graphic background and feature your words synched to your music.

Build, Create, and Service Direct E-mail Lists

While you may already be overwhelmed with the number of Internet strategies available to you, don't forget e-mail marketing. Stanford University professor Monica Lam says, "It is a simple, direct, and still effective method of getting your promotional message out to your public and triggering a customer response." Read on.

Building E-mail Lists

When building your e-mail list, put *quality* before *quantity*. Always ask people if they really want to be on your list and receive information. For those who do, have them e-mail you (this way you can easily log their data and eliminate input errors). And don't forget to offer an incentive in exchange for their e-mail, such as a free record, a free T-shirt, or a just a big ol' hug. [*LOL.*]

Compose Effective E-mails

To stand out from other e-mails and get your target customers' attention, be sure to create personalized, catchy, and complete subject lines, such as: "HI BOBBY/After-Party with FREE Booze/MAY 1/COMING?" (See e-mail inbox graphic.)

In the body of your e-mail, provide more detailed information with links that get your fans to take action and visit your site.

And as a failsafe, indie artist Cheryl Engelhardt suggests that you conduct tests by making several versions of one e-mail message and taking note of which approach and style gets the best results. Getting feedback is always wise.

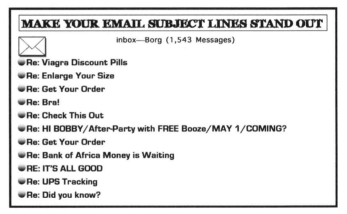

Servicing Your E-mails

Last, when servicing your e-mail lists, be sure to use one of the many e-mail services available today to personalize your e-mail messages, isolate specific territories, increase deliverability, remove dead or bounce-back e-mails, and manage "unsubscribe" lists (the lists of those persons who wish to be removed from your database). GoDaddy, Constant Contact, GroupMail, VerticalResponse, MailChimp, and Bandcamp are all great services to check out. Some of them are free for up to about 500 e-mail addresses, but then charge a small monthly fee based on the number of e-mails you build into your database.

AFTERTHOUGHT: CAN-SPAM ACT Remember that the US Congress strongly regulates the sending of unsolicited e-mail. Not only is it illegal, it pisses people off. Be sure that everyone on your e-mail list truly desires to be on your e-mail list, and always provide a link where they can opt out at any time they want. Practice good Web etiquette. It will pay off!

Start a Direct Online Newsletter

Another effective method of online promotion is to start a newsletter and provide your fans with concise and regular information about your career. *But don't just plan to hype yourself!*

Add interesting music trivia, articles, and even "how to" tips to make your newsletter more informative, useful, and interesting. Avoid sending large blocks of text and/or graphics that can make your newsletter difficult to download on personal computers or view on mobile phones. Instead, include brief announcements that sum up your entire newsletter in one paragraph, and then provide links to your site where further information, pictures, and other media can be obtained.

To help you create customized e-mail newsletters and announcements that get immediate and measurable results, Andreas Wettstein, former VP of new media at Warner Bros. Records, suggests you check out Constant Contact (www.constantcontact.com), Bronto (www.bronto.com), and MyNewsLetterBuilder (MNB; www.mynewsletterbuilder.com).

Use Podcasts to Get Exposure

Podcasts are digital audio shows that can be downloaded and played on personal computers or MP3 players, such as the Apple iPod. Everything from talk shows to political shows to indie music shows can be a perfect fit for your brand and an excellent opportunity for exposure. For a directory of podcasts, check out Podcast Directory (www.podcastdirectory.com).

If you're really proactive, you can start your own podcast show. This can be accomplished by deciding on a theme, writing a script, recording it on Apple Garage Band software, incorporating music files and sound bites, and publishing it to sites such as Apple iTunes Store or a multitude of others. Internet consultant Dave Jackson offers a free tutorial on his website called "Promoting Your Band Through Podcasting" (www.promotingwithpodcasting.com). Script ideas and other general writing tips can be found by reading *Strategic Writing* by Charles Marsh.

Create Online Viral Goodies Such as Screensavers, Wallpapers, and More

Getting close to the end of our discussion on Internet marketing, I'd like to share a few "viral goodies" that can be written into your plan. These include computer screensavers, wallpaper, and customized toolbar skins, which can all be shared easily among your fans.

Screensavers

Screensavers are computer programs that were once used to protect older monitors from phosphor burns. Today, screensavers have a more decorative purpose and can be embedded with pictures, videos, and links to your site. You can provide your screensaver for free to your most loyal fans and get them to pass it along to their friends.

Get your screensaver built by checking out companies like GraFX (www.grafxsaver.com) and SofoTex (www.sofotex.com/download/Screen_Savers/Screensaver_Tools/).

Wallpaper

Wallpaper (see the graphic) is essentially a "desktop picture" or background that you can also provide to your fans for free and encourage them to pass along to others. Keep the design simple, leave the center of the computer screen free of design so that the workplace is not cluttered, and choose a background color that is "easy on the eyes" (light gray works great).

To create your own wallpapers, you can watch some of the many tutorials offered by Adobe Photoshop software. Just conduct a keyword search for "wallpaper + computer + tutorials," and you'll find plenty.

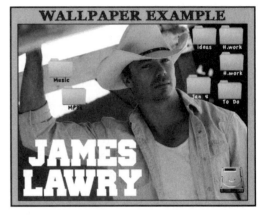

Customized Toolbar Skins

Our final viral goodie, customized toolbar skins, are essentially the designs that wrap around the various toolbars on your computer screen. These can be sold to your fans or just given away for free. You can find the software to create skins through DHX (www.dhtmlx.com).

AFTERTHOUGHT: TELL-A-FRIEND SCRIPT Code that can be placed on your Web pages and gives visitors the opportunity to tell a friend about what they just saw or read is called *Tell-a-Friend Script*. This can help accelerate word-of-mouth promotion about your product. Check out Tell-a-Friend (tellafriend.socialtwist.com).

Leave Announcements on Event Calendars, Message Boards, Groups, and Directories

And last but not least, to add to our long list of Internet promotion ideas, let's briefly discuss event calendars, message boards, and directories.

Event Calendars

Event calendars that announce your upcoming gigs and other events for free can be found in most local newspapers and music magazines. Just scroll through each publication or search its site online for submission policies.

Message Boards

Message boards that cover topics that appeal to your target audience are also great places to leave announcements about your career. The extremely popular Craigslist (www.craigslist.org) is one of many sites that you want to check out.

Groups

Groups, such as the ones found on Yahoo! Groups (www.groups.yahoo.com/neo), are a great way to connect with like-minded people on the Web. For instance, a band could easily tap into a group such as "Extreme Sports Enthusiasts" or "Fans of Metal," and begin communicating and trying to draw fans over to its site.

Web Directories

Finally, Web directories allow you to post your website URL under appropriate categories and announce to the world that you exist. This helps your target market find your site, interact with you, and potentially make a purchase.

Google offers a free directory, but there are literally hundreds more. Conduct a search using keyword phrases such as "bands + free directories."

Got it? Good! You are now on the way to becoming an Internet marketing expert.

So, let's move on to our second promotional strategy of this chapter, which is closely related to Internet promotion: word of mouth. It's not a new form of promotion, but it has recently risen to greater popularity, given its "viral-like" ability to spread at an accelerated rate on the Web.

AFTERTHOUGHT: GOT MORE INTERNET PROMOTION TIPS? Evites (Evite.com) are a useful and free way to announce your special music events, send invitations, and even receive free promotion tips. Also check out Eventful (Eventful.com) and Cvent (cvent.com).

Use Word-of-Mouth Marketing (WOMM)

Word-of-mouth marketing is the process of stimulating natural conversation (or *buzz*) between people about your products and services. Or as Emanuel Rosen says in *The Anatomy of Buzz*, it's the act of generating natural "unpaid" communication between friends, family, and colleagues. Natural communication (especially when it includes recommendations, unbiased opinions, and more) is highly trusted and a big reason why people decide to take action and buy.

Now what follows are a few tips to get the buzz started about you. Be sure to write the ideas you like best into your very own Marketing Plan of Attack™.

Create Products and Services That Are Naturally Contagious

Make no mistake—when people think your products and services are exciting, outrageous, and exceptional, they'll do what they do best: *talk* and diffuse the word naturally.

When Prince first hit the scene, everyone talked about the guy who could play every instrument, sing, produce, dance, entertain, and look like a superfreak on stage. When Ozzy apparently bit the heads off of bats and broke the necks of doves during his live performances, the buzz about him was smoking hot. And when guitarist Stanley Jordan first hit the scene as the guy who could play chord changes and solo at the same time, musicians and enthusiasts couldn't get enough of him.

Yes, I know that creating "naturally contagious" products is easier said than done. It takes finding a market need and capitalizing on your strongest attributes to fill that need better than anyone else. It also takes researching your customers and knowing how to fully satisfy them, as well as analyzing your competitors and striving to differentiate yourself. But by working long and hard, excellence and focus will come, and with excellence and focus, so will the natural word of mouth.

Make Your Communications Special, Scarce, and Memorable

Another method to help stimulate word-of-mouth promotion is to make your communications special, scarce, and memorable. Using special *trigger words*, holding contests, spoon-feeding the information, and making your communications shocking and memorable are just a few methods you can write into your plan.

Use Trigger Words

"Sneak preview," "exclusive footage," and "never before released" are all phrases that you can use when posting and titling video clips on the Internet. Believe it or not, these words are actually what get people more interested in checking you out and telling a friend. Conduct a search on the Internet and examine how highly viewed content is titled. Write down the phrases you see and try to use similarly interesting words in your own posts.

Hold Contests

Short-term contests and scavenger hunts with exciting prizes and rewards are yet another method to stimulate buzz. Jay-Z initiated a scavenger hunt to market his book *Decoded* with great success. On a special website, Jay-Z left clues in mysterious places around New York City (the bottoms of pools at hotels and the bottoms of plates in restaurants) where passages from his book could be found. The person who found the most passages was offered tickets to his New Year's Eve show.

Tease Your Audience

Spoon feeding or teasing your audience with limited and intriguing graphics and words is also worth mentioning. The absurd sticker and street campaign launched by artist Shepard Fairey (www.obeygiant.com) is a classic example. On seemingly every telephone poll in Los Angeles, Fairey tacked up mysterious posters that said no more than the word *Obey*. After several years of doing this and creating a strong buzz, he started his own clothing line and is now doing quite well as a professional artist. That's dedication!

Use Humor, Sex, or Shock Appeal

And finally, keep in mind that humor, sex, or shock appeal can also stimulate natural conversation between folks at a widespread and accelerated rate. As told by David Meerman Scott in *Real-Time Marketing and PR*, indie artist Dave Carroll received millions of hits after he posted a funny video on YouTube about how his guitars were broken by United Airlines. In fact, this led Carroll to signing a deal with an equipment case manufacturer to start a line of cases named after him. Not bad for a low- to no-budget independent artist. He used the power of social media to seize the day.

AFTERTHOUGHT: CREATE PHOTOSHOP PRANKS Rob Blasko Nicholson of Mercenary Management suggests that you create Photoshop pranks to generate word of mouth. For instance, to promote an upcoming show, you might Photoshop a picture of a current celebrity holding your recording or standing next to your band. While it's obviously just a prank, it gets people talking and discussing whether or not it's real and legal.

Spot Customer Hubs and Opinion Leaders

Spotting customer hubs and opinion leaders is yet another idea to consider when creating a word-of-mouth strategy. Some people are more interested in new products and services, and like to talk about them more than others. Some people are also "better connected" and more influential, and can spread the word faster. These people are what author Emanuel Rosen calls *hubs* (a.k.a. *brand ambassadors*): effective centers from which word of mouth is amplified.

To spot these people, look at those within your target audience who are the first to know about that cool new band, where the party is at, and "everyone that's anyone." Come on, you know exactly who I'm talking about—there's one of these people in every school, workplace, town, or social network.

In any case, once you have identified them, you must then use your best networking skills to casually reach out and introduce your products and services. Rest assured, if these folks like what you have to offer, they'll recommend you to their large clique of people, who'll tell their large clique of people, and so on and so forth, thus amplifying the positive word of mouth about your products.

You must then go out of your way to nurture a strong bond with these valuable people by making them feel special, as if they are an important part of your family.

DIG OUT YOUR SOULS ON THE STREETS: WORD OF MOUTH AT ITS BEST

Before releasing their new recording *Dig Out Your Soul*, Oasis leaked four of their songs on the streets, literally. It asked some of New York's most visible street musicians to reinterpret their new songs with whatever arrangement and instrumentation they wanted, and then to perform the songs in subway stations, parks, and anywhere else they wanted. Key fans were then given maps of where the performances were going to be held, and encouraged to post pictures and videos of the performances.

The word-of-mouth results of the campaign were extensive—street musicians and fans alike posted personal pictures on their photo-sharing sites, wrote about their experiences on personal blogs, conversed about the songs and performances with friends on their social networks, and released videos on their video channels.

And to further stimulate word of mouth and get the conversation going, Oasis then created a 10-minute documentary about the entire marketing campaign, posted the video on important video channels, and attracted over 250,000 additional viewers in just one week. Sales in the first week of the album's release were healthy.

You see, creating interesting ideas and getting key fans and opinion leaders to take part and engage in your brand is the essence of word-of-mouth marketing. Okay, so your band is not Oasis, but you can use this example as inspiration to create your own ideas that get people sharing and talking about your career. So start thinking!

Seed Journalists and Other Industry Folk

Getting close to the end of our discussion on word-of-mouth marketing, be clear that journalists and other industry folks can play a major part in spreading the word about your products and services. For this reason, it is essential to provide (or *seed*) local media sources that cover your music scene with important information about your company. Typically this involves sending them a press kit (including a bio and an interesting story about your company), furnishing them with press releases that include relevant and current information that is "newsworthy," tipping them off about publicity stunts that shock and/or amuse your community, and inviting them to charity events that build goodwill toward your company. Remember that publicity and public relations were covered in more detail in a previous chapter, but it's extremely important to mention here as well.

Provide Product and Service Samples and Ask People to "Tell a Friend"

Finally, product and service samples are yet another important aspect of word-of-mouth marketing. Bottom line, people must be able to experience the product or service themselves so that they can get excited about it, discuss it with others, and make recommendations.

Be clear that companies of all shapes and sizes use samples as a promotional method. For instance, in the early '80s, Steve Jobs of Apple donated a computer to every school in California to stimulate excitement and generate the buzz. Pretty cool story considering where it all got him!

So, how might you provide samples and ask people to spread the word? Consider writing a few of the following tips into your own Marketing Plan of Attack™:

• Offer free song downloads on your site, accompanied by friendly verbiage that says, "If you like what you see or hear, please pass it along to a friend."

- Walk around key events, such as industry conventions and conferences where your target customers congregate, pass out samples, and ask them to "spread the word." Better yet, you can get an attractive representative to do it together with you. And . . .
- Throw exclusive private parties in interesting places, require that people RSVP immediately due to limited space, and permit them to "invite a special guest." Then perform a few of your best new songs live and ask people to "tell a friend."

That's all for word-of-mouth marketing. Now, let's move on and take a look at our last form of promotion in this chapter: *guerrilla marketing*. You won't want to miss this low-budget street method of promotion, so read on.

AFTERTHOUGHT: WAIT! GOT MORE TIPS? The Word-of-Mouth Marketing Association (WOMMA) educates its members via webinars, conferences, and articles, and provides guidelines that regulate ethical standards for word-of-mouth marketing. Check them out at womma.org.

Utilize Guerrilla (or "Street Commando") Tactics

While there are many definitions of what guerrilla marketing actually is, I like to think of it simply as this: *any unconventional form of promotion that can be employed on a low budget to no budget.*

The term *guerrilla marketing* actually comes from *guerrilla warfare*, where small groups of soldiers (or independent artist marketers, like you) conduct secret raids to "compete" against their current government (or, for our purposes, companies with large advertising dollars).

The aim of guerrilla marketing is not to win huge battles or have a huge effect on your community all at once, but rather to win small groups of fans gradually over time by exposing your brand everywhere they look.

Street stencils, stickers, posters, postcards, CD-R samplers, and CD-R fliers are all techniques that you might consider writing into your own Marketing Plan of Attack™. Since some of these techniques are considered controversial, I'll offer my legal disclaimer here: proceed at your own risk, and please be sure to respect your local laws. Now read on.

Make Your Mark with Street Stencils

Street stencils are thin sheets of cardboard with your band logo, website URL, and persuasive slogan cut into them. When an adhesive substance like paint or chalk is sprayed on top of the cardboard sheets, it seeps through the cutout designs in the cardboard and leaves the design impression on city sidewalks, walls, and beach boardwalks.

Just remember that using real paint to mark public property is illegal, so spray chalk is a wiser and recommended choice. Chalk-It Spray Chalk by Abrivo Sports is safe to use on virtually any surface and simply washes away with water. It is nonflammable, nontoxic, and environmentally safe. So perhaps you'll give it a try on your next guerrilla marketing raid.

Stick Up Your City with Stickers

Stickers are like secret marketing weapons that can include your logo, an interesting message, and a call to action (e.g., "check out our site"). Stickers can be easily carried in your pants pockets and then quickly stuck on everything from the bathroom stalls of clubs to the walls of record stores where other stickers are placed. Online companies like StickerJunkie and Sticker Guy are rather affordable and can help you get started.

Los Angeles DIY artist Andrew Trout actually helps himself to a handful of free adhesive packing labels found at his local post office, sprays them black with spray paint, and then sprays his band's logo on top of the packing slips with his website URL to create instant stickers. Hey, I'm not advocating this technique, because using these mailing labels to make DIY stickers goes beyond the post office's intended use, but it goes to show just how far some DIY artists are willing to go to generate a response on a low budget to no budget. Again, just be smart and proceed at your own risk.

EXAMPLE: BAND STICKERS

Tack Up Your Town with Fliers and Posters

Fliers and posters are marketing tools that display attractive graphics and important information about your performances and record releases. The best-designed fliers and posters are those that are kept simple and uncluttered, embrace custom fonts (see www.dafont.com), and provide a call to action (such as a QR code where further information can be obtained). Regular sizes include 8.5"×11" sheets of paper (usually called fliers) that you can print at any office supply store. Larger sizes can be as big as 24"×36" made from card stock

EXAMPLE: VARIOUS POSTERS

(usually called posters) that a company like Disc Makers or some other marketing company can print for you. Just keep in mind that the more colors you use, the higher your costs. Fliers and posters can be tacked, taped, or glued to various indoor/outdoor places, slid under dorm doors, and even hung inside clubs where you're going to perform (see the poster graphic).

For the first club gig I played as a kid in Kingston, New Jersey, I actually ran a guerrilla marketing raid in the middle of the night and hung fliers on every telephone pole on Route 27 between my home in Princeton and Kingston. It was great! You could see the bright green announcements for miles. After the gig, I even removed the fliers and disposed of them to avoid potential complaints by the city. So everyone won. Hey, if it worked for me, it can work for you. Perhaps you'll give fliers and posters a try.

Hit the Streets with Glossy Postcards

Glossy postcards (4 1/2"×6"), or as I call them, "mini portable billboards," are yet another guerrilla marketing idea that you might consider. You, or a street team of fans, can easily hand them out to club-goers on the streets.

EXAMPLE: POSTCARD

FREE CONCERT
ONE NIGHT STAND
20 LIVE ACTS ALONG WITH INTERNATIONAL DJs
November 19

The Key Club
Plush Lounge
9093 Sunset Blvd

Age: 18 + Doors: 6:30 Show: 7:00

Any local print shop or online business like Overnight Prints (www.overnightprints.com) can help get the job done.

One club promoter I know in Los Angeles took postcard promotion to a whole new level. He increased the size of the postcards to look like parking tickets and stuck them on cars' windshields. He had the words "City of Hollywood" on the front and put all the information about his club and upcoming events on the back. This definitely got people's attention. So, what will you come up with to help spread the word?

Hand Out Three-Song CD-R Samplers

Three-song CD-R samplers of your music can be handed out together with your glossy postcards, which we just discussed above. Manufacturers like Disc Makers (www.discmakers.com) can print the disc for you in as little as 24 hours and can even sell you a *CD duplicator* so you can print the discs yourself. CD samplers can be handed out on city streets and in front of venues where you are going to perform.

When handing out promotional items, be sure that people really want them. (Never shove stuff in people's hands.) This way you'll end up with a much better return on your investment and fewer CD-Rs in city trash cans. You're lucky. I had to learn this information the hard way.

Give Away CD-R Fliers

CD-R fliers are similar to CD-R samplers, but they specifically have the dates and times of your gigs *directly* printed onto the CD-Rs (hence the name, CD-R flier). These can be handed out in opportune places like city streets and sports venues. Disc Makers also sells *on-disc printers* to help you get the job done.

Organize Guerrilla Performances (a.k.a. "Smart Mob" Events)

And finally, let's talk about organizing guerrilla performances (a.k.a. "smart mob" events) at key locations. What's a guerrilla performance, you ask? It's where you set up your equipment and perform at *unauthorized places* and at *unauthorized times*. It's also where you use your social networks to rally your fans, get them to attend, and spread the word of mouth about your cause.

Rage Against the Machine performed in front of the New York Stock Exchange without the proper permits. Alien Ant Farm set up on a roof across from the BET Awards in Hollywood. And Kascade alerted fans via social networks that he would be DJing from the back of a flatbed truck as it rolled along Hollywood Boulevard.

Okay, so maybe the above examples are more publicity stunts than actual performances, but guerrilla performances can nonetheless be a good way to get the message out about your band—whether you're a more established act or just starting out. Perhaps I'll see you out on the streets too.

=MARKETING PLAN TEMPLATE=

Use the template below, or a template like it, to help you craft important information that you will use in your Marketing Plan of Attack™. For additional help, be sure to refer to the marketing plan example below, the chapter on assembling your plan, and the complete plan provided in the back of this book.

Your Company Promotion Strategy Template (Part 2)

Use this template to craft your promotion strategy. When formatting your marketing plan, you can remove the questions and just keep the headers and your answers. Utilize the points below that best apply to you. Be thorough!

Internet Strategy: Will you build a personal website? If so, what are the various menu items that you will use? Are you planning to use social media? If so, which sites, and what are the various strategies that you plan to use? Does building a mobile website sound like something that you will include in your plan? How do you plan to generate online publicity and reviews? Do you have any specific blogs or web magazines in mind to pursue? Will you use Web video? How about podcasts? And will you create any viral goodies with hopes that fans will pass them around?

Word-of-Mouth Marketing: Will you target customer hubs and opinion leaders? Do you plan on giving out product samples to get the word of mouth started? Will you hold any contests? Don't just rely on these questions; be sure to review the chapter to get more ideas.

Guerrilla Marketing Tactics: Will you utilize street stencils? If so, how and where? Do you plan to use stickers? If so, explain where and how. Do you plan to make fliers and posters? If so, where will you hang them? Do glossy postcards sound like something that would work in your promotional campaign? How about CD-R samplers?

=MARKETING PLAN EXAMPLE=

Now here's an abridged marketing plan example for the band Rally the Tribes, to help you put together your own promotional strategy.

PROMOTIONAL MIX STRATEGY

a) Internet Promotion Plan

★Personal Website at www.rallythetribes.com: RTT will use John Interpoll to develop a website using the free and low-budget services of WordPress. Menu items will include *About*, *Store*, *Media*, *Links*, *News*, and *Mailing List*. Using keywords like "RTT," "Rally the Tribes," "LA Bands," "Political Rallies," and so forth, we will use our designer to optimize the site for search engines and will also have our designer establish reciprocal links on "like-sites."

★Social Media: RTT will utilize social media accounts to ultimately draw traffic to www.rallythetribes.com. Sites like Facebook and Twitter will be at the center of their campaign. RTT will strive to engage people in conversation and listen to what they have to say; post quality, relevant, and current content that people want to share; and investigate what people are talking about on other social networks.

★ Podcasts: RTT will seek spins in cool electronic music podcast shows like *LA Mosh Mix*, *LA DJ*, and *Rock Monsters*. They will also seek interviews and performances on political talk show blogs by people like Princeton University Professor Cornel Ronald West, Dr. Ron Luther, and One People Blog News to attract the interest of new fans.

b) Word-of-Mouth Marketing Plan

★ Product Samples: RTT plans to give away 200 units of their 12-song album *War and Police* to stimulate interest and generate buzz among fans and industry folks. They will ask recipients to "tell a friend." They will also offer free exclusive downloads (at www.rallythetribes.com) of different remixes of songs that are not available on the RTT record.

c) Guerrilla (or Street Commando) Tactics

★ Street Stencils: RTT plans to stencil Los Angeles sidewalks in Hollywood, West LA, Venice, and other places where students, hipsters, and music/fashion-minded people converge. The stencil will feature the RTT man with his fist in the air and nothing more (i.e., there will be no further identification). Note: RTT will use spray chalk.

★ Fliers: We will make fliers (that look like political campaign posters) utilizing the free services of LA EZ Print (a friend and supporter of RTT). In return for the favor, we will include LA EZ Print's logo on the fliers. We will tack these fliers all over city telephone poles and in record stores and tattoo shops before RTT gigs.

Etc.

Formulate a Promotion Strategy, Part 3

Winning Over Fans via Radio Play and Creative Sponsorships

Radio play and sponsorships are yet two more methods of promotion that can help you communicate the unique *features* and *benefits* of your offerings. Similar to the other promotion strategies discussed in parts 1 and 2, the objective of utilizing these strategies is to help you achieve the goals of your marketing plan and also do the following:

- **Get your target customers' attention via radio play and creative alliances.**
- **Stimulate your fans' sense of intrigue and hold their interest.**
- **Help them to decide that they need and want your offerings.**
- **Get them to act by making a purchase.**

I can't stress enough how important it is to keep all of your other strategies and research findings in mind when developing a promotion strategy—from having a clear profile of your target fan and the radio formats and stations to which they are most likely to listen, to having a clear idea of your desired brand image and the companies that would be a perfect fit for sponsorships.

Furthermore, it's important to state again that it's not just a radio campaign or sponsorship that will make or break your career, but rather the perfect blend of all of your other promotional strategies working together as one integrated marketing communications program. Okay? Good!

Now let's get right to work and examine some low-budget promotional strategies, including the following:

1. **Developing a Radio Promotion Campaign**
2. **Aligning with Local and National Sponsors**

Develop a Radio Promotion Campaign

Radio promotion is the process of soliciting your music to radio stations to get airplay, build professional relationships, and make fans. While it is a category of promotion that is not mentioned in general marketing books, it is very specific to the music business and the No. 1 medium for taking music to the masses. A hit song can get played on a commercial radio station at least 14 times in one day—*in one city*—reaching hundreds of thousands of listeners and potential new fans.

But commercial radio stations are not an easy "nut to crack." The majors have always had a tough time getting music added—*and still do today*! This brings us to whether or not commercial radio is even a viable medium for the independent and do-it-yourself artist to pursue. If not, then what are the alternatives and what can you reasonably expect to accomplish?

It's questions like these that make developing a radio promotion campaign so necessary. It's crucial to have a realistic and practical understanding of what you can (and cannot) accomplish, or you could easily spend your valuable time and energy with zero results.

From choosing the appropriate mediums to looking ahead toward hiring an independent radio promoter, you'll find the following points extremely helpful when developing your radio campaign.

Choose the Appropriate Mediums

There are essentially six different radio mediums from which the independent do-it-yourself artist can choose when putting together a radio promotion plan: college radio, National Public Radio, commercial specialty shows, Web radio, satellite radio, and smaller-market commercial stations.

College Radio (or Noncommercial Radio)

College radio is one of the easiest ways for independent artists to receive radio play. Typically, college radio is made up of three-hour individual shows presented by student DJs who are broadcast or communications majors. Most of these student DJs fancy themselves as being "the man" (or woman) who is going to discover that next big local band. Thus, student DJs are very enthusiastic about music and are usually very approachable.

Building relationships with college radio personnel makes good sense because these folks are typically well connected to other local DJs, club owners, local record stores, and the college's own activities director, who books college gigs. The only downside to promoting your music for airplay on college radio stations is that the broadcast range of most stations is very limited. Thus you may not be able to pick up the signal from much farther than a few miles beyond the campus perimeter.

ARRANGE A PROMOTIONAL CHARTING CAMPAIGN FOR CMJ

One of the great things about promoting your music to college radio is that you can also get ranked on College Music Journal, an organization that charts college radio play. CMJ's charts are viewed by a wide array of music industry folk (ranging from A&R to music publishers), so any band showing up in these charts is deemed impressive.

To chart on CMJ, you must convince at least 5 to 40 college stations (depending on the time of year) to add your record to its playlists and report you to CMJ. This is no easy task—it requires organization, tenacity, and persons with great phone skills to make follow-up calls to stations that you service—but it can be accomplished!

To arrange a charting campaign, you can get the pertinent station list from CMJ or by searching online for something like "CMJ reporting college stations," decide on a specific date (a.k.a. *add date*) on which you want to be added to a station's top playlists, and put together a team of people to call the stations every week for several weeks. Perhaps someone from your fan club would be excited to help. Just make sure to script out what you want him or her to say about you.

For further advice on charting, you can visit Bryan Farrish (www.radio-media.com) or contact CMJ (www.cmj.com).

National Public Radio (NPR)

While on the topic of college and noncommercial radio stations, it might be a good idea to briefly mention National Public Radio (NPR) stations, since their programming is often provided as a service of college radio stations.

NPR is a publicly funded radio entity that broadcasts a wide range of eclectic music, interesting news programs, human-interest stories, and more. Overall, it is a great medium for up-and-coming indie artists to receive airplay and get noticed.

In Los Angeles, KCRW, the NPR affiliate that operates out of Santa Monica College, runs several shows that feature talented up-and-comers. Indie artist Gaby Moreno was featured on the station and has since progressed to doing some very cool things, such as a tour with Tracy Chapman.

The only minor downside to NPR stations is that they are publicly funded and rely on donations. Thus, they often have fundraisers for several days every few months and consequently talk much more than broadcast new music. But this is to be expected and a small price to pay. Be sure to search for NPR affiliate stations and programs near you at www.npr.org/stations.

Commercial Specialty Shows

Commercial *specialty shows* are the weekly late-night programs on commercial radio stations that focus on independent artists and the local music scene.

While the music that airs on specialty shows is not part of regular commercial rotation programming, the benefit of getting played on these programs is that the DJ typically sits in on meetings with the station's program director, and it could lead to regular rotation down the line. Another benefit is that the broadcast range of commercial stations could number in the tens (and even hundreds) of miles, so the exposure for just one spin could be pretty significant.

The downside to commercial specialty shows is that they typically feature more alternative styles of music than they do pop music. Furthermore, since they get hundreds of submissions, it is unlikely that you'll be played on any one particular station beyond one or two spins.

For an example of a specialty show, check out Kat Corbett's *Locals Only* at kroq.radio.com/shows/kat-corbett/, or just search for "commercial specialty shows" online.

Web Radio

Web radio stations are yet another way to get your music and brand exposed. To be clear, I am not talking about the bigger commercial stations that broadcast online, but rather the passionate broadcasters who sit in their bedrooms or small studios broadcasting independent music from talented people just like you.

The great thing about these indie Web radio broadcasters is that they are actively looking for new content for their shows, and their submission policies can be as simple as sending a music file via e-mail. Furthermore, the listeners are typically die-hard music lovers who are interested in discovering new and exciting music. Bottom line: *exposure on Web radio stations can lead to more fans, as well as more sales of your music.* Search the Web for stations at Live365 (www.live365.com) and other sites like it.

START YOUR OWN WEB RADIO STATION

Starting *your own* Web radio station to broadcast your music (as well as the music of other indie artists who give you permission) might also be a great option, though one that is extremely ambitious.

One student of mine created his own techno show on which he broadcast the music of a handful of Los Angeles DJs weekly from his studio loft. He would interview these DJs, report on the latest club news, and spin his own music as well. Thousands of fans from all over the world (Amsterdam, London, New York) listened weekly. To start your station today, you can find easy-to-use software packages and services at a very reasonable price. For starters check out Pirate Radio (www.pirateradio.com) and also BlogTalkRadio (www.blogtalkradio.com).

Satellite Radio Stations

While there are just a few satellite service providers in the United States (in fact, Sirius XM Radio Inc. is pretty much it), satellite radio is yet another medium through which artists can receive radio play.

Satellite radio stations can be both ad based and ad free, and provide a number of niche music and talk programs that cannot be found on regular terrestrial radio stations.

Since satellite radio relies on signals beamed from satellites (hence the name *satellite*), the shows can be picked up from automobiles and homes anywhere in the United States—so the exposure can be pretty substantial. Furthermore, since satellite radio requires a subscription and special hardware, the listeners typically tend to be a little more sophisticated—*read: those who have more money and may be more interested in purchasing your music if they like it.*

Perhaps the only downside to satellite radio is that the submission process can be a little difficult, as information for submissions is not readily available, and follow-up calls and e-mails are frowned upon.

Smaller-Market, Low-Rated Commercial Stations

Last on our list of possible radio stations on which to promote your music, let's discuss smaller-market commercial stations.

Peter Petro of Bryan Farrish Radio Promotions says that these stations are far more accepting of indie artists' music than major commercial stations in bigger markets such as Los Angeles, New York, and Nashville. Additionally, smaller-market stations are more accepting of pop music and smooth jazz, which are two formats that most college stations do not cover. While you have to reach out to tens of smaller-market stations just to get one interested, you can succeed at getting airplay. In Petro's exact words, "Radio promotion is not unlike a presidential campaign. You really have to be ready to put in a significant amount of time."

AFTERTHOUGHT: CREATE A STATION LIST Create a target station list of all radio mediums by using Radio-Locator (www.radio-locator.com), Indie Bible (www.indiebible.com), and Live365 (www.live365.com). You can also use annual guides compiled by music magazines such as *Music Connection*. Write down the station name, show name, DJ, contact information, submission policy, and *call time* (the time the DJ accepts calls). This should pretty much do it.

Prepare the Proper Materials for Your Campaign

Before sending out your music to the various radio mediums discussed above, you must have the proper materials together. While there are a few exceptions to the rule (depending on the specific medium and director of the station), you need the following:

- A broadcast-quality master, including metadata, with sounds and performances that are comparable in quality to other material you hear played on your local stations.
- A professionally replicated disc (rather than a disc burned by you at home) to ensure reliable playback at the stations.
- A disc packaged in standard plastic jewel cases (with a spine) or Digipaks (with a spine) to accommodate the configuration of radio station shelves where music is stored. Note that thinner packaging might go undetected and get lost between other CDs.
- A package that is properly labeled, including your name, address, e-mail, website URL, song titles, song lengths, and suggested listening.
- A "one-sheet" that includes important information such as your name, picture, brief bio, and accomplishments.
- A short note or cover letter indicating your objectives for sending your music. And finally . . .
- A digital file of your album in case the station prefers digital online submissions.

Anne Litt, director of music development at KCRW in Santa Monica, sums it all up by saying, "We just need you to make it supereasy—no 8" × 10" photos, no posters, and nothing else that *kills a million trees.* I appreciate quick efficiency that's to the point."

Consider How You Will "Service" Stations

The method by which you get your music in the hands of radio station personnel (a process called *servicing*) is another important consideration when putting together your radio promotion plan. Servicing is done by either sending your packages by first class mail, e-mailing your digital music files, or traveling to the stations and meeting with the appropriate DJs, but the method really depends on the specific radio medium and station director.

At the college level, for instance, servicing can be done by all methods: first class mail, e-mail, or face-to-face delivery. The latter is obviously a more personal approach.

When serving face-to-face, you can find out when a specific DJ is coming off the air and then show up at the station a few minutes before that time. Be flattering (say you are a fan of his or her show), knowledgeable (comment on a previous broadcast or guest), and humble (say you'd love to hear his or her professional and trusted opinion about your music). And remember to keep the meeting brief! If done with tact, servicing stations in person can really make a difference.

Strategize Your Follow-Up

It's not enough to just service your music to radio stations; now you have to promote it. Remember this: *music is usually not broadcast on the radio because it is good, but because it is well promoted.* Thus, creating a well-thought-out follow-up strategy is another crucial step in putting together a solid radio plan.

When calling stations to get feedback, Anne Litt of KCRW advises, "Just be personable, don't be pushy, and make the DJ aware of any other stations that might be playing your music." Great advice, Anne. And if a station decides to add your music to its playlist, I'd advise you to be prepared to do the following:

- Send the DJ a thank-you card for adding your music, and let him or her know that you really appreciate his or her support.
- Request positive quotes from the DJ about your music to use in your promotional packets.
- Schedule station interviews and station performances.
- Offer records, merchandise, and concert tickets that the DJ can give away on his or her show.
- Send in prerecorded *station identifications* (e.g., "This is John Doe and you're listening to KXLU"). DJs typically get a kick out of station IDs.
- Provide prerecorded *station drops* (where you remix a song to include a specific station's call letters or DJ's name).
- Invite the DJ to your shows as a guest.
- Ask the DJ to MC your live performance.
- Ask your fans to listen to the station and inquire about your music when they hear it.

Overall, remember that your promotional goals for radio should be to form long-term relationships that can lead to other promotional opportunities. DJs and other radio personnel are known to refer bands to important contacts like other radio DJs, local club bookers, and owners of mom-and-pop retail stores. They also go on to work at commercial stations, *and this might be an "in" for you down the road.* I call this creating the "clique of the future" and sealing your fate. As English author Samuel Johnson once said, "The future is purchased by the present."

Look Ahead Toward Hiring an Independent Radio Promoter

And as a final step in your radio promotion plan, you might also consider getting an independent radio promoter.

Independent radio promoters are paid for their experience and the number of connections they have that can lead to spins. They offer advice about which songs to service to radio, and they mail out packages, make follow-up calls, work charting campaigns, and send you weekly reports on your music's progress. Some promoters even get your recordings into record stores (albeit there are not many stores left these days).

However, the downside of independent radio promoters is that they cost money. For indie artists, a promoter can charge $3,000 to $10,000 for a four-month professional radio campaign. Also, there may not be any point to getting airplay in a city 3,000 miles away from you, unless you're ready to follow up with a tour of that city.

Despite the aforementioned cons, it's still a good idea to take a look at some of the services that exist out there to get a good sense of the available players in your market. Bryan Farrish Radio Promotion (www.radio-media.com), Tinderbox Music (www.tinderboxmusic.com), and Powderfinger Promotions (www.powderfingerpromo.com) are a few companies you may want to check out.

Now let's move on and briefly examine the next, and last, type of promotion we'll discuss in this chapter: sponsorships.

Align with Local and National Sponsors

Sponsorships are a mutually beneficial relationship wherein each of two (or more) product-based companies market their products via the support and approval of the other. Says Patrick Courrielche of Inform Ventures, LLC: "Simply put, sponsorships are a win-win situation for all."

Artists can develop relationships with local sellers and national manufacturers and get the following:

- Live show promotion.
- Visibility through music samplers.
- Exposure from company advertisements.
- Free merchandise.
- Cash awards.
- Recording time.
- Tour support.
- Promotional giveaways, such as T-shirts, posters, gift bags, and bumper stickers.
- Credibility in the eyes of the public, as well as in the eyes of club bookers who might be interested in having that artist perform.

Companies, on the other hand, can form relationships with artists and get the following:

- Exposure to selective target markets.
- Public awareness and sales.
- Coolness by associating themselves with hip and "in" music.

Though sponsorships are usually reserved for artists already creating a small buzz in their communities, remember that "if you don't ask, the answer is always *no*!" Or to put it another way, sports legend Wayne Gretzky says, "You miss 100 percent of all the shots you don't take."

So from listing the products that are associated with your fans to getting promoted on local music compilations, be sure to write a few of the following ideas into your Plan of Attack™.

List the Products Associated with Your Fans

The first and most important step in uncovering sponsorship opportunities is to review the customer profile you established in chapter 4 and list the various products that are associated with your fans—including their clothing, footwear, headgear, sunglasses, and what they drink. In case that wasn't clear, your customer's psychographic and behavioral characteristics are the key in helping you hone in on what businesses and companies are worth approaching for sponsorships.

For instance, your fans might be drawn to Vans shoes, Doc Martens boots, or Von Dutch headgear. Or they may be into Powell or Flowlab skateboards, Scion cars, or Harley-Davidson motorcycles. They may also be into Jack Daniel's liquor, Newcastle Brown Ale, or Rockstar energy drinks. Lastly, they might be drawn to Zig-Zag rolling papers, Zippo lighters, or Swisher Sweets cigars.

Whatever the products your target audience enjoys, just remember that the more specific you are in describing your fans' preferences, the more focused you'll be on the right companies to approach. So, if you haven't fully analyzed your fans, now may be a good time to go back to chapter 4 and get busy with a customer analysis.

Form Strategic Alliances with Local Sellers via In-Store and Cross-Promotions

After listing all of the products associated with your fans, you're ready to form strategic alliances with local sellers. This is the process of researching local small businesses that sell the specific products your fans use, and then reaching out to these stores to arrange mutually beneficial promotional campaigns. These include in-store promotions and cross-promotions.

Try In-Store Promotions

In-store promotions are simply promotional opportunities within various retail stores. They can include live performances, broadcasts over the store's sound system, posters, listening booths (where your record can be sampled), and consignment agreements.

As part of my DIY marketing class at UCLA, one Los Angeles band approached a hip and fashionable clothing boutique on West Hollywood's Melrose Avenue and arranged a number of these various promotions. The band's record was made available for sale in the boutique, while select tracks blasted over the sound system daily to promote it. The band was even invited to play in the store on a Saturday afternoon, and it attracted a huge crowd and made new fans. What's more, it was given free merchandise to parade in onstage and give out to fans around town. Hey, you can't beat that!

Seek Cross-Promotions

Cross-promotions are situations where two or more companies come together to advertise their products and share the costs 50/50. Let's use a tattoo shop and a band as an example (see the graphic "Hollywood Tattoo Presents"): Could there be a better advertisement for a tattoo shop than one that is attached to a rock 'n' roll show where people have an interest in tattoos? *No.* And is there a better situation for an artist like you to be associated with a cool store while saving money and getting promoted to your public? *No.* Can you see how this works? Of course you can! Everyone wins.

It's not too difficult to find businesses interested in forming alliances with you—you just have to get out there and sell yourself. Artists in your very own city may already even have relationships with local stores and be willing to share the information with you. Be sure to reach out to them and see what you uncover.

AFTERTHOUGHT: WAVE YOUR SPONSOR'S FLAG Always be sure to include your sponsors' names and logos on the flyers and posters you make when promoting your events. This is important. The more you promote them, the longer they'll support you.

Be on the Lookout for Corporate Contests, Campaigns, and Opportunities

After researching local sellers and investigating strategic alliances, you can investigate the companies that *manufacture* the specific "product brands associated with your target fans" to uncover available contests, campaigns, and opportunities. By simply logging on to various corporate websites, you'll be surprised at the number of companies that are getting involved with bands. Consider these:

- Jim Beam supports bands through its National Campus Band Competition with rewards of cash, recording time, and musical gear.
- Zippo Lighters holds its Zippo Hot Tour; the winning prize is a showcase for major-label A&R representatives.
- Taco Bell actually allowed select touring bands to eat for free in any one of their restaurant locations across the United States.
- Jeep sponsored and promoted eight independent artists to go on tour in its jeeps and appear on *The Tonight Show* (indie artist Eric Hutchinson is one example).
- The Gap is known to sponsor and promote band performances in its stores.
- Anheuser-Busch is known to hold a battle of the bands and promote the winners. And finally . . .
- Grey Goose vodka is known to offer free drinks at various events if you can prove you have a large draw that's over 21.

Don't just target companies that are already getting involved in sponsorships—forge your own new ground as well. To illustrate, a local environmentally conscious Los Angeles band got really creative when it approached the manufacturers of a company that built vegetable oil–powered motors and transporters, and arranged a sponsorship for a national tour in a vegetable oil–powered bus. The idea was so creative, it also earned the band a significant amount of news coverage and promotion in both print and television. Kick-ass!

SANGRE AND SAM ASH: A WIN-WIN RELATIONSHIP

Musicians Institute graduate Ralph Castellanos Jr. (of the band Sangre) approached a local branch of a national company and received what he calls an "accessory deal," all by showing his band was creating a buzz. The band received a credit of $250 a month for accessories (strings, picks, skins, sticks) from any Sam Ash music store (www.samash.com). In return, the band contractually agreed to hang a Sam Ash banner onstage everywhere it performed, to include the Sam Ash logo on promotional fliers, and to upload the Sam Ash logo onto the band's website. Furthermore, the band gave Sam Ash the rights to use their music on music compilations. If these compilations were to be distributed for sale, the band would have received a royalty of 20 percent. That's not a bad deal considering the amount of promotion and exposure.

Says Castellanos, "Sam Ash was interested in bands that were performing two times per month, had already created a local name for themselves, and had a professional-sounding demo. We spoke with a store representative in LA and got the corporate phone number. We expressed our enthusiasm and just sold ourselves from there. We were persistent, but we were never pains in the butts. I think this type of sponsorship was a great way for my band to jump into the 'endorsement' world and get that little extra bit of promotional boost and support we needed when starting out. Also, it was a great way for Sam Ash to promote its stores. Our contract was only one year long and everybody won!" [Author's note: Though most contracts at this level of sponsorship are straightforward, never sign anything you do not understand without first seeking proper counsel.]

Build Credibility and Exposure via Equipment Endorsements

Equipment endorsements are yet another way to promote your brand and build awareness about your company. Endorsements are like product sponsorships, but they deal specifically with companies that offer free or discounted musical instruments and mentions in advertisements. In return for this, all you have to do is perform on a specific company's gear in front of a substantial number of people and sound damn good doing it.

To begin forming relations with certain companies, you should make a list of the various brands of musical instruments you play currently, or truly desire to play. Visit the websites of these target companies and write down the artist relations directors' names, addresses, phone numbers, e-mails, and submission requirements. You can then drop these folks a line, or better yet, meet them in person by attending the biannual NAMM show (www.namm.com), which is a large convention that attracts nearly every equipment manufacturer and artist relations director. If going to NAMM is not possible, then get to know your local music store representatives. Remember that these people are on the phone with equipment manufacturers all day long and can certainly help lead you to a professional endorsement down the line. If it worked for me, it can work for you.

Now be sure to check out companies such as Pearl, Sabian, Rhythm Tech, Rickenbacker, and Gibson, which are all known to provide endorsements to musicians who are attracting attention.

AFTERTHOUGHT: ATTENTION Bill Zildjian of Sabian (a cymbal manufacturer) says the best candidates for endorsements are those who can show that they're generating "attention" in their community, and specifically generating the attention of people between the ages of 18 and 30 who aspire to be musicians. A teacher with a large student roster, a band with a huge local buzz, or a group on a small leg of a national tour might qualify for an endorsement.

Get Promoted via Corporate Music Compilations

Corporate music compilations are the last sponsorship method that we'll discuss in this chapter. Created by various corporations as a way to reach their customers more casually, music compilations are albums that feature several singer/songwriters and bands. For instance:

- The automobile company Saturn put together a compilation of unsigned singer/songwriters and distributed it with all of the cars it sold nationwide.
- The Internet service provider EarthLink arranged a compilation to give out to all of its new customers.
- And the social networking site MySpace (when they were still cool) created a compilation with the Vans Warped Tour and distributed it to all ticket holders.

To find opportunities similar to the ones above, Dave Freeman of Falling Elevator Music (a marketing agency) suggests you browse the websites of trendy and relevant corporate brands. Also keep your eyes open for announcements on message boards like Pulse Music Board (www.pulsemusic.proboards.com) and network groups like Yahoo Groups (www.groups.yahoo.com/neo). You might also keep your eyes open for companies, like Freeman's, that specialize in corporate compilation marketing. "Just be skeptical of newer and smaller companies that request an upfront payment to be made on the compilations they create," says Freeman. "*The last thing you can afford is to get ripped off.*"

SEVEN STEPS TO APPROACHING SPONSORS

1. Make a detailed list of the local businesses and national corporations you wish to target. Log on to each company's website for specific information, including the business's name, owner, brand manager, event coordinator, address, phone number, store hours, website URL, submission polices, and more.
2. Be prepared to show various companies how they can benefit by sponsoring you: show that you're creating a buzz in your community, you're reaching their target demographic fan, and you have the right personality that matches and aligns with their brand.
3. Create a press kit (physical and electronic) that is specifically designed with sponsors in mind. Show pictures of you promoting the product, and include biographical information. Check out companies like Sonicbids to help you create your electronic press kit if needed.
4. Remember to express absolute excitement in promoting a company's products. Emphasize your work ethic and commitment to following through on the deal. Many bands flake out on hanging up banners at shows, placing logos on posters, mentioning the company's name in record liner notes, and keeping sponsors up to date with career news. Some bands even attempt to sell or pawn products that were given to them. These are all big mistakes. Paris Hilton has been sued more than once for not honoring her sponsorship agreements. But that's no surprise!
5. Be persistent but never be a pain in the butt. Polish your sales and negotiation skills by reading books like Zig Ziglar's *Secrets of Closing the Sale.*
6. Refer to the global authority on sponsorships, IEG, and its books *The IEG Complete Guide to Sponsorships* and the *IEG Source Book* (www.sponsorship.com). These are two helpful resources that list strategies for obtaining sponsorships. IEG even holds a regular convention that could be a good networking opportunity. And finally . . .
7. Never sign any agreement you do not understand. As I've said before and will say again, consult with a proper business representative, such as a skilled consultant and/or attorney.

=MARKETING PLAN TEMPLATE=

Use the template below, or a template like it, to help you craft important information that you will use in your Marketing Plan of Attack™. For additional help, be sure to refer to the marketing plan example below, the chapter on assembling your plan, and the complete plan provided in the back of this book.

Your Company Promotion Strategy Template (Part 3)

Use this template to craft your promotion strategy. When formatting your marketing plan, you can remove the questions and just keep the headers and your answers. Utilize the points below that best apply to you. Be thorough! Don't just answer the questions below; be sure to review the chapter to get specific ideas for a variety of promotion methods.

Radio Promotion Strategy: What radio mediums will you be pursuing (college, Web, satellite, specialty shows, etc.)? What are the specific stations that you are targeting? How will you service those stations? Is there any particular follow-up plan that you intend to execute? Whatever strategies you choose, list them clearly, as I have done in the marketing plan example below.

Local and National Sponsorship Plan: What are the various products associated with your target fans? Who are the local sellers and where are they located? Who are the corporate manufacturers and where are they located? Will you be targeting equipment manufacturers? If so, which ones and why? What information will you compile as a means to sell yourself to a sponsor or endorser (EPK, physical press kit)?

=MARKETING PLAN EXAMPLE=

Now here's an abridged marketing plan example for the band Rally the Tribes, to help you put together your own promotional strategy.

PROMOTIONAL MIX STRATEGY
a) Radio Promotion Plan

★College Radio: RTT will focus primarily on getting played on college radio stations in Southern California.

★National Public Radio: RTT will target NPR stations for interviews and appearances that focus on music and politics (e.g., *This Is the World* on KCRW).

★Station List: RTT will focus on college radio stations such as KSCR (USC), KXLU (Loyola Marymount), UCLARadio.com (UCLA), KCSN (Northridge), KPCC (Pasadena), KCSB (Santa Barbara), KCSC (Cal State Chico), and KOXY (Occidental College). They will also focus on commercial specialty shows, such as KROQ's *Locals Only* with DJ Kat Corbett. A full list with contact information is available in our database.

★Materials: RTT will submit a full physical press kit, including RTT folder, one-sheet, and *War and Police* CD in Digipak packaging (the suggested listening track will be "Petty Thieves Hang, Big Ones Get Elected" and "LAPD—Treat 'Em Like a King").

★Servicing: RTT will service all Southern California college stations in person. RTT will attempt to service Kat Corbett of KROQ at one of her regularly hosted events as a remote DJ, and also send her a package via UPS.

★Follow-Up: RTT will build relationships with local stations by inviting DJs to MC certain local performances, offering giveaway concert tickets and merch that can be given out on the air, submitting station IDs, getting DJ testimonials that can be used in RTT biographical material, and requesting live interviews and performances on station shows.

b) Local and National Sponsorships

★Products Associated with Fans: Nike designer footwear, Nike clothing, Nike accessories, Coogi jeans and polos, Abercrombie and Fitch polo shirts, Kat Von D tattoos, Ray-Ban sunglasses, Flowlab skateboards, Scion cars, Zig-Zag rolling papers, Zippo lighters, and RockStar energy drinks.

★Local Sellers List: Hollywood Skate on Cahuenga, Melrose Swag on Melrose, Blue Fly Designer Shoes of Beverly Hills, Kat Von D tattoo shop on La Brea, Scion of North Hollywood on Lankershim, and Melrose Smoke and Toke shop on Melrose.

★Corporate Manufacturers List: Ray-Ban corporate office in Rochester, New York; Scion corporate office in Torrance, California; Nike corporate office in Beaverton, Oregon; Zippo corporate office in Bradford, Pennsylvania; Coogi corporate office in Pine Bluff, Arizona; Flowlab corporate office in Long Beach, California; Zig-Zag corporate office in Louisville, Kentucky; Rockstar corporate office in Las Vegas, Nevada; and Kat Von D tattoo shop in Hollywood, California.

Etc.

17

Formulate a Promotion Strategy, Part 4

Utilizing Direct Marketing, Personal Selling, and Sales Promotions to Get Fans

Wrapping up our four-part discussion on promotion, direct marketing, face-to-face selling, and sales promotions are additional strategies you might consider to help you achieve your marketing plan goals. By keeping in mind all of your other strategies and the research tools we discussed in this book thus far (your customer profile, competitor analysis, brand identity etc.), you can create an effective and integrated marketing communication plan that ultimately helps you do the following:

- **Build customers' awareness by grabbing their attention.**
- **Hold your customers' interest by giving them what they want/need.**
- **Provide important information that helps customers decide to buy.**
- **Build customers' relationships by enticing them to take action.**

The objectives and benefits of promotion should all sound pretty familiar to you by now, as we've discussed them in the proceeding promotional chapters. So, let's just cut right to the chase and examine the following low-budget strategies:

1. **Developing a Direct Marketing Plan**
2. **Thinking About Face-to-Face Selling**
3. **Employing Sales Promotions**

Develop a Direct Marketing Plan

As defined by George Belch in *Advertising and Promotion*, *direct marketing* is a system by which organizations bypass intermediaries and *communicate directly with end users to generate sales*. Promotional communications (including order forms, URLs, 800 numbers, coupons, etc.) are delivered primarily via regular mail, phone, the Internet, and broadcast media. Typically, contacts are managed and updated in a database.

There are a number of benefits you get by utilizing direct marketing in your promotional plan. It can be:

- Targeted to specific customer characteristics (by age, city, purchase habits, etc.).
- Personalized to include names on envelopes and in e-mail correspondences.
- Executed inexpensively compared to other forms of promotion. And . . .
- Easily tracked to measure effectiveness.

There are also a number of disadvantages to direct marketing. Typically people are:

- Offended by most promotional correspondences they receive via mail or the Internet.
- Supportive of "do not call" lists and anti-spam laws.

- Uncomfortable purchasing products (like T-shirts) they cannot examine.
- Scared to use credit cards online.

But when weighing the pros and cons, direct marketing is still a very popular form of promotion used by all types of companies.

From examining the various types of direct marketing methods to writing persuasive content that generates a response and leads to sales, let's take a closer look at how you might use direct marketing to achieve the goals of your marketing plan.

Decide on the Direct Marketing Methods

There are a number of direct marketing methods that can help you reach out to your target audience and trigger a buying response. I've already alluded to some of these methods in previous chapters, so let's briefly focus on direct mail, telemarketing, and mobile marketing.

Direct Mail (Using Regular Mail)

Started back in 1733 when Benjamin Franklin sold almanacs through regular mail, direct mail is still used as a major promotional strategy. While you may associate direct mail immediately with junk mail that gets thrown away (typically only 2 percent of all people targeted by direct mail will respond), it can still be an effective way to promote your record releases, concert performances, and news.

There are generally two types of mailing pieces used by independent artists via regular mail: standard letter–sized notices and postcards.

- ***Standard Letter–Sized Notices:*** Standard 8.5"×11" sheets of paper that contain notices about your offerings and events can easily be folded into thirds and stuffed into letter-sized envelopes. In the direct mail world, these notices are often called *broadsides*.
- ***Postcards:*** Eliminating the envelope altogether for a more immediate message delivery, glossy postcards (4.25"×6") can include an attractive picture on one side and a personal note to a fan on the other (see the graphic "Postcard"). By the way, the post office offers reduced rates to organizations sending out postcards in bulk.

Telemarketing (Using the Phone)

Many people are annoyed by telemarketing, but *using the phone* is yet another effective direct marketing method that you might consider for your plan. It includes outbound and inbound calls.

- ***Outbound Calls:*** Outbound promotional calls to invite fans to come out to your shows, among other things, can be executed easily. I actually forgot how special a phone invite could be until I received a call from a Los Angeles club promoter who invited me to her event. Of course, she had an absolutely charming phone voice and was quite personable. That said, if your speaking voice is not your strongest asset, here are three tips: pronounce everyone's name correctly, speak slowly, and smile when you talk.

- ***Inbound Calls:*** Inbound, toll-free 800 numbers can also be executed easily for a rather inexpensive per-minute rate and one-time setup fee. Numbers can be included in your mailings, in e-mails, and on your website to generate buying action. When people call in, you can have an attractive message that announces all of your gigs, leaves a personal greeting to fans, and promises to call them back. Or you can even answer the calls during certain business hours or hire a few interns to answer calls for you.

Mobile Marketing

Next to last in our discussion about direct marketing is mobile marketing, which is sure to get bigger as technology develops. A statistic by Nielsen (www.nielsen.com) states that over half the population of the United States owns a mobile device. So let's take a look at two methods of mobile marketing: text messaging and mobile applications.

- ***Text Messaging:*** There's a sense of immediacy that comes with receiving a text message, and in recent surveys conducted by Nielsen, teenagers between the ages of 13 to 19, and adults 20 to 28, send and respond to text messages as much as three thousand times per month. (Older groups use it less, but the numbers are improving, according to the Pew Charitable Trusts, a nonprofit research organization.) As long as your fans don't mind it, text-messaging marketing may be a good choice for you. There are four basic methods of mobile marketing (see the graphic "Text Message Mobile Marketing," and view it from left to right): *mobile coupon texting, Quick Response (QR) code texting, text-to-vote surveys,* and *group text messaging.* For more information on these various methods, be sure to check out Pro Texting (www.protexting.com), Mobivity (www.mobivity.com), and other companies like them.

- ***Mobile Apps:*** We touched briefly on apps as a distribution strategy in chapter 12. Thus, I'll only use this space as a brief reminder that apps are a method of direct marketing that, if downloaded by your target fans onto their mobile devices, can serve as a constant attention grabber that your Web store and products are just a touch away. It's not that difficult, or expensive, to get a mobile app built. So again, for starters, just check out Mobile Roadie (www.mobileroadie.com). You'll be glad you did.

This only touches the surface of what mobile marketing is all about, so be sure to check out the book *Go Mobile* by Jeanne Hopkins and Jamie Turner for more detailed info.

Personal Websites and E-mail Marketing

And finally, personal websites and e-mail marketing are two more methods of direct marketing that allow you to communicate with fans and do business without any middleperson distributors or intermediaries. Since we've already covered websites and e-mail in previous chapters, just remember to create an informative website that gets fans to act, and use a professional e-mail service that helps your correspondences rise above all of the clutter that exists on the Internet.

GET YOUR MAILING/CALLING/TEXTING LISTS TOGETHER

Once you've chosen your method of direct marketing, you should assemble and maintain a targeted contact list or database. We've been touching on this briefly throughout the book, but here are few more ideas:

- **Fan Lists:** Ask fans to e-mail or text you so that you can immediately log their addresses into your databases. Also, be sure to provide a form on your personal websites where fans can sign your mailing list or subscribe to your blog.
- **Business Lists:** Network at key events, and be ready to exchange business cards with important industry folks. Also refer to handy resource guides and sites like the Music Business Registry (www.musicregistry.com) and SRDS (www.srds.com) to gather the contacts of interesting business leaders with whom you'd like to form relationships.
- **Shared Lists:** Ask other like bands in your area if they can send out announcements on their lists, and you can do the same for them on your lists. And finally . . .
- **Rented Lists:** Call your local music stores, magazines, and other music-related businesses and ask if they'd be willing to rent out their mailing/phone lists. Speak with the ad departments to get the rates and other particulars. Okay?

[Note: The Direct Marketing Association (DMA) provides a wealth of helpful information and statistical data on the practices and methods of direct marketing, and on building up your databases. Why not visit their site at www.newdma.org.]

Create Persuasive Content That Sells

Now that you have a good idea about the various direct marketing methods that exist (mail, telemarketing, mobile marketing, the Internet, etc.), we need to discuss the most important part of direct marketing: *content*! Without great content, everything we've discussed so far is meaningless. You'll find the following brief tips to be extremely useful.

- **Say the Most Important Things First:** State who you are, the most unique benefit that you're offering, and some interesting hook or question that gets your target customers' attention and ultimately entices them to buy.
- **Provide More Detailed Information:** Hold your customers' interest and help them decide to do business with you by indicating your key selling points and "what's in it for them." Be succinct!
- **Include Your Company Logo and Slogan:** When applicable, include your company's logo and slogan (sometimes called a *company signature*) at the bottom or end of your correspondence. Doing this can help build *brand image* and increase *brand recognition*, which are known to lead to repeated sales.
- **End with a Call to Action:** Get your fans to act by including a polite command toward the end of your marketing communication. For instance: "To RSVP for the show and exclusive after-party, be sure to contact www.example.com/JulyParty while tickets last." This stuff really works!
- **Use a Marketing Information System Code:** Be sure to monitor the success of your direct marketing campaign by including a unique reference code. For instance, the special URL in the example above ending in "JulyParty" makes tracking simple, since the Web page it links to is built specifically for the event.
- **Use Attractive Graphics:** If the direct marketing method you're using calls for it, use an attractive graphic that shows off your product or otherwise intrigues (or even shocks) the viewer. Just be sure the graphic ties in well with your opening line.

- *Keep It Simple:* Remember the acronym KISS (keep it simple, stupid) when laying out your designs or crafting your telephone scripts. The more you say, or the more cluttered correspondence appears or sounds, the more confused people can get and unlikely they are to respond to your correspondence.
- *Remember That Every Word Matters:* Craft your correspondences using words that resonate positively with your target audience. When calling someone, don't start with "Sorry to bother you," because you'll essentially put it into their mind that you're a bother. To learn more about the power of words, check out Frank Luntz's work on something he calls *The Word Lab.* Note: While Luntz's political views are known to be controversial, his research on words is still of note and merits mention. Check it out.
- *Use the Right Colors and Fonts:* From the envelopes you choose to the postcards you design, only use colors and fonts that are consistent with the brand image you'd like to project onto your customer. The more customers identify with you, the greater the chance they will buy.
- *Adapt to Each Customer:* And finally, read Zig Ziglar's *Secrets of Closing the Sale* and remember to "think and act like the customer." When calling someone who's upbeat, adopt a high-energy personality. When calling someone who's low-key, adopt a mellow personality. This helps win over customers and make sales. Says Robert Bly in *The Copywriter's Handbook*, "Mirroring your customer establishes trust."

EXECUTE YOUR DIRECT MARKETING CAMPAIGN EFFECTIVELY

To ensure you get the most out of your direct marketing campaign, be sure to check out the following tips:

- *Test Your Offer:* Before putting a direct marketing campaign into full swing and sending out 5,000 e-mails (postcards, text messages, or whatever), be sure to conduct research and get feedback on a small sample group. For instance, you might create three different headlines and test a different one on each of three similar groups of people (say about 30 people per group if possible). The headline that produces the highest response rate in the shortest amount of time (within a few days, tops) should be the one that is used on your entire list.
- *Use Multiple Direct Marketing Methods with Optimum Timing:* Don't just rely on one method of promotion, try to use two or three. For instance, you might send out an e-mail to your list two weeks before a show, send out postcards one week before the show, and call each fan two nights before the show. Since the recipients are hearing about your gig through a number of different sources, one after the other, the results can be optimum.
- *Provide Several Ways to Respond:* Include a number, address, e-mail, URL, and "text to" number to provide a number of different ways with which your target customers can respond.
- *Pay for the Return Response:* Depending on the type of correspondence, you might also consider paying for the response. You can leave an 800 number, SASE (self-addressed stamped envelope) or a postage-paid BRC (business reply card) addressed to you. The easier you make it for people to respond, the better.
- *Investigate Mailing Rates:* Contact the United States Postal Service (USPS) and speak with a direct mail specialist. He or she will help find the best solutions to save you money by weighing, for instance, the difference between first-class mail and bulk mail. The more you can bring down your costs, the better.
- *Send Direct Promotions and/or Gifts with the Product:* Should people respond to an offer and order a T-shirt or record, make the most out of your mailing costs and the trip to the post office, and send additional promotional materials for other products/events in the same package. You might even try to include a small free gift like a sticker or patch to make your fans super happy and motivated to spread the word about your company.

- ***Send Offers People Need, When They Need Them:*** If you have the right data collected, you might strive to send a birthday card and discount offer for your products to those having a birthday within a specific month. Or, you might send a customized offer to attend a club show along with a drink coupon to those fans who are turning 21 and are now of the legal drinking age. The result of this type of marketing is, "Wow, this is exactly what I needed."
- ***Keep Your Lists Updated:*** Statistics say that over 18 percent of the addresses on your mailing list need updating each year. It is absolutely important to your success that you maintain your lists and keep them current.
- ***Look into E-Mail Marketing Programs:*** As stated before, be sure to look into a number of different e-mail services. When handling large lists (over 500 names), you might have problems with e-mails bouncing and keeping your list organized and up to date. Check out companies like Constant Contact, MailChimp, and FanBridge.
- ***Be Patient:*** Remember that your direct marketing efforts can have a residual affect. A person may not respond to one of your mailings or phone calls immediately, but he or she may remember you and get in touch down the line.

Think About Face-to-Face Selling (a.k.a. Personal Selling)

Moving on from direct marketing, the second of three promotion strategies we'll discuss in this chapter is face-to-face selling.

Face-to-selling is *the process of getting eye-to-eye with target customers and influencing them to act.* You can use your looks, intellect, and scent to get their attention, interpret their needs, and adjust your delivery. Ultimately, you can get your prospects to *like you* and *feel good about themselves* as well.

Face-to-face selling techniques are useful when speaking with fans at your merch booth, conversing with music publishers at conventions, and announcing sales promotions during your live performance sets. Bottom line, face-to-face selling is an important promotional skill that helps close the deals and pay the bills.

Now let's examine the face-to-face selling process. From deciding on whom you intend to pitch to preparing to follow up, be sure to write these tactics in your own Marketing Plan of Attack™.

Decide on Whom You Intend to Pitch Face-to-Face

The first step in the face-to-face selling process is to decide with whom you'd like to schedule an appointment, build a relationship, and close that deal.

When compiling your list, include names, addresses, phone numbers, faxes, e-mails, websites, and company secretaries or assistants. Remember that you can use a variety of different resources to create these lists, ranging from directories and yellow pages to personal referrals and contacts.

Your list might include some of the following people:

- ***Event Promoters:*** To discuss bookings.
- ***Retail Store Managers:*** To get them to carry your recordings on consignment.
- ***Radio Station Music Directors and DJs:*** To get them to play your music.
- ***Brand Managers:*** To converse about sponsorships.
- ***Street Team Members:*** To convince them to promote your band.
- ***Merch Booth Personnel:*** To arrange for them to sell merch at your shows.

- *Equipment Manufacturers:* To consider you for endorsements.
- *Personal Managers:* To discuss management or auditions for other bands.
- *Music Producers:* To consider your next recording project.
- *Music Library Personnel:* To talk about licensing your music.
- *Public Relations Firms:* To convince them to take you on as a client at a discount rate.
- *Record and Publishing Company A&R Reps:* To persuade them to take your press kit or come out to your show.
- *Bank Managers:* To discuss a personal loan. And . . .
- *Investors:* To get them to fund your project.

Get the Right Tools Together

After gathering the names of the people with whom you want to set up a meeting, make sure that you have all the necessary devises and software in place to hold a successful meeting.

These tools might include:

- A tablet computer or laptop to access your digital music files.
- Microsoft Word documents in which to write and take notes.
- A calculator (which can usually be found on a computer) to figure out pricing or budgets.
- PowerPoint files to give more formal presentations.
- Appointment books or software to schedule meetings.
- Database software (such as Access or Excel) to keep important information about all your contacts together.
- A smartphone that makes contacting clients and getting directions a snap.
- A credit card swiper app (like Square [squareup.com]) to take payments. And . .
- A pen, pad of paper, press kit, physical recording, and business cards.

Get Your Sales Look Together

Like buying clothes for the new school year or a new job, shop for a few presentable items (suit, dress, slacks, etc.) to accommodate a variety of sales occasions. This is an important consideration—*even in the casual business of music.* Showing up to a bank to get a loan dressed in your winged bat outfit for the stage might not go over so well. [*Laughing but serious.*]

Prepare a Tight "Elevator Pitch" or Opener

To grab a prospect's immediate *attention* and hold his or her *interest*, you must also prepare and rehearse a tight pitch that includes the following information: who you are, what you want, and how what you have to offer can benefit your prospect.

At the close of your pitch, ask permission to discuss your business in more detail. Your pitch in total should be no longer than about 20 seconds—the time a short elevator ride takes.

Here's what I used to approach a book editor at a convention:

> Paul, hi, I'm Bobby Borg. Listen, I absolutely love your books and I'm confident that I have the perfect title to fill a void in your music business catalogue. I'm a former artist on Atlantic Records and have a unique position for the book in mind that I believe will lead to healthy and continued sales. Can we talk over coffee or a cocktail?

Prepare a Full Business Overview

Once you have your audience's attention and interest with your elevator pitch, you'll need to provide a full business overview to help your potential customer *decide* to do business with you. Remember that the more clear and concise your information is, the easier it will be to win over a prospect.

Be sure to prepare the following:

• A summary of your business idea.
• The unique benefit you can offer the company you're pitching.
• The amount of money your business idea might require to execute.
• A specific timeline for how it can be executed. And . . .
• A brief history of your company and the other team players involved.

Be Prepared to Meet Sales Objections

It's not always enough to just prepare a tight sales pitch and presentation; now you have to plan for the objections. An objection is *when a potential prospect gives you a reason why he or she shouldn't buy, a feeling of disapproval, or an argument in opposition to what you are pitching.*

Here are a few techniques to consider:

• *Use Empathy:* Show that you understand each prospect's thoughts and feelings by acknowledging his or her concerns. If a music supervisor says, "We're not looking for anything right now," express your understanding of how annoying it must be to get pitched all day by new artists who are usually not any good, and then offer a few testimonials that prove your competence and experience level, and try once again.

• *Prepare Questions to Common Objections:* Get to the heart of each disagreement. If someone says, "Sorry, but I'm not interested in starting private lessons at this time," you might respond with, "Do you mind me asking what you're basing your decision on?" If they respond wholeheartedly, you can work at solving their problem.

• *Break Down the Objections:* Help people see the issue in bite-sized and digestible "pieces." If someone says a $25 T-shirt is too expensive, you might explain that it will look like new for the next two years and help save the earth too (given its high-quality environmentally safe materials)—all for just a buck a month. This works. Seriously!

• *Provide Proof of Your Claims:* Be prepared to support everything you say. Using the T-shirt example above, you might have literature from a credible source that speaks about the high-quality fabrics and inks used to make your shirts and the positive effects these materials have on our planet.

• *Know the Right Body Language:* Finally, be prepared to respond to an objection with confidence and a smile, and never make that "you idiot" face or roll your eyes around in the back of your head. Your posture should always be upright and the distance you stand (or sit) from a customer should never be closer than a few feet. Keep it real and be a pro.

Have Several Closing Techniques on Hand

After you've clearly presented your products/services/ideas to a potential customer, and you've met all objections to his or her satisfaction, you may be ready to close the sale. The word *close* refers to the *actions taken by a salesperson to finalize the sale.*

The particular close you use will differ depending on the product you're pitching, but two techniques you might want to consider are the "positive two choices" close (e.g., ask them if they want the T-shirt in black or in white), and the "Ben Franklin" close (e.g., create a list of all the pros to buy, given their situation, versus all of the cons). The pros should obviously trump the cons.

Prepare a "Follow-Up"

And finally, the last step in the sales process deals with following up. This alleviates any concerns a customer may have with a purchase, builds trust, and even stimulates future purchases. A courtesy call or card in the mail should suffice. The idea is to make people feel good about themselves and about doing business with you.

That's about it for face-to-face selling. Now, let's check out the last form of promotion (that is closely related to face-to-face selling and direct marketing): sales promotions.

AFTERTHOUGHT: WANT TO READ MORE? For information about sales, negotiations, and interpersonal skills, be sure to read books like Gerald Manning's *Selling Today*, Zig Ziglar's *Secrets of Closing the Sale*, Tom Hopkins' *How to Master the Art of Selling*, Gerard Nierenberg's *How to Read a Person Like a Book*, Robert Greene's *48 Laws of Power*, Sun Tzu's *Art of War*, Miyamoto Musashi's *Book of Five Rings*, and Niccolò Machiavelli's *The Prince*.

Employ Sales Promotions (Short-Term Incentives)

Sales promotions are *short-term incentives* intended to stimulate a *quick buying response in your target customer*. While we already discussed a few of these strategies in the pricing chapter, let's take a closer look at a few more types of sales promotions that exist, from coupons to one-time exclusive offers.

Utilize Coupons

Coupons are often perceived like real money. They might offer free admission to one of your shows, half off the price of your T-shirts, or an opportunity to take lessons at a limited "introductory discount rate."

One great thing about coupons is that they can be e-mailed to your fans, included as part of a magazine ad, or even posted on your website in PDF format, allowing interested parties to download them and present them to you in person.

Offer a Limited-Time Prize with Each Purchase

This is a type of sales promotion where customers are entered into a drawing and given an opportunity to win valued gifts after they purchase your products.

For instance, a band might announce on its website that when you buy its recordings, you are entered into a drawing to win an all-expenses-paid trip with the band on tour. This serves as an inspiration for people to take immediate action.

Are you starting to see how this stuff works?

Offer Promotional Products (Specialty Advertising)

Promotional merch products that bear your name and logo (such as shot glasses, key chains, and beer koozies) can also be used as part of a sales promotion.

For instance, for a limited time, when a customer wants to make a purchase of your recordings or T-shirts, you might offer them a promotional product at no extra charge.

Hold a Special-Event Raffle

Raffles are a type of sales promotion where people are given the opportunity to buy a ticket (or several tickets) and win something of value on the night of the event.

One of your raffle items might include an album, T-shirt, hoodie, sticker, and ticket to an upcoming party all bundled together in an attractive bag. Another item can even be the very same acoustic guitar on which you perform your set on a given night. On the latter note, see if you can get a local music store (like Sam Ash or Guitar Center) to donate the guitar for the raffle. I did!

All in all, raffles cause people to take action, and they are fun. The money raised by the raffle could even be given to a special charity to boost your public image and do some good for the world as well.

Use Sweepstakes

Moving on, sweepstakes give your fans the opportunity to enter their names into a drawing (without making a purchase) and win some sort of valued prize. There will be one happy winner, and you'll have tens and even hundreds of new contacts on which to act at a later date. Everybody wins.

Execute a Customer Loyalty Program

This is a type of sales promotion whereby a small wallet-sized card is given out to fans during a short-term period and they are rewarded for the number of purchases they make. Car washes utilize this strategy: with each wash you get, your card gets marked with a unique stamp, and by the tenth wash, you get one wash free. Perhaps artists can use a similar approach: each time fans come to a show, they get their cards stamped, and by the third show they receive a free T-shirt or some other prize.

Implement One-Time Exclusive Offers (While They Last)

And finally, sales promotions that are built around the perception of limited availability and exclusivity can be quite effective.

As previously stated in another chapter, Trent Reznor created a box set that included his songs on high-quality vinyl together with attractive print images—all personally signed by Reznor. As there were only 2,500 copies manufactured and fans were urged to "act immediately," the sets sold out quickly for a whopping $300 each.

Okay, so you're not Trent Reznor, but you can execute a similar strategy on a smaller scale. Do what works for your brand.

SEVEN STEPS TO CREATING AN EFFECTIVE SALES PROMOTION STRATEGY

Now that you know about the various types of sales promotions that exist, let's talk about creating an effective sales promotion strategy that's right for you. Consider these seven steps:

1. ***Decide on the Type of Sales Promotion That Fits Your Brand:*** Whether you choose to utilize coupons or a one-time exclusive offer, remember that you must always stay in synch with the desired image you'd like to project into the marketplace. Let's face it, some sales promotions are not for everybody. Don't use them if they are not right for you.
2. ***Decide on the Different Media You'll Use to Deliver Your Sales Promotion:*** Remember that sales promotions can be delivered using Internet techniques (via e-mail and your personal website), guerrilla marketing (via postcards and flyers), direct marketing (via broadsides and text messaging), and face-to-face selling techniques—all discussed in subsequent sections

and chapters. The idea is to utilize a few different mediums to ensure that you really get the message out there.

3. ***Decide Exactly When the Sales Promotion Will Begin and End:*** Sales promotions must have a clearly defined beginning and an end. Will it be for just the night of a show, two weeks, or the entire holiday season? Whatever it is, make it very clear.

4. ***Test the Sales Promotion on a Limited Number of People:*** Before printing a few hundred coupons to send off to your fans, be sure to get some feedback on the words and graphics you use. The idea is to create the most effective promotion that will push your fans' buttons and get them to take action.

5. ***Keep the Purpose of Your Sales Promotion Clearly in Mind:*** Be clear on why you are holding a sales promotion and what you'd like to achieve. Is your goal to sell a specific number of units? Is it to introduce your new record and build awareness in the marketplace?

6. ***Control the Number of Promotions You Hold:*** Remember that too much of a good thing is a bad thing. Sending out e-mails every other week telling people that they can record in your studio at a "one-time specially reduced price" just looks bad.

7. ***Stick to the Rules of the Promotion:*** Finally, don't be tempted to make an offer that is not in line with the rules of the promotion. Doing this can clearly compromise the integrity of the promotion and even your brand. Stick by your own rules!

=MARKETING PLAN TEMPLATE=

Use the template below, or a template like it, to help you craft important information that you will use in your Marketing Plan of Attack™. For additional help, be sure to refer to the Marketing Plan Example below, the chapter on assembling your plan, and the complete plan provided in the back of this book.

Your Company Promotion Strategy Template (Part 4)

Use this template to craft your promotion strategy. When formatting your marketing plan, you can remove the questions and just keep the headers and your answers. Utilize the points below that best apply to you. Be thorough! Don't just answer the questions below. Be sure to review the chapter to get specific ideas for a variety of promotional methods.

Direct Marketing Plan: Will you utilize direct mail? How about telemarketing? What about mobile marketing? How about e-mail? How will you create a database of names? What type of content will you include in your direct mail pieces?

Face-to-Face Selling Strategy: To whom do you intend to pitch your products/services/ideas and use face-to-face selling techniques? What are the various sales tools that you'll use (iPad, iPhone, calculators)? Do you have a sales presentation pitch in mind?

Sales Promotions: What are the various sales promotions you might employ? Will you use coupons and/or one-time exclusive offers? If so, what are the various media channels you'll use to deliver your sales promotions? Will you use e-mail, postcards, broadsides, and/or text messaging? Do tell.

=MARKETING PLAN EXAMPLE=

To help you put together your own promotional strategy, here's an abridged marketing plan example for the band Rally the Tribes.

PROMOTIONAL MIX STRATEGY
a) Direct Marketing Plan
★Mobile Marketing: RTT will collect fans' numbers in their database and text these fans before live-performance events. RTT will also provide a mobile phone app for free to their fans. The app will include easy access to pictures, video, and concert dates that both engage them and educate them about the unique benefits of being an RTT fan.
★Database: RTT will put together a database that includes fans who visit the www.rallythetribes.com website, join RTT social networks, and speak with RTT personally at clubs and other networking events. RTT will also put together industry lists by networking at important industry events, asking for referrals from people they trust, and utilizing compiled lists available in the Music Business Registry. RTT will use Excel software to store these names, using data fields such as name, e-mail, address, number, age, and birthday.

b) Face-to-Face Selling Strategy
★Face-to-Face Meetings: RTT will attempt to pitch event promoters, retail store managers, radio station music directors, brand managers, equipment manufacturers, music supervisors, and others to arrange various deals. RTT will utilize Excel software to organize, manage, and utilize the contact information of these various professionals.

c) Sales Promotions Plan

★Coupons: RTT will place coupons on their site (www.rallythetribes.com) and allow fans to download them in exchange for their e-mail addresses. For instance, before their show, RTT might create a coupon that allows fans to buy the RTT rugby shirt or jersey for the regular price of $19.99 and get the military hat for free (a savings of $11.99 to the customer). The term of this promotion will be limited to just that live performance. The purpose of this promotion is to stimulate excitement and ultimately increase awareness about the band.

★Special Event Raffles: RTT will seek items from their various sponsors that they can raffle off at their live performances. For instance, if securing an agreement with Ray-Ban, RTT might provide fans the opportunity to buy a number of $1 tickets to win a new pair of Ray-Ban sunglasses. The money collected will then be donated to special charities and help solidify RTT's brand as being a socially conscious band. Note that the raffle also serves as an added customer benefit that RTT can use when promoting their live performances to their fans. Announcements about the raffles will be communicated via www.rallythetribes.com and through e-mails and text messages.

Etc.

18

Prepare a Measuring Strategy
Tracking, Analyzing, and Adjusting Your Marketing Campaign

A final strategy that is often overlooked by marketers is measuring. Measuring is *the process of creating systems to collect, analyze, and act on information that is relevant to the goals of your marketing plan.*

A measuring strategy can help you *get* and *keep* your career on track, and determine what *is* and what *is not* working. Bottom line: without a strategy in place, you can easily flush thousands of marketing dollars down the drain. As John Wanamaker, a pioneering marketer and merchant, is noted for saying: "Half the money I spend on marketing is wasted—the problem is, I don't know which half!" This is why creating a measuring strategy is so important.

A well-thought-out and -executed measuring strategy can help you to do the following:

- **Work smarter and faster, not harder.**
- **Use your time and financial resources to their fullest potential.**
- **Understand what your target audience truly responds to.**
- **Assess how your efforts compare to those of your competitors.**
- **Stay abreast of the never-ending and unpredictable changes in the marketplace.**

Despite these benefits, a surprising number of companies neglect to develop a measuring strategy. They argue that measuring is too time consuming and that the overlap between different marketing activities makes it difficult to measure cause and effect.

But keep in mind that we're not looking to develop the most complex systems. The agenda is to develop an easy-to-execute measuring strategy to help you informally "keep score" and be more efficient. A laptop computer, Excel software, filing cabinet, index cards, notebook, and some free online tools (discussed later) might be all you need.

So now let's get to the following topics:

1. **Knowing What to Measure**
2. **Considering Your Sources and Methods of Measuring**
3. **Converting, Analyzing, and Taking Action**

Know What to Measure

Knowing what to measure is the first step in preparing an effective measuring strategy. While there are complete books written on the topic of measuring, here are a few ideas for you to consider.

Opportunities, Strengths, Weaknesses, and Threats

Your external environment, where opportunities and threats exist, and your internal environment, where strengths and weaknesses can be found, are forever changing with time. Thus, periodically conducting a SWOT analysis (from chapter 3) can help you stay abreast of new and major changes in the marketplace.

Customer Markets and Dimensions

Keeping a watchful eye on your desired target market can help you determine whether you're actually pursuing the "right" target fans or neglecting a market segment altogether. Using the techniques you already learned in chapter 4 makes analyzing customers easy.

Competitive Variables

An ongoing scan of your competition's strategic activities (branding, product, price, place, and promotion), and of how they might be responding to your own marketing decisions, can help you especially maintain a true competitive advantage in the marketplace.

Company and Product Brand Image

Measuring your customers' awareness of your brand and whether you are at the "top of their minds" when discussing a certain category (such as "local bands in LA" or "Studios in Nashville") can be extremely helpful in determining the success of your public relations and other promotional strategies.

Products and Services

Measuring your fans' attitudes about your products and services can easily help you determine their level of satisfaction with you and their likelihood to recommend you to friends and family. This is all important stuff.

Pricing Strategies

To determine the ideal price for which you are willing to sell your products and for which customers are willing to buy, your pricing strategies should be measured continually. Of course, you must also keep a close eye on sales and other financial records to determine how your pricing affects your company's profitability.

Place Decisions

You should always pay attention and measure how well your products and services perform in each of your distribution outlets. Doing this will help you see where you're generating the most sales and where you're wasting the most time.

Promotion Effectiveness

And finally, knowing everything from the number of people who respond to an ad to the amount it costs you in promotion for each customer to respond can be extremely important in evaluating where you're getting the most bang for your promotional buck. Okay? Good. Then let's move on.

Consider Your Sources and Methods of Measuring

Now that you have an idea of *what* you can measure, let's consider *how* you'll do it. What follows are several sources and methods of measuring, including everything from examining sales records to utilizing the help of professional organizations. Pick the ideas that best fit your measuring needs.

Examine Your Company's Sales Records

One of the most basic ways for your company to determine its successes and failures is to look at its various sales records and consider its *net profitability* (i.e., its revenue minus expenses).

In the simplest form, your company's sales records might include:

- Excel spreadsheets where you log (in both units and dollars) all of the sales you make and expenses you pay out.
- Invoices (or bills) that you provide to each customer who does business with you.
- Packing slips that you use when fulfilling Internet orders for your various products.
- Financial records from various distributors. And . . .
- Bank account statements associated exclusively with your business.

Remember that the more thorough and consistent you are in keeping and filing accurate records, and in training all of the members of your team to do the same, the more useful these records will be to you—from measuring the profitability of your company and individual products, to measuring the performance rating of individual sales reps, and so much more. So if you decide to write this measuring strategy into your marketing plan, be sure to stay extremely organized.

Count Inventory

Counting inventory is another basic method you can use to measure your company's success and profitability. In the merch business, this is often called *counting in* and *counting out*. In other words, at the beginning of the evening, you count the quantity of T-shirts, records, and patches you bring into the venue, and at end of the night, you count the remaining quantity you load into the truck and take home. By subtracting the number of units at the end of the night from the number of units at the beginning of the night, you'll get the number sold.

The key to this system is, of course, counting the inventory carefully, and then making sure that your count matches up with the total money you've collected. Among other things, measuring your inventory provides you with a basic way to check the performance of sales personnel and analyze the various places (venues, stores, Internet sites) that produce the best results.

Use Bar Codes and SoundScan Reports

As you already know after reading the chapter on distribution (chapter 13), bar codes and SoundScan reports can also help you measure the sales success of your various products.

When a bar code, which must be included on all products sold at retail, is scanned at the point of purchase, information about that product and sale can be tracked by Nielsen SoundScan.

SoundScan data has many uses, but it is particularly important to companies that need to verify the numbers of recordings they've sold when negotiating with traditional brick-and-mortar distributors, record/publishing companies, or interested investors. The data is also useful when determining royalty payments that might be due to you.

While SoundScan reports can be very expensive, limited packages are available to smaller record companies and independent artists just like you. For further information on SoundScan, contact Nielsen (www.nielsen.com). For information on bar codes, you can simply contact a disc manufacturer such as Disc Makers (www.discmakers.com) that resells bar codes.

AFTERTHOUGHT: WHAT ABOUT MEASURING INTERNET AND LIVE SALES? When selling music online, you must also use an ISRC Code (International Standard Recording Code) to help identify each song. Codes can be obtained via ISRC's site (www.usisrc.org) or CD Baby (www.cdbaby.com). When selling music in live venues, you must ask the venue promoter if the club is registered with SoundScan and has a *venue verification form* for you to fill out and send in. Beyond this, make sure to at least collect credit card slips and make copies of checks as proof of payment.

Count People/Fans/Friends

To measure your awareness in the marketplace and determine whether your promotional and other efforts are paying off, another basic method is to count people/fans/friends and more and look for increases and decreases in your numbers.

You can count easily the number of fans you have on your mailing list, the number of friends who are part of your social networks, and the number of people who come to your shows.

Just keep in mind that counting people/fans/friends works especially well when you do it *before* and *after* implementing a particular marketing strategy to see if that strategy caused any spikes in your numbers.

For instance, you might run a print ad for your next gig and measure the audience attendance in comparison to a previous gig's attendance. If you see that your numbers increased after running the ad, it can be unscientifically concluded that it was the ad that brought about the change. Make sense? Good, then let's move on.

Take Advantage of Internet Services and Tools

The Internet also provides a variety of measuring tools of which to take advantage. Search engine tools, social networking tools, and direct marketing tools can all help you determine the success of your online promotion strategies, the specific costs of marketing online, and more. Read on . . .

Search Engine Tools

Search engines (such as Google, Yahoo! Search, and Bing) provide analytic tools that can help you collect a variety of different data according to your needs.

This includes things like *cost per click* (or CPC—what an ad costs you per each person who clicks on it), *click-through rate* (or CTR—the number of people who see and click on your ad), and *page views* (the number of times that a certain page on your website is visited). There are even tools that will alert you every time something is posted about you or your competitors online.

So for more on these tools, be sure to check out Google AdWords, Google AdSense, Google Analytics, and Google Alerts. Also see the back of this book for a list of more resources.

Social Networking Tools

Social networking sites (such as Facebook, Twitter, Google+, YouTube, and others) also provide some very sophisticated analytical tools.

You can track, measure, and analyze the number of people who respond to the content you post, share your content, "like" you, click on (and open) your links, and say positive or negative things about you.

There are even tools to help you monitor the geographic region from which your fans originate.

And let's not forget that social networks are also "real time" measurement tools that help assess customers' attitudes instantaneously. Remember the Roxy's owner discussed in chapter 10, who stayed glued to the Web, spotted a recent negative post, and tracked down the customer to remedy her issues while she was still in the venue? Now that's a pretty cool move.

Direct Marketing Tools

And finally, direct-mail Internet services (such as Constant Contact and MailChimp) can help you determine the success of your e-mail campaigns, newsletters, and other promotional activities.

Direct marketing tools can provide you with information about how many recipients actually opened your direct e-mail, how many people have asked to be removed from your e-mail list, how many e-mails bounced back and were duds, and so much more. All of this information is extremely important and can help you save time and money when marketing online.

For more detailed information on Internet measuring methods and tools, be sure to check out books like *Web Analytics* by Avinash Kaushik and *Social Media Metrics for Dummies* by Leslie Poston. You should also check out blogs like Kaushik's *Occam's Razor* (www.kaushik.net).

Use a Marketing Information System Code (MISC)

Getting to the halfway mark in our discussion on sources and measuring methods, it's a good time to mention *marketing information system codes*. A marketing information system code is an identifier unique to each marketing communication, and yet another great way to measure the effectiveness of your various promotion strategies.

For example, when handing out fliers for one of your live performances, you could stamp each with an MISC unique to specific territories, such as the beach and downtown. The fliers you hand out on the beach might urge people to verbally use the phrase "Code Beach" upon entering the club, and the fliers you hand out downtown could urge people to verbally use the phrase "Code Downtown." By counting the number of responses and measuring which phrase was used the most, you'll be able to determine which promotional effort was more effective.

Or, for another example, you or your webmaster could create a special page on your website that is specifically connected to a magazine advertisement you run to entice people to buy your products. The advert might ask people to visit this unique page by typing a URL (e.g., www.rallythetribes.com/magazinepromo) into their favorite Internet browser, or otherwise use their cell phones to scan a QR code linked to the page. By tracking the number of page views and sales, you'll have an excellent idea of how well that ad performed.

Bottom line: you can, and should, put an MISC on everything and then track and analyze the results. It can save your company a great deal of time and money. Sounds good to me!

Create Promotional Effectiveness Forms

Next up in our discussion about methods of measuring are *promotional effectiveness forms*. These help you determine which promotional strategies are performing the best and are most worthy of your continued investment.

Here's how you can make a promotional effectiveness form work for you:

1. Collect important information from your customers (such as name, contact, how they heard about you, and sales status) and log it into a client database form.

2. Transfer the information from your client database form into a "promotion report card" that indicates the specific strategy used, the number of people who responded to a specific strategy, and the number of sales made as a result of that strategy. And finally . . .

3. Determine which marketing mix strategies performed the best, and focus on these in your campaign.

Promotional effectiveness forms are not the most scientific method (because there are so many factors that can influence the success and failure of a particular strategy), but they can certainly help you draw some useful conclusions about how to be more effective with your marketing efforts.

Now check out how I used promotional effectiveness forms when starting my teaching business in Boston, Massachusetts. Viewing the tables "Prospect/Client/Fan Database" and "Monthly Promotion Report Card," see if you can figure out what strategies worked most effectively for me and what strategies I discontinued.

Example: Part 1: Record data from your customers.
Prospect/Client/Fan Database

Name (Last, First)	Contact Info	Heard About Us, How?	Sales Status
Doe, John	Johndoe@gmail.com	Print Advert	Hot: Signed up
Doe, Jane	janedoe@gmail.com	Print Advert	Hot: Signed up
Smith, Joe	Smith@gmail.com	Networking	Cold
Thomas, Rain	rain@gmail.com	Networking	Cold
Victors, Jon	victors@yahoo.com	Print Advert	Hot: Signed up
Walts, Jackson	walts@gmail.com	Street Fliers	Hot: Signed up

Example: Part 2: Insert the appropriate data from Form 1 here.
Monthly Promotion Report Card

Promotion Source	# of Leads/Inquiries (X)	# of Sales (✔)
Print Advert	X X X	✔ ✔ ✔ (This worked best)
Rented Mailing List	(Zero leads)	(Zero sales)
Word of Mouth	(Zero leads)	(Zero sales)
Networking	X X	(Zero sales)
Street Fliers	X	✔

Conduct Primary Research: Surveys, Focus Groups, and More

We already discussed primary research methods in chapter 5, but it's necessary to review it here, since it can also be extremely useful in measuring important information about your customers and what they think and feel. In case you forgot, primary research is project-specific research conducted by you. It includes survey questionnaires, intercept interviews, and observational methods.

Survey Questionnaires

Survey questionnaires, which typically consist of multiple-choice questions and short-answer choices, can be easily distributed among your customers on postcards via your live gigs and/or websites and blogs via the Internet. Questions ranging from "How did you hear about us?" to "Would you recommend us to a friend?" could really help gage your marketing efforts. Be sure to check out free online survey tools like SurveyMonkey (www.surveymonkey.com), and Zoomerang (www.zoomerang.com).

Intercept Interviews

Intercept interviews, which typically consist of more open-ended and detailed customer questions, can be easily conducted orally as people are leaving a studio or concert venue. They can also be submitted in a more formal sit-down interview that lasts for several minutes. The great thing about interviews is that they can help uncover the true deeper motivations of what your customers really think about your company's products and services, and they can be recorded on a digital video or audio camera to be reviewed and studied at a later time.

Observational Methods

And finally, observational methods, where your target market is studied as it interacts with various products and services, can be easily executed at your live performances or various retail environments. For instance, it's amazing how much can be learned by hiring a representative to stand at the back of a club to observe what people are saying and doing as you perform your set. If you've never done this before, you're missing out on some really valuable data. Why not give it a try?

For additional information and methods of primary research, be sure to check out *The Market Research Toolbox* by Edward McQuarrie.

Utilize Secondary Research: Media Sources, Industry Charts, and More

Secondary research (research published by other people) is yet another form of monitoring you might consider using. It includes media sources, industry charts, and trade associations.

Media Sources

By checking out certain blogs, message boards, and review sites, you can monitor the positive and negative comments that various journalists and customers are making about your career. Just conduct a search for your name and see what comes up.

Industry Charts

By reading certain charts (like those published by College Music Journal), you can see how your radio promotional efforts and charting campaign are measuring up. Be sure to check out CMJ's website (www.cmj.com).

Trade Associations

And finally, through trade associations (like the Recording Industry Association of America, National Music Publishers Association, and National Association of Music Merchants), you can monitor your entire industry to identify new opportunities and threats, and get a sense of how well music and sales are doing as a whole and how badly music piracy is hurting the business. Check out www.riaa.com and www.nmpa.org.

Utilize the Help of Consultants and/or Professional Organizations

And last, but certainly not the least, on our list of methods and sources of measuring are professional consultants and organizations. While you're probably thinking that they are too expensive, you just might be pleasantly surprised.

Professional Consultants

Professional consultants are experienced experts in the field of marketing who can work on a more personal basis with you and give you the real scoop on your company's profitability, promotion effectiveness, customer satisfaction, and so much more. There may be some professionals in your area who are between projects and available to work with you at a reduced price, and you may even be able to find retired consultants who will work for free just to keep themselves busy. In fact, the Small Business Administration (www.sba.gov) is known for providing a number of low-budget and free services to young business owners. Also be sure to ask for referrals from industry people in your area that you trust, or just conduct a search on the Web. You may also contact me, Bobby Borg Consulting (www.bobbyborg.com/consultations).

Professional Organizations

Professional organizations, such as the American Marketing Association or the American Advertising Federation, consist of thousands of professional members. Sometimes these organizations have available mentors and/or marketing plan/advertising campaign competitions where you can get some very valuable marketing feedback pro bono (yup, that means for free). Be sure to look up both of the aforementioned organizations and others just like them.

So, that's it for methods and sources of measuring. Now, let's move on to converting, analyzing, and taking action. Hang in there, we're almost done.

Convert, Analyze, and Take Action

After deciding which sources and methods of measuring you'll use, you must consider what you'll do with all the resulting data. There are typically three steps: converting your data into readable form, analyzing your data's quality, and taking action.

Convert Your Data into Readable Form

It is not enough to just collect data; you must put it into a language everyone on your team can understand, just as we discussed in chapter 6. To demonstrate, you might use the data in your promotion report card (discussed earlier), calculate the percentage of people who heard about you through each of the various strategies in your marketing mix, and then create a handy bar chart.

Converting your data into readable form can really help get your point across to your other team members (partners, investors, etc.) about which strategies are performing well and which are not. Take a look at the graphic "Promotion Effectiveness: Live Show." The results are pretty clear.

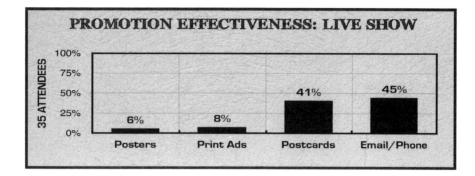

Analyze Your Data's Quality

After you've converted your data into readable form, you must consider its actual quality and how accurate it is. We discussed this already in chapter 6, but as a brief review, consider whether your data is the following:

- Representative and derived from a sample of 30 or more of your most likely fans.
- Reliable and derived from consistent conditions from one test to the next.
- Valid and based on unbiased responses to your questions.

Look, your data can never be 100 percent accurate, no matter how sophisticated a researcher you are. But striving to meet the above criteria to the best of your ability will truly help make the difference. Be sure to review chapter 6 if needed.

Take Action

The last stage in preparing a measuring strategy is to decide what to do with all of the data you've acquired. Will you adjust a certain part of your plan immediately to save time and money? Will you pull an advertisement that doesn't seem to be performing well? Or will you wait and give certain promotional endeavors further time to see if you get better results?

Whatever you do, remember that measuring is all about keeping your eyes and ears open for ways to continually improve your business and yourself. As W. Edwards Deming (the founder of the Japanese management process *kaizen*) once said, "It's not enough to *do* your best—you must *know what to do*, and *then* do your best." Believe that!

DRY AS THE SAHARA DESERT, BUT WORTH THE TROUBLE

I know that all the following left-brain info and formulae are dry and somewhat tedious to learn. However, when you're speaking with investors or bankers, using terms like ROI and GPM (and understanding their meaning) shows that you've got business sense. You want that backer's money, right? Then show that you understand how it works. Now consider this:

- *Net Profit:* Sales revenue minus your total costs (including taxes, research, etc.) equals your net profit. This metric is one of the most commonly used methods for looking at the general success or failure of a company.
- *Gross Profit Margin:* Gross profit margin (GPM) tells you the percentage of the price, minus your costs, that you keep as gross profit. It can be calculated using the following equation: (price − costs) ÷ price.

- *Return on Investment (ROI):* This tells you the percentage your initial investment should grow on a specific product or service. The following equation is used for ROI: (price − cost) ÷ cost.
- *Response Rate:* The number of people who buy your products/services, divided by the number of promotional pieces you send out, equals your response rate. If 30 people of the 1,000 you solicited attend your show, then your response rate is 3 percent: 30 ÷ 1,000 = .03, or 3 percent.
- *Cost per Order (CPO):* The cost per promotional piece, multiplied by the number of leads contacted, divided by the people who buy, equals your CPO. For instance, if it costs you 50 cents per postcard (including postage), and you mail 1,000 cards to your fans, then your total cost is $500 ($.50 × 1,000). If only 30 people come to your show, your costs to promote that show are $16 per person: $500 ÷ 30.
- *Cost per Thousand Impressions (CPM):* A standard metric to help marketers measure advertising costs and media performance is *cost per 1,000 impressions*, or "cost for 1,000 people to see, hear, and/ or listen to an ad." CPM data is typically provided in the media packets from the various media sellers you contact, along with demographic/psychographic/geographic data.
- *Cost per Click (CPC):* Cost per click is a Web metric based on how often ads are "seen and clicked on" for a potential purchase, in proportion to what you pay for the ad. Typically, these stats are provided by the publisher of the ad.
- *Click-Through Rate (CTR):* The percentage of people who click on your Internet ad (like sponsored search links or banner advertisements), divided by the number of people who see the ad (i.e., the number of times the ad is served up) equals your CTR. CTR can help measure the effectiveness of an ad, but is not a reflection of whether people were actually converted to customers and made a purchase. Note that typically CTR stats are provided by the publisher of the ad.
- *Customer Net Promoter Score:* The percentage of your total fans that are likely to recommend you to friends and family is called your customer net promoter score. It can be found by simply conducting a survey and asking, "Would you recommend us to friends?" Overall, this can tell a lot about customer loyalty.
- *Customer Retention Rate:* The ratio of the number of customers *retained* over a specific period of time to the number of original customers. For instance, if only 30 of 50 music students renew their monthly lesson plans, you have a retention rate of 60 percent: 30 ÷ 50 = .60, or 60 percent.
- *Churn Rate:* The ratio of the number of customers *lost* over a specific period of time to the number of customers retained. For instance, if 20 of your 50 music students do not renew their monthly lesson plans, you have a churn rate of 40 percent: 20 ÷ 50 = .40, or 40 percent.
- *Customer Lifetime Value (CLV):* In short, CLV is a projection of what each customer could be worth in net profit over his or her lifetime as a customer (usually calculated on a lifetime of three to five years). While calculating CLV is rather complex and involves formulas that are beyond the scope of this book, an overly simplified version involves taking the total amount in dollars you collect in a year, dividing it by the number of customer transactions in the year, and multiplying that by the number of years you expect they will buy from you. Say what? Is your head spinning yet? Relax! We're done.

For more detailed information on business/marketing metrics and their uses, be sure to check out *Measuring Marketing* by John Davis or *Marketing Metrics* by Paul Farris, or just speak to an accountant or beloved nerd!

=MARKETING PLAN TEMPLATE=

Be sure to use the template below, or a template like it, to help craft important information that you will use in your Marketing Plan of Attack™. For additional help, refer to the marketing plan example below, the chapter on assembling your plan, and the complete plan provided in the back of this book.

Your Measuring Strategy Template

Use this template to craft your measuring strategy. When formatting your marketing plan, you can remove the questions and just keep the headers and your answers. Use the points below that best apply to you.

Reason for Measuring: What do you plan to achieve by implementing a monitoring and measuring strategy? (Do you plan to: Gauge customer awareness? Discover customers' reactions to pricing? Determine your return on investment? Find the places your products sell best? Discover where customers hear about you? Determine which promotional strategies are the most effective? Figure out the lifetime value of a customer? Calculate your net profit?)

Methods of Measurement: What sources and methods of monitoring and measuring will you use? (Will you: Examine sales records? Count inventory? Count fans? Use marketing information system codes? Create promotional effectiveness forms? Conduct primary and secondary research?)

Plan of Action: After converting your data and carefully considering its quality, how will you decide what to do with all of the information? (Will you: Take a more cautious approach and conduct several tests before making adjustments to your marketing plan? Take a more aggressive approach and immediately move forward with the necessary changes? Hold regular meetings with your organization and discuss a plan of action?)

=MARKETING PLAN EXAMPLE=

Now here's an abridged marketing plan example for the band Rally the Tribes, to help you put together your own measuring strategy.

MEASURING STRATEGY

a) Reason for Measuring: RTT plans to achieve the following with their monitoring and measuring strategies: Gauge customer awareness, discover customers' reactions to pricing, and determine return on investment. Find the places products sell best, discover where customers hear about us, and determine which promotional strategies are the most effective. Find the number of people who click on an ad, analyze how long visitors stay on the RTT site, find the number of customers who buy in proportion to the number of people who visit the RTT site, and find their net profit.

b) Methods of Measurement: RTT will use the following sources and methods of monitoring and measuring:
★Basic Accounting Methods: As a general means of checking the effectiveness of certain marketing strategies, RTT will simply count sales (i.e., they will count sales of their products and services at consignment, live performances, www.rallythetribes.com, iTunes, and other locations where RTT products and services are sold). They will look particularly for spikes in sales (for instance, on the Internet) and try to draw a correlation to recently executed promotional activities.

★Marketing Information System Codes (Posters/Postcards): All postcards and posters will include a marketing information system code and text that asks persons to use that code when, for instance, entering at the door of a club. When handing out cards on the Sunset Strip in front of the Whisky, the code "Whisky" might be written on a certain number of cards distributed at that location. The number of people who use a specific code will then be counted to help determine the effectiveness of marketing in a particular location.

★Personal Website Tools: Since a great deal of RTT's promotional efforts consist of driving current and potential fans over to www.rallythetribes.com to offer information and entice sales, they will use Google Analytics to monitor the number of people who visit the site, what pages the visitors view, and how long visitors look at a page.

★Social Analytics: RTT will utilize the tracking tools offered by social networks to count the number of friends/fans they acquire on a specific social service, the number of people who listen to their songs on a specific service, and the locations of people who communicate with RTT on a specific social service.

★Search Engine Hit Results and SEO: RTT will monitor the effectiveness of their overall promotional efforts, particularly those of publicity and PR, by counting the number of websites that feature reviews or mentions of RTT. For instance, at the beginning of the campaign, they will count their search engine hit results and match those to the hit results at the end of each month. They will also monitor their Google position and strive to be at the top of each Google search when using a variety of different keyword searches.

c) Plan of Action: After converting their data and carefully considering its quality, RTT will conduct regular research before making any marketing plan adjustments. They will hold regular weekly meetings to discuss their plan of action.

19

Assemble Your Marketing Plan of Attack™

Presenting Your Business and Marketing Ideas Effectively

Now that you have completed all of the marketing plan templates in each chapter of this book, it's time to compile them in a detailed Marketing Plan of Attack™. This will serve as your playbook and *battle plan* for taking your career from the streets to success, a communication tool to keep all the members of your organization on track, and a sales document to attract potential investors, distributors, and others.

A Marketing Plan of Attack™ will also help you to:

- **Gather your research, goals, and strategies into one easy-to-access document.**
- **Organize all of your marketing activities into a structured timeline.**
- **Present your business/marketing ideas in a clear and logical manner.**
- **Establish a professional image in the eyes of potential stakeholders.**
- **Present an itemization of your marketing costs.**

Your plan of attack will include a cover, binding, and even colorful charts and graphs, but always remember that it's a "living and breathing document." In other words, this chapter discusses the finalization of your marketing plan, but the truth is your plan will never be *final*. It should be continually revised and improved as information is collected from the marketplace and new marketing opportunities ensue.

It's true that marketing plans can come in all shapes, sizes and looks, but you'll find that this chapter presents a simple and effective method—no matter if you are a band recording an album to release to fans or a composer building a studio to deliver tracks to ad agencies.

So let's take a look at precisely how your plan will be laid out from beginning to end, and learn a few more important marketing concepts not yet discussed. These include:

1. **Presenting a Front Cover**
2. **Providing an Executive Summary**
3. **Inserting a Table of Contents**
4. **Completing and Formatting All of the Templates**
5. **Building an "Allocation of Costs Table"**
6. **Incorporating a Timeline**
7. **Adding an Appendix**

YOUR COMPLETE MARKETING PLAN OF ATTACK™—A BIRD'S-EYE VIEW

This book has been organized close to the way that your marketing plan should be organized, but here's a bird's-eye view of what should be included in your complete plan. Note that certain items are yet to be discussed in this chapter.

- *Front Cover:* A front cover with your photograph or logo, artist name, and website URL.
- *Executive Summary:* A one-page summary briefly describing your complete plan.
- *Table of Contents:* A TOC outlining each section of the plan with page numbers.
- *Vision Paragraph:* Your company's vision, describing where you want to be in seven to ten years.
- *SWOT Analysis:* An internal and external examination of your company and ideas. This includes your research in bullet points and a conclusion paragraph.
- *Customer Analysis:* A profile of your most likely customer. This also includes your research in bullet points and a conclusion paragraph.
- *Competitor Analysis:* A study of your direct competitors. Yes, this also includes a competitor table and a conclusion paragraph.
- *Testing and Feedback:* Results (and methods) from research tests to confirm that your idea is viable.
- *SMART Goals:* A one-paragraph goal set in the context of one year.
- *Company Brand Strategy:* The company name, logo, slogan, mascot, personality, and position of your company.
- *Product Brand Strategy:* The structure, names, slogans, materials, and position of your products.
- *Product/Service Strategy:* Plans for the finalization of your offerings and customer service policies.
- *Price:* The various amounts for and timeframes during which you will sell your products/services.
- *Place:* Where you intend to make your offerings available so that customers can find them.
- *Promotion:* An integrated mix of the activities that will best get your target fans to take action, which could include publicity, advertising, Internet, word of mouth, guerrilla marketing, radio, sponsorships, direct marketing, face-to-face selling, and sales promotions.
- *Measuring:* Methods for ensuring that your marketing is working effectively.
- *Allocation of Costs Table:* A detailed budget delineating expenses involved in executing your strategies.
- *Timeline:* A timeline to help organize the execution of your plan over the period of a year.
- *Appendix:* An appendix containing extra charts, graphs, or research findings (this is optional).

[Special Note: Once you have the parts in the right order, make sure it's edited for grammar and spelling. Staple the pages together at the upper-left corner, or get it spiral bound at a print shop for a more professional look. Okay?]

Present a Front Cover

The front cover of your Marketing Plan of Attack™ is extremely important, since it's the first thing people will see. That's why it's so necessary that you follow these three simple steps:

1. In an 8.5"×11" Microsoft Word document (or Adobe Photoshop canvas, etc.), include the name of your company at the top of the page and the words "Marketing Plan of Attack™."
2. Below your company name and heading, include an attractive picture of your band, album cover, studio, and so forth. Beneath this, offer a brief description of the focus of your marketing plan (e.g., "Record, DVD, Merch, & Performance Release," "Studio Launch," or

"Business Loan Proposal"). Be as specific and concise as possible. And finally . . .

3. Include your website URL at the bottom of the page and the correct copyright notice (for example, Copyright © 2020 by Bobby Borg). That's pretty much it. Now check out the front-cover graphic "Rally the Tribes."

Provide an Executive Summary

Though an executive summary is *the last part of your marketing plan you'll write*, it should be provided at the very front of your plan.

An executive summary is a *one-page overview* of your research findings, marketing goals, product strategies, costs, challenges, and more. According to the Small Business Administration (www.sba.gov), an executive summary sums up why your business idea will be successful. Some people even say that an executive summary qualifies whether or not your entire plan is worth reading by business professionals, such as investors, distributors, and others.

To ensure that you provide an effective summary in your marketing plan, below are the key elements that should be included, along with a brief mention of how to create these elements.

Lead Off with a Company Biography

List the city and state in which you reside, your company's full name, and its type/style. You might even list three "like bands" to give people a sense of your sound. Include the names of your company representatives and the role they all play in your firm. Consider the following example for the band Rally the Tribes:

> Formed in 2015 in Los Angeles, California, Rally the Tribes (RTT) is a rock/rave band that can be described as "Tupac meets Skrillex meets Rage Against the Machine." Founding key members include Kennedy Robert Jr. on vocals and K. Luther Martin on turntables.

Add a Brief and Personal Story

Now, you must hook your readers and give them a true sense of your experience and history by including information about how your company came together and why the individual people involved are special and important. Interesting and newsworthy accomplishments are also very useful here. For instance, RTT might write:

> Traveling for most of their young lives, both Robert Jr. and Martin were exposed to a variety of cultures and musical styles. They decided to merge their experiences and views after meeting in Cambridge while studying at Harvard University and MIT, respectively.

Summarize Your Vision

Your vision discussed in chapter 2 must also be summarized. Include where you intend your company to be in seven to ten years and what image it will project in the marketplace. A simple line will suffice:

> RTT's vision is to create a rock/rave band that projects a message of peace, justice, and equality.

Offer Your Market Need

Using information from your SWOT Analysis in chapter 3, now offer the market need or void in the marketplace you identified, and the approach to filling that void or need better (*more uniquely*) than anyone else. Be sure to offer supporting data to verify the existence of this need. Consider this:

> RTT will capitalize on the young-adult generation's need to hear new and exciting music and to be part of an important and higher cause. They will do this by uniquely providing a blend of rock, rap, and techno rave styles, and by uniquely focusing on extremely sensitive political and world issues. Research via *Billboard* and CMJ charts affirm that there are no other bands that fuse rock, rap, and techno rave styles with a strong political message. Research via the National Center for Education Statistics indicates that there is a growing interest among young Americans in political news and change since the Obama election of 2008.

Summarize Your Key Revenue Generators

Now summarize the key products and services that will generate revenue for your company. Remember that without revenue, a company can only survive for so long. Check out what RTT has to offer:

> RTT will release their first 12-song album, which will also serve as the soundtrack for a documentary DVD film they are writing and producing. The band will also produce a live show featuring a 7-song set of their music. A line of T-shirts bearing political slogans, hats, and hoodies will also be sold at shows and on their personal website at www.rallythetribes.com. They will run a fan club called Change Agents.

State Your SMART Goals

Moving along (hang in there, we're almost done), you must now briefly state the specific and measurable aspects of your goals from chapter 7. Consider this:

> RTT's first-year objective is to increase awareness in Los Angeles with a database of 5,000 active fans, sell 1,000 recordings (800 CDs, 100 USB flash drives, and 100 downloaded albums), sell 500 DVDs, play 12 rock/rave shows, attract an average of 350 people per regular live performance, and sell all of the merch they produce.

Provide an Overview of Your General Strategies

Referring to chapters 8–18, you must now provide a general overview of the strategies you'll use to accomplish your goals. RTT might write the following:

> RTT's marketing communications will employ a more serious/dramatic tone. Slogans might include: "Music That Matters" and "Music with a Mission." They will perform at political rallies, donate a portion of their proceeds to charities, and primarily utilize the following marketing strategies: low-budget Internet, word of mouth, guerrilla street marketing, and direct marketing.

Briefly List Your Resources

To build your credibility in the eyes of executive readers of your plan, you must also list important strengths (finances, skills, equipment, etc.) from your SWOT analysis. The band RTT might write:

> RTT is composed of highly educated band members who are well versed in national and global political issues, have 20 aggregate years of songwriting and performance training and experience, and are able to reduce certain production and promotion costs through barter deals and professional relationships. They own state-of-the-art recording gear and have access to a rehearsal facility, which was acquired mostly through funds from fan donations and professional relationships. RTT's strong management skills facilitate their day-to-day operations.

Provide Your Costs

Getting close to the completion of your executive summary, you must now provide a brief explanation of all of your marketing activities and their total costs. RTT might write the following:

> We estimate our total recording, manufacturing, printing, Web design, and other promotional costs to be $26,719.35. This number does not include the $16,000 saved in recording costs alone by using creative bartering arrangements.

Identify the Challenges

Finally, you must identify the threats your company faces and the general tactics it will use to minimize these threats (refer to your SWOT analysis from chapter 3). This is the perfect way to wrap up your executive summary, since it shows that you are both realistic and business minded. RTT might write:

> RTT faces threats including opposition from members of the public and potential sponsors who don't share the political stances on sensitive issues expressed in our lyrics' subject matter (such as pro-choice and pro-marijuana). To reduce these threats, we plan to be peaceful and respectful always when getting our message out to the people.

So that's about it on creating an executing summary. Just be sure to lay out all of the sections on one sheet of paper and use the following headers in bold: Company Biography, Personal Story, Vision, Market Need, Key Revenue Generators, SMART Goals, General Strategies, Resources, Costs, and Challenges. (See the graphic "Executive Summary.") Cool? Then let's move on to the next section.

EXECUTIVE SUMMARY

Biography: Your Writing Goes Here...

Personal Story: Your Writing Goes Here...

Vision: Your Writing Goes Here...

Market Need: Your Writing Goes Here...

Revenue Generators: ETC...

Resources: ETC...

Costs: ETC...

ETC...

Insert a Table of Contents (TOC)

Now comes a pretty basic part of your plan: a table of contents (or TOC). This should highlight the main sections of your marketing plan, including everything from your vision to your appendix. On the far right of the page, be sure to include the corresponding page numbers.

Most word processing applications like Microsoft Word and Apple Pages allow you to automatically create and update TOCs in a few clicks of a mouse. If you don't know how to create a TOC, just type the words "table of contents + Microsoft Word" into your favorite search engine and learn how. This should be all it takes to get the job done. Now check out the graphic "Table of Contents."

Complete and Format All of the Templates

Next, to ensure that you put together the absolute best Marketing Plan of Attack™ possible, let's take a look at filling in all of the information and getting it formatted correctly.

TABLE OF CONTENTS

Fill In All of Your Information

Completing the marketing plan templates involves answering all of the questions exactly as directed in chapters 2–18 (your vision statement to your measuring strategy). Just remember that your information can be written in first-person plural (we), first-person plural possessive (our), or third person (company name, or *it* or *they*). The amount you write and the total page count of your plan is unimportant (shoot for quality, not quantity), but expect to write at least 10 pages and as many as 30.

Format Your Templates Correctly

After filling out all of your templates, it's important that you transfer all of the information into your Marketing Plan of Attack™ using the right format. The most important thing to remember is that it is not necessary to include all of the questions provided in the templates, but you should include nearly all of your answers.

Each section must also be clearly labeled (organized) with consistent headings, subheadings, and bullet-point styles to make each section as easy to read and locate as possible. While it is perfectly okay to brand your marketing plan with specific fonts and styles, it's also not a bad idea to use common, easy-to-read font styles, like Times New Roman at 10- to 12-point size with 1.1 or 1.2 line spacing. Be sure to number each page of your plan as well. That should pretty much do it.

Now be sure to study the template "Your SWOT (or OSWT) Matrix and Conclusion Template" that was first presented at the end of chapter 3, only now the questions are answered in the way that our sample band, RTT, might fill it out.

Your SWOT (or OSWT) Matrix and Conclusion Template
Use this template to help you craft your SWOT analysis.

Opportunities: Identify and explain voids or needs in the *external* competitive, political, societal, technological, economic, distribution-related, industry-specific, and/or consumer marketplace and the opportunities to fill these needs. If possible, provide secondary or primary data that supports your claims.

★According to data collected by the National Center for Education Statistics, there is a growing interest among young Americans in political news and change, especially since the Obama election of 2008.

★According to the *Billboard* and *CMJ* charts, there are currently no other bands that fuse rock, rap, and techno rave styles with a strong political undertone.

Strengths: Internal aspects like finances, equipment, and skills that will help fill the above needs.

★Intangible Resources: Highly educated band members who are well versed in national and global political issues, have 20 years' aggregate training in songwriting and performance, play multiple instruments, and have professional relationships where barter deals can be arranged to reduce certain production costs.

★Tangible Resources: State-of-the-art recording gear, turntables, and access to a rehearsal facility that has been acquired mostly through donations and professional relationships.

Weaknesses: Deficiencies in internal company resources, finances, skills, company management, and more.

★Processes: Minimal marketing experience and number of followers.

★Financial Resources: Rely heavily on fan donations and bartering.

Threats: Identify *external* issues (competitive, political, social, technological, economic, etc.) of which you are not in control and that can get in your way.

★Censorship from radio stations that prefer not to broadcast our controversial subject matter.

★Public opposition and backlash (over sensitive issues like pro-choice and pro-marijuana viewpoints), and companies' disinterest in associating their brands via sponsorships with a politically minded group.

SWOT Conclusion Template: Now use your research from the information above to help you write your SWOT paragraph below. Feel free to adjust the template to fit your needs.

Given our company's vision of becoming a nationally known rock/rave band, *we monitored* the external political and societal landscape *and identified an opportunity to* create recordings, performances, and documentaries that give a voice to the political youth movement, fill society's intrinsic need to be part of a bigger cause for change, and provide new and exciting music unlike the competition. *Our company strengths are well suited to take advantage of this opportunity, given our* academic credentials, musical training, and innovation processes. *Our weaknesses are our* lack of financial resources and minimal fan base, *but being that they are* ~~are not~~ *critical to growth, we will* ~~will not~~ *convert them to strengths by* seeking donations, utilizing limited-budget marketing techniques, and building a database of fans drawn from political rallies, live performances, and social networks. *Our most serious threat is* backlash and opposition from opposing political groups, *but to reduce these threats, we plan to* be peaceful and respectful when getting our message out to the people.

Now see an example of how the SWOT (or OSWT) matrix and conclusion template may look when the very same information is transferred from the template, labeled, formatted, and included into your Marketing Plan of Attack™. By the way, it's okay to just glance over the example to get a sense of the look of it.

SWOT (or OSWT) ANALYSIS
a) Opportunities:
★According to data collected by the National Center for Education Statistics, there is a growing interest among young Americans in political news and change, especially since the Obama election of 2008.
★According to the *Billboard* and CMJ charts, there are currently no other bands that fuse rock, rap, and techno rave styles with a strong political undertone.

b) Strengths:
★Intangible Resources: Highly educated band members who are well versed in national and global political issues, have 20 years' aggregate training in songwriting and performance, play multiple instruments, and have professional relationships where barter deals can be arranged to reduce certain production costs.
★Tangible Resources: State-of-the-art recording gear, turntables, and a rehearsal facility that has been acquired mostly through donations and professional relationships.

c) Weaknesses:
★Processes: Minimal marketing experience and number of followers.
★Financial Resources: Rely heavily on fan donations and bartering.

d) Threats:
★Censorship from radio stations that prefer not to broadcast our controversial subject matter.
★Public opposition and backlash (over sensitive issues like pro-choice and pro-marijuana viewpoints) and companies' disinterest in associating their brand via sponsorships with a politically minded group.

e) SWOT Conclusion:
Given our company's vision of being a nationally known rock/rave band, we monitored the external political and societal landscape and identified an opportunity to create recordings, performances, and documentaries that give a voice to the political youth movement, fill society's intrinsic need to be part of a bigger cause for change, and provide new and exciting music unlike the competition. Our company strengths are well suited to take advantage of this opportunity, given our academic credentials, musical training, and innovation processes. Our weaknesses are our lack of financial resources and minimal fan base. However, because these are critical to growth, we will convert them to strengths by seeking donations, utilizing limited-budget marketing techniques, and building a database of fans drawn from political rallies, live performances, and social networks. Our most serious threat is backlash and opposition from opposing political groups, but to reduce these threats, we plan to be peaceful and respectful when getting our message out to the people.

Build an Allocation of Costs Table

As if filling out and completing all of the templates at the end of each chapter were not enough, building an allocation of costs table is yet another important step in assembling your marketing plan. It shows you and your readers precisely where your company stands in both dollars and "sense" (ha ha, and cents too).

So let's first discuss the following topics: identifying how you expect to fund your project, listing all of your marketing activities, and including the approximate costs. Then we'll take a brief look at what the allocation of costs section of your marketing plan might look like.

Identify How You Expect to Fund Your Project

The first step in putting together the allocation of costs section of your marketing plan is to identify your financial sources in a short introductory paragraph. While this book encourages you to utilize low-budget and even no-budget methods to market your company, you should identify how you expect to fund your project. Sources might include one (or some) of the following:

- Small loans from family members or commercial banks.
- Barter exchanges (trade-offs of goods or services with others).
- Spec deals (agreements to make payments only if your company makes money).
- Donations from various suppliers, service providers, friends, fans, and so forth.
- Interested investors.

No matter what financial sources you intend to use, be sure to also provide the grand total of all your costs in your opening paragraph, as I have demonstrated below for the band RTT.

> We are a do-it-yourself band and are able to work on a limited budget because of our professional relationships, internal strengths, and access to free tools and services. We use our own professional equipment and have arranged barter deals with recording studios, printers, and sound and light crews. We also have set up "merch on demand" accounts (where T-shirts and other items are created only after ordered) to reduce certain initial expenditures. The allocation of costs estimates only reflect the actual money we have to spend, and not the services we plan to get for free or barter for: One Year Total: $26,719.35.

List All of Your Marketing Activities

Now, using an Excel spreadsheet or just a Word document with tables, list all of your marketing activities and their associated expenses in separate tables. For instance, a band like RTT might create nine different tables with titles clearly marked as follows:

a) **Research Tools**
b) **12-Song Album**
c) **DVD Soundtrack**
d) **Merchandising Line**
e) **Live-Performance Set**
f) **Internet Promotion**
g) **Guerrilla Marketing**
h) **Publicity**
i) **Direct Mail**
j) **Paid Advertising**

Under each heading, the band might now include all of the applicable expense items. For instance, under the table I've provided, "12-Song Album," I've listed the manufacturing of CDs, flash drives, and digital distribution in the rows on the left. Remember, your allocation of costs table only includes items that you have to pay for, so don't worry about listing free activities.

a) 12-Song Album

Manufacturing Costs for Six-Panel Digipak CDs		
Manufacturing Costs for Wristband Flash Drives with Logo		
Setup Costs for Digital Distribution, Including Bar Code and ISRC Code with CD Baby		

Research and List Approximate Costs

The last step in building an allocation of costs table deals with listing all of your *per-unit costs*, *total costs*, and *subtotals*. You should already have researched these costs when filling out your chapter templates (especially when creating your product and pricing strategies), so you can simply transfer that information here. If you need to conduct further research, get on the phone and start asking for quotes. Or you might want to go to various websites, such as Disc Makers (www.discmakers.com) that allow you to type in all of your specs and quantities, and obtain an immediate quote. This can feel like a tremendous amount of work, but remember the well-known proverb "Rome wasn't built in a day." Now check out the table "12-Song Album" with all of the cells filled in to give you an idea of what I'm talking about.

a) 12-Song Album

Manufacturing Costs for Six-Panel Digipak CDs	1,000 Units @ $1.20	$1,200.00
Manufacturing Costs for Wristband Flash Drives with Logo	100 Units @ $7.45	$745.00
Setup Costs for Digital Distribution, Including Bar Code and ISRC Code with CD Baby	N/A	$69.00

Subtotal: $2,014.00

So that's pretty much it. See, that wasn't too bad, right? Just be sure to study the more complete allocation of costs example I've provided for the band RTT before moving on to the last section.

ALLOCATION OF COSTS

We are a do-it-yourself band and are able to work on a limited budget because of our professional relationships, internal strengths, and access to free tools and services. We use our own professional equipment and have arranged barter deals with recording studios, printers, and sound and light crews. We also have set up "merch on demand" accounts (where T-shirts and other items are created only after ordered) to reduce certain initial expenditures. The allocation of costs below only reflects the actual money we have to spend. One year total: **$26,719.35**.

a) 12-Song Album

Manufacturing Costs for Six-Panel Digipak CDs	1,000 Units @ $1.20	$1,200.00
Manufacturing Costs for Wristband Flash Drives with Logo	100 Units @ $7.45	$745.00
Setup Costs for Digital Distribution, Including Bar Code and ISRC Code with CD Baby	N/A	$69.00

Subtotal: $2,014.00

b) Live-Performance Set

Bullhorn	1	$120.00
Strobe Lights	3 @ $66.66	$200.00
Police Lights	4 @ $87.50	$350.00

Subtotal: $670.00

c) DVD Soundtrack-Umentary™: *Occupy World*

DVD Manufacturing Costs	1,000 units @ $1.54 (Note: The goal is to sell 500 in the first year, but it was cost effective to make 1,000.)	$1,540.00

Incorporate a Timeline or Schedule

Next up are timelines, which are systems that help you break your yearly SMART goals and strategies into smaller bite-sized pieces. Timelines help ensure that you'll get things done "on time" and hopefully "on budget," and "on the level of quality desired."

While there are complete courses and books written on the subjects of time and project management, with detailed charts such as *Gantt* (that shows the start and finish date of every task in relationship to every other), let's keep things simple and just focus on outlining all of your marketing strategies, organizing tasks into the most logical sequence of steps, and adding some finishing touches.

Outline All of Your Marketing Strategies

Outline all of your marketing strategies, including branding, product, price, place, promotion, and measuring. The specific tasks associated with each strategy must also be listed in bullet-point form, but that will be discussed momentarily. First see the table that I've provided to examine what the band RTT might create.

[Branding]
★Marketing tasks listed here . . .
★
[Product]
★
★
[Price]
★
★
[Place]
★
★
[Promotion]
★
★
[Monitoring/Market Information]
★
★

Organize Your Tasks into the Most Logical Sequence of Steps

Next, you must fill in all of your marketing tasks for each strategy. To ensure that you get all of your tasks completed in the most efficient, logical, and timely manner throughout the year, be sure to organize them in a way that helps you tackle *all of the important stuff that is due first*. In other words, you have to *consider the sequence* of things.

For instance, you can't schedule a record release party on March 31 without considering that the promoter must be called in late January to book the show. You can't schedule the promoter to book the show in late January without having a website up and a sample track and picture where he or she can take a look and listen. And you can't put up a sample track and picture for the promoter to take a look and listen to unless you've already started to lay tracks and take photos in early January. On the latter note, remember that some tasks can—*and should*—be scheduled *simultaneously to maximize resources and ensure you meet your goals on time*. For instance, while laying tracks in the studio, you can also have a photographer capture cool live shots for your website and video. You get the idea!

An effective method of organizing your tasks throughout the year is to start at the end of each quarter (or month, week, etc.) and work backwards with consideration to how long each task is likely to take. I know this is a challenge and takes a little work, but be reassured that this is what it takes to get organized and succeed. If you'd like to read more about time management, check out the classic book *The Seven Habits of Highly Effective People* by Stephen Covey, *The Fast Forward MBA in Project Management* by Eric Verzuh, or *A Guide to the Project Management Body of Knowledge (PMBOK Guide)* by the Project Management Institute.

MARKETING PLAN TIMELINE (ONE YEAR)
a) January 1–March 31 (Q1): Pre–Record Release

[Branding]

★ Complete any needed testing/research to ensure that we have the best branding strategy in place.

★ Strive to maintain and promote a consistent brand image in all of our marketing activities executed in this quarter and throughout the year.

[Product]

★ *War and Police* Album (release slated for March 31):

> Finish writing songs, test songs on fans, consult with songwriter Brian Wilston, record tracks and mix/master with Bob Sloan, create branded album artwork, and manufacture CDs and flash drives with Disc Makers.

★ RTT Merch:

> Create branded merch artwork with Adobe software, and print it with Bob Fiero at Zebra Marketing. Set up CafePress merch-on-demand site, and build merch table.

★ Live Performances ("Gatherings"):

> Work up RTT live set No. 1 with band and the Jensen Brothers Sound and Lights at Hollywood Rehearsals, build stage props with Hollywood Movie Set and Design, and buy all lighting.

[Price]

★ All Products/Services: Establish all policies on www.rallythetribes.com store, on packaging, with consigners, and more.

★ CD: Initiate special-event discount price for the record release party on March 31.

[Place]

★ CD/DVD Place: Arrange consignment agreements with Amoeba Music and Truth Clothing (and others). Set up physical/digital distribution with CD Baby, and load files on www.rallythetribes.com by March 20 at the latest.

★ Live-Performance Place: In the first week of January, set up a performance at Sundance Film Festival (to be held Jan. 24—with RTT Digital only), book album release party with Key Club, and arrange for after-party at Hollywood Rehearsals (to be held March 31—with complete band).

★ Songs: Upload compositions to the Creative Commons site (www.creativecommons.org).

[Promotion]

★ Internet Promotion: Set up Facebook and Twitter accounts and begin hyping record release. Build mobile phone app with Mobile Roadie. Reach out to electronic music magazines and political blogs for release blurbs about *War and Police*. Load short clips of *Occupy World* on YouTube and Vimeo with teaser ad "coming soon." Reach out to political blogs for prerelease interviews and discussions about charities, and acknowledge the video contest winner ("The Change Agent of the Month") and make sure he or she is mentioned on the RTT site.

★ Word-of-Mouth Promotion: Invite Los Angeles opinion leaders (music critics, rave promoters, fans, artists, popular journalists, and cool college kids) into the studio and rehearsal room and give a "sneak preview" performance/party of RTT's work. Give out free CDs to key influencers and ask them to "tell a friend."

★ Guerrilla (or Street Commando) Tactics: Stencil streets with RTT logo, place stickers all over Hollywood clubs, and hand out cards and CD-R samplers (three weeks prior to record release party on March 31).

[Monitoring/Market Information]

★ Monitor all promotional and other strategies for effectiveness and return on investment.

Add Some Finishing Touches

And finally, you can add some finishing touches to your timeline by simply titling it. Your decisions will be based on the time periods used (quarterly, monthly, weekly, daily, etc.) and whether your timeline starts before or after an important event, such as before the release of your recording. For example, a band might use the title "January 1–March 31 (Q1): Pre–Record Release." Works for me.

Now, to wrap up this section on timelines, please see the table "Marketing Plan Timeline" for the band RTT.

Add an Appendix

And finally, as an addendum to your plan, you can create an appendix that includes detailed lists of concert venues, radio stations, magazines, blogs, sample survey cards, research charts, and so forth, that may be too large to stick into the body of your plan. An appendix is not mandatory, but it can certainly be useful.

Whew! You're finished with assembling your plan. Now you better do something with it other than let it collect dust on your coffee table. This brings us to the next, and most important, chapter on "executing" your plan.

So, what are you waiting for? *Turn the page!*

[Note: Be sure to check out the back of this book to examine a complete and detailed Marketing Plan of Attack™.]

Execute Your Marketing Plan Effectively
Adopting the Right Policies
That Get Your Company Results

Congratulations! You've come a long way. Creating and assembling a marketing plan is an impressive feat of which you should be extremely proud—*but don't get too comfortable just yet.*

In the words of Ralph S. Larsen, CEO of Johnson & Johnson: *The best-thought-out plans in the world aren't worth the paper they're written on if you can't pull them off.*

This brings us to an extremely important stage in the marketing process known as *execution*, which is the art of getting things done. In general terms, execution involves adopting the right *policies* to help you close the gap between what you *want to achieve* and what your organization *delivers.*

Adopting the right set of execution policies can also help you to:

- **Follow through flawlessly with everything you say.**
- **Make things that are supposed to happen, happen. And . . .**
- **Correct your company's shortcomings and stay on track.**

This chapter emphasizes a number of important execution policies, including everything from collecting the necessary funds to delegating the workload appropriately. There is no particular order in which these policies must be carried out, so feel free to skip through them as you'd like.

Make Sure Your Plan Passes the Bullshit Test

Proper planning and strategy methods should already be drilled into your head, but it's important to take another quick look at them just to be sure. Bottom line, if your plan is a bunch of "hyped bullshit," you don't stand a chance of effectively executing it. Consider the following:

1. Do you have a business vision for the future that is clear and realistic? Or is it overly fantasized, with language like "I want to rule the universe" and "I want achieve world domination"?
2. Have you conducted research thoroughly, found a void or need in the marketplace, and found a uniquely profitable way to fill that need better than anyone else, even through the most difficult times? Or are you just copying what everybody else has already done before?
3. Is your plan truly based on legitimate strengths (skills, resources, and people power)? Or are you just fooling yourself and living in some "fake it, hope ya' make it" world?
4. Are your goals truly attainable, with clear systems for monitoring and measuring your progress? Or are they overreaching and ultimately setting you up for failure? And . . .
5. Have you put into place an *integrated mix* of marketing strategies and allocated your available funds accordingly? Or is your plan based on nothing more than the misguided expectation that Internet promotion alone will propel you to superstardom?

If you have a few changes you'd like to make to your plan, remember it's never too late for improvements; a marketing plan is a living, breathing document. I know the above questions are tough, but your response to them can mean the difference between successful execution and failure.

Secure the Needed Funds Now

Before even attempting to execute your Marketing Plan of Attack™, be sure to secure the necessary funds long in advance, or you could easily get delayed and/or left permanently stranded.

I have seen countless indie artists start a project they couldn't finish because they either ran out of money, or they naïvely expected that someone would appear magically to offer them help.

So whether the funds are in the form of currency or a legally binding agreement that states the resources will be there for you when needed, *secure the needed funds now!* You'll be so glad you did.

AFTERTHOUGHT: REINVEST IN YOURSELF Should you be fortunate enough to secure the necessary funds for your project, and actually have a few bucks at the end of the day in profits, don't be afraid to reinvest back into your company. These funds can help you buy better and more efficient equipment, which can be used to produce even greater profits, which can be reinvested (and so on and so forth), until eventually you become a sustainable business. Remember, it takes money to make money. Or as Samuel Johnson once said, "The future is purchased by the present."

Remember Not to Wait Around for Others to Help You: Do-It-Yourself (DIY) or Die

Even after reading this book and writing a plan based on a proactive approach, some of you may still be less than enthusiastic about rolling up your sleeves and getting things done. So, let me remind you, you better get pumped up on doing-it-yourself, *because it's unlikely that anyone is going to do it for you just yet.*

Remember that doing-it-yourself (DIY), which is also called *self-leadership* by Richard Leider in the book *The Leader of the Future*, is a proactive approach to marketing your company, firmly based on the idea that until you stimulate excitement on your own, no one will care about your success more than you—not A&R reps, not managers, and not agents. These professionals, especially the ones who have clout, are motivated by money, and the last time I checked, a percentage point of zero was still zero (i.e., zero incentive). Thus, you better get excited about *attracting the attention of those who can help you by first helping yourself.*

Bands like Clap Your Hands Say Yeah had record companies throwing deals at them after they built a strong buzz by themselves. The artist Owl City went on to sign a major recording deal with Universal Republic after getting hundreds of thousands of plays from a song recorded at his mom's house. And Linkin Park impressed Warner Bros. Records after playing sold-out shows with legions of fans who were already singing their lyrics as if the band were already a platinum act.

So to be sure: Don't rely on luck or the fantasy that you're God's gift to music and you're soon to be miraculously discovered. No one is going to save you and whisk you from your garage to superstardom. Adopt a healthy attitude about work. It's not a "four-letter word." *It's a necessity.* The motto you should confidently employ is *DIY or die!*

Be Ready and Willing to Go the Distance with Persistence

Proactivity and hard work are extremely important, but being able to hang in there for *as long as it takes*, in spite of the many challenges you'll face, is crucial. As business consultant Brian Tracy states, "You have to put in many, many, many tiny efforts that nobody sees or appreciates before you achieve anything worthwhile."

Yet, it still amazes me how many young musicians approach me at music business conferences and complain about how long they've been working and how frustrated they are that they haven't yet arrived. The crazy thing is that most of these artists have only been at it for a few short years. This behavior reeks of immaturity and "weekend warrior" syndrome.

Malcolm Gladwell writes in *Outliers* that you have to put in your "ten thousand hours" before getting what you truly want. He points out that the Beatles played in clubs for years while honing their performance and songwriting skills. They didn't make it; they *earned* it.

Look, there are no guarantees for any of you who are pursuing your goals and long-term visions. But one thing is certain: *success won't come to you overnight.* So get ready to push forward for the long haul and remain determined that you're going to achieve the success you desire. As Kevin Spacey says in the movie *Swimming with Sharks:* "Be willing to earn it, take it, and make it yours."

AFTERTHOUGHT: FINISH EVERYTHING YOU START Successful execution requires that you work long and hard, but also that you follow up and follow through with everything you do. It took me seven months just to get a review of my book in *Modern Drummer* magazine. This is par for the course. Stay organized, don't give up, and get the job done.

Burn, but Don't Burn Out: Nutrition, Sleep, Exercise, and More

While we've already established that hard work and long hours are par for the course in the music industry, we must not forget to mention the importance of getting adequate rest, nourishment, and exercise (things that are typically overlooked in most business books, but nonetheless, things that are crucial to your success).

Without good health and a balanced lifestyle, your ability to execute efficiently can be reduced dramatically, and may even cause you to make critical mistakes that cost you a lot of time and money. (Heck, it can even cost you your life—I fell asleep once while driving. Yikes. Close call!) And don't overlook the effects of neglect on your appearance. If you look tired, drag your feet, and put on excess pounds, you can negatively affect how people respond to you and to your career.

I know. I know. You don't need a lecture, but this stuff is important. So, just be sure to take the little I've written here very seriously and read the books *Psychology* by Douglas Bernstein and *Health and the Domino Effect* by Sharon Price. Your ability to execute really does depend on staying healthy.

Choose Employees and Band Members Wisely

Moving on to one of the most important factors in the successful execution of your Marketing Plan of Attack™, let's look at the relationships you'll have with other musicians. If you haven't hired or partnered with anyone just yet, and you plan on doing it, be sure to pay close attention. Your ability to get things done will be determined largely by the people you bring into your organization.

Choosing employees and members is one area where musicians tend to make big mistakes. Somehow they're likely to choose their employees, band members, and partners based on whether they live in the same area and/or have the right hair color and tattoos.

While location and looks can be important, here are other more serious considerations:

1. Does the candidate share a passion for your long-term vision and overall values?
2. Does the candidate possess important internal strengths (skills, equipment, resources, etc.) that can make up for your weaknesses?
3. Does the candidate have the ethic and tenacity needed to work harder and longer (if necessary) than anyone else, even through the most difficult time?

4. Does the candidate show a desire to commit to the organization, or does he or she have other obligations (school, relationship, career) that might distract him or her?
5. Does the candidate have a problem with any serious addictions such as drugs and alcohol? And . . .
6. Is the candidate a good follower, as well as a good leader?

If the thought of raising these questions makes you feel a little uncomfortable, remember that they can save you a great deal of time and hassles in the long run. Trust me on this, gang. I'm speaking from years of experience. Bottom line: if you don't have the right people in place, *you don't have a fighting chance!*

AFTERTHOUGHT: GOT MUSICIANS? Note that the best method for finding musicians is through personal recommendations from trusted sources, such as other musicians, producers, managers, music teachers, club promoters, and even music store clerks. You can also attend local jam sessions and open mics, check out the hottest bands in your area, place ads in your local music paper, post announcements in social networks and blogs, and call your local musicians' union.

Delegate the Workload Within Your Organization

One of the advantages of working with other people, whether you are in a band with three other partners or you are a solo artist who hires ambitious musicians, is that you can delegate the workload within the entire organization.

One musician can be the website guy, another the club booker, and you can be the spokesperson. Even the fans of your organization can be delegated certain tasks, such as helping with street promotion or working in your merch booth.

As long as you can get everyone excited about the long-term vision of the company, to feel empowered to take on certain tasks that match their strengths, and to hold themselves accountable for both the successes and failures of their responsibilities, delegating the workload is a productive step toward executing your marketing plan effectively. It can also save you a great deal of time and money. By the way, successful delegation is the hallmark of great leadership and is what makes teams succeed.

For more on this, see *The 17 Indisputable Laws of Teamwork* by John C. Maxwell, *The Leader of the Future* by the Peter Drucker Foundation, and *Lead by Example* by John Baldoni.

Link Rewards to Performance Execution

While on the topic of motivation and getting people to act, let's talk about *money*. Money is a tremendously motivating force. Yet so many musical organizations fail to discuss their reward system and instead treat the issue like it's taboo and something that should not be mentioned in the same sentence as the word *art*. But in the long run, this attitude can drain people of their willingness to get things done. That's why considering the following tips is so important:

- If you're in a band, write out a clear and simple band membership agreement that defines how things like copyright ownership for songwriting collaborations will be split and what percentage of income will be reinvested back into the band. Sample agreements can be found on the Web.
- If you are a solo artist and employer, explain to your musicians precisely how and when they'll get paid, and give them incentives for helping you with things like promotion.
- If you have people who are helping you with sales at your merch booth, explain how they'll be rewarded for their efforts with special perks like a small commission of the merchandising sales if a certain gross amount is reached.

THE MANY QUALITIES OF A GREAT LEADER

Leadership is the process of getting people focused on a vision, influencing them to take action, and causing them to initiate change. It takes great leaders (both self-leaders and team leaders) for effective execution. Here is a list of a few adjectives that apply to great leaders:

accepting	composed	energetic	inquisitive	open-minded	self-aware
accountable	confident	engaged	inspired	organized	skilled
adaptable	courageous	ethical	intelligent		socially adept
aggressive	credible	exemplary	intuitive	people-centric	strong
articulate	curious			perceptive	
attentive	customer-	fair	kind	persistent	teacherly
	centric	firm		persuasive	tenacious
balanced		flexible	loyal	positive	trustworthy
believable	decisive			proactive	
bold	definitive	generous	mature		unafraid
brave	determined	grateful	mindful	realistic	
	disciplined		moral	relevant	values-driven
calculated	diverse	honest	motivated	respectful	victorious
calm		humble		responsible	
ceremonial	effective	humorous	nimble	responsive	willing
comfortable	efficient	influential	noble		well-connected
communicative	empathetic	innovative		secure	
competent					

Overall, the idea is to create an appreciative culture that boosts your entire organization's morale and gives them an incentive to come together as a team. In the long run, you'll improve your ability to execute efficiently and increase your chances of achieving your goals. So take this point seriously!

Communicate the Sense of Urgency to Get Things Done Now, Before It's Too Late!

Moving on to yet another thought that deals with the important topic of motivation, communicating a sense of urgency that *certain tasks must be done by certain times* is a great way to get others, as well as yourself, to act right *now*!

Take *age* and *time* for instance. The fact is this: *we're all getting older each day.* And in this fast-paced music industry, which is largely based on youth, freedom, sacrifice, and risk, *failure to act right now can mean the failure to capitalize on your golden window of opportunity.* That's right! Think about that for a moment. Surely there are exceptions to this rule depending on the genre of music you are pursuing and other factors, but the point is that urgency and time can get you fired up and cause you to get the most out of every single day of your life.

Another factor to consider is competition. The longer you wait around to get your idea to the marketplace, the greater the chance that someone will get there first and make you look like a copycat. It wouldn't be the first time that something like this happened, would it? Surely you've said before: "I thought of that idea first"? Are you going to let that happen again? I didn't think so!

I always say, why wait for tomorrow for something you can do today. If you want to read more on the subject of urgency and the various methods you can think about to get motivated, see John P. Kotter's *A Sense of Urgency*. Hurry up, before it's too late!

Get Rid of Complacency, Negativity, and Flakiness, and Do It Quickly

Even after reading books on how to effectively execute your plan and motivate people, you may still find that certain partners (employees, etc.) are not on the same page as you. They display continuous complacency, negativity, and flakiness that suggest they don't believe in the vision and values of the organization.

If you find yourself in this predicament, it is extremely important to rid yourself of this problem immediately before it does any long-term damage to your organization. Does this sound harsh? Well, be assured there is nothing more harmful to your cause than the toxic fumes of complacency, negativity, and flakiness.

In *The Prince*, a classic book read by many top business executives, Niccolò Machiavelli puts it bluntly: "Unless a *disease* has been diagnosed and treated at the outset, it will become easy to diagnose but difficult to cure." Unfortunately for me, I know this all too well from my own experiences with certain ex-partners. Referring to these folks as a disease is putting it nicely.

Bottom line: Attack problematic people head-on, and part ways if needed. Don't prolong the inevitable and jeopardize your ability to execute effectively. Move out the old, and move in the new!

Embrace Industry Types, Movers and Shakers, and Company Deals Carefully

After doing-it-yourself and building up a strong buzz in your marketplace, there may come a time when you'll be approached by some industry professionals (managers, producers, agents, investors, etc.) who express an interest in offering you some help. *Awesome!* But just be careful. Getting stuck in the wrong situation could easily derail your career and ability to execute at your own free will. Thus, be sure to assess all potential team players carefully by doing the following:

1. Listen to the ideas this person has for you, and determine whether they are truly in line with your vision and values.
2. Assess the track record or experience of this person by checking references and speaking with people you trust.
3. Assess the person's ethical code and whether he or she has any potential ulterior motives, such as wanting to sleep with you, instead of wanting to help you (hey, I'm being real!).
4. Weigh what you're giving up (a fee, percentage, creative and business control) for what you're going to get. And finally . . .
5. Assess all legally binding agreements that you're asked to sign (which might mean that you have to hire a music business attorney).

I'm not going to get into the details of your professional team here, since that is beyond the scope of this book. But the point is that you must be careful to get into the *right* relationships with industry folks, and not simply *any* relationship. This goes for relationships with record companies, music libraries and publishing companies too.

If you want to read more about the business of music, be sure to check out Don Passman's *All You Need to Know About the Music Business* and/or *The Musician's Handbook* by yours truly. Both of these books are being used at major educational institutions across the country and can be found easily online.

Always Give Thanks to Those Who Help by Practicing the Attitude of Gratitude

Getting close to the end of our discussion on execution, let's take a look at a quote by James Allen, the British philosopher and author of the pioneering self-help book *As a Man Thinketh*, who once said, "No duty is more urgent than that of returning thanks." If that wasn't clear enough: *nurturing healthy relationships and making people feel appreciated is a big part of effective execution and getting things done.*

When someone offers you assistance and/or gives you a break in this crazy business, it's your karmic responsibility to go out of your way to show that person thanks and appreciation. Send a card, thank him or her on your recording, pay homage to him or her in interviews, and always remember this person helped you when you needed help the most. Remember that by doing this, *you'll increase the likelihood he or she will help you again.* And in this business, folks, you need all the help you can get.

"And don't just reach out to your contacts when you need something or after they've helped," says Keith Ferrazzi in the book *Never Eat Alone*, "reach out to those in your circle of contacts all the time." Heck, if applicable, you might even return the favor and hook them up with some work or hire them yourself.

Showing gratitude is not only good business and marketing sense, it's a good way to live a full life! Okay? So just do it!

Remember That Life Is Not Just a Box of Chocolates

And finally, my last thought about effective execution is really one that sums up this whole chapter and book— it deals with being fully aware of every business decision *you make*, and the ones that *you do not make*. This brings to mind a famous quote from the classic movie *Forrest Gump*.

Forest compares life to a box full of chocolates because, in his words, "You never know what you're going to get."

Well, for a slightly different take on this, I compare life to a jar of jalapeños, because *everything you do [or don't do] today can burn your ass tomorrow!* Be wise. Think ahead! And make every day count. And that, folks, is all I have to say!

A FEW MORE TIPS FOR THE ROAD: FAMOUS QUOTES ON EFFECTIVE EXECUTION

- "A mighty oak tree was once a nut that stood its ground." —Proverb
- "Riches do not respond to wishes, only to definitive plans and constant persistence." —Napoleon Hill
- "All that we are is the result of what we thought." —Buddha
- "If you want to change your future, change your thoughts." —Lisa Nichols
- "Feed your faith and your doubts will starve to death." —Proverb
- "Act the way you'd like to be and soon you'll be the way you act." —Leonard Cohen
- "*Impossible* is a word only to be found in the dictionary of fools." —Napoleon Bonaparte
- "Success is 10 percent inspiration and 90 percent perspiration." —Thomas Edison
- "Being in the right place at the right time won't make you a success unless you're ready." —Johnny Carson
- "I'm far from being God, but I work Goddamn hard." —Jay-Z
- "Hire people who are larger than you are and become a company of giants." —David Ogilvy
- "Leaders are not born, they are grown." —James Kouzes
- "Great leaders create great communities of people." —Gifford Pinchot
- "Leadership is not a position, it is a process." —James Kouzes
- "All leaders must learn to follow if they are to successfully lead." —Douglas K. Smith
- "The first responsibility of a leader is to define reality." —Max De Pree
- "Perpetual optimism is a force multiplier." —Colin Powell
- "Success is the ability to go from one failure to another with no loss of enthusiasm." —Winston Churchill
- "To subdue the enemy without fighting is the acme of skill."—Sun Tzu
- "Life is like boxing: you can be losing in the ninth round and still win by knockout in the tenth." —Unknown
- "A year from now you will wish you had started today." —Karen Lamb

21

Continue to Learn About Marketing

Strengthening Your Marketing Muscles with 20 Exercises

The best way to *end a book on marketing* is to read how to *continue learning about marketing*. Doing this will force you to keep your eyes and ears open to the world around you, apply the basic principles of this book to everyday business issues, and absorb new marketing concepts and perspectives. Just like exercising in a gym and keeping your body fit, continuing to learn about marketing will keep your marketing muscles strong.

Continuing to learn about marketing will also help you to:

- **Absorb marketing concepts into your "DNA" through repetition and exposure.**
- **Expand your horizons to tackle concepts beyond the scope of this book.**
- **Stay current on new marketing practices and techniques.**
- **Take away the most useful lessons from every marketing experience.**

What follows are 20 concise and helpful learning exercises that you can practice in any order. They include everything from studying the life stories of successful and innovative artists you admire to attending industry conventions.

Be sure to think of your own exercises to add to the list, and feel free to share them with me and other readers via my website (www.bobbyborg.com). Cool?

And now, let's roll up our sleeves and get ready to keep those marketing muscles in shape.

Study the Life Stories of Successful and Innovative Artists You Admire

Look closely at the careers of successful artists and ask how these artists succeeded.

Did they work hard to develop their strengths and remedy their weaknesses? Did they work hard at discovering and developing their unique sound and style? And did they set specific goals and execute powerful marketing strategies to achieve these goals?

The answers to all of these questions can provide the keys to your own success. Read books, watch documentaries, and listen to podcasts online to conduct your own research.

Analyze the Careers of Artists Who Have Failed

Learning *what not to do* is just as important as learning *what to do*.

So what causes a group to fail? Is it lack of uniqueness? Is it a lack of great songs? Is it being in the wrong place at the wrong time? Is it drug abuse? Or is it just poor execution?

DVD documentaries such as *Dig* and *Anvil, the Story of Anvil* are particularly enlightening, but there are so many more. Conduct a search online and watch everything you can find.

Study the Histories of Companies Outside the Music Industry That You Respect

What made companies like Apple Inc. successful? How about companies like Walmart? Target? Budweiser or Harley-Davidson?

While it's hard to imagine, many of these companies started out in the same place everyone else starts out—with nothing but a vision. But they were able to take that vision to fruition.

So what is it that makes companies like the ones above succeed? Was it a great idea? Was it innovation? Was it hard work? Was it great customer service?

Soak this stuff up! Get tuned into it! Feel those marketing muscles grow!

Examine and Learn from the Marketing That Is Around You Each and Every Day

Since there are only so many hours in a day to dedicate to studying marketing, it is helpful to examine the marketing around you in your daily life.

The next time you're in a grocery store, pay attention to its pricing strategies and coupons, and consider how you might apply these ideas to your own business.

When looking at a magazine or driving down the street, pay close attention to the ads and billboards and ask yourself how you can make your next poster and postcard more effective (in fact, you might even start saving ads you like in a notebook so you can refer to them now and again).

And when approached by a salesperson at the mall, consider whether his or her approach is effective and what you might do better when approaching a music industry veteran at the next conference you attend.

Marketing is all around you. Pay attention and learn!

Consider How Companies Handle Themselves in the Face of Adversity

It's not enough to just study how to build a successful business—you must also learn how to protect one. This brings us to the topic of conflict resolution. Remember, it takes years to build a brand but just a day to wreck one.

Thus, be sure to do the following:

- Learn from examples like Coca-Cola and their handling of their disastrous attempt to release New Coke.
- Consider how Johnson & Johnson handled the Tylenol scandal of 1982.
- Think about how BP handled the oil spill in the Gulf of Mexico.
- Think about how the record companies handled Napster and what they could have done better.
- Consider how Chris Brown handled his charges of assault against Rihanna.
- Observe how that person that's facing adversity today (whoever it might be) is dealing with bad publicity.

There are countless more examples that you can study. Just conduct a search on the Internet using keywords like "conflict resolution" and "marketing case studies" and you'll be surprised at how many hits you get. Read them all and learn.

Analyze Why Some Artists Can Stand the Test of Time and Others Fade Away

Why do terms like "one-hit wonder" exist? Why do bands have a lifespan of just a few years—even those that sell millions of records? And what is it about artists like Madonna and Metallica that allows them to reinvent themselves and have careers 30 years (and more) strong? What are their secrets to success and longevity? Is there anything that you can learn and apply to your own career? After all, you want more than just your "15 minutes of fame"—you want a career. Right? Okay, then, get studying.

Study the Lives of Great Leaders Throughout History

No matter how much you know about marketing, you can never be successful without successful execution.

That being said, be sure to examine the stories of great leaders, whether they be presidents, athletes, or inventors. What was it that helped these people accomplish exactly what they set out to accomplish? Are there any common characteristics you can adopt?

Biographies worth reading include *Steve Jobs* (by Walter Isaacson), *A. Lincoln—A Biography* (by Ronald White), *Andrew Carnegie* (by David Nasaw), and *The Lombardi Rules: 26 Lessons from Vince Lombardi—The World's Greatest Coach* (by Vince Lombardi Jr.). Check them all out and find more like them.

Read the Greatest and Latest Business and Marketing Books

As Confucius once said, "You cannot open a book without learning something." How true! There are so many classics that will remain relevant for years to come and new ones being published every day. You can't read them all, but I highly recommend these works by the following greats:

- Philip Kotler: *Marketing Management*
- Ira Kalb: *Nuts and Bolts Marketing*
- William Perreault: *Essentials of Marketing*
- Edward McQuarrie: *The Market Research Toolbox*
- Lynn Upshaw: *Building Brand Identity*
- David Ogilvy: *Ogilvy on Advertising*
- John Caples: *Tested Advertising Methods*
- Robert Bly: *The Copywriter's Handbook*
- Zig Ziglar: *Secrets of Closing the Sale*
- Mark Jeffery: *Data-Driven Marketing*
- John Davis: *Measuring Marketing*
- Max De Pree: *Leadership Jazz*
- SAGE Publications: *SAGE Brief Guide to Marketing Ethics*
- Dave Chilton: *The Wealthy Barber*
- Eric Verzuh: *The Fast Forward MBA in Project Management*
- Daniel Goleman: *Emotional Intelligence*

Also be on the lookout for works by popular names such as:

- Theodore Levitt
- John P. Kotter
- Peter Drucker
- Brian Tracy
- Tom Hopkins
- David Aaker
- Malcolm Gladwell
- Al Ries and Jack Trout
- Peter Lynch
- Richard Czerniawski and Michael Maloney
- Rosser Reeves
- Don Peppers and Martha Rogers
- Dan Ariely

- Guy Kawasaki
- Brian Solis
- Daniel H. Pink
- Seth Goodwin

There are many more, but these will keep you busy for a long time.

Follow a Variety of Marketing Experts on Their Social Networks

You'd be surprised at the number of amazing articles, tips, and inspirational quotes you can discover just by following the social networks of many of the greatest names in marketing. Use the list I offered above, add a few of your own, and get signed up now. You'll be glad you did.

Subscribe to a Variety of Blogs for the Latest Business and Marketing Information

Blogs are a great way to get updated on the latest marketing and business information. Connecting to the RSS (Really Simple Syndication) feed on blog sites conveniently sends information directly to your inbox by e-mail. Be sure to check out information via popular sites and blogs such as:

- Harvard Business Review
- Mashable
- MarketingSherpa
- Wired
- Hypebot
- MediaPost
- Advertising Age
- Adweek
- eMarketer
- ClickZ
- Fast Company
- McKinsey Quarterly
- Stanford Social Innovation Review
- TEDTalks

Become a Member of a Popular Marketing and Business Organization

Organizations are a great way to get invited to local mixer events, get access to useful webinars (some free and some low cost), and learn about major marketing and business conventions. While there are so many organizations, you can start by checking out the following:

- The American Marketing Association (where I sit on the board as VP of Special Events)
- The Direct Marketing Association
- The Market Research Association
- The Word of Mouth Marketing Association
- The American Association of Advertising Agencies (4A's)

Take a Continuing Education Class in Marketing

Reaching the halfway point in our discussion about furthering your marketing education, it's time to mention continuing education classes.

There are a number of excellent classes on marketing that you can take online or at local community colleges and universities. Classes are held conveniently both day and night to accommodate any schedule. There are even extension programs that offer certificates and courses that can be taken for college credit.

The University of California Los Angeles, Berklee College of Music in Boston, and Musicians Institute in Hollywood are all examples of continuing education institutions that have marketing courses. Be sure to check these schools and others like them, and consider signing up today. You just might end up with me as your instructor.

Take Advantage of "Open Course" Materials from Major Institutions

Did you know that a number of world-class colleges and universities have decided to offer notes, podcasts, and other materials online for free? That's right! They call it *free-share*, *open learning initiatives*, or just *open courses*.

While you have to be rather proactive and self-motivated to find the material you want and get through it on your own (there are limited subjects offered, and you don't have access to students and professors), this information can still be invaluable. Okay, so there may also be some applications that you have to download to get the materials, and there may be a few books that you have to buy, but hey, beggars can't be choosers.

Check out Yale University (oyc.yale.edu), Berklee College of Music (www.berkleeshares.com), University of California at Berkeley (webcast.berkeley.edu), Massachusetts Institute of Technology (ocw.mit.edu/index.htm), Stanford University (itunes.stanford.edu), and University of Notre Dame (ocw.nd.edu).

Get an Internship in a Marketing Company

A great internship in a marketing company will provide you the opportunity to get behind the scenes and see how experienced professionals make important decisions in the real world.

No matter what your age, internships provide you with an opportunity to gain insight, make connections, build confidence, and prove yourself.

Getting an internship will usually require that you be enrolled in an educational program at a local college. So why not get in touch and ask the internship coordinator at your local institution for more information. You might also check out MyMusicJob (www.mymusicjob.com), ShowBizJobs (www.showbizjobs.com), and Monster (www.monster.com) for available paying gigs too. Good luck!

Find a Mentor

Unlike a formal internship, discussed above, a mentorship is typically a situation where an experienced professional agrees to provide you with guidance on a more casual basis, such as accepting your e-mail questions and providing advice now and again.

A mentor may be a former teacher, someone you met at a convention, or an executive of a music company. It might even be a volunteer referred to you by the Small Business Administration's service called Score (www.score.org). One thing is for sure: a mentor is someone who sees you as having a great deal of potential, work ethic, and trustworthiness.

But just be very sure to remember this vital point: don't just *take* from mentors—be prepared to *give back and show thanks*. Offer to assist them in conducting research or even running small errands. Even if they decline, they'll appreciate your professionalism. Remember: practice the "attitude of gratitude." It really does go a long way. Okay?

Teach Others What You Know, and Thus Grow

There is a Latin proverb that says, "By learning you will teach, and by teaching you will learn."

So, why not practice writing a marketing plan for an artist friend of yours? You can prepare a series of interview questions, meet with him or her with your laptop or tablet in hand, and follow the marketing process from beginning to end.

Or you might teach the materials you learned in this book to your band members so that everyone can be on the "same page" and speak the same language. In fact, you might even buy them a copy of this book or lend them your own. Makes sense, right?

Look, by teaching others, you too will learn a great deal about yourself and about modern marketing principles. And it's a great way to get those marketing muscles in shape. So just do it.

Listen to Educational Radio Programs While You Drive

Learning about marketing doesn't have to stop while you're in the car—you can listen to incredible radio programs on the go offered on networks like NPR (National Public Radio).

For instance, in Los Angeles, I keep KCRW-FM: 89.9 tuned in whether I'm making a short or long drive. I especially like the NPR program *All Things Considered*, where you can hear and learn about many of the same business and marketing concepts we discussed in this book. It's really a great way to get marketing and business into your DNA.

To find an NPR station in your area, conduct a search at www.npr.org. Or you can just hook up your iPod to your car and play some of those awesome podcasts you download from the Web or audio books you buy from Amazon. Just be sure to keep your eyes on the road at all times. Okay?

Read the Local Trades

Winding down to our last few exercises in this chapter, remember that every big city has a music magazine that offers marketing and business tips for musicians. Boston has *Performer Magazine*, Los Angeles has *Music Connection*, and New York has the *Village Voice*, to name a few. These are all great papers that offer excellent advice. What is your local magazine? Find out, use it, and excel!

Just Get Out There and Do It

Marketing guru Philip Kotler said, "Marketing takes a day to learn, but unfortunately it takes a lifetime to master." It's not the understanding of marketing alone that will make you a master; it is the experience that comes with years of practice. Thus, one of the best ways to master the art of marketing is to just do it—*and to do it for a very long time*. There is nothing more valuable in this business, or in life, than experience.

Hire a Consultant

And finally, speaking of experience, a great way to learn about music marketing is to witness a seasoned professional in action. Ask around in your city for recommendations from people you trust. Of course, you are always welcome to visit me at www.bobbyborg.com to set up a phone/Skype meeting, or to just browse through some free articles and videos. Well, that's about all folks.

And now, it's time to say goodbye. I would like to thank you for reading this book and allowing me to be part of your history in the making. Just remember to invite me to all of your backstage parties. Seriously! I wish you a very warm farewell and an extra sincere "good luck." Peace!

RALLY THE TRIBES

MARKETING PLAN OF ATTACK™

RECORDING, DVD, MERCH, AND PERFORMANCE RELEASE

WWW.RALLYTHETRIBES.COM

EXECUTIVE SUMMARY

Company Biography: Formed in 2015 in Los Angeles, California, Rally the Tribes (RTT) is a rock/rave band that can only be described as Tupac meets Skrillex meets Rage Against the Machine. Founding key members include Kennedy Robert Jr. on Vocals and K. Luther Martin on Turntables and robotic switches. Musicians include Ace Lincoln on guitar, Robbie Roosevelt on electric drums and classical percussion, and Churchill Preston on electric cello and turntables.

Brief Story: Leader Kennedy Robert Jr. is a first-generation American whose father won a Nobel Peace Prize for spearheading a government agency that diligently pursued and prosecuted World War II criminals. K. Luther Martin is the son of an acclaimed photographer who focused his works on the injustices visited upon Tibetan Buddhists and other repressed peoples of the world. Traveling for most of their young lives, both Robert Jr. and Martin were exposed to a variety of cultures and music. They decided to merge their experiences and views after meeting in Cambridge while studying at Harvard and MIT respectively. They recently relocated to their native Los Angeles.

Vision: RTT's vision is to create a rock/rave band that projects a message of peace, justice, and equality.

Market Need: RTT will capitalize on the young adult generation's need to hear new and exciting music and to be part of an important and higher cause. They will do this by uniquely providing a blend of rock, rap, and techno rave styles, and by uniquely focusing on extremely sensitive political and world issues. Research via *Billboard* and CMJ charts affirm that there are no other bands that fuse rock, rap, and techno rave styles with a strong political message. Research via the National Center for Education Statistics indicates that there is a growing interest among young Americans in political news and change since the Obama election of 2008.

Revenue Generators: RTT will release their first 12-song album, which will also serve as the soundtrack for a documentary DVD film they are writing and producing. The band will also produce a live show featuring a seven-song set of their music. A line of T-shirts bearing political slogans, hats, and hoodies will also be sold at shows and on their personal website at www.rallythetribes.com. They will run a fan club called Change Agents.

SMART Goals: RTT's first-year objective is to increase awareness in Los Angeles by building a database of 5,000 active fans, sell 1,000 records (800 CDs, 100 USB flash drives, 100 download albums), sell 500 DVDs, play 12 rock/rave shows, attract an average of 350 people per regular live performance, and sell out all merch they produce.

General Strategies: RTT's marketing communication approach will be that of a more serious/dramatic tone. Slogans might include "Music That Matters," and "Music with a Mission." They will perform at political rallies, donate a portion of their proceeds to special charities, and utilize the Internet (social media, political blogs, and personal websites), word of mouth (giving out samples and targeting key tastemaker fans), guerrilla street marketing strategies (postcards, stickers, and street stencils), direct marketing (e-mail and text messaging), and more.

Resources: RTT is composed of highly educated band members that are well versed in political issues of the nation and world, have an aggregate of 20 years' training in songwriting and performance, and have professional relationships where barter deals can be arranged to reduce certain production and promotion costs. They possess state-of-the-art recording gear, turntables, and a rehearsal facility that has been acquired mostly through donations and professional relationships. RTT has strong management skills that are helpful to their day-to-day operations.

Costs: Total recording, manufacturing, printing, web design, and other promotional costs are estimated at around $26,719.35 (including a 5 percent contingency). Keep in mind that this reflects great savings as a result of creative bartering deals and other means.

Challenges: The threats that RTT faces include public and sponsor opposition over sensitive lyric subject matter (like pro-choice and pro-marijuana viewpoints). To reduce these threats, RTT plans to exercise peaceful and respectful methods for getting their message out to the people.

TABLE OF CONTENTS

1. COMPANY VISION

In seven to ten years, we envision our organization becoming a nationally known rock/rave band in the business of "music and activism," whose main products/services will be recordings, performances, merch, photography and poetry books, documentary films, and fan clubs. Twenty percent of the proceeds will be donated to special causes around Los Angeles and our nation, such as the Los Angeles Coalition to End Hunger and Homelessness. Our music, words, and actions will be known for projecting a message of peace, justice, and equality to our target audience and the nation.

2. SWOT (or OSWT) ANALYSIS

a) Opportunities:

★ According to data collected by the National Center for Education Statistics, there is a growing interest among young Americans for political news and change, especially since the Obama election of 2008.

★ Since the formation of the American Youth Congress in 1930, groups such as the National Youth Rights Association and Advocates for Youth have shown a continual influence in politics. Similar groups are expected to form and be of great influence on younger generations over the next twenty years.

★ Social science is a growing field in psychology and one that recognizes a strong human need to be part of a greater cause or social movement, particularly one for the betterment of the world.

★ According to the *Billboard* and CMJ charts, there are currently no other bands that fuse rock, rap, and techno rave styles with a strong political undertone.

b) Strengths:

★ Processes: Highly innovative individuals who have the ability to write and record material fast.

★ Capabilities: Strong management skills that are helpful in day-to-day operations.

★ Intangible Resources: Highly educated band members who are well versed in political issues of the nation and world, have 20 years aggregate training in songwriting and performance, play multiple instruments, and have professional relationships where barter deals can be arranged to reduce certain production costs.

★ Tangible Resources: State-of-the-art recording gear, turntables, and a rehearsal facility that has been acquired mostly through donations and professional relationships.

c) Weaknesses:

★ Processes: Minimal marketing experience and number of followers.

★ Financial Resources: Rely heavily on fan donations and bartering.

d) Threats:

★ Competition from other bands that have more financial backing and leverage to gain a greater share of the market.

★ Censorship from radio stations that prefer not to broadcast our controversial subject matter.

★ Laws that prevent rallies and protests.

★ Public opposition and backlash (over sensitive issues like pro-choice and pro-marijuana viewpoints), and companies' disinterest in associating their brands via sponsorships with a politically minded group.

e) SWOT Conclusion:

Given our company's vision of being a nationally known rock/rave band, we monitored the external political and societal landscape and identified an opportunity to create recordings, performances, and documentaries that give a voice to the political youth movement, fill society's intrinsic need to be part of a bigger cause for change, and provide new and exciting music unlike the competition. Our company strengths are well suited to take advantage of this opportunity, given our academic credentials, musical training, and innovation processes. Our weaknesses are our lack of financial resources and minimal fan base. However, because these are critical to growth, we will convert them to strengths by seeking donations, utilizing limited-budget marketing techniques, and building a database of fans drawn from political rallies, live performances, and social networks. Our most serious threat is backlash and opposition from opposing political groups, but to reduce these threats, we plan to be peaceful and respectful when getting our message out to the people.

3. CUSTOMER ANALYSIS

a) Demographic:

★ Age: 18–28.
★ Gender: Male 70 percent/ Female 30 percent.
★ Education: BA and MA: UCLA, Stanford, Berkeley, and so forth.
★ Income: $30,000–$70,000.
★ Ethnicity: White (60 percent), black (15 percent), Hispanic (15 percent), Asian (10 percent).

b) Psychographic:

★ Activities: Listening to alternative music, reading literature, attending political rallies, volunteering for special causes, listening to NPR radio stations like KCRW *This Is the World*, reading blogs like the *New York Times* and the *Washington Post*, and listening to podcasts by Princeton University professor Cornel Ronald West.
★ Interests: Photography, documentary films, poetry, social technology, and higher education.
★ Opinions: Pro-choice, anti-war, pro–legalization of marijuana, pro-Democrat, pro–gay marriage, and so forth.

c) Behavior:

★ Attributes Sought: Wanting to feel as though they are part of a larger movement or tribe, wanting to mix and mingle with like-minded intellects and proponents for change, wanting to blow-off steam.
★ Rate of Use: Attends concerts and raves in clubs and alternative venues on the weekends, purchases music regularly from sites like iTunes, buys at least one piece of merch at shows each month.
★ Adopter Type: "Early adopters," who take ownership and pride in discovering new music and bands early on.

d) Geographic:

★ City: Los Angeles and surrounding cities.
★ Online Territory: United States.

e) Customer Analysis Conclusion:

Given that our most likely customers' demographic includes 18-to-28-year-olds, we could plan to play college campuses, focus on airplay on college radio stations, and support local college students' campus political groups and movements.

Given that our customers' psychographics include activities revolving around literature and political rallies, we could name our first album War and Police *(as a spinoff on Leo Tolstoy's classic novel* War and Peace*) and design artwork to demonstrate police at war with peaceful protesters. Furthermore, based on our audience's interest in documentary films, we could create a documentary called* Occupy World *that uses our music as the soundtrack. The band could eventually release an 80-page book of rare photographs in effort to draw attention to oppressed and marginalized societies, and we could hold a contest to get fans to submit their very own pictures. Our logo might be a shadow of a man imposed over a globe holding his fist in the air, similar to a victory salute. The font we'll use in various marketing communications could be a stencil font to indicate a military or battle theme, and the colors we use might be red (as a symbol of revolt) and black (as a symbol of honor). Finally, in biographical materials included on our website and when submitting to the press, we could share our story and heritage (being that we come from families of political activists and Nobel Peace Prize recipients), since we feel the fans will appreciate that we are truly the real thing.*

Given that our customers' behavioral traits include wanting to be part of a greater and important cause in the world, we could create a slogan that draws on this emotional appeal, such as "Music That Matters," "Advocates for Change," or "We Are Change Agents." We could also run a fan club called Change Agents.

And given that our customers' <u>geographic</u> dimensions include Los Angeles, we could plan to center our promotional campaigns in this area, utilize symbols of LA in our marketing communications, write songs that mention California and its news, and support charities that are localized in the LA community.

4. COMPETITOR ANALYSIS
a) Competitor Matrix: National and Local Acts:

	National Act A **Rage Against the Machine**	National Act B **Rise Against**	Local Act A **The Local Rebels**	Local Act B **Stand Up and Fight**
Company Brand Identity	Style: Alt rap rock. Musicianship: Very strong (unique guitarists). Overall Image: A very strong and believable political vibe (projected in their lyrics, cover art, videos, actions [they speak on the floor of the US senate], website [which has a calendar of political activism events], and heritage [their families are all famous political activists]). Logo: Revolutionary—is that of the Zapatista Army. Individual Members: Very diverse— each is of a different ethnicity. Dress: They regularly wear political statements on shirts and hats. Overall Assessment: A very strong and consistent brand.	Style: Hardcore punk. Musicianship: Good. Overall Image: Mild political undertone (projected vaguely in their lyrics, calendar of activism events on their site, their affiliation with animal rights groups, and straight-edged vegetarian lifestyle [the band is even sponsored by Vans shoes with a line called the "Vegan Shoe"]). Logo: Cool: a fist through a heart. Individual Members: Not very diverse—each is of the same ethnicity (white). Dress: Bland: Black T-shirts and black pants. Overall Assessment: A mildly strong brand that seems contrived.	Style: Heavy alt rock. Musicianship: Fair (singer and guitarist steal the show). Overall Image: Mild political undertone, but comes across more angry and without any particular focus. Logo: Nothing special—a wordmark with their name in IMPACT font. Individual Members: Not very diverse—band is all white. Dress: Weak—plain street clothes (nothing outstanding). Overall Assessment: Weak branding—unsure what they stand for and nothing really to identify with.	Style: Metal/alt rock. Musicianship: Fair at best. Overall Image: Mild political undertone, but comes across more like an angry band that doesn't really have any solutions regarding how to make things better. Logo: A little cliché—a circular lettermark with the acronym SU&P and a lightning bolt in the middle. Individual Members: Not ethnically diverse: all white. Dress: Weak from a political standpoint—black T-shirts, wallet chains, tattoos, and boots. Overall Assessment: There is nothing that is visually current or strong about this band.
Product Brand Identity	Album titles, song titles, and album artwork strongly convey the band's political brand. The band's live performances include air raid sirens, searchlights, and American flags hanging upside-down, which is a signal of distress. The band also uses their live show as a platform to make strong political statements (members give speeches, stand nude on stage, wear orange prison suits, etc.). Their merch products convey political messages and slogans.	Album and song titles could be stronger and better hold a more consistent political vibe. Album art could also convey a stronger political brand. Their live performance is cool and highly produced with a lot of lights and smoke. Their merch items simply consist of the band's name, without any real interesting designs.	There seems to be a lack of consistency between what the band's name implies and what the album title and song titles convey. The album artwork also does not convey anything political. The live performance is not particularly outstanding in any way, just a band playing their set of songs with an angry kind of vibe (they say *fuck* a lot and occasionally go into a political rant). Merch items, like T-shirts, just convey the band name.	The band's name implies a rebellious attitude, but this doesn't really match with the record name, the song titles, and the lyrics. The live performance is intense in that the band is ear-bleeding loud, but there is nothing "stand-out" about the show other than the massive wall of Marshall stacks. Merch items, like T-shirts, just convey the band name.

	National Act A **Rage Against the Machine**	National Act B **Rise Against**	Local Act A **The Local Rebels**	Local Act B **Stand Up and Fight**
Products/ Services	Records (CDs, downloads, streams), movies (DVDs), live concerts, placements in movies and soundtracks, syndicated politically based radio show, and merch (line of T-shirts, hats, posters, wristbands, cinch bags, bracelets, and bandanas). They also have a website store.	Records (CDs, downloads, streams, vinyl), movies (DVDs), live concerts, video game placements, live concerts, and merch (line of T-shirts, coats, hoodies, posters, bandanas, buttons, and messenger pack). Strangely, they also have a large line of kids' shirts. They also have a website store.	Records (CDs, downloads, streams), live performances, and merch (they only have one offering—a short-sleeved T-shirt with band logo).	Records (CDs, downloads, streams), live performances, and merch (they have one short-sleeved T-shirt design with logo). They have TV placements in the reality series *Intervention*.
Price	T-shirts ($23), hats ($14), posters ($14), wristbands ($5), cinch bag ($14), bracelet ($10), and bandana ($10). Live concerts (often free to benefit political causes). Records ($9.99), movies ($14.95).	T-shirts ($17.95), poster set ($19.95) coat ($44.95), hoodies ($34.95), bandanas ($7.95), button pack ($4.95), messenger pack ($34.99), and signed photo ($5). The band has a lot of bundle offers for their merch, including: hoodie, messenger pack, and glove ($74.95). Live performance show ($70). Records ($9.99), movies ($14.95).	T-shirt ($15). Live performance (pay-to-play/percentage at door). Records ($10).	T-shirt ($12). Live performance (pay-to-play/percentage at door). Records ($10). TV placements (gratis for promotion).
Place	They perform in large venues as well as political rallies in front of city halls. They distribute records through a major label. They have a merch deal with a merchandiser. They get placements in edgy films and soundtracks via a music publisher.	They perform in large venues and at political rallies. They distribute records through a major label. Products are sold at shows and at live performances via a merch deal they have in place.	They perform in clubs. They distribute records and merch at live show and via their website. They distribute online via CD Baby on iTunes.	They perform in clubs. They distribute records and merch at live shows and via their website. They distribute online via TuneCore and on iTunes. They get music placements via TAXI (an independent A&R company).
Promotion	The band uses a website (which features a blog, downloadable viral wallpaper, news, videos, events, music, video journals, and a fan club). Their social networking seems inactive. The band has appeared on television and talk shows. They conduct interviews in mags and on radio shows.	They use a website (with news, concert dates, music, videos, and pictures of fans who have tattoos). They use social networking heavily. They hold meet-and-greets at various locations. They participate in interviews with mags and radio shows.	They have no personal website (social networks only). They distribute postcards in front of the clubs where they perform.	They use a website (which features news, concert dates, bios, music, a store, and a link to iTunes). They use direct e-mail marketing, street stenciling, stickering around town, and postcards handed out in front of clubs where they perform. The band is heavily into networking and can be seen socializing every night in town.

b) Competitor Analysis Conclusion:
Given that Rage Against the Machine is defunct, and given that our other competitors' musical style and political brand image is somewhat watered-down, we could capitalize by pushing our unique rock/rave sound and the political youth movement message in all of our marketing communications as follows:

1) The brand identity we convey could be centered around our political seriousness and commitment to higher musical and academic educations (Berklee, Harvard, MIT), our family heritage and long-lasting tradition in political activism, our look (collegiate jocks with mohawks, rugby shirts, and piercings), and our alliances and sponsorships with major political movements and public figures (like local poets, journalists, and political leaders who strongly resonate with our message and our audience).

2) The songs we release could focus exclusively on important political subject matter, our music videos could have a documentary vibe and key in on failing world economies and other important political/legal topics, and our merchandising (shirts, hats, and bumper stickers) could feature short and daring political slogans that get people's attention. RTT's live-performance set can also be centered on a theme similar to a political activist rally or protest march.

3) The promotional strategies we implement could focus on charity and benefit concerts to build community goodwill, college and National Public Radio interviews and appearances that focus on music and politics, social media and interactive personal websites to get the message out about important political activism events, and guerrilla street marketing techniques (using posters and stickers that include a political campaign–styled look) that can be posted across college campuses.

Overall, our competitive advantage could be as follows: "Real musicianship and thought-provoking lyrics fueled by a tradition for change, to create music that matters and music that's heard."

We anticipate that the competition may respond to this move by adopting a similar political brand identity, so we could push our credibility and family heritage by adopting the slogan "The Original Change Agents." For a completely different approach, we could form a local rock/rave coalition or label, sign our local competitors, and earn a place in our fans' minds as being these artists' "creators" or "producers." This all will be to remain a step ahead and continue to be a dominant competitive force in our own right.

5. DEMO AND FEEDBACK (R&D)
a) Products/Services and Other Items Tested:
★ Products: Songs (fans' opinions of the likability of our musical style and subject matter).
★ Other Items: Overall brand identity (fans' interest in politics and important matters of the world).

b) The Problem:
According to secondary data we observed from the National Center for Education Statistics, there is a growing interest among young Americans in political news and change—especially since the 2008 election of President Barack Obama. And according to the preliminary research we conducted using casual observational methods, no one else is mixing rock/rave genres and focusing on important causes. However, while the aforementioned data is certainly encouraging, we still wanted to test out our brand of politically minded rock/rave music on our most likely fans to determine the level of receptivity and interest. It makes sense to do this before moving forward with a full, permanent band, recording a 12-song professional album, and performing out regularly.

c) Methods:
★ Surveys: Survey questionnaires were submitted to three separate audiences that attended live rehearsal-room performances at our Hollywood rehearsal complex.
★ Observation: Participants were observed during the performances, and informal field notes were recorded.
★ Depth Interviews: After the performances, participants were telephoned randomly and then interviewed to get their deeper thoughts about the music and political content.

d) Sample Audience:
★ Participants: Sixty persons (20 per performance) were recruited from various college campuses in the Los Angeles area via a qualifying questionnaire that was read to *all* students as they passed by. Only fans and recent consumers of rock and rave were chosen.

e) Example of Tests (Survey and Interview Questions):
a) On a scale of 1 to 5, how would you rate our music and why [one being "don't like it" and five being "love it"]?
b) On a scale of 1 to 5, how concerned are you with important events and crises of the world [1 being "not at all" and 5 being "very concerned"]?

c) On a scale of 1 to 5, how interested would you be in attending RTT shows and rallies [1 being "not at all" and 5 being "very interested"]?

f) Analysis:

★ Percentages: For questions using a Likert scale, we added up the total scores and divided that number by the total possible scores of 300 (i.e., 60 research persons × 5 possible points = 300 total possible points). The results: For question A, "How would you rate our music?" we collected an average score of 276/300, or 92 percent (also see chart below for further breakdown). For question B, "How concerned are you with important events and crises of the world?" we collected an average score of 238/300, or 79 percent. And for question C, "How interested would you be in attending RTT shows and rallies?" we collected an average score of 292/300, or 97 percent.

★ Trends: We scanned for recurring words and phrases in our surveys and interviews and found the following in regard to our musical vibe and people's interest in supporting the cause: "intense," "passionate," "real," "explosive," "insane," "true," "honest," "important," "original," "unique," "music with substance," "music with a message," "music with meaning," "a musical movement," "a force to be reckoned with," and "music that will make you listen." The most used phrases were "amazing to watch," "master musicians," and "intense performances."

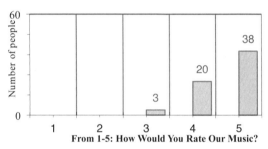

On Closer Examination

g) Conclusion:

Given our initial concern about whether our target audience would be interested in our rock/rave sound and heavily politically based subject matter, we conducted research during live rehearsal-room performances using survey cards with a Likert Scale model; observational methods by having the crowd monitored as we performed; and depth interviews held after the performances. The number of people we used in our surveys was three groups of 20 that we identified from the student body of Los Angeles–area colleges. The data we retrieved from our work shows that people's interest in our music was hot, with a score of 92 percent; people's level of concern about important events and crises of the world was medium high, with a score of 79 percent; and people's interest in attending our shows and supporting our cause was very hot, with a score of 97 percent. The most-recurring comments were "amazing to watch," "master musicians and DJs," and "intense performances." As a result of this information and our findings, we feel confident that the best course of action for our organization is to write more material in our chosen style and vibe, move forward with our professional 12-song recording, and capitalize on our raw live energy, musicianship, and visual appeal.

6. MARKETING PLAN SMART GOALS

To work toward our long-term vision of becoming a nationally known rock/rave band with a strong political message, we plan to offer a 12-song album tentatively titled War and Police, *a documentary DVD film titled* Occupy World, *a line of T-shirts and other merchandising products bearing political slogans, and a 12-song live-performance set. Our goal is to sell 1,000 records (800 CDs, 100 USB flash drives, 100 download albums), sell 500 DVDs, sell out all merch produced, and perform 12 RTT rock/rave performances. We also plan to increase our consumer awareness in Los Angeles, to be indicated by a database of 5,000 fans and an audience attendance of 350 per show. The general strategies to accomplish this goal will consist of Internet marketing (social media, political blogs, and personal websites), word of mouth (giving out samples and targeting key taste-maker fans), guerrilla street marketing strategies (postcards, stickers, and street stencils), and direct marketing (e-mail and text messaging). This goal will be accomplished within one year of the execution of this plan.*

7. COMPANY BRAND STRATEGY

a) Company Band Name: Rally the Tribes.

b) Description of Name: The name represents our vision of bringing together people of many cultures via our music to fight for important causes of the world.

c) Logo: The logo is a circular shape (perfect for patches and stickers) with a shadow of a man holding his fist in the air, similar to a victory salute. At the top of the circle, the name Rally the Tribes is presented in the upper arc. At the bottom of the circle, the band's home city of Los Angeles is presented in the lower arc. The logo also features the Knights of Malta Cross—not only does founder Robert Jr. have family roots in Malta, the Knights were a valiant group founded to protect the sick, poor, and needy no matter what religion or race, and they were known for winning the Great Siege of Malta against all odds in the 1500s. The logo's font is PortagoITC TT to project a military or battle theme. The colors are mostly black, which is a symbol of honor.

d) Slogan: "Music with a Mission," "Music That Matters," and "The Original Change Agents."

e) Mascot: N/A

f) Personality
★ Attitude: Politically motivated, serious, angry, and determined to cause change.
★ Dress: Our look is that of fashion-trendy collegiate jocks with mohawks, rugby shirts, track jackets, baseball and soccer jerseys, tattoos, piercings, skinny jeans, and Nike footwear.
★ Associations: Public relations activities will include our associations with the Coalition for Humane Immigrant Rights of Los Angeles and the Los Angeles Coalition to End Hunger and Homelessness.

g) Enhancement Methods: We will use the name, logo, and slogans on websites, blogs, social networks, the drummer's bass drum head, live-performance banners, equipment cases, T-shirts, stickers, street stencils, and more.

h) Positioning: "A politically minded rave/rock band fueled by a tradition for change, to create music that matters and music that's heard."

[Note: Founder Kennedy Robert Jr. on vocals and K. Luther Martin will also have a side project called RTT Digital, performing their DJ set in select dance clubs when Rally the Tribes is not performing. This, of course, will also help establish RTT's brand as being serious-minded and hard-working musicians.]

8. PRODUCT/SERVICE BRAND STRATEGY

a) 12-Song Album
★ Brand Structure: Combined.
★ Album Title: *War and Police* (a spin-off on Leo Tolstoy's classic novel *War and Peace*).
★ Song Titles: "LAPD—Treat 'Em Like a King," "Petty Thieves Hang, Big Ones Get Elected," "Protest/Anti-Test," and many more in the works. [Note: Songs will feature guest DJs.]
★ Slogan/Taglines: The slogan "Music That Matters" will be used in promotional campaigns.
★ Colors/Fonts/Graphics: The album cover will be primarily black and white to give a news

editorial vibe. Fonts will be PortagoITC TT to project a military vibe and American Typewriter to project an editorial vibe. It will feature a picture of police clashing with protesters.

★ Design Concepts: The album will make a very serious political statement about misuse of power. It will also project an image of quality—CDs will include a six-panel insert featuring photographs of injustices around California and the world.

★ Materials/Formats/Packaging: CDs will be manufactured and packaged in Digipak material, which uses less plastic and is better for the environment. We will also manufacture USB flash drives and offer digital downloads and streams to project a current and technologically savvy vibe.

★ Positioning: Politically minded rock/rave music powered by jock punks and special guest DJs who can play.

b) Soundtrack-Umentary™ DVD

★ Brand Structure: Combined.

★ DVD Title: *Occupy World* (a spin-off on the Occupy Wall Street Movement started in 2011).

★ Slogan/Tagline: "A Soundtrack-Umentary™" on failing economic systems and what we can all do about it." [Note that the word *Soundtrack-Umentary™* is a play on the words *soundtrack* and *documentary*. The tagline uses fear appeal to get people's attention.]

★ Colors/Fonts/Graphics: The DVD packaging will mostly be in black and white to give a news editorial vibe. Fonts will be PortagoITC TT to project a military vibe. There will be a graphic featuring fists in the air imposed over a world map.

★ Design Concepts: The DVD album will project an overall image of revolt and anarchy.

★ Materials/Formats/Packaging: DVDs will be packaged in Digipaks, which use less plastic and are better for the environment. The packaging will include a two-panel insert with basic information like track listings and thank-yous. RTT will also use on-disc printing.

★ Positioning: *"The Original Soundtrack-Umentary™* on world politics and change, featuring the rave/rock sounds of RTT."

c) Merchandising Line

★ Brand Structure: Combined.

★ Names/Titles (as shown below): The Change Agent Hoodie, the RTT Jock/Rock Jersey with George Cross, the Rally the Tribes Military Hat, the RTT "Man Not Mouse" Pad, the "Petty Thieves Hang, Big Ones Get Elected" T-shirt, and the Rugby Rally with Logo.

★ Slogans/Taglines: The slogan "Merch That Matters" will be used in promotional campaigns.

★ Colors/Fonts/Graphics: Mostly black and white with splashes of red and yellow using PortagoITC TT font. The graphics used will include RTT's logo, fan club name, and song lyrics.

★ Design Concepts: We will project our politically based brand and jock/rock vibe. Baseball jerseys and rugby shirts with logo will help project the collegiate element of RTT's brand.

★ Materials: T-shirts will be made from hemp to help make a statement about the environment.

★ Positioning: *"Merch That Matters:* 20 Percent Donated to Local Charities."

d) Live-Performance Set and Production

★ Brand Structure: Combined.

★ Names/Titles: Rock/Rave.

★ Slogans/Taglines: The tagline "Gathering at the . . ." will be used to help convey the rally or protest vibe.

★ Stage Design Concepts: Overall, the design of the show will be visually captivating, ominous, and intense. The idea is to emulate a protest march. It will open with a recording of air raid sirens to convey an ominous mood. There will be police lights and strobe lights on each side of the stage to add to the effect. RTT will build 2′ × 2′ light boxes with Plexiglas tops and spotlights inside (when a performer stands on these boxes, a light will shine up into his face and create an eerie and stunning visual effect). RTT's drummer will face backward to the audience with a three-panel reflecting mirror set up in front of him so that the audience can see both what he is playing and his facial expressions. In between songs, RTT's singer will regularly speak into a bullhorn, similar to what an organizer might do at a rally or protest. Last, we will hang a large vinyl banner behind the band, which features the RTT logo as well as thought-provoking political statements from historical leaders like Martin Luther King, Jr., Abe Lincoln, and others. RTT will also feature their logo on their drummer's bass drum heads.

★ Positioning: RTT would like fans to think of their shows as a rock/rave gathering or rave/mosh rally, rather than just a show or performance.

e) Fan Club
★ Brand Structure: Combined.
★ Name/Title: Change Agents.
★ Slogan/Taglines: "We Are Change Agents."
★ Positioning: "The Original Change Agents."

9. PRODUCT/SERVICE STRATEGY
a) 12-Song Album: *War and Police*
★ Production: In-house and outsourced. Founders Kennedy Robert Jr. and K. Luther Martin will compose the album material while consulting with an outside professional. RTT's album artwork will be created in-house utilizing graphic arts software such as Adobe Illustrator. RTT will also record their music in-house utilizing their home-recording gear, consisting of MacBook Pro laptop computers, Logic recording software, Reason software, keyboards with soundcards, and external microphones like Shure SM57s. Utilizing their professional relationships to arrange barter deals, they will also outsource certain production needs, such as the recording of the drums, mixing, and mastering. RTT will also outsource their regular musicians and guest DJs.

★ Manufacturing: The manufacturing of recordings (both CDs and USB flash drives) will be outsourced. We will also consider outsourcing a limited run of vinyl should the demand justify this decision.

★ Companies: RTT will outsource Berklee songwriting coach Brian Wilston. RTT's outsourced recording needs will be handled by LA producer Bob Sloan and Sloan Productions. RTT will use musicians Ace Lincoln, Robbie Roosevelt, and Churchill Preston. Records will be manufactured using Disc Makers in Pennsauken, NJ.

★ Quantities: RTT will manufacture 1,000 CDs and 100 USB flash drives. They will also release their records as a digital download and stream utilizing CD Baby.

★ Explanation of Choices: Founders have extensive graphic arts experience using Adobe Illustrator, as well as recording experience using Logic and other home recording gear. Producer Bob Sloan is known for his work with electronic music in Amsterdam and will enhance RTT's rock/rave direction and brand. He has also agreed to do all the work on spec until RTT gets a deal. Musicians Ace Lincoln, Robbie Roosevelt, and Churchill Preston are some of the best in Los Angeles and are already known for their work in the popular punk band the Crooked Presidents. They have agreed to barter their services. Disc Makers is the leading company in disc manufacturing for independent artists and offers fair prices: approximately $1,200 for 1,000 CDs, $745 for 100 wristband flash drives, and minimal charges for digital distribution. All of this will help keep quality up and profits high.

★ Customer Service Strategy: All customers who purchase the album, whether live or online, will receive a thank-you card in the mail. RTT will also feature each customer's profile picture on the RTT site. At the end of the month, RTT will call each person who purchased the record and ask for feedback. All customers will also receive a birthday card.

b) DVD Soundtrack-Umentary™: *Occupy World*
★ Production: In-house and outsourced. RTT's DVD artwork will be created in-house utilizing Adobe Illustrator. RTT will fully outsource filming and editing needs utilizing their professional relationships with a friend in film school.

★Manufacturing: The manufacturing of the DVDs will also be outsourced.

★Companies: RTT's outsourced filming needs will be handled by Josh Jordon, a USC film student and assistant to the film department chairman. DVDs will be manufactured using Disc Makers in Pennsauken, NJ.

★Quantities: While their goal is to sell 500 units, RTT will manufacture 1,000 DVDs to benefit from "economies of scale" (note that the price difference between manufacturing 500 units and 1,000 is only $200).

★Explanation of Choices: Founders have extensive graphic arts experience using Adobe Illustrator. Student/ documentarian Josh Jordon is a great friend and local award-winning filmmaker. RTT can also get all of Jordon's services for free and utilize his school equipment at no cost. Disc Makers is the leading company in disc manufacturing for independent artists and manufactures at a reasonable cost: approximately $1,500 for 1,000 units. This will help keep quality up and profits high.

★Customer Service Strategy: A similar approach will be taken as with the recordings. All customers who purchase the DVD film, whether live or online, will receive a thank-you card in the mail. We will also feature each customer's profile picture on the RTT site. At the end of the month, RTT will call each person who purchased the DVD film and ask for feedback. All customers will also receive a birthday card.

c) RTT Merchandising Line

★Production: In-house and outsourced. RTT will create their slogans and designs using Adobe Illustrator.

★Manufacturing: RTT will outsource their merchandising needs to professional printers and utilize "merch on demand" services online.

★Companies: RTT's outsourced printing needs will be handled by Bob Fiero at Zebra Marketing in North Hollywood. Merch on demand will be handled by CafePress at www.cafepress.com.

★Quantities: RTT will initially manufacture small runs of merchandising products to test the market as follows: the Change Agent Hoodie (sold only online as merch on demand), the Rugby Rally with Logo (36 units: 12 small, 12 medium, 12 large), the RTT Jock/Rock Jersey with George Cross (36 units: 12 small, 12 medium, 12 large), the "Petty Thieves Hang, Big Ones Get Elected" T-shirt (36 units: 12 small, 12 medium, 12 large), the Rally the Tribes Military Hat (one size fits all adjustable: 36 units), and The RTT "Man Not Mouse" Pad (sold only online as merch on demand).

★Explanation of Choices: Printer Bob Fiero at Zebra Marketing has over 30 years' experience in the merchandising business working with top acts like the Red Hot Chili Peppers and others. He produces quality high-end work and has agreed to print shirts at cost: the Rugby Rally @ $6, the Jock/Rock Jersey @ $5, and the "Petty Thieves Hang, Big Ones Get Elected" T-shirt @ $4. Hats will cost $5. This will help keep quality up and profits high. CafePress is a reputable company perfectly suited for the creation of mouse pads and hoodies. Working with CafePress eliminates the up-front capital needed to manufacture these items.

★Customer Service Strategy: All products shipped online will be guaranteed satisfaction, or your money back.

d) Live-Performance Set

★Production: In-house and outsourced. RTT's founding key members Kennedy Robert Jr. on vocals and K. Luther Martin on turntables and robotic switches will outsource work to their regular musicians. RTT will also outsource a regular sound person and light person on each show. Utilizing their connections at a movie set company in Hollywood, they will also outsource all set-design needs: the $2' \times 2'$ light boxes with Plexiglas tops and spotlights inside, the drum kit three-panel reflecting mirror, the artwork on the drummer's bass drum head featuring the RTT logo, and the large vinyl banner that features the RTT logo. The police lights, strobe lights, and bullhorn will all be purchased.

★Rehearsals: Rehearsals to produce the show will be held in RTT's rehearsal facility at Hollywood Rehearsals in North Hollywood.

★Companies: RTT's will use Ace Lincoln on guitar, Robbie Roosevelt on electric drums and classical percussion, and Churchill Preston on electric cellos and turntables. For sounds and lights, RTT will utilize Jensen Brothers in Van Nuys, CA. Set design and props will be built by Hollywood Movie Set and Design on Cole Street. RTT will utilize their rehearsal facility at Hollywood Rehearsals in North Hollywood.

★Quantities: RTT will attempt to put on 12 rock/rave performances (or "gatherings") in a year.

★Explanation of Choices: Musicians Ace Lincoln, Robbie Roosevelt, and Churchill Preston are some of the best musicians in Los Angeles, already known for their work in the punk band the Crooked Presidents. They are willing to work with RTT on an exchange basis—since founders Robert and Martin provide their performance and recording services to the Crooked Presidents for free. The Jensen Brothers Sound & Lights in Van Nuys are a reliable concert production company that are friends of RTT; thus the gear is free. Owners of Hollywood Movie Set and Design also donate their services and do incredible work. Hollywood Rehearsals is conveniently located in North Hollywood; it is safe, it has excellent soundproofed rooms, and our friend Max Roster built it; thus the rehearsal costs are minimal to nothing.

★Customer Service Strategy: After every Rally the Tribes "gathering," RTT will throw an after-party at their rehearsal complex. They will make an effort to shake hands, collect e-mail addresses, and thank people for coming out.

e) RTT Fan Club

★Production: In-house/Outsource: We will utilize free online services, and the design skills of John Interpoll, to create an online fan club.

★Companies: WordPress (www.wordpress.com), FanBridge (www.fanbridge.com), and John Interpoll.

★Explanation of Choices: Both WordPress and FanBridge provide free and easy-to-use content management systems. John Interpoll is a friend and recent grad of a local art school that is willing to design and set up the site for free.

★Customer Service Strategy: Each person that joins the fan club will be privy to special news and updates around Los Angeles, such as private BBQs and parties, and private brainstorming sessions with the band. Members will be treated as part of the family.

Product Features and Benefits Chart (PFB Chart)		
Products/Services	Feature(s) of Product/Service	Benefit(s) Important to Audience
a) Album: *War and Police* **by RTT**	Twelve songs featuring four intellectual and highly skilled musicians creating music that can only be described as Skrillex meets Tupac meets Rage Against the Machine. Recorded in one of LA's top studios. Available in CD, flash drive, digital format, and streaming.	This album's unique blend of rock and rave will grab the listener by both his throat and mind and pull him onto the dance floor turned mosh pit for 60 minutes of entertaining music that really matters. Fans will feel like they are contributing to an important cause (20 percent of the price goes to special charities such as the Los Angeles Coalition to End Hunger and Homelessness).
★Track 1 from *War and Police*: "Petty Thieves Hang, Big Ones Get Elected" (lead track from the album).	A mid-tempo rock/rave song featuring the thought-provoking lyrical rhymes of Kennedy Robert Jr.	This three-minute power-packed song empowers the listener with the idea that everyone can make a positive change in this world. It could also be perfect for music in a video game like *Call of Duty*.
★Track 2 from *War and Police*: "LAPD—Treat 'Em Like a King" (second single to push from the album).	An upbeat, foot-stomping raver mixed with trancelike synth sounds, heavy guitar, and an anthemlike chorus lyric.	Music that pulls you out of your chair and gets your fists swinging in the air. This would be perfect music for an edgy cop drama TV show or movie.
★Track 3 from *War and Police*: "Protest/Anti-Test" (third single from the album).	A mid-tempo battle cry song featuring the genius turntable techniques of K. Luther Martin.	These lyrics enlighten the listener about the challenges of civilian protests throughout history. The lyrics teach people how to organize and cause change in the world today.

Product Features and Benefits Chart (PFB Chart)		
Products/Services	Feature(s) of Product/Service	Benefit(s) Important to Audience
b) DVD Soundtrack-Umentary™: *Occupy World*	Featuring the music of RTT, *Occupy World* includes rare and candid interviews with top elected officials and university professors discussing failing world economies.	This 90-minute documentary educates the viewer on what is really going on in the world and teaches him or her what can be done to help before things get far worse for all of us. The footage and music are mesmerizing and entertaining.
c) Merchandising Line by Rally the Tribes	Features shirts, hoodies, a military hat, and accessories bearing interesting slogans. Made from hemp materials.	Perfect for the fan who wants to make a strong political statement, feel good about not harming the environment, and make a positive change in the world (20 percent of the price goes to special charities). Products shipped from the RTT website are guaranteed.
d) Live-Performance Set	Features 10 high-energy songs played back to back in a powerful set with a fully customized light show, professional sound, and highly trained intelligent musicians with a mission.	This 40-minute high-energy and visually entertaining set will keep fans fully engaged all evening, get them raving and moshing, and make them feel like they are truly part of an important gathering to cause change and make a difference in the community. Fans also have the opportunity to buy $1 raffle tickets and win great sponsored prizes. Other sales promos are also offered.
e) The Change Agents Fan Club	A group of like-minded fans, followers, and change makers privy to special news and updates around Los Angeles, private BBQs and parties, and private brainstorming sessions with the band.	This group provides "change agents" all around LA and the world to be part of a bigger and more important cause. Fans will feel like part of an important family that comes together to make a real difference in the community.

10. PRICE STRATEGY

Utilizing personal connections to arrange barter deals with recording studios, video crews, printers, and sound and light techs, and utilizing their own equipment, a number of DIY tools, and "on-demand" services, RTT is able to keep costs down and thus earn higher profit margins on certain products/services. Overall, their pricing strategies will be on the higher end to validate a higher-quality brand image, but 20 percent of the total proceeds collected will be donated to various charities.

a) 12-Song Album: *War and Police*

CD Pricing		
Strategy Names (Initial and Alternate)	**Prices/Amounts**	**Units and Time Period**
Top-Line Price for Records	$10 (Note: Manufacturing cost per unit is $1.20. Estimated GPM is 88 percent.)	On 800 units (of a 1,000 unit pressing). Term of one year.
Free Price	$0 (Note: Manufacturing cost per unit is $1.20. Will take a loss.)	On 200 units (of a 1,000 pressing). Term starting at least one month prior to the official release date and continuing until all units distributed.
Money-Back Guarantee Price Offer	$10 Full refund with shipping and handling will be mailed to customer.	On all paid units sold online. Term is for one year.

CD Pricing		
Strategy Names (Initial and Alternate)	**Prices/Amounts**	**Units and Time Period**
Zone Pricing (On Shipping and Handling from Web Sales)	$3 (US and Canada orders) added to price. $5 (all other orders) added to price.	On all paid units sold online. Term is for one year.

USB Flash Drive Pricing		
Strategy Names (Initial and Alternate)	**Prices/Amounts**	**Units and Time Period**
Top-Line Price for Records	$10 (Note: Manufacturing cost per unit is $7.45. Estimated GPM is 25 percent.)	On 100 units (of a 100 unit pressing). Term of one year.
Money-Back Guarantee Price Offer	$10 full refund with shipping and handling will be mailed to customer.	On all paid units sold online. Term is for one year.
Zone Pricing (On Shipping and Handling from Web Sales)	$3 (US and Canada orders) added to price. $5 (other) added to price.	On all paid units sold online. Term is for one year.

Digital Album and Singles Pricing		
Strategy Names (Initial and Alternate)	**Prices/Amounts**	**Units and Time Period**
Establishment Price (iTunes)	$9.99/$0.99 for downloads. (Note: iTunes and CD Baby take a cut of sales. Small setup fees. Estimated average GPM is 55 percent.)	On all units sold. Term for one year or as long as record stays up on iTunes.

b) DVD Soundtrack-Umentary™: *Occupy World*

DVD Pricing		
Strategy Names (Initial and Alternate)	**Prices/Amounts**	**Units and Time Period**
Top-Line Price/Psychological "End in 9 Price" for DVD Documentaries	$14.99 (Note: Manufacturing cost per unit is $1.50. Estimated GPM is 89 percent.)	On 500 units (of a 1,000 unit pressing). Note: The goal is to sell 500, but manufacturing 1,000 was cost effective. Term of one year.
Money-Back Guarantee Price Offer	$14.99 full refund with shipping and handling will be mailed to customer.	On all paid units sold online. Term is for one year.
Zone Pricing (On Shipping and Handling from Web Sales)	$3 (US and Canada orders) added to price. $5 (other) added to price.	On all paid units sold online. Term is for one year.

c) RTT Merchandising Line

The Rugby Rally and the RTT Jock/Rock Jersey		
Strategy Names (Initial and Alternate)	**Prices/Amounts**	**Units and Time Period**
Top-Line Price/Psychological "End in 9 Price" for Rugby and Jersey Shirts	$19.99 (Note: Manufacturing cost per unit is $6. Estimated GPM is 70 percent.)	On all units (of an initial printing of 36 units) less those used in special sales promotions. Term is for one year.
Money-Back Guarantee Price Offer	$19.99 full refund with shipping and handling will be mailed to customer.	On all paid units sold online. Term is for one year.
Zone Pricing (On Shipping and Handling from Web Sales)	$5 (US and Canada Orders) added to price. $7 (other) added to price.	On all paid units sold online. Term is for one year.
Special Event Discount Price (Buy Rugby or Jersey and Get Military Hat for Free)	$19.99 (Note: Manufacturing cost per shirt is $6. Cost per hat is $5. Estimated GPM is 44 percent.)	Term: Short-event sales promotions planned throughout marketing year.

The "Petty Thieves Hang, Big Ones Get Elected" T-Shirt		
Strategy Names (Initial and Alternate)	**Prices/Amounts**	**Units and Time Period**
Top-Line Price/Psychological "End in 9 Price" for T-Shirts	$14.99 (Note: Manufacturing cost per unit is $4. Estimated GPM is 84 percent.)	On all units (of an initial printing of 36 units). Term of one year.
Money-Back Guarantee Price Offer	$14.99 full refund with shipping and handling will be mailed to customer.	On all paid units sold online. Term is for one year.
Zone Pricing (On Shipping and Handling from Web Sales)	$5 (US and Canada orders) added to price. $7 (other) added to price.	On all paid units sold online. Term is for one year.

The Rally the Tribes Military Hat		
Strategy Names (Initial and Alternate)	**Prices/Amounts**	**Units and Time Period**
Top-Line Price/Psychological "End in 9 Price" for Hats	$11.99 (Note: Manufacturing cost per unit is $5. Estimated GPM is 58 percent.)	On all units (of an initial printing of 36 units)—less those used in special sales promotions. Term is for one year.
Money-Back Guarantee Price Offer	$11.99 full refund with shipping and handling will be mailed to customer.	On all paid units sold online. Term is for one year.
Zone Pricing (On Shipping and Handling from Web Sales)	$5 (US and Canada orders) added to price. $7 (other) added to price.	On all paid units sold online. Term is for one year.
Special Event Discount Price (Buy Rugby or Jersey and Get Military Hat for Free)	$19.99 (Note: Manufacturing cost per shirt is $6. Cost per hat is $5. Estimated GPM is 44 percent.)	Term: Short-event sales promotions planned throughout marketing year.

The RTT "Man Not Mouse" Pad (Sold by Merch on Demand Only with CafePress)		
Strategy Names (Initial and Alternate)	**Prices/Amounts**	**Units and Time Period**
Bottom-Line Price	$7 (Note: Manufacturing out-of-pocket cost to RTT per unit is $0. GPM is 0 percent.) Shipping/handling by CafePress.	On all units sold through CafePress. Term is for one year.

Change Agent Hoodie (Sold by Merch on Demand Only with CafePress)		
Strategy Names (Initial and Alternate)	**Prices/Amounts**	**Units and Time Period**
Bottom-Line Price	$16 (Note: Manufacturing out-of-pocket cost to RTT per unit is $0. GPM is 0 percent.) Shipping/handling by CafePress.	On all units sold through CafePress. Term of one year.

d) Live-Performance Set

Regular Club, College, and Other Performances		
Strategy Names (Initial and Alternate)	**Prices/Amounts**	**Units and Time Period**
Establishment Price	Pay-to-play/free/guarantees up to $1,000 and more per show.	Each show is subject to different policy. Term of one year.

e) RTT Fan Club

RTT Fan Club		
Strategy Names (Initial and Alternate)	**Prices/Amounts**	**Units and Time Period**
Free Price	$0.	Term: For six months from the date the marketing plan launches (quarters 1 and 2)
Donation Pricing	$10.00 suggested minimum fee.	Term: For six months starting six months after the launch of the plan (quarters 3 and 4)

11. PLACE STRATEGY
a) 12-Song Album: *War and Police*
★ Brick-and-Mortar (Record Store) Consignments: RTT will set up a consignment agreement with Amoeba Music in Hollywood, CA.
★ Brick-and-Mortar (Non–Record Store) Consignments: RTT will set up consignments with local college bookstores (like UCLA, USC, and Loyola), as well as fashion boutiques on Melrose like Truth Clothing and others.
★ Brick-and-Mortar DIY Friendly Distributor: RTT will utilize the services of CD Baby to facilitate the ordering of *War and Police* in retail stores.
★ Online Personal Website: We will build a Web store at www.rallythetribes.com where physical recordings will be sold utilizing the e-commerce services of PayPal and the US Postal Service. We will also provide a link to iTunes where *War and Police* will be available for digital download.
★ Online DIY Friendly Distributor: RTT will utilize CD Baby to get on sites like iTunes, Rhapsody, and Spotify.

★Live-Performance Venues: We will create a merch booth and sell product at live performances in clubs, political rallies, and other places we play. We'll accept cash, checks, and credit cards (using Square on our smartphones).

b) DVD Soundtrack-Umentary™: *Occupy World*
★Online Personal Website: Using our store at www.rallythetribes.com, we will sell our DVD film by accepting PayPal payments and checks, and utilizing the United States Postal Service.
★Live-Performance Venues: Using their merch booth, RTT will sell their DVD film at live performances; they will accept cash, checks, and credit cards (using Square on their smartphones).

c) RTT Merchandising Line
★Online Personal Website: Utilizing their web store at www.rallythetribes.com, RTT will sell their line of merch products, and they will include a link to www.cafepress.com where they will sell their "Man Not Mouse Pad" and the "Change Agent Hoodie." For product sold on their website, RTT will accept payment utilizing PayPal and personal checks, and will send product using the United States Postal Service.
★Live-Performance Venues: Utilizing their merch booth at live performances, RTT will proudly display their line of merch products (except for the "Man Not Mouse Pad" and the "Change Agent Hoodie)." They will accept cash, checks, and credit cards (using Square on their smartphones).

d) Live-Performance Set
★Clubs: RTT will perform at local LA clubs like the Key Club and make every effort to set up a monthly residency with this club.
★Alternative Venue Performances: RTT will perform at college frat parties at UCLA and USC, small film festivals (like the Silver Lake Film Festival and the Temecula Valley Film Festival), and corporate holiday parties (like at their buddies' shops—Vortex Skate Shop in Hollywood and Truth Clothing on Melrose).
★Anchor Events: RTT's founders will invest in attending and performing at SXSW, Sundance Film Festival, and Winter Music Festival in Miami. They will also play at select anchor gigs and local clubs and raves.

[Note: Between RTT gigs, founders Kennedy Robert Jr. and K. Luther Martin will also make select appearances as "RTT Digital" in DJ and rave clubs (like Vanguard and LAX) to spin a short set and promote RTT shows.]

e) RTT Fan Club
★Personal Website: RTT fan club will originate at www.rallythetribes.com.

f) RTT Songs (Licensing Opportunities)
★College Films: Songs like "Petty Thieves Hang, Big Ones Get Elected," "LAPD—Treat 'Em Like a King," and "Protest/Anti-Test" will be used in the student documentary film produced by RTT called *Occupy World*.
★Creative Commons Website: RTT will load their music at www.creativecommons.org and allow for student game developers and student independent documentarians to use the music in their student projects and film festivals.
★Songplugger: Pen Music Group, a personal friend of RTT, will strive to plug songs in television shows like *Intervention* and *Gang City*.
★ Out-of-the-Box and Local Business Licensing: RTT will pitch their music to local activist and cause groups (like PETA) that do cable advertising and video blogging.

12. PROMOTIONAL MIX STRATEGY
a) Internet Promotion Plan
★Personal Website at www.rallythetribes.com: RTT will use John Interpoll to develop a website using the free and low-budget services of WordPress. Menu items will include: *About* (to include band history), *Store* (to sell all products and provide product information and customer service info), *Media* (to post live-concert videos, political rally pictures, and photos of fans), *Links* (to social network sites, charities, voter registration, and important congresspeople, *News* (to post current events and a calendar of political activist events around LA), and *Mailing*

List. Using key words like "RTT," "Rally the Tribes," "LA Bands," "Political Rallies," and so forth, we will use our designer to optimize the site for search engines and will also have our designer establish reciprocal links on "like-sites."

★ Social Media: RTT will utilize social media accounts to ultimately draw traffic to www.rallythetribes.com. Sites like Facebook and Twitter will be at the center of their campaign. RTT will strive to engage people in conversation and listen to what they have to say; post quality, relevant, and current content that people want to share; and investigate what people are talking about on other social networks.

★ Mobile Phone App: RTT will provide a mobile phone app for free to their fans. The app will include easy access to pictures, video, and concert dates that help educate and engage fans about the unique benefits of being an RTT fan.

★ Online Publicity (Reviews and More): RTT will target online rock and electronic music magazines like *Spin Club*, *Fresh Club Beats*, and *TurnTable* magazine. RTT will also target music, lifestyle, and political blogs they find using the blog directory service of Technorati (www.technorati.com/blogs/directory).

★ Web Video: On their YouTube and Vimeo channels, RTT will post exclusive and shocking short clips (30 seconds to 3 minutes) of their documentary movie *Occupy World* to ultimately draw fans to www.rallythetribes.com and get them to make a purchase. These clips will be titled with lines like "Exclusive Video" and "Sneak Preview" to give a feeling of scarcity and stimulate word-of-mouth buzz. They will also post live clips from political rallies they attend, live shows they perform, and speeches they give around Los Angeles. RTT will also hold a video contest called "Change Agent of the Month," where fans can submit short video clips of themselves protesting for an important cause in their community, or otherwise doing something for the betterment of their community. The best video gets featured on the YouTube and the RTT site.

★ Podcasts: RTT will seek spins in cool electronic music podcast shows like *LA Mosh Mix*, *LA DJ*, and *Rock Monsters*. They will also seek interviews and performances on political talk show blogs by people like Princeton University Professor Cornel Ronald West, Dr. Ron Luther, and One People Blog News to attract the interest of new fans.

★ Viral Goodies: RTT will provide the "RTT wallpaper," a desktop picture that includes the RTT logo, a list of charities in LA, and the numbers and addresses of senators where fans are encouraged to write. Fans will be asked to "share it with a friend."

b) Word-of-Mouth Marketing Plan

★ Contagious Products and Services: As laid out in the Performance Brand Strategy, RTT will strive to put on the most intense and unique live-performance concert possible every time it performs and do something "shocking" and strange to get people talking. Furthermore, they will always have a very cool and fun "after-party" after each of their shows.

★ Customer Hubs and Opinion Leaders: To amplify the positive word of mouth, RTT will target Los Angeles opinion leaders (music critics, rave promoters, fans, DJs, artists, and popular journalists) and provide samples and other promotional materials (free exclusive merch, invites to RTT parties, etc.) with hopes that they'll tell their large clique of people, who'll tell their large clique of people, and so on and so forth.

★ Product Samples: RTT plans to give away 200 units of their 12-song album *War and Police* to stimulate interest and generate buzz among fans and industry folks. They will ask recipients to tell a friend if they like the material. They will also offer free exclusive downloads (at www.rallythetribes.com) of different song remixes that are not available on the RTT record.

c) Guerrilla (or Street Commando) Tactics

★ Street Stencils: RTT plans to stencil Los Angeles sidewalks in Hollywood, West LA, Venice, and other places where students, hipsters, and music/fashion-minded people converge. The stencil will feature the RTT man with his fist in the air and nothing more (i.e., there will be no further identification). Note: We will use spray chalk.

★ Fliers: We will make political election themed fliers utilizing the free services of LA EZ Print (a friend and supporter of RTT). In return for the favor, we will include LA EZ Print's logo on the fliers. We will tack these fliers all over city telephone poles and in record stores and tattoo shops to announce RTT gigs.

★Stickers: RTT will have 5,000 stickers manufactured, utilizing the free services of LA EZ Print, and will place them in hip Hollywood and Los Angeles clubs (on the bathroom stalls and walls), and at comic and record shops (such as Amoeba) where other stickers are placed and permitted.

★Glossy Postcards: RTT will make 4.25″ × 6″ postcards utilizing the free services of LA EZ Print. RTT will distribute these postcards at venues where they perform, at tattoo and head shops, and at surf and skate shops.

★Three-Song CD-R samplers: RTT will also burn their own disks and hand out CD-R samplers, together with the postcards, in front of venues, tattoo and head shops, and surf and skate shops.

d) Local and National Sponsorships

★Products Associated with Fans: Nike designer footwear, Nike clothing, Nike accessories, Coogi Jeans and polos, Abercrombie and Fitch polos, Kat Von D tattoos, Ray-Ban sunglasses, Flowlab skateboards, Scion cars, Zig-Zag rolling papers, Zippo lighters, and RockStar energy drinks.

★Local Sellers List: Hollywood Skate and Pharmacy Skateboards on Cahuenga, Melrose Swag on Melrose, Blue Fly Designer Shoes of Beverly Hills, Kat Von D Tattoo Shop on La Brea, Scion of North Hollywood on Lankershim, and Melrose Smoke and Toke Shop on Melrose.

★Corporate Manufacturers List: Ray-Ban corporate office in Rochester, New York; Scion corporate office in Torrance, California; Nike corporate office in Beaverton, Oregon; Zippo corporate office in Bradford, Pennsylvania; Coogi corporate office in Pine Bluff, Arizona; Flowlab corporate office in Long Beach, California; Zig-Zag corporate office in Louisville, Kentucky; Rockstar corporate office in Las Vegas, Nevada; and Kat Von D Tattoo Shop in Hollywood, California.

★National Equipment Manufacturers: Gibson guitars, Philips turntables, Shure microphones, Zildjian cymbals, DW drums, and Fender bass.

★Press Kit: RTT will submit both physical press kits (with folder, one-sheet, and live-performance pictures) and an electronic press kit (utilizing Sonicbids).

[Note: Given our lyrical approach to sensitive issues, we understand that setting up sponsors may be a challenge.]

e) Radio Promotion Plan

★College Radio: RTT will focus primarily on getting played on college radio stations in Southern California.

★National Public Radio: RTT will focus on NPR stations for interviews and appearances that target music and politics (e.g., *This Is the World* on KCRW).

★Commercial Specialty Shows: RTT will submit to commercial specialty shows in Los Angeles.

★Station List: RTT will focus on college radio stations, such as KSCR (USC), KXLU (Loyola Marymount), UCLARadio.com (UCLA), KCSN (Cal State Northridge), KPCC (Pasadena), KCSB (University of California Santa Barbara), KCSC (Cal State Chico), and KOXY (Occidental College). They will also focus on commercial specialty shows, such as KROQ's *Locals Only* with DJ Kat Corbett. A full list of contact info is available in our database.

★Materials: RTT will submit a full physical press kit including RTT folder, one-sheet, and *War and Police* CD in Digipak packaging (the suggested listening tracks will be "Petty Thieves Hang, Big Ones Get Elected" and "LAPD—Treat 'Em Like a King").

★Servicing: RTT will service all Southern California college stations in person. RTT will endeavor to service Kat Corbett of KROQ at one of her regularly hosted events as a remote DJ, and also send her a package via UPS.

★Follow-Up: RTT will build relationships with local stations by inviting DJs to MC certain local performances, offering giveaway concert tickets and merch that can be given out on the air, submitting station IDs, getting DJ testimonials that can be used in RTT biographical material, and requesting live interviews and performances on station shows.

f) Publicity and Public Relations Plan

★Press Kit: RTT will create a 9″ × 12″ two-pocket customized presentation folder with RTT logo, business card, one-sheet, and bio. We will have the folders and cards made at Vistaprint and pay local writer Bob X of *Music Connection Magazine* to write the bio (a move that will help build a stronger relationship with the magazine). We will also build an electronic press kit utilizing the services of Sonicbids or ReverbNation.

★ Target List of Local Media: To stimulate reviews and mentions, RTT will submit to local music magazines such as *Music Connection*, *Skinnie*, *Alternative Press*, *Campus Circle*, and *Rock City News*. RTT will also submit to student and lifestyle papers and magazines like *Daily Bruin*, *Thrasher* skateboard magazine, and *Tattoo* magazine.

★ Media Relationships: RTT will strive to build solid relationships with local press and writers by regularly congratulating them on their stories and work, and by sending thank-you cards when any mentions are made of the band.

★ Networking: RTT plans to build local and national media contacts at events like SXSW in Texas, Winter Music Conference in Florida, and Sundance Film Festival in Utah. It will also attend local events in LA (such as the Los Angeles Music Festival), parties and showcases thrown by local magazines, various charity events hosted by music and industry folk in the Los Angeles area (such as the Toys for Tots Harley Ride), local art and film festivals (such as the Silverlake Film Festival), and parades (such as the LA Gay Pride Parade in June).

★ Publicity Stunts: Occasionally, RTT will play "Commando Raids," where it performs on the street (in front of City Hall and other government offices, college campuses, etc.) in protest of certain important issues. RTT will motivate fans to attend these events, and ask them to create their own personally designed picket signs. RTT will also arrange "imitation police" to raid their record release party on March 31 and drag the band away.

★ Record Release Party: Upon the release of RTT's record *War and Police*, RTT will throw a record release party on March 31 at the Key Club.

★ Charity Events: RTT will promote their live-performance charity events for local LA organizations like the Coalition for Humane Immigrant Rights of Los Angeles and the Los Angeles Coalition to End Hunger and Homelessness. Local magazines will be invited to these events and furnished with official press releases. RTT will also participate in events to help feed the hungry during the holiday season (such as Thanksgiving and Christmas/Chanukah time) and take photos of these events to be posted on their websites and social media profiles.

★ Expanded Territories: RTT will utilize the "hometown done good" technique in various territories by contacting their alma maters (Berklee, MIT, Harvard, Fairfax High School, etc.) to receive press. They will then collect these clippings and links and include them in their press kit to generate even more press.

g) Direct Marketing Plan

★ Direct Mail: RTT will use the United States Postal Service to submit press kits to various businesses (club promoters, music supervisors, and journalists) that give them permission.

★ Outbound Telemarketing: RTT will utilize their database to invite fans to live performances.

★ Mobile Marketing: RTT will collect fans' numbers in their database and text these fans before live-performance gatherings. RTT will also provide a mobile phone app for free to their fans. The app will include easy access to pictures, video, and concert dates that both engages them and educates them about the unique benefits of being an RTT fan.

★ E-mail: RTT will utilize the services of Constant Contact to send targeted e-mail correspondences to fans, personalized announcements about shows, personalized birthday greetings, and an informative quarterly RTT newsletter.

★ Database: RTT will put together a database that includes fans who visit the www.rallythetribes.com website, join RTT social networks, and speak with RTT at clubs and other networking events. RTT will also put together industry lists by networking at important industry events, asking for referrals from people they trust, and utilizing compiled lists available in the Music Business Registry. RTT will use Excel software to store these names and use data fields such as *Name*, *E-mail*, *Address*, *Number*, *Age*, and *Birthday*.

★ Content: RTT will craft persuasive communications that get people's attention and cause them to act. They will use catchy hooks in the form of questions (like "Did you know that 500 children under the age of 12 will sleep on the streets of LA tonight?"), detailed information in the body copy, and an enticing call to action in the close. They will also use persuasive graphic pictures and photos of political rallies and other pictures that cause people to take a second look and read the text. (Some of these graphics will be donated by the father of founder K. Luther Martin, who is an acclaimed photographer.) Fonts will include Impact, American Typewriter, and PortagoITC TT. Colors will include black, gray, white, red, and yellow (to match the RTT websites, album covers, and other branding).

h) Sales Promotions Plan

★ Coupons: RTT will place coupons on their site (www.rallythetribes.com) and allow fans to download them in exchange for their e-mail addresses. For instance, before their show, RTT might create a coupon that allows fans to buy the RTT rugby shirt or jersey for the regular price of $19.99 and get the military hat for free (a savings of $11.99 to the customer). The term of this promotion will be limited to just that live performance. The purpose of this promotion is to stimulate excitement and ultimately increase awareness about the band.

★ Special Event Raffles: RTT will seek items from their various sponsors that they can raffle off at their live performances. For instance, if securing an agreement with Ray-Ban, RTT might provide fans the opportunity to buy a number of $1 tickets to win a new pair of Ray-Ban sunglasses. The money collected will be donated to special charities and help solidify RTT's brand of being a socially conscious band. Note that the raffle also serves as an added customer benefit that RTT can use when promoting their live performances to their fans. Announcements about the raffles will be communicated via www.rallythetribes.com and through e-mails and text messages.

i) Face-to-Face Selling Strategy

★ Face-to-Face Meetings: RTT will attempt to pitch event promoters, retail store managers, radio station music directors, brand managers, equipment manufacturers, music supervisors, and others to arrange various deals. RTT will utilize Excel software to organize, manage, and utilize the contact information of these various professionals.

★ Sales Collateral: RTT will have a handy notebook that they can reference when pitching various bookers, music supervisors, and music stores. This book will include company strengths, competitive advantages, and testimonials. When hiring people to run the merch booth at live shows and conventions, RTT will construct a FAQ sheet outlining detailed information about their products (such as where the record was recorded, on what cameras they recorded the DVD film, the materials that each merch product is made of, and the charities that RTT supports). Of course, a price sheet will also be handy, along with a product/feature/benefit chart.

★ Sales Tools: At conventions, networking situations, and their merch booth, RTT will have their trusted iPads available with access to video clips and music files. They will also have their iPhones with a Square (squareup.com) credit card swiper handy.

★ Sales Presentation: RTT will always have a detailed and well-prepared sales presentation with an opener, body, and close for any type of sales pitch. A follow-up pitch will also be written. Some of the key selling points that RTT will use include: They create music that truly matters, they donate 20 percent of all profits to charities, and they come from a long tradition of activists who care.

j) Paid Advertising Strategy

★ Search Results Page Advertising: RTT will utilize the services of Google AdWords. Since RTT can decide on the amount they want to spend for keywords, pay only when someone clicks on their ad, and access data on the number of people who actually clicked through to their website, this is an attractive form of online advertising. Estimated bid per keyword is 20 cents per click with a capped expense of $1,000. Keywords might include "RTT," "Rally the Tribes," "LA Bands," "Music That Matters," "Political Rallies," and so forth.

13. MEASURING STRATEGY

a) Reason for Measuring: RTT plans to achieve the following with their monitoring and measuring strategies: gauge customer awareness, discover customers' reactions to pricing, determine return on investment, find the places that products sell best, discover where customers hear about them, determine which promotional strategies are the most effective, find the number of people who click on an ad, analyze how long visitors stay on the RTT site before leaving, find their net profit, and find the number of customers who buy on the RTT site in proportion to the number of people who visit the site.

b) Methods of Measurement: RTT will use the following sources and methods of monitoring and measuring:

★ Basic Accounting Methods: As a general means of checking the effectiveness of certain marketing strategies, RTT will simply count sales (i.e., they will count sales of their products and services at consignment, live performances, www.rallythetribes.com, iTunes, and other locations where RTT products and services are sold). They will look in particular for spikes in sales and try to draw a correlation to any recent promotional activity that was executed.

★ Business Reply Cards (BRP): RTT will include business reply cards in the packaging of their album *War and Police* and their DVD film *Occupy World* to retrieve important data from consumers. A BRP card might ask basic information, such as "How did you hear about us?" and "What do you think of our record?" Responses can be sent back via snail mail, e-mail, or even text messaging.

★ Sales Coupons: To determine the effectiveness of certain sales promotions that RTT establishes, they will simply count the number of coupons that are redeemed during their limited-time promotions.

★ Marketing Information System Codes (Posters/Postcards): All postcards and posters will include a marketing information system code and text that asks people to use that code when, for instance, entering at the door of a club. For example, when handing out cards on Sunset Boulevard in front of the Whisky, the code "whisky" might be written on a certain number of cards that are distributed in that location. The number of people who use a specific code will then be counted to help determine the effectiveness of marketing in a specific location.

★ Direct Marketing Services and Strategies: RTT will utilize the e-mail services of Constant Contact to measure the effectiveness of certain e-mail blasts. Note that Constant Contact helps manage returned e-mails and even the names of persons who want to opt out of the mailing list. It also measures the number of people who clicked on, and opened, an e-mail announcement. Additionally, with all correspondences that are sent out to fans via snail mail, RTT will ask fans to fill out a brief survey. They will also have a survey on www.rallythetribes.com that asks the question "How did you hear about us?" And finally, they will call random people in their database after a live performance to conduct brief interviews regarding the live performances.

★ Personal Website Tools: Since a great deal of RTT's promotional efforts consist of driving current and potential fans back to www.rallythetribes.com to offer information and entice sales, they will use Google Analytics to monitor the number of people who visit the site, what pages the visitors view, and for how long visitors look at a page.

★ Social Analytics: RTT will utilize the tracking tools offered by social networks to count the number of friends/fans they acquire on a specific social service, the number of people who listen to their songs on a specific service, and the locations of people who communicate with RTT on a specific social service.

★ Web Advertising Return on Investment (ROI): RTT will utilize the services of Google AdWords and count the number of clicks against the number of conversions into sales.

★ Search Engine Hit Results and SEO: RTT will monitor the effectiveness of their overall promotional efforts, particular that of publicity and PR, by counting the number of websites that feature reviews or mentions of RTT. For instance, at the beginning of the campaign, they will count their search engine hit results, and match those to the hit results at the end of each month. They will also monitor their Google position and strive to be at the top of each Google search when using a variety of different keyword searches.

★ Intercept Interviews: RTT will regularly have members of their team ask fans questions as they are leaving a venue, store, or rehearsal.

★ Focus Groups: RTT will hold regular brainstorming and focus group sessions with their fan club members and others to gauge how people are feeling about certain shows, merch products, songs, and more.

★ Survey Cards and Rehearsal Performances: RTT will hold regular rehearsal performances where they invite people to offer feedback via survey cards that are distributed.

★ Observational Methods: RTT and their team will carefully observe and make note of fans as they interact with RTT (i.e., they will carefully take note of the number of people who are on the dance floor and for what songs they are on the floor, the lengths of the audience applause, the gestures people are making during a live-performance set, and more).

c) Plan of Action: After converting their data and carefully considering the quality, RTT will conduct regular research before making any marketing plan adjustments. They will hold regular weekly meetings to discuss their plan of action.

14. ALLOCATION OF COSTS

Note: RTT is a do-it-yourself band that is able to keep costs down by utilizing the professional equipment they own, arranging a number of barter deals with recording studios, printers, and sound and light crews, and setting up merch on demand accounts. The allocation of costs below only reflects the money RTT has to spend. One year total: **$26,719.35**.

a) Market Research

Two-Drawer Filing Cabinet	1	$240
Files	100	$60
Microsoft Office Suite	1	$120
Magazine Subscriptions	3	$299

b) 12-Song Album: *War and Police*

Manufacturing Costs for Six-Panel Digipak CDs	1,000 Units @ $1.20	$1,200
Manufacturing Costs for Wristband Flash Drives with Logo	100 Units @ $7.45	$745
Setup Costs for Digital Distribution, Including Bar Code and ISRC Code with CD Baby	Flat rate (no per unit charge)	$69

c) DVD Soundtrack-Umentary™: *Occupy World*

DVD Manufacturing Costs	1,000 units @ $1.54 (Note: The goal is to sell 500 in the first year, but it was cost effective to make 1,000.)	$1,540

d) RTT Merchandising Line

The Rugby Rally with Logo	Initial printing: 36 units @ $6 = $216: (12 small, 12 med, 12 large). Estimated number of printings = 12.	$216 ×12 $2,592
The RTT Jock/Rock Jersey with George Cross	Initial printing: 36 units @ $5 = $180: (12 small, 12 med, 12 large). Estimated number of printings = 12.	$180 ×12 $2,160
The "Petty Thieves Hang, Big Ones Get Elected" T-shirt	Initial printing: 36 units @ $4 = $144: (12 small, 12 med, 12 large). Estimated number of printings = 12.	$144 ×12 $1,728
The RTT Military Hat	Initial printing: 36 units @ $5 = $180. Estimated number of printings = 12.	$180 ×12 $2,160

e) Live-Performance Set

Bullhorn	1	$120.00
Strobe Lights	3 @ $66.66	$200.00
Police Lights	4 @ $87.50	$350.00

f) Internet Promotion

Custom Mobile Application with Mobile Roadie	N/A	$300.00
GoDaddy Website Hosting	12 months	$100
ATT Cable	12 months	$480

g) Guerrilla Marketing Tactics

Chalk Spray Paint for Stencils	40 cans	$160
CD-R Sampler Disc Duplicator Machine from Disc Makers	1	$699
CD-R Discs	50 packs of 100 (5,000 discs)	$850

h) Publicity

RTT Printed Folders at Vistaprint	300	$175
EPK at Sonicbids	12-month subscription	$400
Bio to Be Written by Local Writer	N/A	$200
Networking: Winter Music Fest, SXSW, Sundance (Admission, Flights, Hotel, Food)	2 persons	$7,200

i) Direct Mail

E-mail Service Constant Contact 500 to 3,000 names	12 months	$300

j) Paid Advertising

Google AdWords (Bid for .20 per Click with a Cap at $1,000)	12 months	$1,000

Subtotal: $25,447

Contingency (5%): $1,272.35

One Year Total: $26,719.35

15. MARKETING PLAN TIMELINE (ONE YEAR)
a) January 1–March 31 (Q1): Pre–Record Release

[Branding]
★ Complete any needed testing/research to ensure that we have the best branding strategy in place.   ★ Strive to maintain and promote a consistent brand image in all of our marketing activities executed in this quarter and throughout the year.

[Product]

★ *War and Police* Album (Release Slated for March 31): Finish writing songs, test songs on fans, consult with songwriter Brian Wilston, record tracks and mix/master with Bob Sloan, design album artwork, and manufacture CDs and flash drives with Disc Makers.

★ *Occupy World* DVD Film: Shoot documentary with Josh Jordon, design DVD artwork, manufacture DVDs with Disc Makers.

★ RTT Merch: Design/prepare merch artwork with Adobe software, print with Bob Fiero at Zebra Marketing, set up CafePress merch-on-demand site, and build merch table.

★ Live Performances ("Gatherings"): Work up RTT live set No. 1 with band and the Jensen Brothers Sound and Lights at Hollywood Rehearsals, build stage props with Hollywood Movie Set and Design, and buy all lighting.

★ Fan Club: Build www.rallythetribes.com with fan club and store using John Interpoll.

★ Customer Service: Get customer service policies in place for RTT Web store. Strive to give customers something unique.

[Price]

★ All Products/Services: Establish all policies on the RTT Web store, on packaging, with consigners, and more.

★ CD: Initiate special event discount price for the record release party on March 31.

[Place]

★ CD/DVD Place: Arrange consignment agreements with Amoeba Music and Truth Clothing (and others), set up physical/digital distribution with CD Baby, and load files on www.rallythetribes.com by March 20 at the latest.

★ Live-Performance Place: In the first week of January, set up a performance at Sundance Film Festival (to be held in Jan.—with RTT Digital only). Book album release party with Key Club and arrange for after-party at Hollywood Rehearsals (both to be held March 31—with complete band).

★ Songs: Upload compositions to the Creative Commons site (www.creativecommons.org).

[Promotion]

★ Internet Promotion: Set up Facebook and Twitter accounts and begin hyping record release, build mobile phone app with Mobile Roadie, reach out to electronic music mags and political blogs for release blurbs about *War and Police*, load short clips of *Occupy World* on YouTube and Vimeo with teaser ad "coming soon," reach out to political blogs for prerelease interviews and discussions about charities, and acknowledge the video contest winner ("The Change Agent of the Month") and make sure he or she is mentioned on the RTT site.

★ Word-of-Mouth Promotion: Invite Los Angeles opinion leaders (music critics, rave promoters, fans, artists, popular journalists, and cool college kids) into the studio and rehearsal room and give a "sneak preview" performance/party of RTT's work. Give out free CDs to key influencers and ask them to "tell a friend."

★ Guerrilla (or Street Commando) Tactics: Stencil streets with RTT logo, place stickers all over Hollywood clubs, hang up posters, and hand out cards and CD-R samplers (two weeks prior to each show).

★ Sponsorships: Hit up local stores in Hollywood (like Hollywood Skate on Cahuenga and Melrose Swag on Melrose) to get them to play *War and Police* in their stores, and put up posters for the record release party.

★ Radio Promotion: Service local college radio (KXLU) to play prerelease single, tighten up relationships with DJ, and ask DJ to MC record release party.

★ Publicity and PR: Complete press kits (physical and electronic, which includes paying an important local journalist to write the bio), network at area clubs and like shows (and at Sundance Film Festival), confirm the charity (Los Angeles Coalition to End Hunger and Homelessness) for the record release party on March 31, inform local press about charity/record release performance, and organize "imitation police" for the publicity stunt on the night of the record release party (phony police will break up the party and haul RTT away in an unmarked cop car).

★ Direct Mail: Establish Constant Contact account and begin building database, e-mail an announcement about the record release party to any fans and industry people on list, and call fans and industry people to personally invite them to the record release party.

★ Sales Promotion: Establish raffle items for the record release party on March 31.

[Monitoring/Market Information]
★ Monitor all promotional and other strategies for effectiveness and return on investment.

---

b) April 1–June 30 (Q2): Post-Release

[Branding]
★ Strive to maintain and promote a consistent brand image in all of our marketing activities executed in this quarter and throughout the year.

[Product]
★ Songs: Continue writing new material for album 2. Contact Pen Music for licensing and placement.
★ Remixes: Remix single tracks from *War and Police* to make them available for free download on the RTT site.
★ Merch: Continue to manufacture shirts and experiment with new designs.
★ Fan Club: Launch www.rallythetribes.com fan club and site on April 1.
★ Live Performances ("Gatherings"): Continue rehearsing live-performance set.
★ Customer Service: RTT will call all fans to thank them for their support, and will mail fans birthday notices.

[Price]
★ Merch Sales Promo: Put up coupon for sales promotion at www.rallythetribes.com (April 15–31) that allows fans to buy the rugby or baseball T for $19.99 and get the RTT military hat for free (a savings of $11.99).

[Place]
★ Live Performance: Continue setting up more performances and after-parties. Call Key Club to set up monthly residency. Arrange for performances with RTT Digital at SXSW and Winter Music Festival.

[Promotion]
★ Internet Promotion: Launch www.rallythetribes.com (April 1). Also continue to communicate with target fans on social networks to hype upcoming gigs and parties and tactfully get them to visit www.rallythetribes, provide mobile phone app and "RTT Wallpaper" for free download at www.rallythetribes.com, continue to reach out or to/follow up with electronic music mags and political blogs for reviews about *War and Police*, load short clips of *Occupy World* on YouTube and Vimeo video channels with the notice "exclusive footage," continue to reach out to political blogs for interviews and discussions about charities, reach out to political podcasts for interviews, and acknowledge the video contest winner (the "Change Agent of the Month") and make sure he or she is mentioned on site.
★ Word-of-Mouth Promotion: Continue to invite Los Angeles opinion leaders (music critics, rave promoters, fans, artists, popular journalists, and cool college kids) into the studio and rehearsal room and give a "sneak preview" performance/party of new work being created.
★ Guerrilla (or Street Commando) Tactics: Continue to hang up posters and hand out cards and CD-R samplers (two weeks prior to each show).
★ Sponsorships: Continue to hit up more local stores in Hollywood (like Blue Fly Designer Shoes of Beverly Hills, Kat Von D Tattoo Shop on La Brea, Scion of North Hollywood on Lankershim, Melrose Smoke and Toke Shop on Melrose) to get them to play *War and Police* in their stores, put up posters for upcoming shows, and provide giveaways. Also begin contacting corporate manufacturers (like Ray-Ban corporate office in Rochester, New York; Scion corporate office in Torrance, California; Nike corporate office in Beaverton, Oregon) to arrange partnerships.
★ Radio Promotion: Continue to service local college radio stations (like KXSC, KXLU, UCLARadio.com, KCSN, KPCC, KCSB, KCSC, and KOXY) to play tracks and arrange interviews. Also go after commercial specialty shows (KROQ *Locals Only* with DJ Kat Corbett).

★ Publicity and PR: Submit press release to local press about record release success, send thank-you cards out to all that helped make the record release possible, continue to send out press kits (physical and electronic) to important journalists and bloggers, expand territories by contacting home towns and alma maters (Berklee, MIT, Harvard), network at area clubs and like shows (and at SXSW and Winter Music Conference), continue volunteer work for charities and veterans (like on Memorial Day), inform local press about charity work to build PR, and support gay pride parade (in June) and other important "rights events."

★ Direct Mail: Continue to send out e-mail blasts to fans and industry on our list, and call fans and industry to personally invite them to live performances. Send out quarterly RTT newsletter.

★ Sales Promotion: Put up coupon for sales promotion at www.rallythetribes.com (April 15–31) that allows fans to buy the rugby or baseball T-shirt at the regular price of $19.99 and get the military hat for free (a savings of $11.99).

★ Personal Selling Strategy: Hire and train sales staff with best practices for selling at merch booth.

★ Paid Advertising: Set up campaign with Google AdWords.

[Monitoring/Market Information]

★ Continue to monitor all promotional and other strategies for effectiveness and return on investment.

---

c) July 1–September 30 (Q3): Post-Release

[Branding]

★ Strive to maintain and promote a consistent brand image in all of our marketing activities executed in this quarter and throughout the year.

[Product]

★ Songs: Continue writing new material for album 2 and start testing new material on fans. Contact local activist groups (like PETA) for placement opportunities in campaigns and adverts.

★ Remixes: Continue to remix single tracks from *War and Police* and make them available for free downloads on RTT site.

★ Merch: Continue to manufacture shirts and experiment with new designs.

★ Fan Club: Hold RTT Change Agent brainstorming meetings.

★ Live Performances ("Gatherings"): Work up new RTT live set (No. 2) with band and the Jensen Brothers Sound and Lights.

★ Customer Service: RTT will call all fans to thank them for support, and send out birthday notices.

[Price]

★ Merch Special Event Discount/Sales Promotion: Initiate a special live-performance event promotion: chance to win a free CD, DVD, T-shirt, and hat.

[Place]

★ Live Performance: Continue setting up more performances and after-parties. RTT Digital continues spinning in local clubs.

[Promotion]

★ Internet Promotion: Keep site at www.rallythetribes.com current by uploading activist news, fan profiles, and more. Also continue to hype upcoming gigs and parties on social networks and tactfully get target fans to visit www.rallythetribes.com, provide mobile phone app and the "RTT Wallpaper" for free download at www.rallythetribes.com, reach out to or follow up with electronic music mags and political blogs for reviews about *War and Police*, load short clips of *Occupy World* on YouTube and Vimeo with notice "exclusive footage," reach out to political blogs for interviews and discussions about charities, pitch political podcasts, and acknowledge the video contest winner (the "Change Agent of the Month") and make sure he or she is mentioned on site.

★ Word-of-Mouth Promotion: Continue to invite Los Angeles opinion leaders (music critics, rave promoters, fans, artists, popular journalists, and cool college kids) into the studio and rehearsal room and give a "sneak preview" performance/party of new work being created.

★ Guerrilla (or Street Commando) Tactics: Continue to hang up posters and hand out cards and CD-R samplers (two weeks prior to each show).

★ Sponsorships: Nurture partnerships with local stores in Hollywood by keeping them up to date with all RTT happenings and successes and sending them pictures of us promoting their gear. Continue to contact corporate manufacturers (like Ray-Ban corporate office in Rochester, New York; Scion corporate office in Torrance, California; and Nike corporate office in Beaverton, Oregon) to arrange partnerships.

★ Radio Promotion: Continue to promote to the local college radio stations that are on our list to set up in-station performances, offer giveaways, and submit station IDs. Also get a quote from DJ Kat Corbett after she plays RTT on her *Locals Only* show.

★ Publicity and PR: Continue to send thank-you cards out to all that help spread the word about RTT, continue to send out press kits (physical and electronic) to important journalists and bloggers, network at area clubs and like shows, continue volunteer work for charities, inform local press about charity work to build PR, and organize anti-war/911 event on September 11 in Westwood.

★ Direct Mail: Continue to send out e-mail blasts to fans and industry on list, call fans and industry to personally invite them to live performances, and send out quarterly RTT newsletter.

★ Sales Promotion: Offer a special live-performance event promotion: chance to win a free CD, DVD, T-shirt, and hat. Record the giveaway as a nonsale and be sure to collect all contestants' e-mail addresses and cell numbers.

★ Paid Advertising: Continue to advertise with Google AdWords.

[Monitoring/Market Information]

★ Continue to monitor all promotional and other strategies for effectiveness and return on investment.

d) October 1–December 31 (Q4): Post-Release

[Branding]

★ Strive to maintain and promote a consistent brand image in all of our marketing activities executed in this quarter and throughout the year.

[Product]

★ Songs: Continue writing new material for album 2 and seeking out a songwriting consultant once again.

★ Remixes: Remix single tracks from *War and Police* to make them available for free download on RTT site.

★ Merch: Continue to manufacture shirts and experiment with new designs.

★ Fan Club: Hold RTT Change Agent brainstorming meetings.

★ Live Performances ("Gatherings"): Work up new RTT live set (No. 3) with band and the Jensen Brothers Sound and Lights.

★ Customer Service: RTT will call all fans to thank them for support, and will mail select fans birthday notices.

[Price]

★ Merch Sales Promotion: Put up coupon for sales promotion at www.rallythetribes.com (Oct. 15–31) that allows fans to buy the RTT rugby or baseball T-shirt for $19.99 and get the military hat for free (a savings of $11.99).

[Place]

★ Live Performance: Continue setting up performances and after-parties (make this after-party a huge Halloween blowout). RTT Digital will continue spinning in local clubs.

[Promotion]

★Internet Promotion: Continue to keep site at www.rallythetribes.com current by uploading activist news, fan profiles, and more. Also continue to hype upcoming gigs and parties on social networks and tactfully get target fans to visit www.rallythetribes.com, provide mobile phone app and the "RTT Wallpaper" for free download at www.rallythetribes.com, reach out to or follow up with electronic music mags and political blogs for reviews about *War and Police*, load new short clips of *Occupy World* on YouTube and Vimeo with the notice "exclusive footage," reach out to political blogs for interviews and discussions about charities, pitch political podcasts, and acknowledge the video contest winner (the "Change Agent of the Month") and make sure he or she is mentioned on the RTT site.

★Word-of-Mouth Promotion: Continue to invite Los Angeles opinion leaders (music critics, rave promoters, fans, artists, popular journalists, and cool college kids) into the studio and rehearsal room and give them a "sneak preview" performance/party of the new work being created.

★Guerrilla (or Street Commando) Tactics: Continue to hang up posters and hand out cards and CD-R samplers (two weeks prior to each show).

★Sponsorships: Continue to nurture partnerships with local stores in Hollywood by keeping them up to date with all RTT happenings and successes and by sending them pictures of RTT promoting their gear. Continue to nurture partnerships with corporate manufacturers (like Ray-Ban corporate office in Rochester, New York; Scion corporate office in Torrance, California; and Nike corporate office in Beaverton, Oregon) to arrange partnerships.

★Radio Promotion: Continue to promote to the local college radio stations to set up in-station performances, offer giveaways, and submit station IDs.

★Publicity and PR: Continue to send thank-you cards to all that help spread the word about RTT, continue to send out press kits (physical and electronic) to important journalists and bloggers, network at area clubs, continue to do volunteer work for charities (like at food banks for Thanksgiving and Christmas/Chanukah and Toys for Tots Harley Ride), and inform local press about charity work to build PR.

★Direct Mail: Continue to send out personalized e-mail blasts to fans and industry people, call fans and industry to personally invite them to live performances, and send out quarterly RTT newsletter.

★Sales Promotion: Put up coupon for sales promotion at www.rallythetribes.com (Oct. 15–31) that allows fans to buy the RTT rugby or baseball T-shirt at the regular price of $19.99 and get the military hat for free (a savings of $11.99).

★Paid Advertising: Continue to advertise with Google AdWords.

[Monitoring/Market Information]

★Continue to monitor all promotional and other strategies for effectiveness and return on investment.

16. APPENDIX

a) Film/TV Links

•*The Hollywood Reporter* (www.hollywoodreporter.com)

•*Film and Television Music Guide* (www.musicregistry.com)

b) Live-Performance Links

•*The Billboard Musician's Guide to Touring and Promotion* (www.musiciansguide.com)

•The Musician's Atlas (www.musiciansatlas.com)

c) Internet Links

•Technorati (blog search tool) (www.technorati.com/blogs/directory)

•Podcast Directory (www.podcastdirectory.com/)

d) Radio Promotion Links

•Radio-Locator (www.radio-locator.com)

•NPR (www.npr.org)

e) Publicity

•Charity Navigator (www.charitynavigator.org)

•PR Newswire (www.prnewswire.com)

f) Sponsorships Links
•IEG Source Book (www.sponsorship.com)
g) Direct Marketing Links
•Standard Rate and Data Service (SRDS) (www.srds.com)
•Direct Marketing Association (DMA) (www.newdma.org)
h) Mobile Marketing Links
•Mobile Marketing Association (www.mmaglobal.com)
i) General Business Links
•Small Business Administration (www.sba.gov)
•Federal Trade Commission (www.ftc.gov)

Glossary of Terms Found in This Book

A

adoption of innovation. A behavioral characteristic that examines the tendencies by which customers adopt a product as it moves through its life cycle. People can be characterized as innovators, early adopters, one of the early majority, one of the late majority, or laggards.

advertgaming. Interactive ads that include short videos and small games.

AIDA. A promotional model that stands for attention, interest, decision, and action.

allocation of costs. A table that includes your marketing activities and approximate costs to show readers precisely where you stand in both dollars and cents.

alternate format performance. A performance that features a different approach than usual (e.g., an electric band performs acoustically, and vice versa).

alternative venue. A place to perform your music that is dissimilar to your typical club or concert venue; colleges, conventions, and corporate parties are a few examples.

anchor event. A gig you book at or around a larger or more established event (such as a large music industry convention or film festival) in order to capture the draw from this event and/or maximize your resources.

annotations. Notes, comments, or links added to various media (video, pictures, text).

app. A computer software application that performs specific functions for the user. Apps are most commonly downloaded for use on mobile phones, but their code is also embedded frequently into website pages.

attainable. Represented by the letter *A* in the business model SMART; helps a company assess whether it is truly creating goals that are realistic and "doable."

B

band. A group of individuals united in the pursuit of a common goal in which each person plays a unique and integral part in achieving a dream.

bar code. A UPC (Universal Product Code) on the packaging of products that aids retailers with tracking inventory and helps companies with tracking sales.

barter system. The trading of goods and services as currency to satisfy payment.

behavioral dimension. A segmentation dimension that looks at a customer's rate of use of a product/service, the attributes customers seek in that product/service, and the tendencies with which customers adopt a product/service.

benefit. What a product/service does for the customer.

bias. A prejudice for or against something that can tarnish an objective research study and lead to inaccurate results.

bill poster (poster). One of the large, colorful concert (and movie) posters that you've seen glued side by side all over buildings and construction areas.

blog. A distinctive type of website that enlists contributors to update posts in chronological order, utilizes a web format called Really Simple Syndication (which alerts subscribers of all updates), and allows visitors to leave comments.

bottom-line costs. The costs required to bring your product or service to the marketplace.

brand. A company, product, or service (and the tangible and intangible elements that distinguish it from another company, product, or service).

brand ambassador. A passionate fan who voluntarily spreads positive messages about a company.

brand association. A relationship that one company instigates with another to strengthen its public image.

brand attitude. The overall posturing a company chooses to project to its public (bad boy, bad girl, gangsta, ghetto, intelligent, all-American wholesome, etc.).

brand identity. The name, logo, slogans, associations, and behavior a company uses to ensure that the right image forms in the minds of fans.

brand image. The perception that is formed in the customer's mind about a product/service/company.

brand logo. A design (composed of graphics, words, and/or letters) that conveys a company's brand name and character in the marketplace.

brandmark. A company logo composed of only a graphic (i.e., no words or letters).

brand name. The label given to a company or product/service to help create a strong and memorable image in the minds of fans.

brand personality (or character). The attitude, look, and vibe of a company.

brand structure (a.k.a. brand architecture). The manner in which a company brand and a company product brand relate to each other. There are three possibilities: company dominant, company endorsed, and company silent.

break-even analysis. An analytical process in which the total costs (both fixed and variable) equal the total revenue. Fixed costs ÷ (price – variable costs) = your break-even point.

brick and mortar. Any walk-in store on the street, including record shops and alternative (non-record) shops.

broadside. A form of direct mail; standard 8.5" × 11" sheets of paper that can be easily folded into thirds and stuffed into letter-sized envelopes.

bundle pricing. The process of grouping several products together and selling them at a price that is lower than if each product were sold separately, but still yield a profit to the seller.

C

cannibalization. When a company's product or service takes sales away from another of its existing products or services.

channel contention. Competition that exists between the various sellers of your products in the distribution chain.

channel of distribution. Wholesale distributors, street and online retailers, bookers, and film/TV pluggers that participate in the flow of products and services from creators to end users.

churn. The percentage of your total customers who stop purchasing your products within a certain period of time.

citizen journalist. A new breed of media expert; the customer who spreads news on blogs, social networks, and other media channels.

click-through rate (CTR). The percentage of people who click on your Internet ad, divided by the number of people who are exposed to the ad.

close. Refers to the last step in the sales process when a seller obtains a final commitment from a buyer.

cobranding. Where two different brands team up to market their products and services together, and thus collectively benefit from the value each one brings to the table.

code of ethics. In the name of company integrity and the public's best interest, organizations often write their own set of guidelines (specific to their company culture and business) that all team members must read and execute.

combined or undifferentiated approach. A method where two or more target market segments are combined together to form one larger segment, and only one marketing strategy is created.

combinedmark. A logo that incorporates a graphic with the band name or acronym.

commercial specialty show. A weekly late-night program on a commercial radio station that focuses on independent artists and the local music scene.

company branding. The process of delivering clear, relevant, consistent, and long-term messages about a company with the intention of creating a positive image in the minds of the customers.

company dominant (or combined) brand structure. A type of product brand architecture in which the identity of the company supports the overall image of all of its products and services.

company endorsed brand structure. A type of brand architecture in which the company uses its identity to support the image of products and services outside the realm of its usual line of products and services.

company silent (or separated) brand structure. A type of brand architecture in which the identity of the company is separated from the various products and services it provides so that the image of one product/service can't affect the image of another product/service.

competition. Forces that exist when there are: 1) other businesses trying to do the same thing, 2) new entrants in the marketplace due to a low barrier of entry, 3) substitute products that can satisfy fans as well as you can, 4) buyers with bargaining power who can force you to charge lower prices, and 5) suppliers with bargaining power who can force you to pay higher prices.

competitive advantage. The differentiating factor between one organization's product/service and others that is seen by customers as an attractive and relevant benefit.

competitor. A company that your most likely customers could see as offering similar products and services; or in broader terms, any company that could draw attention away from you.

competitor analysis. A market research tool that allows marketers to examine the strengths and weaknesses of competing companies/products/services in order to find a true competitive advantage.

consignment. The process of leaving recordings (or other products) in stores and collecting payment after they sell.

consumer price boundary. What your target customer is used to paying and willing to pay for a particular product/service category.

contract employee. Anyone who agrees to work under a set of conditions specified by a contract and in a continuing relationship (a talk show band, a concert tour, etc.).

co-op advertising. The practice whereby two companies share the cost of advertising, thus making the costs more affordable for each company.

cost of sales (bottom-line costs). The costs required to bring your product or service to the marketplace.

cost per click. A web metric based on how often ads are "seen and clicked on" by potential customers, in proportion to what you pay for the ad.

cost per order (CPO). The cost per promotional piece, multiplied by the number of leads contacted and divided by the people who buy, equals your CPO.

coupon pricing. A sales promotion strategy that offers a product or service at a reduced price (and for a limited time) using cutouts or downloadable offers that represent a form of currency.

CPM (cost per thousand people). The cost for 1,000 people to actually see, hear, and listen to an ad in a specific media channel.

Creative Commons. Provides a simple way to license your music for free while setting parameters for how your music can and cannot be used.

crisis management. The methods by which an organization responds to, and attempts to prevent, certain rumors and events that may tarnish its brand image.

crowdsourcing. A process of using fans to make certain decisions (about set orders, T-shirt designs, artwork, etc.).

customer hub. An effective center from which word of mouth is amplified.

customer lifetime value. The amount customers are worth to you in sales if they keep on buying from you.

customer ownership. The pride a customer takes in your brand, and the feeling that he or she is part of your success.

customer profile. A detailed description (and even portrait) of fans, including demographic, psychographic, technographic, behavioral, and geographic factors.

customer profile conclusion paragraph. A detailed description of target fans, and how this data might be used to better market products and services for these target fans.

customer service. The level of care that's provided to customers at every stage of the relationship (i.e., before they buy, when they buy, and after they buy).

customer service policy. A written declaration of how a company will treat its customers at every brand touch point. A customer service policy might contain everything from your commitment to quality, to your warranty and return policies, to how well you'll treat customers long after the sale.

D

demographic. A segmentation dimension consisting of age, sex, education, economic status, and nationality.

depth interview. A thorough research method designed to get to the heart of a customer's drives and motivations.

dichotomous question. A type of question used in market research surveys where participants can answer with a yes or no.

Digipak. A type of CD packaging that contains less plastic than standard, jewel case CD packaging and is thus more environmentally friendly.

direct marketing. A form of promotion where companies communicate to end users directly without using intermediaries to generate a customer response or transaction.

direct route. A method of distribution where the creator moves products directly to end users.

disguised pricing. A pricing strategy where the seller hides or shifts the price of the product or service into another product or service to make the consumer feel as though he or she is getting something for free.

distributor. Anyone in the channel of distribution between creators and end users.

donation pricing. A pricing strategy that allows the customer to set the price for the goods and services he or she wishes to procure.

duplicate. The process of using your own computer and special software to copy your own files onto CDs or DVDs and then use your own printer to print onto the disc surfaces. It can also involve purchasing a CD/DVD duplicator, which can get the job done much faster and more professionally.

E

economic price. The perfect price at which "supply" and "demand" intersect.

economies of scale. A concept whereby the cost per unit of a product or service gets smaller as more units are manufactured.

elicitation techniques. A research method that attempts to draw out deeper subconscious thoughts and feelings about a product or service that people may not even know they have.

empowerment. Usually applies to the topic of leadership; it's the strength, autonomy, and trust an employee (band member, etc.) is given to feel ownership in/of a project, make decisions, and get the job done.

end-in-9-or-5 pricing. A pricing technique where prices end with the numbers 9 or 5 to make them appear to be lower (e.g., $99 instead of $100 or $195 instead of $200).

endorsement. A win-win relationship between instrument manufacturers and artists—companies get their equipment exposed, and artists get to play new gear for free.

end user. The final customer.

EPK (electronic press kit). A collection of materials (bios, pictures, videos, songs) in digital format used to get gigs, blog reviews, and more.

ethics. The legal and moral decision-making criteria that companies are obligated to apply to their everyday operations.

ethnographic research. A study of human cultures whereby researchers "live like the natives live."

evangelist. A superloyal fan who is so passionate about you that it becomes his or her mission to spread the word of mouth about your brand everywhere he or she goes.

event advertising. Promotional communications at sporting events, fairs, circuses, concerts, and more.

exclusive distribution rights. Companies handling digital distribution typically request permission to be the sole provider of your recordings, since no two companies can digitally distribute the same recordings on download sites at the same time.

execution. The art and management of getting things done.

executive summary. A one-page concise overview of the key sections of a marketing plan (vision, goals, strategies, allocation of costs, etc.) placed at the front of a marketing plan. An executive summary sums up why your business idea will be successful and qualifies whether or not your entire plan is worth reading.

experiment. A test of two different research conditions (or treatments)—such as two different headlines for the same ad. If only 60 percent of a research group likes an ad when it uses headline A, and 90 percent of another research group likes an ad when it uses headline B, it can be said that the condition (the headline) is what caused the outcome, and that headline B is better.

extension. Refers to both *brand extensions*, where new products outside the realm of a company's typical offerings are created, and *line extensions*, where different variations of an existing product are offered.

external environment. The domain outside your company and your control, where both opportunities and threats can be found.

F

face-to-face selling (personal selling). The process by which you influence a prospect *eye-to-eye* to make a decision in both your and his or her favor.

fan awareness. A measure of how many fans know (or will know) about your brand; the number of devoted followers who attend your shows, the number of followers' addresses in your database, and more.

feature. What a product is/has; one of the parts that make up a product.

focus group. A method in which a small number of fans are asked questions by a moderator and are then observed while they participate in a discussion about a product.

free pricing. A strategy based on the idea that the easier it is for people to experience your company's offerings, and the more people start to talk about your offerings, the sooner people will pay for all of your company's offerings.

G

genre. A category or subcategory of music.

geographic dimensions. The characteristics that help a company define where its fans live and where its marketing efforts will be concentrated.

geomarketing. Marketing based on a prospect's precise location and specific device (i.e., mobile phone, tablet, computer, etc.).

gig swap. A situation where one band invites another to play on their show and exposes them to their fans and territory, and vice versa.

goal. A short-term product/service objective set to increase awareness and revenue.

goal setting. The process of dissecting your long-term vision into smaller product/service objectives that will help your organization increase awareness and profits.

Gracenote Media. After entering the data about your music into the Gracenote Media database (www.gracenote.com), your song data will show up when people play your recording in their computers.

graphical map. A visual representation of the overall layout of a website.

gross profit margin (GPM). The percentage of the price, given your costs, that you can keep as gross profit; (price − cost) ÷ price.

guerrilla marketing. An unconventional form of promotion that can be employed on a low budget to no budget.

H

hall fee. A commission a venue charges for allowing you to sell your T-shirts, hats, posters, and other goods.

headline. The part of a marketing communication intended to attract attention.

historical method. A method of forecasting your sales by looking at what your company sold in the previous year.

homogeneous customers. Customers who share common characteristics and are likely to respond to marketing messages in the same way.

I

incremental goals model. A model created by Bobby Borg that helps show the yearly steps a marketer must take on the path to achieving his or her long-term vision.

independent contractor (self-employed performer). Anyone who makes his or her services available for hire for shorter-term relationships (studio work, casuals, etc.), usually without unemployment, medical, and other benefits.

independent radio promoter. A professional promotion person who, by virtue of his or her experience and connections in the radio business, helps get records played on the radio. While many independent radio promoters are hired by record companies, they are independent of them.

indirect route. A method of distribution where the creator moves products through intermediaries such as online and physical distributors, retailers, agents, and songpluggers.

in-flight advertising. Promotional communications broadcast on airline audio programs.

in-house. The process of using your own company and resources to complete a job.

innovation. The uniqueness, inventiveness, and modernization of your products and services.

intercept interview. A research technique designed to get feedback from customers as they are leaving a venue (club, music store, or other music-related center).

intermediary. Intermediaries include anyone (e.g., various online and physical distributors, retailers, agents, songpluggers, etc.) who is in the distribution channel between creators and end users.

internal environment. The domain within your company and your control.

Internet marketing. The process of educating customers online about the features and benefits of your offerings for the purposes of stimulating sales.

inverted pyramid. In press releases, a style of writing that includes the most important information at the top, followed by less important information.

ISRC Code (International Standard Recording Code). An international identification system used for identifying content (sound, music, and video recordings) online.

J

jingle. A short song or instrumental that a company uses to help brand its image on radio, on TV, or online.

K

kaizen. An approach for the continuous improvement of management performance. It was established by Dr. William Deming, an American consultant; initially used in Japan, but now employed internationally.

L

leadership. The process of focusing on a vision, taking action toward it, influencing others to treat the vision as it were their own, and getting results.

lettermark. A logo that features the initials of a brand name with or without the name spelled out beneath, alongside, or above the name.

Likert scale. A widely employed research tool used in surveys, where participants indicate their level of preference (from 1 to 5 or from "strongly agree" to "don't agree at all").

loss leader pricing. A strategy wherein a product is sold at a lower price as a way to draw customers in, with the intention that they'll also buy higher-priced products that can make up for any losses.

loyalty program. A type of sales promotion whereby a small wallet-sized card is given out to fans during a short-term period, and they are rewarded for the number of times their card is stamped (i.e., the number of purchases they make).

M

Marketing Information System Code (MISC). An identifier unique to each marketing communication that makes tracking that communication easy.

marketing myopia. A business term derived from the title of an important marketing paper written by Harvard Business School professor Theodore Levitt. In his paper, he criticized companies for being shortsighted and asserted that all CEOs must ponder the question "What business am I in?"

market penetration. A company's sales goals represented as a percentage of its industry's projected total sales for that year (data that can only be acquired through trade journals, business magazines, or research consultants).

market share. An actual measure of a company's performance compared to its competitors in a specific industry.

markup. The amount (or percentage) that is added to the cost of a product to derive its selling price (cost + markup = price).

mascot. Often used interchangeably with the word *spokescreature*, a mascot is a graphical representation of something memorable, relatable, and relevant to a company's personality (or the personality of its target market) and is intended to create a positive image in the minds of fans.

maven. Someone who actively initiates conversation and spreads the word about new products and services.

measurable. The countable or quantifiable element of an organization's SMART goals.

measuring. The process of collecting, analyzing, and acting on information relevant to the goals of your marketing plan.

merchandising (merch). Items (such as T-shirts, hats, rolling papers, mouse pads, etc.) that can provide a significant source of revenue for your company, while helping to advertise and establish your brand image.

merchandising company. A company that offers advances and royalties in return for the rights to manufacture and sell merch products bearing your name, likeness, and logo.

mind map. An exercise that helps you discover what your brand is all about; it's created by writing a relevant keyword (adjective) in the center of a sheet of paper, and freely associating several different words based on that keyword.

mission statement. A short paragraph that helps your entire organization focus on a collective idea so that it can work in a uniform, aligned, and consistent manner. It identifies a company's purpose, target audience, and point of differentiation.

mobile advertising. A process of marketing via cell phones including text and graphic messages.

money-back guarantee pricing. A strategy where you charge a slightly higher price for your products and services and then justify the price by offering a money-back guarantee.

most likely customer. A person or business that is most likely to come out to your shows, buy your music, or license your songs.

multichannel network (online video studios): A large (often well funded) video organization that offers individual YouTube channel owners (like you) partnership agreements and assistance in a variety of areas (audience development, cross-promotion, digital rights management, product development, programming, funding, and monetization and sales) in exchange for a percentage of the ad revenue from your channel.

multiple or differentiated approach. A method where two or more target market segments are chosen—such as a primary market built around your most likely fan and a secondary market built around your next likely fan—and separate marketing strategies are specifically tailored to cater to the needs of each of these segments.

music library. A business that makes a wide variety of music available to song users (directors, producers, music supervisors, ad agencies, etc.) who are looking for music.

music publisher. A company that is in the business of songs, including plugging your songs, offering advances, handling administrative duties, and collecting generated incomes.

music supervisor. An individual who chooses music for films and television shows and handles business and licensing issues.

N

NACA (National Association for Campus Activities). An organization that holds regional and national events for college bookers and entertainers.

need. A void in the marketplace and/or something a customer deems as necessary or important.

net profit. Revenue minus your expenses.

net promoter score. The percentage of your total fans that are likely to recommend you. It can be found by asking your customers the question "Would you recommend us to a friend or family member?"

next likely customer. The next likely customer (after your most likely group) to come out to your shows, buy your music, or license your songs.

Nielsen SoundScan. An organization that collects data recorded from bar codes that are scanned at retail and makes it available to record companies and others for a fee.

NPR (National Public Radio). A publicly funded radio entity that plays alternative or eclectic music, interesting news programs, human-interest stories, and more. It is a great medium for up-and-coming indie artists to receive airplay and get noticed.

O

objection. A reason why a prospect feels he or she *shouldn't* purchase.

one-sheet. Information about your career (accomplishments, short bio, contact, picture) that fits on one page and can be absorbed with one quick reading.

one-stop shop. A term used in the music publishing world to mean an owner of both the master recording and composition.

opinion leader. A person who strongly influences others to act; these are the folks who are instrumental in starting a buzz about a product or service.

opportunity. A void or consumer need in the marketplace, and a unique and profitable approach to fill that void or need better than anyone else.

out of home advertising (OOH). Advertisements that are placed outside (on bus benches, billboards, cars, etc.).

outreach strategy. A strategy that focuses on contacting media folk to build strong relationships long before asking them to review your press kits.

outsource. The process of using "outside" companies to finalize your products/services for the marketplace or to complete a certain objective or marketing activity.

P

paid advertising. Any paid form of promotion (e.g., ads in newspapers, on radio stations, etc.).

participant observation. A method of primary research that involves watching target customers interact with a product/service so as to better understand how to fulfill their needs.

percent occupancy method. A pricing strategy that establishes an early lower price for customers when the available occupancy in a venue is high, and a subsequently higher price for customers as the venue fills up and the available occupancy space is low.

per-inquiry ad. Any ad that requires no upfront costs, but rather a percentage of income that comes directly from the ad.

photo story. Photodocumented proof of a "newsworthy" event in your career.

place. The process of making goods and services convenient for end users to find and buy.

placement service. A company that helps you place your music in film, television, and video games.

pledge pricing. A creative method of raising money for a project whereby you present a variety of package deals to consumers, such as prebuying your record plus an autograph for $8, or prebuying your record plus an autograph and lunch date for $75.

pop-under ad. An ad that appears under the Web page, so that when you leave the Web page, you see the ad.

pop-up ad. An ad that pops up in front of the Web page, so that you are forced to see the ad before you see the Web page.

positioning. The process of getting your target audience to see your product and service in a way that is unique from your competitors.

press release. Current and newsworthy bits of information released to the media and citizen journalists to help generate exposure for your company.

price. The amount for which an organization is willing to sell its products/services, and for which a customer is willing to buy.

primary research. Information that is specifically collected by an organization (via focus groups, surveys, interviews, etc.).

print on demand. A process whereby a company has its products manufactured only when there is an order for them.

problem. As it relates to market research, this is one of five steps in the scientific method of research whereby researchers identify the issues they want to test. As it relates to customers, this is a need or void in the marketplace where customers are seeking solutions.

product. The goods and services (songs, CDs, live performances, DVDs, etc.) that are created to satisfy the needs of the target audience, increase awareness, and generate profits.

product life cycle. The stages a product goes through in the marketplace (introduction, growth, maturity, and decline).

product placement. When companies pay to have their products placed prominently in TV shows and movies.

product/service branding. The process of delivering clear, relevant, consistent, and long-term messages about a product/service with the intention of creating a positive image in the mind of the customer.

promotion effectiveness form. A tool that measures the success and failure of your marketing efforts.

prototype. A product, service, or concept developed by a company before mass production in order to obtain feedback and/or investment.

psychographics. An analysis of customers' lifestyles based on their activities, interests, and opinions.

publicity (earned media). The exposure you get when journalists and others publish stories, reviews, and interviews about you.

public relations (PR). The various activities performed by a company to promote and protect its brand image in the eyes of the public.

Q

qualitative data. Information that is open-ended and less scientifically precise than quantitative data.

quantitative data. Information that can be summarized in numbers and other statistics.

Quick Response (QR) code. A type of bar code placed on posters, adverts, and products that, when scanned by a mobile phone with a special app, directs consumers to further information and even an e-commerce system.

R

radio promotion. The process of sending and promoting your music to radio stations to get airplay, build relationships, and stimulate sales.

reliable data. Information derived from tests that produced consistent results.

replicate. The professional manufacturing process of letting a factory laser read your original disc and embed it onto a glass master, which is then used to create high-quality (and high-quantity) replications of your work.

representative sample. A group of research participants that symbolize a snapshot of the total population of a company's target customer.

research and development (R&D). The process of developing and demoing your products and services, getting feedback from your most likely fans, and making necessary improvements *before* using your valuable resources.

residency. A live-performance booking for several nights in one venue.

retention. The number of customers retained over a period of time divided by the number of customers lost.

return on investment (ROI). The percent of your initial investment that should or did grow ([price – cost] ÷ cost).

road-mapped. Represented by the *R* in the goal-setting model SMART goals; reminds an organization to choose strategies that will realistically get it from point A to point B.

S

sales handbook. A document (stored in a three-ring binder, computer file, etc.) containing important information about your products and services to aid you in the sales process.

sales promotion. A short-term incentive to stimulate a quick buying response from your target customer.

sample audience. A group of people in a research study that is representative of your target audience, from which data can be derived and conclusions can be drawn.

search engine advertising. A popular method of promotion that enables you to place small classified-style text ads on the results page of a specific keyword search made by a consumer.

secondary research. Published materials (via census reports, trade magazines, and blogs) that are readily available to an organization.

segmentation. The process of breaking down a market into a well-defined group of customers who share common characteristics and respond to marketing messages in a similar way.

segmentation dimensions. The characteristics widely used by companies to define their market, including demographic, psychographic, technographic, behavioral, and geographic factors.

SEO (search engine optimization). The process of ensuring that people who are looking for you, or are looking for a product/service similar to yours, will find you. *Optimization* is also the process of ensuring that your website has a consistent look on various web browsers.

service. An act a company provides (via live performances, clinics, instruction, production, etc.) to satisfy the needs of a target audience.

servicing. Radio lingo that refers to the process of getting your music into the hands of radio station personnel.

single or concentrated approach. A method where only one target market segment is chosen (such as the one built around your most likely fans) and a marketing plan is tailored specifically to meet the needs of this select group.

slogan. A philosophical, emotional, or clever short statement about a company or product that is often part of a brand logo.

SMART goals model. A goal-setting model used for the purpose of creating specific, measurable, attainable, road-mapped, and time-based goals.

smart mob. A guerrilla marketing method in which a group of people covertly come together in a public place to promote a product or make a statement.

sniper. A person who illegally hangs posters on telephone poles and city walls.

social media. The content published on social networking sites.

solo artist. A talented musician with instrumental/writing/acting/modeling skills who has a strong desire and ability to lead others, and the resources to hire a team of professionals to work for him or her.

specialty advertising. Promotional items (such as keychains, calendars, and pens) that feature your company's brand name, logo, and/or slogan.

specific. Represented by the *S* in the goal-setting model SMART goals; helps an organization focus on a clear and exact product/service objective over the next year.

spokescreature. Often used interchangeably with *mascot*, a spokescreature is a graphical representation of something memorable, relatable, and relevant to a company's personality (or the personality of its target market) and is intended to create a positive image in the minds of fans.

sponsorship. A relationship between artists and product-based companies in which artists receive products and/or assistance with promoting their events, in return for allowing companies to advertise their products or services in creative ways.

spot buy. An ad that is bought on local television and radio stations in select regions.

strength. One of the capabilities, resources, processes, and geographic factors of a company that enable it to pursue certain marketing opportunities.

subhead. The part of a marketing communication (usually below the headline) intended to hold people's interest and entice them to read more.

supply and demand. An economic theory that says the following: when supply exceeds demand, there is a surplus (which usually causes prices to fall), and when demand exceeds supply, there is a shortage (which usually causes prices to rise).

survey questionnaire. A research tool that typically consists of a short set of questions with specific answer choices that can be analyzed using numbers and percentages.

sweepstakes. An opportunity to win a valued prize without having to make a purchase; all that is required is a name entry.

SWOT analysis (OSWT analysis). An acronym for strengths, weaknesses, opportunities, and threats; its key purpose is to help companies discover a market need and an opportunity to fill that need better than anyone else.

SWOT conclusion paragraph. A short paragraph that identifies a company's opportunities and the strengths it possesses, the weaknesses it must turn into strengths, and the threats it must minimize to successfully pursue these opportunities.

T

tagline. A philosophical, emotional, or clever short statement that usually represents the philosophy of a particular ad campaign. Note that *tagline* is often used interchangeably with *slogan*. However, a slogan is usually a statement about a company or product brand and is often used together with the company logo.

talent agent. A licensed professional who sells your act to venue promoters, negotiates fees, collects deposits, routes the direction of a tour, and helps decide for whom you should open (or who should open for you).

target audience. A group of customers on whom a company focuses its marketing. These groups are comprised of people who all share common characteristics and are likely to respond to a marketing message in the same way.

target driven approach. A positioning technique that involves targeting specific groups with the intention of creating a strong image of your products in their minds.

technographics. A segmentation dimension that looks at new technology and people's interactions with it.

threat. One of a number of inevitable factors in the external marketplace, such as competition and business/legal regulations, that can harm a company during its pursuit of certain marketing opportunities.

time-based. Represented by the T in the goal-setting model SMART goals; ensures that an organization gives its marketing goals a time frame of typically one year.

timeline. A system that helps you to schedule your yearly SMART goals and strategies in smaller increments (quarterly, monthly, weekly, daily, and even hourly).

top-level domain (TLD): The last part of a web address (such as .com, .net, .org, etc.).

traditional independent distributor. A distributor that serves independent labels and artists. It warehouses recordings, fulfills orders, handles accounting functions, and sets up retail promotions with stores.

trailer house. Trailer houses produce short advertisements (trailers) or previews for production and film companies.

turn time. The time it takes to receive a product, from the point at which an order is made to the time it arrives on your doorstep.

U

UPC (Universal Product Code). See bar code.

usability testing. A research technique that examines a consumer's interaction with a product.

V

valid data. Quality information that accurately and scientifically represents what a researcher sets out to learn.

vision statement. Defines the type of career you'd like to have, the style or genre you'd like to pursue, and the vibe you'd like to project onto the world in seven to ten years.

vocal down mix. A mix specifically for film and television with the vocal mixed extremely low so that it does not get in the way of the film's dialogue and sound.

voice of customer. A market research technique where a company focuses on the question "What would the customer think?"

W

weakness. One of a number of internal capabilities, resources, processes, and geographic factors of a company that can disqualify it from pursuing certain marketing opportunities.

Web developer. A Web developer (or Web master) is a person experienced in computer science whose role is to polish up your website design, generate Web pages, observe traffic and other statistical data, and make sure that people can find you on the Web.

Web widget. Application software provided by a sponsoring company that allows users to perform a variety of different functions, such as selling music from personal websites and collecting e-mail addresses.

wordmark. A logo that features the brand name in a simple and unique typeset.

word-of-mouth promotion. The process of stimulating natural conversation between people about your products and services.

Z

zone pricing. A pricing strategy that focuses on setting shipping and handling charges by geographical territory.

Directory of This Book's Resources and Beyond

Additional Learning Resources

Associations
- American Marketing Association (www.ama.org)
- Direct Marketing Association (www.the-dma.org)
- Market Research Association (www.marketingresearch.org)
- Word of Mouth Marketing Association (www.womma.org)
- American Association of Advertising Agencies (www.aaaa.org)
- Small Business Administration (www.sba.gov)

General Business Advice
- *All You Need to Know About the Music Business* by Don Passman
- *The Musician's Handbook* by Bobby Borg
- *Marketing Management* by Philip Kotler

Informational Blogs
- Harvard Business Review (hbr.org)
- Mashable (mashable.com)
- MarketingSherpa (www.marketingsherpa.com)
- Wired (www.wired.com)
- Hypebot (www.hypebot.com)
- MediaPost (www.mediapost.com)
- Advertising Age (adage.com)
- Adweek (www.adweek.com)
- eMarketer (www.emarketer.com)
- ClickZ (www.clickz.com)
- Fast Company (www.fastcompany.com)
- McKinsey & Company (www.mckinsey.com/insights)
- Stanford Social Innovation Review (www.ssireview.org)
- TED Talks (www.ted.com/talks)
- CBS MoneyWatch (www.cbsnews.com/moneywatch)
- Lefsetz Letter (lefsetz.com/wordpress)

Jobs
- MyMusicJob (www.mymusicjob.com)
- ShowBizJobs (www.showbizjobs.com)
- Monster (www.monsterjobs.com)

Mentoring
- Score (www.score.org)

Open Source Learning Sites
- Yale University (oyc.yale.edu)
- Berklee College of Music (www.berkleeshares.com)
- University of California at Berkeley (webcast.berkeley.edu)
- Massachusetts Institute of Technology (ocw.mit.edu/index.htm)
- Stanford University (itunes.stanford.edu)
- University of Notre Dame (ocw.nd.edu)

Assembling Your Marketing Plan

Funding
- Small Business Administration (www.sba.gov)
- Kickstarter (www.kickstarter.com)
- Pledge Music (www.pledgemusic.com)
- Indiegogo (www.indiegogo.com)
- Gofundmenow (www.gofundmenow.com)

Branding Resources

Band Names
- US Patent and Trademark Office website (www.uspto.gov)
- Thomson Compumark (trademarks.thomsonreuters.com)

Fonts and Styles
- DaFont (www.dafont.com)
- *Big Book of 5,000 Fonts* by David Carter
- DeviantArt (www.deviantart.com)
- Logotournament (logotournament.com)

General
- *Building Brand Identity* by Lynn Upshaw
- *Building Strong Brands* by David Aaker
- *Branding for Dummies* by Bill Chiaravalle and Barbara Findlay Schenck
- *Creating Brand Loyalty* by Richard D. Czerniawski
- *Advertising Slogans of America* by Harold S. Sharp

Execution Resources

Ethics/Legal
- American Marketing Association's Statement of Ethics (www.ama.org/AboutAMA/Pages/Statement-of-Ethics.aspx)
- Federal Trade Commission (www.ftc.gov)

- Word of Mouth Marketing Association's Code of Ethics (www.womma.org/ethics)
- SAGE Publications: *SAGE Brief Guide to Marketing Ethics*

Help Groups
- Alcoholics Anonymous (www.aa.org)
- Sexaholics Anonymous (www.sa.org)
- Narcotics Anonymous (www.na.org)

Leadership Books
- *Leading Change* by Philip Kotler
- *The Leader of the Future* by the Drucker Foundation
- *Execution* by Larry Bossidy and Ram Charan
- *The Art of War* by Sun Tzu
- *48 Laws of Power* by Robert Greene
- *Leadership Jazz* by Max De Pree
- *The Leadership Challenge* by James M. Kouzes and Barry Z. Posner
- *Lead by Example* by John Baldoni
- *Steve Jobs* by Walter Isaacson
- *A. Lincoln—A Biography* by Ronald White
- *Andrew Carnegie* by David Nasaw
- *The Lombardi Rules: 26 Lessons from Vince Lombardi—The World's Greatest Coach* by Vince Lombardi Jr.

Motivational Books
- *The Secret* by Rhonda Byrne
- *The Power of the Subconscious Mind* by Joseph Murphy
- *The 21 Indispensable Qualities of a Leader* by John C. Maxwell
- *Creative Visualization* by Shakti Gawain
- *The Alchemist* by Paulo Coelho
- *Outliers: The Story of Success* by Malcolm Gladwell
- *The Power of Now* by Eckhart Tolle
- *Getting Things Done* by David Allen

Measuring and Monitoring Resources

General
- *Data-Driven Marketing* by Mark Jeffery
- *Measuring Marketing* by John Davis

Tools
- Disc Makers Bar Codes (www.discmakers.com)
- Nielsen SoundScan (www.nielsen.com)
- International Standard Recording Code (www.usisrc.org)
- Mention (www.mention.com)
- Google Analytics (www.google.com/analytics/)

- Google Alerts (www.google.com/alerts)
- Tagboard (www.tagboard.com)
- Sproutsocial (sproutsocial.com)
- Quickbooks (quickbooks.intuit.com)
- Mint (www.mint.com)

Surveys
- SurveyMonkey (www.surveymonkey.com)
- Zoomerang (www.zoomerang.com)

Place and Distribution Resources

Live Performance Opportunities
- The Musician's Atlas (www.musiciansatlas.com)
- The Musician's Guide to Touring and Promotion (www.musiciansguide.com)
- Theme Park Jobs (www.themeparkjobs.com)
- Music Business Registry Calendar of Events (www.musicregistry.com)
- Armed Forces Entertainment (www.armedforcesentertainment.com)
- House Concerts (www.houseconcerts.com)
- National Association for Campus Activities (www.naca.org)
- Bonnaroo (www.bonnaroo.com)
- Vans Warped Tour (www.warpedtour.com)
- Voodoo Music Festival (www.voodoomusicfest.com)
- Sasquatch Festival (www.sasquatchfestival.com)
- The Booking Agency Directory (store.pollstar.com/c-2-Directories.aspx)
- International Talent & Touring Guide (www.billboard.com)
- Sonicbids (www.sonicbids.com)

Recorded Music

Independent Distributors
- Alternative Distribution Alliance (www.ada-music.com)
- Red (www.redmusic.com)
- Redeye Distribution (www.redeyeusa.com)
- Nail (www.naildistribution.com)

Independent Stores
- Amoeba (www.amoeba.com)
- Newbury Comics (www.newburycomics.com)
- Grimey's (www.grimeys.com)
- Other Music (www.othermusic.com)
- Waterloo Records (www.waterloorecords.com)
- Princeton Record Exchange (www.prex.com)
- Aquarius Records (www.aquariusrecords.com)
- *Time* list of indie record shops (www.time.com/time/arts/article/0,8599,2065345,00.html)

Online Retailing/Tools
- CD Baby (www.cdbaby.com)
- The Orchard (www.theorchard.com)
- TuneCore (www.tunecore.com)
- IRIS (www.irisdistribution.com)
- Amazon Advantage Program (advantage.amazon.com/gp/vendor/public/join)
- CafePress (www.cafepress.com)
- Classic Music Vault (www.classicmusicvault.com)
- Nimbit (www.nimbit.com)
- Myxer (www.myxer.com)
- Bandcamp (www.bandcamp.com)
- TopSpin (www.topspinmedia.com)
- INgrooves (www.ingrooves.com)
- Wikipedia List of Social Network Sites (www.en.wikipedia.org/wiki/List_of_social_networking_websites)

Sales Tools
- Nielsen SoundScan (www.nielsen.com)
- Square (squareup.com)

Song Placements

Conventions/Festivals
- American Film Institute Festival (www.afi.com)
- Temecula Valley International Film & Music Festival (www.tviff.com)
- Sundance Film Festival (www.sundance.org/festival)
- E3 Expo (www.e3expo.com)
- Wikipedia List of Festivals (en.wikipedia.org/wiki/List_of_film_festivals#North_America)

Groups
- Music Supervision Exchange (www.linkedin.com/groups/Music-Supervision-Exchange)
- Synch Music Professionals (www.linkedin.com/skills/skill/Music_Clearance)
- Film & Music Connection (www.linkedin.com/groups/Film-Music-Connection-96311/about)
- TV/Film Music Opportunities (www.linkedin.com/groups/Film-Music-Jobs-2276889)

Film Schools
- Los Angeles Film School (www.lafilm.com)
- USC School of Cinematic Arts (cinema.usc.edu)
- UCLA School of Theater, Film & Television (www.tft.ucla.edu)
- Tisch School of the Arts (about.tisch.nyu.edu)
- Watkins College of Art, Design, and Film (www.watkins.edu)

Game Schools
- ITT Technical Institute (www.itt-tech.edu)
- The Art Institutes (www.artinstitutes.edu)
- DeVry University (www.choosedevry.com)
- Westwood College of Technology (www.westwoodcollege.com)

Music Libraries/Pluggers
- Opus1 Music Library (www.opus1musiclibrary.com)
- APM Music (www.apmmusic.com)

- Megatrax (www.megatrax.com)
- RipTide Music (www.riptidemusic.com)
- Killer Tracks (www.killertracks.com)
- pigFACTORY (www.pigfactory.com)
- Choicetracks (www.choicetracks.com)
- PEN Music Group (www.penmusic.com)
- Extreme Music (www.extrememusic.com)
- Jingle Punks (www.jinglepunks.com)
- Production Music Association (www.pmamusic.com)

Music Publishers
- Warner/Chappell Music (www.warnerchappell.com)
- Universal Music Publishing Group (www.umusicpub.com)
- Sony/ATV Music (www.sonyatv.com)
- BMG Chrysalis (www.bmgchrysalis.com)
- Music Publishers Association Directory (www.mpa.org/directory-of-music-publishers)

Song Placement Services
- TAXI (www.taxi.com)
- Pump Audio (www.pumpaudio.com)
- AudioSparx (www.audiosparx.com)
- Song U.com (www.songu.com)
- Smashtrax Music (www.smashtrax.com)
- The Orchard (www.theorchard.com)
- SongCatalog (www.songcatalog.com)
- CrucialMusic (www.crucialmusic.com)
- MusicXray (www.musicxray.com)
- Musicclout (musicclout.com/contents/)

Tools and Helpful Sites
- The Hollywood Reporter (www.hollywoodreporter.com)
- Film & Television Music Guide (www.musicregistry.com)
- Internet Movie Database Pro (www.imdb.com)
- TV Show Music (www.tvshowmusic.com)
- MTV Soundtrack (www.soundtrack.MTV.com)

Large File Storage and Submission Services
- Dropbox (www.dropbox.com)
- Hightail (www.hightail.com)

Pricing Resources

Government Regulatory Agencies
- Federal Trade Commission (www.ftc.gov)

Pledge Pricing Sites
- Kickstarter (www.kickstarter.com)
- PledgeMusic (www.pledgemusic.com)
- Indiegogo (www.indiegogo.com)

Product Resources

Customer Service
- Temkin Group Customer Experience Research (www.temkingroup.com)
- *Raving Fans* by Ken Blanchard

General
- *Start and Run Your Own Record Label* by Daylle Deanna Schwartz

Merch
- CafePress (www.cafepress.com)
- Spreadshirt (www.spreadshirt.com)
- Zazzle (www.zazzle.com)
- Fat Rat Press (www.fatratpress.com)
- Vistaprint (www.vistaprint.com)
- StickerJunkie (www.stickerjunkie.com)
- Branders.com (www.branders.com)

Songwriting
- *Shortcuts to Hit Songwriting* by Robin Frederick
- *Shortcuts to Songwriting for Film & TV* by Robin Frederick
- *The Craft and Business of Songwriting* by John Braheny
- *Songwriters on Songwriting* by Paul Zollo

Recordings
- Pro Tools (www.avid.com)
- Apple Logic (www.apple.com/logic-pro/)
- Shure (www.shure.com)
- Reason Software (www.propellerheads.se)
- Adobe Photoshop (www.adobe.com)
- Adobe Illustrator (www.adobe.com)
- iStockphoto (www.istockphoto.com)
- Graphicriver (www.graphicriver.net)
- Disc Makers (www.discmakers.com)
- Disc Makers Barcodes (www.discmakers.com)
- Oasis (www.oasiscd.com)
- Rainbo Records (www.rainborecords.com)
- Nielsen SoundScan (www.nielsen.com)
- International Standard Recording Code (www.usisrc.org)
- Gracenote Media Database (www.gracenote.com)
- Apple MacBook Pro (www.apple.com/macbook-pro/)

Video
- Sony Camcorders (www.sony.com)
- Apple Final Cut Pro (www.apple.com/finalcutpro/)
- Apple Imovie (www.apple.com/mac/imovie/)
- Sony Vegas Pro (www.sonycreativesoftware.com/vegaspro)
- JumpCam (jumpcam.com)

- Videoblocks (www.videoblocks.com)
- Animoto (animoto.com)

Website and Store
- Adobe Dreamweaver (www.adobe.com/products/dreamweaver)
- Hostbaby (www.hostbaby.com)
- WordPress (wordpress.com)
- GoDaddy (www.godaddy.com)
- Network Solutions (www.networksolutions.com)
- PayPal (www.paypal.com)
- Google Checkout (checkout.google.com)
- Zen Cart (www.zen-cart.com)
- Shop Script (www.shop-script.com)

Promotion Resources

Advertising
General
- *Ogilvy on Advertising* by David Ogilvy
- *Tested Advertising Methods* by John Caples
- *The Copywriter's Handbook* by Robert Bly
- *Kiss and Sell* by Robert Sawyer
- *Integrated Marketing Communications* by Robyn Blakeman

Online Ads
- Google AdWords (adwords.google.com)
- YouTube (ads.youtube.com)

Web Classifieds
- Yakaz (www.yakaz.com)

Wraps
- Buswraps.com (www.buswraps.com)

Direct Marketing
Database Resources
- Standard Rate and Data Service (SRDS) (www.srds.com)
- Indie Bible (indiebible.com)
- The Music Phone Book (www.musicpage.com/musicphonebook)
- BurrellesLuce (www.burrellesluce.com)
- The Musician's Atlas (www.musiciansatlas.com)
- *Film and Television Music Guide* by the Music Business Registry
- *The Billboard Musician's Guide to Touring and Promotion* by Billboard

General
- Slide Share (www.slideshare.net)

Organizations
• The Direct Marketing Association (DMA) (www.newdma.org)

Postcards/Printing Resources/Mailing
• Overnight Prints (www.overnightprints.com)
• Vistaprint (www.vistaprint.com)
• United States Postal Service Business Solutions (www.usps.com/business)

Quick Response Codes
• QRStuff (www.qrstuff.com)

Face-to-Face Selling Tools
• Square (squareup.com)
• *Secrets of Closing the Sale* by Zig Ziglar

Internet Marketing

Blogging Tools
• Blogger (www.blogger.com)
• WordPress (www.wordpress.com)
• Tumblr (www.tumblr.com)
• Typepad (www.typepad.com)
• Musician's Cooler (www.musicianscooler.com)

Communities
• DatPiff (www.datpiff.com)

E-mail, Newsletters, and More
• GroupMail (www.group-mail.com)
• VerticalResponse (www.verticalresponse.com)
• MailChimp (www.mailchimp.com)
• Bandcamp (www.bandcamp.com)
• Constant Contact (www.constantcontact.com)
• Bronto (www.bronto.com)
• FanBridge (www.fanbridge.com)
• MyNewsLetterBuilder (www.mynewsletterbuilder.com)
• CampaignerCRM (www.campaignercrm.com)
• Noisetrade (noisetrade.com)

Event Calendars, Message Boards, Groups, Tools
• Craigslist (www.craigslist.org)
• Yahoo! Groups (www.groups.yahoo.com/neo)
• Pulse Music Board (www.pulsemusic.proboards.com)
• Evite (www.evite.com)
• Cvent (www.cvent.com)

Internet Publicity (Generating Reviews): Blogs, Fanzines, Podcasts, and More
• PitchFork Media (www.pitchforkmedia.com)
• Cokemachineglow (www.cokemachineglow.com)
• Stereogum (www.stereogum.com)

- Technorati Blog Search (www.technorati.com/blogs/directory)
- Google Blog Search (www.blogsearch.google.com)
- Podcast Alley (www.podcastalley.com)
- Podcast Pickle (www.podcastpickle.com)
- IndieFeed (www.indiefeed.com)
- Coverville (www.coverville.com/submissions)

Online Profile
- SoundCloud (www.soundcloud.com)
- MySpace (www.myspace.com)
- ReverbNation (www.reverbnation.com)
- PureVolume (www.purevolume.com)
- Facebook (www.facebook.com)

Personal Websites
- Web.com (www.web.com)
- Flavors Me (www.flavors.me)
- Virb (www.virb.com)
- Band Zoogle (www.bandzoogle.com)
- WordPress (wordpress.org)
- BandPage (www.bandpage.com)
- NING (www.ning.com)
- Google (www.thinkwithgoogle.com)
- Webby Awards (www.webbyawards.com)
- Adobe Dreamweaver (www.adobe.com/products/dreamweaver)
- TopSpin (www.topspin.com)
- *Online Marketing Heroes: Interviews with 25 Successful Online Marketing Gurus* by Michael Miller

Podcasting
- Promoting Your Band with Podcasting (www.promotingwithpodcasting.com)
- Apple iTunes Podcasts (www.apple.com/itunes/podcasts/)
- Podcast Directory (www.podcastdirectory.com/)
- Liberated Syndication (www.libsyn.com)

SEO
- Wordtracker (www.wordtracker.com)
- WebRing (dir.webring.com/rw)
- Search Engine Watch (www.searchenginewatch.com)
- Search Engine Land (www.searchengineland.com)
- *Search Engine Optimization Bible* by Jerri Ledford
- *Web Analytics* by Avinash Kaushik

Social Media
- Facebook (www.facebook.com)
- Twitter (www.twitter.com)
- LinkedIn (www.linkedin.com)
- YouTube (www.youtube.com)
- Google+ (www.plus.google.com)
- Instagram (www.instagram.com)
- Reddit (www.reddit.com)

- Squidoo (www.squidoo.com)
- Pinterest (www.pinterest.com)
- Vine (vine.co)
- Wikipedia List of Social Network Sites (www.en.wikipedia.org/wiki/List_of_social_networking_websites)
- *Socialnomics* by Erik Qualman
- *The Zen of Social Media Marketing* by Shama Hyder Kabani
- *Social Media Metrics for Dummies* by Leslie Poston
- *The Tipping Point* by Malcolm Gladwell

Social Networking Tools
- Bitly (www.bitly.com)
- Tweetdeck (www.tweetdeck.com)
- HootSuite (www.hootsuite.com)
- Stumbleupon (www.stumbleupon.com)
- Artistdata (www.artistdata.com)
- Mention (www.mention.com)
- Chirpify (chirpify.com)

Streaming and Discovery Sites
- Spotify (www.spotify.com)
- Beatsmusic (www.beatsmusic.com)
- Last.fm (www.lastfm.com)
- Rdio (www.rdio.com)
- Pandora (www.pandora.com)

Video Sites
- Fox Sports (www.msn.foxsports.com)
- Stupid Videos (www.stupidvideos.com)
- eBaum's World (www.ebaumsworld.com)
- Break (www.break.com)
- Vimeo (vimeo.com)
- DailyMotion (www.dailymotion.com/us)
- StageIt (www.stageit.com)
- Ustream (www.ustream.tv)
- YouTube (www.youtube.com)

Video Multichannel Networks
- Fullscreen (www.fullscreen.com)
- Maker Studios (www.makerstudio.com)
- Machinima (www.machinima.com)

Cloud Storage
- Dropbox (www.dropbox.com)
- Hightail (www.hightail.com)

Viral Goodies: Savers, Wallpapers
- GraFX Saver Pro (www.grafxsaver.com)
- SofoTex (www.sofotex.com/download/Screen_Savers/Screensaver_Tools/)
- DHX (www.dhtmlx.com)

Mobile

Apps
- GoDaddy's Goodnight and dotMobi Feature (www.godaddy.com)
- MobiSiteGalore (www.mobisitegalore.com)

Associations
- Mobile Marketing Association (www.mmaglobal.com)

Services
- ProTexting (www.protexting.com)
- Mobivity (mobivity.com)

Publicity and Public Relations

Charities
- American Cancer Society (www.cancer.org)
- Muscular Dystrophy Association (www.mdausa.org)
- The Foundation for AIDS Research (www.amfar.org)
- American Lung Association (www.lungusa.org)
- March of Dimes (www.marchofdimes.com)
- American Red Cross (www.redcross.org)
- People for the Ethical Treatment of Animals (www.peta.org)
- Charity Navigator (www.charitynavigator.org)

General
- *Harvard Business on Crisis Management* by Harvard Business Review
- *The New Rules of Marketing and PR* by David Meerman Scott

Networking
- South by Southwest SXSW (www.sxsw.com)
- West Coast Songwriters (www.westcoastsongwriters.org/Conference)
- Durango Songwriters Expo (www.durango-songwriters-expo.com)
- ASCAP "I Create Music" Expo (www.ascap.com)
- NAMM Convention (www.namm.org)
- Meetup (www.meetup.com)

Press Kits
- Vistaprint (www.vistaprint.com)
- Pocketfolder.com (www.pocketfolder.com)
- StickerJunkie.com (www.stickerjunkie.com)
- Sonicbids (www.sonicbids.com)
- Naldz Graphics (naldzgraphics.net)

Press Releases
- PR Newswire (www.prnewswire.com)
- PRWeb (www.prweb.com)
- GlobeNewswire (globenewswire.com)
- Marketwired (www.marketwired.com)

Regional Music Trades
- *Performer Magazine*—Boston (www.performermag.com)
- *Music Connection*—Los Angeles (www.musicconnection.com)
- *The Village Voice*—New York (www.villagevoice.com)

Radio

Build Your Own Radio Station Tools
- Pirate Radio (www.pirateradio.com)
- SHOUTcast (www.shoutcast.com)
- BlogTalkRadio (www.blogtalkradio.com)

Independent Radio Promotion
- Bryan Farrish Radio Promotion (www.radio-media.com)
- Tinderbox Music (www.tinderboxmusic.com)
- Powderfinger Promotions (www.powderfingerpromo.com)

Radio Submission Services
- Airplay Direct (www.airplaydirect.com)
- musicSUBMIT.com (www.musicsubmit.com)

Station Resources
- Live365 (www.live365.com)
- Radio-Locator (www.radio-locator.com)
- Indie Bible (www.indiebible.com)
- NPR (www.npr.org)
- Kat Corbett's Locals Only (kroq.cbslocal.com/show/kat-corbett/)
- SiriusXM Satellite Radio (www.siriusxm.com)

Sponsorships/Endorsements

Active Sponsors
- Sabian (www.sabian.com)
- Rhythm Tech (www.rhythmtech.com)
- Rickenbacker (www.rickenbacker.com)
- Gibson Guitars (www.gibsonguitars.com)
- Sam Ash Music (www.samash.com)
- Jägermeister (www.jagermeister.com)
- Jim Beam (www.jimbeam.com)
- Zippo Lighters (www.zippohottour.com)
- Red Bull (www.redbull.com)
- The Gap (www.gap.com)
- Anheuser-Busch (anheuser-busch.com)
- Grey Goose Vodka (www.greygoose.com)

General
- IEG Source Book (www.sponsorship.com)

Word-of-Mouth Marketing

Associations
- Word of Mouth Marketing Association (www.womma.org)

General
- *The Anatomy of Buzz* by Emanuel Rosen

Tools
- Tell-a-Friend, Socialtwist, Inc. (tellafriend.socialtwist.com)

Research Resources

Customer Segmentation
- US Census Bureau (www.census.gov)
- CIA World Factbook (www.cia.gov)
- Quantcast (www.quantcast.com)
- Arbitron (www.arbitron.com)
- Stanford Research Institute (SRI) (www.sric-bi.com)
- Nielsen Claritas PRIZM (www.claritas.com/MyBestSegments/Default.jsp)
- ClickZ (www.clickz.com)

Formats/Genres
- AllMusic (www.allmusic.com)

Market Need
- Quick MBA (www.quickmba.com)
- *Blue Ocean Strategy* by W. Chan Kim and Renée Mauborgne
- *Funky Business* by Jonas Ridderstråle and Kjell Nordstrom

Testing and Feedback
- SurveyMonkey (www.surveymonkey.com)
- Zoomerang (www.zoomerang.com)
- Marketing Profs (www.marketingprofs.com)
- *The Market Research Toolbox* by Edward McQuarrie
- *Survey Research Methods* by Floyd Fowler
- *The Complete Idiot's Guide to Marketing Basics* by Sarah White

Index